Bunkers, Pits & Other Hazards

BUNKERS, PITS & OTHER HAZARDS

A Guide to the Design, Maintenance, and Preservation of Golf's Essential Elements

FORREST L. RICHARDSON

and

MARK K. FINE

WILEY

John Wiley & Sons, Inc.

This book is printed on acid-free paper. ∞

Copyright © 2006 by John Wiley & Sons, Inc. All rights reserved

Published by John Wiley & Sons, Inc., Hoboken, New Jersey
Published simultaneously in Canada

No part of this publication may be reproduced, stored in a retrieval system, or transmitted in any form or by any means, electronic, mechanical, photocopying, recording, scanning, or otherwise, except as permitted under Section 107 or 108 of the 1976 United States Copyright Act, without either the prior written permission of the Publisher, or authorization through payment of the appropriate per-copy fee to the Copyright Clearance Center, Inc., 222 Rosewood Drive, Danvers, MA 01923, (978) 750-8400, fax (978) 750-4470, or on the Web at www.copyright.com. Requests to the Publisher for permission should be addressed to the Permissions Department, John Wiley & Sons, Inc., 111 River Street, Hoboken, NJ 07030, (201) 748-6011, fax (201) 748-6008, or online at http://www.wiley.com/go/permission.

Limit of Liability/Disclaimer of Warranty: While the publisher and author have used their best efforts in preparing this book, they make no representations or warranties with respect to the accuracy or completeness of the contents of this book and specifically disclaim any implied warranties of merchantability or fitness for a particular purpose. No warranty may be created or extended by sales representatives or written sales materials. The advice and strategies contained herein may not be suitable for your situation. You should consult with a professional where appropriate. Neither the publisher nor author shall be liable for any loss of profit or any other commercial damages, including but not limited to special, incidental, consequential, or other damages.

For general information on our other products and services or for technical support, please contact our Customer Care Department within the United States at (800) 762-2974, outside the United States at (317) 572-3993 or fax (317) 572-4002.

Wiley also publishes its books in a variety of electronic formats. Some content that appears in print may not be available in electronic books. For more information about Wiley products, visit our Web site at www.wiley.com.

Library of Congress Cataloging-in-Publication Data:
Richardson, Forrest L.
  Bunkers, pits & other hazards : a guide to the design, maintenance, and preservation of golf's essential elements / Forrest L. Richardson and Mark K. Fine.
    p. cm.
  Includes index.
  ISBN-13: 978-0-471-68367-4 (cloth)
  ISBN-10: 0-471-68367-1 (cloth)
    1. Golf courses--Design and construction. 2. Golf courses--Maintenance. I. Title: Bunkers, pits, and other hazards. II. Fine, Mark K. III. Title.
  GV975.R52 2006
  796.352'068--dc22
                                                        2005030961

Printed in the United States of America

10 9 8 7 6 5 4 3 2 1

Contents

FOREWORD		*vii*
ACKNOWLEDGMENTS		*ix*
PREFACE		*xi*
CHAPTER 1	*The Evolution of Hazards*	*1*
CHAPTER 2	*Types of Hazards*	*17*
CHAPTER 3	*Twenty Famous Hazards*	*41*
CHAPTER 4	*Philosophies of Legendary Architects*	*97*
CHAPTER 5	*Psychological Effects of Hazards* by Dr. Edward Sadalla	*133*
CHAPTER 6	*Design & Strategy of Hazards*	*147*
CHAPTER 7	*Constructing Hazards*	*177*
CHAPTER 8	*Restoration & Maintenance of Hazards*	*205*
CHAPTER 9	*Opinions about Hazards*	*237*
AFTERWORD		*258*
GLOSSARY		*259*
BIBLIOGRAPHY		*293*
RESOURCES		*299*
INDEX		*303*

"Two roads diverged in a wood, and I—
I took the one less traveled by,
and that has made all the difference."

———

From "The Road Not Taken,"
by Robert Frost (1874–1963)

Foreword

Hazards are essential to the game of golf. I cannot imagine playing without experiencing that marvelous feeling of hitting a great recovery shot from a hazard, or the anticipation of my opponent trying to recover from a deep pot bunker only to have the ball just catch the upper lip and roll back down toward his feet. This is what makes the game of golf exciting and keeps the players coming back for more.

The designers of the Donald Ross era favored bunkers over water hazards. Years ago, bunkers had different grades of sand and were furrowed in such a manner that a bunker truly was a hazard. I wish my bunkers played more like the bunkers of that era. Today, golf clubs that have PGA Tour professional tournaments insist the sand be smooth and totally uniform so that every shot plays the same.

Hazards have changed the mindset of the touring professional. Many fairway bunkers designed to direct players' shots are safe havens and easier to recover from than shots from the adjacent rough. Sand bunkers beside the green are easier to recover from than many grassy chipping areas surrounding the green.

Water is the only hazard from which there is no recovery. The appeal of the island green on hole No. 17 at TPC Sawgrass is the psychological effect the water has on all golfers. That hole would be just as intimidating and intriguing if it were surrounded by deep furrowed sand or rough similar to the 17th hole at Whistling Straits, site of the 2004 PGA Championship.

Intimidating and intriguing. These two words might well sum up the definition of a perfect hazard. Forrest Richardson and Mark Fine have put together a complete look at hazards and the game of golf in *Bunkers, Pits & Other Hazards*. The golfer in all of us is bound to take away something to remember about hazards—if not to improve our games, at least to give us a better appreciation of hazards and their essential role in this wonderful game.

—Pete Dye

ACKNOWLEDGMENTS

When you read an acknowledgment for a book, it is difficult to fully appreciate the level of sincerity that the author is putting forth in his or her thanks to others. That is, until you write a book yourself. While the names Richardson and Fine appear together on the cover, perhaps a hundred should be listed right beside them. Writing a book, almost any book, requires a team effort, as the amount of information and support needed to complete it is enormous. We cannot possibly list everyone who contributed, but we'll do our best.

It was in the winter of 2003 that the concept for this book was first discussed. An exchange of e-mails eventually solidified our pursuit of this interesting and sometimes controversial topic. We occasionally heard wonderment (Why would anyone want to write a book about golf hazards?), but as it turned out, the topic was met with enthusiastic interest by our publisher and all who reviewed our plans.

This book was truly a team effort and wouldn't contain nearly the information it does without the contributions of people like Patty Moran at the Golf House. Patty never hesitated to help track down an old book or an obscure article from some bygone architect. Dr. Wayne Wilson of the Amateur Athletic Foundation Sports Library in Los Angeles, our West Coast research site, was of invaluable help. As we sorted through the Ralph Miller Collection of golf books, photos, and old publications, Dr. Wilson and his staff shared our enthusiasm.

Speaking of enthusiasm, Ran Morrissett not only sent us a few photos, he sent us seven full photo albums with hundreds of pictures of golf holes and hazards from his travels around the world. Patrick Burton, a golf course architect with Forrest Richardson & Associates, spent countless hours augmenting research and looking through boxes of his personal photos of hazards from around the world. As explained in an introduction to Chapter 5, "The Psychological Effect of Hazards," we eventually convinced ourselves that Dr. Ed Sadalla should stop trying to enlighten us, but instead simply guest-author this chapter. "Simply," of course, is the wrong word. The psychology of hazards is not only fascinating but highly complex. We appreciate Dr. Sadalla's elegance in making this essential topic so understandable.

Many top superintendents contributed as well. People such as Matt Shaffer of Merion, Mike Burke of Cherry Hills, John Zimmers of Oakmont, and John Chassard of Lehigh shared their time and expertise, providing valuable information and insight that we never could have uncovered at any library or Web site. John Chassard went so far as to assist us in drafting and editing our sections on the maintenance of hazards.

What might have been endless surveys and interviews became terrific opportunities to talk with old friends and meet new ones. People like Ian Andrew, Chris Clouser, Gil Hanse, Tom Doak, Elwood Williard, Norm Klaparda, George Bahto, Tom Ferrell,

Martin Hawtree, Craig Disher, Tom Paul, Geoff Shackelford, Brian Phillips, Brad Klein, Gregg Feinberg, Phred Bartholomaei, Bill Yates, Lisa Thomas, Brian Boyle, Tom Vogt, Joel Stewart, Tommy Naccarato, Rick Wolffe, George Skawski, Michael Moore, Daniel Wexler, Wayne Morrison, James Collier, Michael Fay, Bill McBride, Jeff Brauer, Art Hills, Bill Coore, Mike Houska, Bob Cupp, Geoffrey Cornish, Graham Marsh, Ed Easley, Jim Engh, Tom Fazio, Tom Weinert, Rees Jones, Mike Hurdzan, Mike Devries, Mitchell Hantman, and Michael Sweeny were there when we needed them. We are certain to have left out some important names and will be repenting until a second printing sets the record straight.

We like to think that the two chapters on the philosophies of famous past architects and the opinions of many of the great ones living today are invaluable to anyone with an interest in course design. If a summary like this were available a year or two ago, our lives would have been very different. Countless hours of research time could have been used to take vacations, play with the kids, take our wives to dinner, or lower our handicaps. Many of the "golden age" golf architects never wrote a thing; endless searching was required to uncover insights into their thought processes. As far as the living architects go, on more than one occasion during interviews, we were told jokingly (but with a strong hint of seriousness thrown in) that we were asking them to divulge all their design secrets. Fortunately for us, and for you, most of them acquiesced. In all honesty, every one of them was a real pleasure to talk to and extremely forthcoming with thoughts and ideas about hazards.

Thank you to the designer of this book, Brian Richardson, who persevered hours on end, in order to fit all of our findings into 320 readable pages. And to Margaret Cummins and Shannon Egan at John Wiley & Sons for your editing and expert coordination.

Much of our inspiration for writing this book came from our mutual passion for the courses of the British Isles. Between us, we have played and studied hundreds of the famous and not-so-famous courses where hazards were first conceived. There is no better way to appreciate the magnitude of the role that bunkers, pits, and windswept dunes play in the game of golf than to study them on these hallowed grounds. Our love for golf and golf course design continues to be enhanced and nurtured every time we make that trip across the pond.

With that said, we need to thank our families for their patience and support throughout the process. Without them, this book would never have made it to print. During all the late nights, the time we spent away reading, studying, writing, and researching, it was our families who had to grin and bear it. To the Fine family on the East Coast—Mark's wife, Laurie,[1] and their three great kids, Andy, Megan, and Kevin—and to the Richardson family on the West Coast—Forrest's wife, Valerie,[1] and their daughter, Haley—we thank you for your confidence and patience throughout. You are the best.

—FORREST L. RICHARDSON & MARK K. FINE

---

[1] Laurie Fine and Valerie Richardson are infinitely more organized than either of us. The proof of this lies in the piles and stacks of books, papers, copies, images, and sometimes-messy notes both of us generated throughout this work. These two were always there to help sort things out, edit, find "lost" documents, and do their best to make up for our bad habits.

PREFACE

You are holding a book about inconveniences. But unlike such inconveniences in life as biting into a sour strawberry or encountering a pothole that costs you an expensive new tire, the inconveniences covered here lead a dual life. While they are inconvenient on the surface, they are essential to the core. They force decisions. The correct routes will bring triumph and even fame. The bad choices will bring long-term fears and even ruin. The risky paths—whether conquered or failed—intensify the experience.

We point out the subject matter so you might better prepare for that occasional nongolfer who will inquire why anyone would bother putting hazards on a golf course, let alone read a book about the subject. After all, in soccer there are few books about setting up fields with goals that are purposely camouflaged. In baseball one cannot find a title about creating obstacles between first and second base. Nor has there been any classic written for park directors along the lines of *Laying Out Nature Trails: How to Create Difficult Walks That Will Perplex and Frustrate Even the Best of Hikers.*

Golf is so essentially different from other sports and games because the participants have no chance at claiming any exclusive right to what is interesting. If we played golf across identical courses, perhaps it would be different. But we do not. The thousands upon thousands of variables that crisscross the landscape of a golf course (and that must include the very condition of the grounds and the weather forecast each day, not to mention the temperament of the employee who decides that the cup at No. 6 might be better "just a few feet farther over that way") define the very nature of golf. And in turn, hazards define the nature of golf courses.

Our goal here is to celebrate the game of golf by discussing the various ways in which nature and the designer have made the game so interesting. Nature has provided conditions and terrain for golf. The designer has dug into these raw ingredients, time after time, experimenting like a mad scientist to create just the right recipe for the moment. The golf course architect arranges golf holes around natural forms and features and places hazards in the way of the golfer. And why? Because without such obstacles, the game would be lame and boring.[1]

Your authors are admittedly not sitting in one room writing on a single piece of paper. However, we knew early on that we could speak with one voice on this subject: A golf course is made interesting by the intrigue, the temptation, and the risk of its hazards. This is our thesis, pure and simple. With one of us primarily involved in

---

[1] We are certain you have played such a golf hole, or even an entire golf course, made up of lame experiences. Typical traits include repetitive hazards, little interest, and poor thought in the design. From here on, we shall refer to such places as *Boredom Links*. This fictitious course will serve as a signal of our disappointment with a certain approach or lack of attention regarding hazards — the heart and soul of the game of golf.

painstaking research, the other was given the task of arranging it all into words. The images and architects' philosophies included have never before been brought together in one volume. In our humble opinion, they are worth the price of admission all on their own.

As convenient as it might be to stop at our "pure and simple" thesis, we are goaded forward by the words of H. S. Colt and C. H. Alison. These two, coincidentally, were coauthors on the very cherished work *Some Essays On Golf Course Architecture* (1920). Messrs. Colt and Alison write: "It would be necessary to write a very long book, copiously illustrated with diagrams of famous and infamous holes, in order to deal exhaustively with the placement of bunkers."

While bunkers consume much of our discussion, we delve into other hazards as well, including the use of wind direction and even the psychological aspects of hazards. We have tried not to make this book long or elaborate. If you find parts that are, we apologize. That is simply the rub of the green.

—FORREST L. RICHARDSON & MARK K. FINE

CHAPTER 1

The Evolution *of* Hazards

Not far from Slains Castle is a great expanse of seacoast. Here we find dunes shaped by the wind and small rivers that deliver a daily cargo of silt to the North Sea. While no one knows for sure, we can guess the date to be sometime in the early 1600s. Perhaps it is June.

During the summer, the native marram grass along the beach is green up to one's knees. But at the tips, small yellow buds steal the show. Against meadows of lower green grasses, the marram rises up on windblown piles of sand and falls away into sunken pits. It waves goodbye to us with the help of gentle breezes. In and around these pits is an occasional wild orchid, joined by a rare blue-flowered butterwort or an iris. Our painting is nearly complete.

What could be missing?

Golf, of course. For we are not resting on the beach picnicking or looking lazily out across the horizon enjoying idle thoughts. Our trip back in time has us focused on the dunes, and also on a band of dedicated locals partaking in an ancient game of precision, skill, and patience. We are witnessing golf as it was played by its earliest players. Or, depending on the Scottish spelling rules du jour, we might write it as *golfe, gouff, goiff, goffe, goff, gowff,* or even *golph.*

There, beyond that rise, a group is about to whack small balls fashioned from leather pouches filled with goose feathers. Their clubs look rather like farm tools, with heads of beaten metal in oddly curved shapes. There is no course here. At least none that seems laid out in the patterns we have come to know in the twenty-first century. Our painting reflects just the dunes, the marram grass, that tiny bit of color provided by the orchid and its friends the butterwort and the iris, that gang of dedicated players trampling over matted swards of grass, a few high-flying clouds, and one last item of tremendous importance: *a bunker.*

Fig. 1-1 A natural setting of dunes and, as some will call them, "bunkers" at the 18th hole at Deal, England, c.1900. (Source: Golf Illustrated)

This Ancient Game

Our little bunker—the one near Slains Castle, which is not far from the place we now call Cruden Bay in Scotland—is there by more than just happenstance. Some people will tell you it came to be purely by the natural transformation of the land. Their theory is one of natural erosion and movement of the sandy soils. As winds and rains changed the contours of the land, grasses took hold.

Fig. 1-2 Cruden Bay in Scotland, designed by Old Tom Morris and Archie Simpson and founded in 1899. (Courtesy of P. Burton)

Some areas were held intact while other bits blew away. As patches of grasses died, they decomposed. This created nutrients and more grasses grew. Birds and other animals enjoyed the habitat, too. As they ate and left droppings, the area could support more life. One must not think too hard about this—it's simply a natural cycle. According to these believers, our little bunker "just happened."

Others will suggest that mankind helped shape the little bunker, that sheep were raised for food and wool, and it was their instinct to get out of the cold and wind that caused burrows to be formed. A herd of decent-sized, 175-pound sheep hunkering down against an otherwise ordinary sand dune, on the leeward side, will form such a bunker, they will say. This is what caused the hollow, and it only seemed logical that our band of golfers put it to use as a golf hazard, arranging play so it purposely brought the bunker into account.

But why a hazard at all? This is the essential question. In order to attempt an answer, it is necessary to look at the ancient game itself. Many theories exist about how golf came to be. Most certainly the game originated from a combination of two pastimes: (1) the lure of striking a ball with a stick, and (2) the excitement of a hunt. Who wouldn't suggest that swinging a stick to strike a ball as accurately as humanly possible is not only therapeutic, but also a bit addicting? Or that the drive to conquer an obstacle course laid out for the taking is not somehow inherent within our human blood? These two components are at the heart of golf, no matter who you believe invented the game or from what previous games golf may have originated. The latter, the idea of an obstacle course, is the essence of *Bunkers, Pits & Other Hazards*.

Fig. 1-3 The presence of civilization brought sheep to the linksland. Their presence of mind to seek shelter from the cold helped to form many of the pits that eventually became bunkers. An engraving of Dornoch from the picture by George Reid from the National Gallery, Edinburgh, Scotland (Source: Golf Illustrated)

Many people have speculated about the ancient stick and ball games that may have influenced golf. For our purposes, these predecessors are not so important. Golf certainly has within its DNA games involving sticks and balls, but until the custom of carrying multiple clubs was combined with a separate ball for each participant, the game had not yet become golf. And until the unique tradition of negotiating this ball into a small hole was conceived, golf was still not quite formed.

Fig. 1-4 Not to be outdone by sheep, cattle in the Sandhills of Nebraska (U.S.A.) are quite adept at developing cavernous pits through their paths and lying areas. This leads to erosion, and perhaps a future bunker.

The first reference to golf known thus far is from the year 1457. This is when King James II of Scotland (27 years old at the time) banned the playing of golf because it interfered with archery, a decidedly more important skill for winning battles for land and the all-important throne of England. What is not well known is that James became king at the tender age of six. One can only surmise what his outlook on territorial disputes or the banning of golf would have been as a young and energetic boy—a first-grader had he lived in our time.

Fig. 1-5 Natural bunker pits, such as this one in a moorland setting, are formed when surface vegetation is disturbed and erosion takes over.

So we have come to accept that it was in Scotland that golf, the unique game in which each individual renders a ball into a hole and utilizes multiple clubs to do so, originated. At least this is the belief of your authors. Scotland is where the escalating popularity of golf[1] eventually gave us our first golf courses. Although not known as courses in ancient days, the routes from where golfers began their play to the hole where they completed their treks, were "holes." Any number of these holes attacked in succession were "courses."

Fig. 1-6 A fifteenth-century engraving by Hensrick van Schoel shows participants enjoying the Dutch sport of het kolven (kolf) which was largely played on ice and between teams, not individuals as golf. (Source: Golf Illustrated)

---

[1] The argument for the Dutch game *het kolven* or *kolf* being linguistically linked to the word *golf* has been duly dispelled by many experts who will explain to us that there is no historical connection between pronunciation or spelling of the Dutch and Scots. That the modern word *golf* is so close to the ancient word *kolf* is simply a coincidence. The word *golf* is more likely derived from Scottish *howffe* (gathering place) or *gulfe* (bay). But a word to the wise: We recommend that you not attempt this argument to a staunch supporter of the Dutch origin theory without much further reading on your part.

Fig. 1-7 Early golf as it may have been in the period prior to the 1700s. Reproduction of a painting by G. Hilliard Swinstead. (Source: Golf Illustrated, October 1901)

Ultimately, it is the land on which these holes were laid out in ancient times that has defined golf through the ages.

From Town to Country

Early accounts of golf place the game both in the center of towns and across the open countryside. While no one knows the exact time frame of golf's beginning, we can deduce that, for the game to have become popular enough to be banned in 1457, it was probably around for quite some time before then. Throughout its ancient development, a period we shall estimate in these pages to be from the 1200s to the 1600s, golf was played as a test of accuracy through streets and along roads. Golf was just as much at home in the urban setting as it was on the open land on the outskirts of villages. The

Fig. 1-8 Even as golf moved toward open landscapes, it was not uncommon to find many hazards, that were obstructions in nature. In this photo from around 1900, the approach to the green is directly behind a stone wall. (Source: Golf Illustrated)

winner was the one who arrived at the target in the fewest number of strokes. Hazards could be virtually anything in the way: a wall, a road, a tree, a pig, a grassy knoll, or someone's barn. At some point, the target in golf became a hole in which the ball, after being masterfully negotiated to avoid hazards, was put to rest at the finish.

Fig. 1-9 An old photo from St. Andrews shows what appears to be a large match contemplating bunker shots. The deteriorating edges of the bunker are evidence that the links were under continual change, not only by the forces of nature, but from the continual wear and tear of golfers. (Source: Golf Illustrated)

Bunkers, Pits & Other Hazards

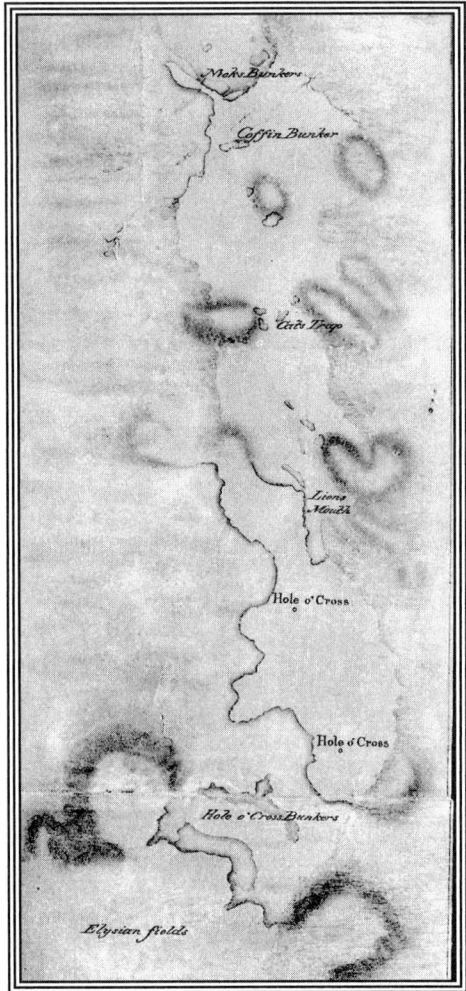

Fig. 1-10 William Chalmers' 1836 map of the "Golfing Course" at St. Andrews (see page 51) contains nine details of the holes and bunkers. Shown here is the detailed area of the Hole o' Cross holes, Holes 5 and 13 of what we now refer to as The Old Course (see color insert). (Reproduced by kind permission of the Royal and Ancient Golf Club of St. Andrews)

Assuredly, golf was more enjoyable in the wide open space of the countryside. While such hazards as cobblestone streets, walls, and buildings may once have been commonplace for the game, the freedom of undulating terrain, open landscapes, and natural hazards seems much more rewarding. Exactly when golf abandoned the streets of town will never be pinpointed. Very likely it was toward the first half of the 1500s, when golfing grounds such as Leith, East Lothian, and St. Andrews were being thought of as permanent courses on which the game could be played. It is noteworthy that, until this time, even such courses as St. Andrews were not at all set in stone. The links—that ground on which people would gather to golf and watch golfers—were simply wide open land dotted with occasional holes and natural obstacles (hazards) to overcome along the trek to these holes. The St. Andrews Links of the 1500s, 1600s, and 1700s, and like many other golfing links, doubled as common ground for local citizens. The links were places to recreate, picnic, and so on.

The Importance of Linksland

Linksland is land located near an open sea or bay that happens also to be connected directly to the sea through natural drainage patterns. It is low lying land that has been formed by centuries of drainage, tidal changes, and the brisk weather along the sea. It generally possesses the characteristics of naturally rolling sand dunes and other natural features that have been formed by the wind, the ocean, and the action of receding tides.

The word *links* comes from the Old English *hlincas*, meaning "ridges." It has come to mean the undulating sandy ground near a shore, full of windswept ridges and hills formed by the forces of the weather and sea. In no other language is there a word to define, with such precision, this distinctive type of land.

Fig. 1-11 The expansive links of St. Andrews as it was in 1901. This photo was taken looking toward the Swilcan Burn where it empties into St. Andrews Bay with The Old and New Courses extending out beyond. (Source: Golf Illustrated, February 1901)

It is no coincidence that *links* also came to mean a golf course, for this is where golf took hold for good. Today, *links* is often used as a synonym for any seaside golf course, and sometimes for any golf course at all. Yet there is a valid point of contention concerning these latter uses. A true links golf course requires linksland. And while linksland may be approximated in 100 ways or more, and it may be that a few inland dunes have nearly the same qualities, courses that are not on linksland are technically not links, at least not when we think carefully about the word and its origin.

In *A History of Golf in Britain,* by Sir Guy Campbell (1952), the formation of golf courses upon linksland is put into sequence. Our condensed summary is as follows:

1. Over the ages the sea gradually recedes.

2. It leaves behind natural channels cut through a sandy terrain, some serving as rivers and streams that carry rainwater from higher ground back to the sea.

3. Coastal winds dry the sand and blow it into dunes. Over time, ridges, knolls, and hollows result.

4. The protected areas of this landscape become a haven for birds, and with their presence come bird droppings, and with this comes an upper layer of rich silt.

5. Seeds blown toward the ocean, some from bird droppings, take hold and germinate.

6. Grasses, such as marram and fescues, take hold and adapt to the sandy soils and wind, as do a few bushes and the occasional tree.

Fig. 1-12 The Cape Bunker at Royal North Devon, England, is a prime example of rugged dunes and broken ground. Royal North Devon, established in 1864, was laid out by Old Tom Morris. (Source: Golf Illustrated)

7. The lower areas, those in between dunes and ridges, are naturally greener and easier to traverse. Animals—rabbits and the foxes who prey upon them, and finally the hunter and his dogs after the fox—wear these areas into tidy pathways.

8. The golfer discovers these areas and puts them to use. They are forgiving compared to the dunes, the taller grasses, and the dense brush. These lower areas, trampled and worn by animal and man, become the golfer's fairways and greens. The rugged dunes and ridges become the challenge—the obstacle course. The combination produces the first golf courses.

The many landforms of natural linksland are the ancestors of all golf hazards. Bunkers originated among the sand dunes as natural hollows and blowouts in towering sand held in place by natural grasses. Bumps and undulations are the hallmark of linksland terrain; it is no wonder that they are replicated in modern courses. Natural ground left in place, and even artificial landscaping for the modern golf course, take a cue from the pockmarked broken ground that runs between tee and fairway and throughout any true links course. The drainage channels, either natural rivers or channels dug to carry runoff from towns back to the sea, were the predecessors of today's artificial channels and streams. The lakes and ponds on our modern courses are responses to the sea itself, placeholders for bays, inlets, and lowlands that are components of a links environment. Even trees, while much higher in profile than gorse,[2] are mere reinterpretations of the stretches of unimproved land that border fairways and pop up at often inopportune places to add challenges across linksland courses.

The thoughtful Robert Hunter, writing in *The Links,* explains the association between linksland and golf hazards in this way: "Golf was born on the crumpled and corrugated areas along wind-swept dunes. Wind and water, hillocks and hollows, mounds and pits, marram grass and bents—these are the hazards of the links." Hunter goes on to sum up

---

[2] Gorse, *Ulex europaeus,* grows typically no more than 6 feet high. It is not used medicinally and fits the following drab description from an 1864 botanical journal: "[Gorse] is used for burning, being cut down every few years in places where it grows naturally." It is quite fitting that golfers find it a dreadful hazard, despite its low growing height.

the very nature of golf: "There can be no real golf without hazards."

The Links Are Improved

In October 1764, at a meeting of the Gentlemen Golfers of St. Andrews, it was decreed "That it would be for the improvement of the links that four first holes should be converted into two." The late Fred Hawtree, in his book, *Aspects of Golf Course Architecture,* suggests that this marks the moment when "the first tiny seed of golf course

Fig. 1-13 Portrait of Allan Robertson, considered by many to be the "Father of Golf Architecture" as a result of his work to improve The Old Course, notably the expansion of greens to accommodate two holes on each green instead of just a single hole that served play going out and also coming in. For the entire year in 1858, Robertson was paid £4 for his work to "repair the links." (Courtesy USGA Archive)

architecture was sown." Whether or not this particular change was the actual beginning of golf course architecture, it was indeed such changes by golfers that opened the door to the practice of improving holes and hazards. As golfers met to contemplate their courses and what made them interesting, it was the relocation of holes and hazards, the enlargement and replication of features, and—heaven forbid—the creation of hazards where none had been before that took hold. The notion that nature was the architect and that hazards were wherever they fell upon the land was forever to be combined with the artistry of a new breed of professional: *the golf course architect.*

Alpinization

The idea of "alpinization" was discussed by many legendary golf architects after a breakthrough experiment in 1910 by J. H. Taylor, the acclaimed British golfer and five-time winner of the Open. The concept was simple enough: Create mounds[3] on flattish inland parcels of land with the goal of emulating the bumpy terrain of seaside linksland. As golf flourished across the world, there was an intense desire to copy the holes and hazards of golf's original courses—those on the natural linksland. Hazards had been driven naturally on early terrain by the coast. The dunes and uneven landscape provided nearly endless hazards for the taking, and in a spot where a new hazard might be interesting to consider, a never-ending supply of land features from which to develop them was readily available. The slopes of dunes and the low points in between needed only a modest nudge to create hazards of dramatic quality.

---

[3] It strikes us as funny that the word *mound* has no decent substitute here, for we sought one during the writing. But mounds were at Royal Mid-Surrey. In today's circles of golf architecture critics, there is a mob out to get the word *mound*. Here in the twenty-first century the word is passé. It is associated with replicated features, uniformity, and a path toward "containment." (Another topic altogether.) Replacements such as *landform, rise,* and *hummock* are used by architects and writers to describe what? Mounds, of course. We submit that a mound can be well formed and quite natural looking. Not all mounds are created equal.

Fig. 1-14 There may be no more beautiful links land than the terrain of Royal Dornoch in the north of Scotland with its dense gorse and undulating terrain (see color insert). (Courtesy of P. Burton)

But as golf moved inland from the seacoasts to meet a population hungry for the game, the charm of the links needed to be cloned to reshape the often less interesting land[4] away from the sea. On many occasions, those responsible for laying out new courses would conduct investigative trips to study early links courses. Whether the new course was being created in the heart of England, just a day's drive from the sea, on the European continent, or in America, re-creating some of the ambiance of natural linksland was a major objective.

It was Taylor's attempt to transform Royal Mid-Surrey's Outer Course in England that spurred the discussion. Mid-Surrey is located at the edge of both Middlesex and Surrey and was founded in 1892. One is able to get a picture-perfect image of the course before Taylor began his tinkering from the words of the late Bernard Darwin. In describing the land's unsuitability for golf, Darwin (as usual) deployed just the right words, writing that it was "flat as a pancake." What more does one need to know? Thank you, Mr. Darwin.

Fig. 1-15 The concept of alpinization is to mimic natural landforms by moving quantities of dirt into rises and valleys. This image of the 10th hole at the Shawnee Country Club, is from an article by A. W. Tillinghast. (Compliments of the Tillinghast Association)

[4] To be sure, not all heathland or land away from the coast is uninteresting. Taylor's experiment with alpinization proved above all else that land that is, indeed, uninteresting is not where golf belongs if other land is available.

Taylor's solution involved many plows and laborers. He was assisted by Peter Lees, a greenkeeper. Together the two men directed this combination of animal and manual labor, creating a scene as if ants were forming pile upon pile of soil. Eventually the flat landscape was transformed into one of peaked mounds and humps. Some of these were very large and impressive. The objective was to re-create linksland, and at the same time eliminate the need for so many penal bunkers. Without dunes or other natural landforms, inland courses were being defined by too many cross bunkers and cop bunkers. These bunkers were becoming a crutch of sorts. Taylor reasoned that hillocks and hollows created artificially would be a better approach and, besides, these would provide a more natural setting to place bunkers.

As the work of Taylor and Lees progressed, those busy planning new courses around the world took notice. Soon there was a buzz about alpinization everywhere golf was being considered. George Crump at Pine Valley attempted a version of alpinization, but soon abandoned it. Crump preferred to use the terrain Pine Valley had to offer. Alpinization did not seem to fit every canvas. In the span of just a few years, the concept of alpinization went from being admired to being shunned. Taylor's abrupt mounds and their artificial look were thought of as hideous and revolting.

Fig. 1-16 At Ballybunion New in Ireland, a natural bunker awaits the golfer who strays from the gentle fairway. (Photograph by Paul Daley, Full Swing Golf Publishing)

Taylor, who had been quoted during his Mid-Surrey effort as saying "it should be made to look as close to nature as the hand of man admits," is still shunned today. Many golf architecture critics and enthusiasts continue to describe his work as a failure—unnatural and unnecessary. But Taylor's laboratory at Mid-Surrey forever gave golf a major breakthrough. The notion that Taylor failed is without merit. Although the result of alpinization at first was perhaps too abrupt and overdone, it opened the door to thinking beyond the use of bunkers as hazards. Taylor taught us to think outside the box when it comes to mixing golf with inland sites. The lesson learned from Mid-Surrey was that the earth could be sculpted, not only by the hand of Mother Nature, but also through the vision of the golf architect. The hazards of the natural linksland were never intended to be bunker after bunker or sand pit after sand pit. Taylor sent a reminder toward the future that the nuances of the undulating land are as much a part of the challenge of golf as anything else.

Fig. 1-17 In this 1900 photo of a bunker at Haylings Island, England, the bunker takes on the look of a volcano. Established in 1883, Hayling was laid out by Tom Simpson. (Source: Golf Illustrated, January 1900)

The Hazard Concept

When the game of golf was first played, a hazard was surely not an actual thing or object. It was a concept, a situation a player got himself into. A problem not avoided caused your ball to be in trouble and the outcome was not known until you performed. Only as time progressed did such perilous situations become known as *hazards*. The concept became a defined term: "Your ball is in a hazard." The definition of a hazard has varied over the years, but the term was mostly used for bunkers and water. In the game of many generations ago, a hazard could be any obstacle that impeded play, making progress impossible without some relief. Today many such features are not hazards, but are instead called *obstacles, impediments,* and *ground under repair*.

Two of the first 13 Rules of Golf established in 1744 by the Honorable Company of Edinburgh Golfers are quoted:

> 5. *If your Ball comes among watter, or any wattery filth, you are at liberty to take out your Ball & bringing it behind the hazard and Teeing it, you may play it with any Club and allow your Adversary a Stroke for so getting out your Ball.*

> 13. *Neither Trench, Ditch or Dyke, made for the preservation of the Links, nor the Scholar's Holes, or the Soldier's Lines, Shall be accounted a Hazard; But the Ball is to be taken out teed and play'd with any Iron Club.*

These two rules shed light on what was considered a hazard in 1744. The other 11 rules, by the way, were about such things as teeing and holing. No mention of *hazard* per se. As golf evolved, so did our concept of a hazard. Partly a reflection of the links themselves, and partly a result of ideas such as alpinization, courses tended to combine natural features of the land with manmade features. Whether for good or ill, golf crossed a line sometime near 1900. And that line has rarely been revisited.

CHAPTER 1 | THE EVOLUTION *of* HAZARDS

The development of hazards on new courses is much more about creating than about discovering. This may be a response to golf's movement from the coast to inland regions. It is also because many who propose new courses are no longer of the school that the site must be "ideally suited for golf," as we have read so many times in so many books. The new school embraces golf on extremely flat land, through home developments, and on jigsaw-puzzles of land that are ill-suited for golf altogether. Amazingly, decent and well-regarded courses have been created from such land. Shadow Creek in Las Vegas is one such example. While critics disagree (they always will), it cannot be contested that Shadow Creek, a course created from nothing and at great expense, we might add, is a wonder to behold. It is alpinization at its strongest, and each hazard—sand, pond, hill, valley, ridge, and bump—is manufactured, through a Disneyland approach, with artificial rock and materials trucked in from miles away. It represents a new concept of golf, but one that coexists with the original concept of naturalness and use of the land whenever possible. Golf now embraces both, sometimes on the same course or hole.

The Bunker Fetish & Other Trends

For many years, bunkers were little more than torture chambers across open links. But as golf courses became better thought out and planned, bunkers became more intellectual. In the story of golf course architecture, bunkers play the dual roles of villain and enchantress. They are indelible characters, often with lives and names of their own: Hell's Half Acre; the Devil's Asshole; the Church Pews; the White Faces of Merion; the Maiden; Sahara; Principal's Nose; the Beardies; Hell and Strath. We have become accustomed to the bunker. It is the quintessential golf hazard.

Historically, the word *bunker* meant "a chest or box," such as one finds on a ship. In 1500s Scots, the word is also recorded as meaning "an earthen seat or bank located in a field." The golf meaning emerged in the 1800s and reflected the deep, chestlike qualities of these hazards, perhaps combining both meanings. One wonders what pits of sand were called before. Likely not *traps,* as this term came into popular use in America after the late Harry Vardon's caddie exclaimed, "Mr. Vardon, you're *trapped*" during the 1913 U.S. Open at The Country Club. But traps they are, these common occurrences on our golf courses.

Fig. 1-18 It is a well known fact that ginger beer was popular on the links, especially at St. Andrews. The refreshing beverage was said to have "eased the pain" of a bad round, acting as an "asprin" in liquid form. (Source: *Golf Illustrated,* May 1902)

13

Bunkers originally formed from natural dunes and hollows, as we have discussed. Some of the ancient examples were pushed along by sheep or other animals seeking shelter. Still others may have been created over time by the continual wearing of a particular spot in the turf by numerous golfers using lofted clubs. Regardless, they became expected in golf and were easy to build.

The bunker is perhaps among the most overused of hazards in golf. Its popularity, if we might use that term while not being in one, results from its having its own set of rules, construction specifications, and even line items within budgets for new courses. How shameful that we have allowed such narrow thinking to infiltrate a game built on the principles of no rules and no standard playing board. While bunkers are useful as hazards, and their variation significant, they are too often an easy way out. Too often they are the same, drawn as little dabs on plans and sketchbooks by well-meaning golf architects.

The water hazard, another hazard that has become somewhat standard, has been formalized and is now defined, marked, and corralled. It no longer needs to be seamless with broken ground and the natural dunescape of the course. The unruly pattern of ancient golf, in which you "play ye ball" where it lies no matter what, is now a ballet of procedure. We "determine." We "drop." We count an extra stroke and we get on with the round.

We are not at all sure that hazards have matured for the better. Many today are lame versions of their ancestors, unable to fight a battle against the golfer. Many look pretty but have little bite.

The Essence of the Game

Hazards are essential. This is the one constant that is evident as we trace the evolution of the hazard in golf. It is our position that you cannot—under any circumstances—have worthwhile golf without hazards. And the more interesting the hazards, the more interesting the golf. Golf and its hazards go hand-in-hand.

Bobby Jones once said, "Every golfer worthy of the name should have some acquaintance with the principles of golf course design, not only for the betterment of the game, but for his own selfish enjoyment. Let him know a good hole from a bad one and the reasons for a bunker here and another there, and he will be a long way towards pulling his score down to respectable limits. When he has taught himself to study a hole from the point of view of the man who laid it out, he will be much more likely to play it correctly."

Whatever your personal viewpoint on hazards, we cannot leave the topic of how they have developed over time without mentioning some of the very recent influences that have affected them. Four major factors have played a role:

1. *Hazards are dumbed down.* In the 1950s, golf architects began taking hazards out of the way. Play that used to go over or around began to be dictated between. There is a big distinction.

The difficulty of the course was lessened to accommodate the new golfer. It was as if bowling alleys had their gutters filled in so the ball would have only one route to follow.

2. *Golf becomes an industry.* The real-estate market, uniformity, and production plans took hold of hazards. As the design of golf courses became a business, architects copied and used quantity instead of quality. Some efforts were great; others were horrid. Under the industrial standard, hazards could be for other purposes than the game itself. Bunkers were placed not for strategy, but often to protect residential lots, for aesthetics, and for "balance," whatever that meant on any given day. Water features today can mean an amenity for home sales.

3. *Nail-clipper precision.* Following the lead of places like Augusta National Golf Club and courses prepared for television broadcast, hazards became manicured and edged so there were no scruffy bits. Sand now has a specification. There are examples of sand being trucked into new courses in Ohio on pallets—in bags marked "100% White Silica from Florida." Grasses too high for comfort, banks too steep to traverse, and areas too unkempt to tolerate were considered bad for the course's image. In the past, they had been bad only for the golfer.

4. *The game changes.* Match play gave way to stroke play in the mid-1900s. Match play is still popular in the United Kingdom, but the American influence on golf has most of the world's golfers playing a laborious game of count the shots. A hazard so dangerous that it sends chills into one's spine has, in many cases, become a token appearance on modern golf courses. We now have such ridiculous sound bites as "He's better off in that bunker Johnny—it's a much easier shot to the green from there."

Fig. 1-19 Sand Hills Golf Club in Mullen, Nebraska (U.S.A.) is an example of a modern course with an approach to hazards that is reminiscent of natural links courses (see color insert).

Most of us are not bothered by these changes. Or are we? Trends come and go. We are seeing today a resurgence of naturalness, of discovering hazards, of selecting suitable sites for golf courses, of designing and constructing hazards that have soul and variation, of not overdoing bunkers, of restraining artificial water hazards. Is this trend here to stay? Likely not, and hopefully not. As Pete Dye and the late Mike Strantz have proven with their innovative approaches to hazards, a book will never be written that can say once and for all: *A golf hazard is from this to this, and nothing else.*

CHAPTER 2

Types *of* Hazards

BUNKERS, PITS & OTHER HAZARDS

There is little debate about the influence of sand on the game of golf. Ever since the first golfers made their way along the beaches and over the dunes, sand has been a constant component of golfing grounds. This partially explains why so many golf architects in modern times have fashioned a crutch out of depressions filled with sand, and then used this crutch to prop up their designs.

Look carefully at golf courses created after the Great Depression. Even as recently as the writing of this book, it was common for a golf architect to unleash 75 or more sand bunkers upon a single 18-hole course. Arranged in predictable patterns and shapes, these thrown-at-the-plan bunkers often represent nothing more than a preprogrammed response from the designer. One might compare this approach to those obligatory holiday decorations we see at the dentist's office, the local dry cleaner, or hanging over the counter at the airline ticket counter. A month or so before Christmas, you will be reminded of our analogy. Polite? Cute? Of course. But not usually engaging. Though some have good intentions, there is nothing terribly thoughtful about ripping open a plastic bag full of Santa Claus figures, snowmen, and candy canes, and then taping them to the ceiling or wall.

Throwing elements at a golf course site for the sake of convenience is not a reputable solution. There must be a careful plot written into the golf architect's plan—one that draws out emotion, stimulating decision making and judgment from the golfer. Most of all, the finished design needs to engage the golfer in a game of temptation and challenge. And for many, an aesthetic sense must shape the course. Meeting these goals involves using a variety of hazards, whether concentrating on a particular type (configurations of sand, for example) or mixing types (introducing sand *along with* water, hillocks, undulations, and a smattering of broken ground just for good measure).

Fig. 2-1 Early-1900s photo of a natural dune bunker at Lahinch Golf Club, Ireland. The bunker was named the "Pons Asinorm Bunker," a reference to an elementary theorem in geometry which means "asses' bridge," referring to the fact that fools would be unable to pass this point in their geometric studies. (Source: Golf Illustrated)

What is it about our little bunker that is engaging? Have you imagined it resting there at the bottom of a hill, or is it out in the open, surrounded by fairway? Is it deep? Banked? Partially hidden? Is it alone, or part of some family gathering of other bunkers? Does it offer an escape route? Or is it one of those perilous pits of tremendous grief that beckons all, conveying a message to future generations of golfers through those who could not resist the temptation to carry over it?

If the essence of golf is hazards—and it is—then we must think of hazards as food. Hazards are the energy of all golf courses. They define the experience. Their makeup shows us what the course is all about. To golfers, some hazards are appetizers, while others work together to form the main course. Some are seasoning, others the finale—dessert or perhaps a satisfying coffee.

Like any good meal, a golf course is a sum of its parts. The golf architect uses raw ingredients to concoct recipes that will tantalize and intrigue. The menu is the design. Our enjoyment and performance are the memories we take away with us. The ambiance. The aromas. The satisfaction. If it all seems lame—sameness and based on formula—we know exactly where we are playing golf. We are at Boredom Links.

Classifying Hazards

When all types of hazards that may be integrated on a golf course are considered, the variety appears enormous, nearly exponential. Our aim here is to separate the different types of hazards, discussing them in terms that will make us think. In order to attack a very big salami, one must begin by slicing it. The result is still a big salami, but in pieces, it appears much more manageable and easier to digest.

Natural vs. Artificial

We begin with the simplest of divisions: Natural vs. artificial. In golf course architecture today, natural hazards are favored over artificial ones. Beginning with the process of selecting and evaluating a site on which to form a golf course, the advice of embracing and preserving the natural ebb and flow of the land is very clear. One should identify the most dramatic and interesting features of the land, and then work these into the design whenever it is possible

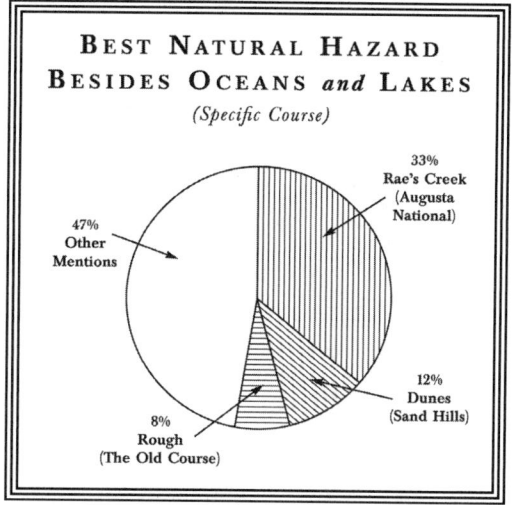

Fig. 2-2 Results of a written survey among 75 officials from golf organizations, greenkeepers, golf architecture writers, golf professionals, and golf course architects conducted during 2004. The survey, conducted by the authors, covered several aspects of hazards, their design, and their maintenance. Results appear throughout the book.

and practical to do so. This is exactly what ancient golfers were practicing when they set out across the linksland toward a target. Would they *avoid* the bumps and obstacles in the way? No. They would purposefully see to it that these bumps and obstacles fell between their starting points and their targets. The punishment was self-inflicted. The routes of holes and courses took the difficult path in many instances, and this was by design.

Fig. 2-3 A natural limestone formation is left exposed about 40 yards short of a par-3 green at Soulliac Golf Club in France. Golf course architect, Jeremy Pern. © J. Pern

Natural hazards are whatever the land offers up. In the case of the site with sand dunes, it would be malpractice if the rises of sand and the grasses that dot the landscape were not integrated as natural hazards. On other sites, it may be a lake, a stream, a ravine, or an outcropping of rock that comes into play as a natural element. And if a course is fortunate enough to find such a home, a natural feature may be an inlet of ocean with waves crashing against rocks and beaches.

Fig. 2-4 The famous Postage Stamp at Royal Troon Golf Club's Old Course, the 8th hole, was originally called Ailsa for its perfect view of the rocky islet by the same name. Willie Park, writing in Golf Illustrated, described the green as, "A pitching surface skimmed down to the size of a Postage Stamp." The smallness of the putting surface, a type of "hazard" in its own right, accounts for its now-famous name. (Courtesy of P. Burton)

Mouthwatering descriptions of natural hazards are supposedly what drive the golf architect to build artificial hazards. The pursuit of natural hazards is, after all, a response to the first golf courses, which were set on land that was as ideal as it was natural. The original golf courses were found, not built. Golf was played in this natural state. As time passed, golfers realized they could do more than carve a hole and clear a place to tee a ball. Hazards could be created that would make things even more interesting. This became a necessity as golf moved inland where there were often few if any natural features similar to those found on seaside links. Alas, the building of golf courses commenced. While the first "man made" golf courses were rudimentary and not so natural in appearance, the golden age[1] designers in particular used all their energy to emulate the natural features of golf's earliest layouts.

---

[1] The "golden age" was that period of golf course architecture that began with the opening of the National Golf Links by C. B. Macdonald in 1911 and lasted roughly until the stock-market crash of 1929, though some extend it to 1937, when Perry Maxwell built nine holes at Prairie Dunes in Kansas.

CHAPTER 2 | TYPES of HAZARDS

Fig. 2-5 Chocolate-drop features can take many forms, but most are geometric. This example of an island drop within sand is from the Tamarack Country Club In Connecticut.

Our idea of imitating nature on the golf course—with artificial hazards and features—is grounded partially in the work of eighteenth-century landscape design, namely that of Lancelot Brown (1715–1783). Known as Capability Brown because of his customary promise that the garden estates of his wealthy clients would have tremendous "capability for landscape improvement" if only turned over to his direction and rebuilding, Brown was responsible for a new age in landscape design. As a "gardener" his doctrine was to convert the grounds of estate property from formal gardens of perfect hedges and rectangular pools to a style of undulating grasses, random clumps of trees, and serpentine lakes. It was shocking to the English landscape, not to mention the English themselves. The new style brought both praise and criticism. Some 15 percent of his masterpieces from long ago, including Stowe in Buckinghamshire and Ashridge in Hertfordshire, have been turned into golf courses since his time. The era of Capability Brown sent a wake-up call to the future. It demonstrated that the artistry of the human race did not have to be based on geometry and formality—that mimicking nature is an acceptable approach when it comes to altering the land.

While it is not a requirement that artificial hazards take their lead from nature, almost all do so. Exceptions are the abrupt features created during the geometric age of golf architecture. This American movement during the late nineteenth and early twentieth century took off with a penchant for the angular, the perpendicular, and the manufactured. Many of America's early golf course designers had come from the business of building and maintaining tennis courts and settings for other lawn sports. They went off in this angular and constructed-looking direction because it was familiar. They had not yet been exposed to Brown's beliefs.

Fig. 2-6 Abrupt chocolate drops from a c.1910 photo at the College Arms Golf Club, Florida. The look was part of a short-lived era of golf course architecture in America that began at the very end of the 1800s and ended shortly after the turn of the century.

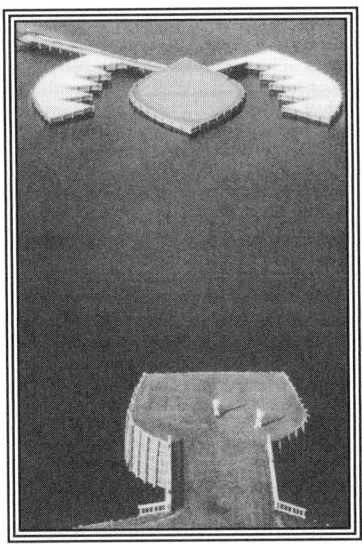

Fig. 2-7 The late Desmond Muirhead began his work as a golf course architect creating innovative, but still classic, designs. His work during the 1960s and 1970s was no indication of what was to come in the 1990s when Muirhead turned to symbolism in golf design. Pictured is the 7th hole, Clashing Rocks, from his famous, Stone Harbor Golf Club, New Jersey. The hole is based on the Greek mythology of Jason and the Argonauts, in which Jason is sent on a journey through a narrow sea guarded by two "clashing rocks." The green (60 feet wide by 125 feet long) represents Jason's boat; the two water-born traps on either side emulate the clashing rocks (see color insert). (© Paul Barton)

Eventually the philosophy of mimicking nature migrated to the States. The notion caught on that golf, in particular, might be better off if it offered good natural hazards and if manufactured hazards followed the pattern of nature. This new ideal was brought to America by men such as Charles Blair Macdonald and A. W. Tillinghast. Macdonald especially can be credited with fostering this direction. He spent time discussing the great links courses of the British Isles with Horace Hutchinson, author of many books and articles about golf and its roots. Hutchinson advocated using nature and variety in 1898 when he began a series of articles on Britain's great links courses. In analyzing the attributes of St. Andrews, Prestwick, and North Berwick, Hutchinson lauded the use of natural and natural-looking features. Even on the many inland courses that had begun to pop up, the golf landscape across the sea from America was embracing the natural look.

In modern times, we have seen the occasional golf architect venture down a creative path that reverts back to the geometric age. For example, in 1993, Bob Cupp created an entire golf course, hazards included, that remains an array of straight lines, polygonned mounds, and bunkers that look like they were created by the animators of *The Jetsons*. The Cupp Course at Palmetto Hall Plantation has the retro look of the geometric era. The late Desmond Muirhead also visited the land of unnatural hazards—more than once. At Lippo Village in Jakarta, Indonesia, Muirhead created a rectangular reflecting pool, a spiral bunker of trigonometric exactness, and straight-edged hazards that could easily have been transported there from old English gardens. In the 1990s, Muirhead aligned his designs with symbolism. He created golf features and hazards

Fig. 2-8 Sometimes a hazard is created through a need other than that of strategy. Such is the case with this drainage ditch at Dooks Golf Club, Ireland. The ditch has become part of the strategy out of default.

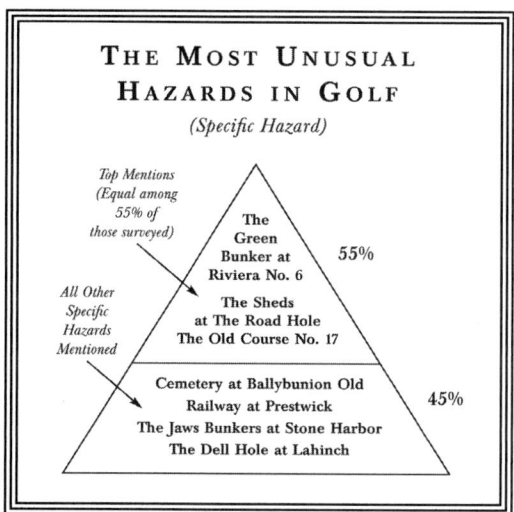

Fig. 2-9 *Results of our survey indicating the most unusual hazards and types of hazards.*

that could be appreciated on the ground, but were even more spectacular when seen from the air. Fish, jaws, perfect circles, eyeballs, and breasts were all a part of Muirhead's repertoire during this time.

In between the pursuit of the all natural or the all unnatural was the idea of introducing functional man-made forms and materials to create hazards. Many man-made materials were first used for practical purposes to reinforce the often deteriorating banks of natural bunkers that would have been a shame to lose to erosion from wind, rain, or the wear and tear of golfers. Sleepers[2] were used on early golf courses for the purpose of holding back sand and soil. Photographic evidence, such as that from North Berwick in Scotland where the famous Redan Hole is flanked by sleepers, shows that the practice was around quite early in golf's evolution. Stone walls, stacked sod walls, and bulkheads are all examples of devices used as retaining walls to keep the edges of hazards upright. But these were out of necessity and practicality. The effort was not in response to a design trend, as was the case of geometric design.

Another rationale for mixing naturalness with man-made forms was to handle drainage. The ditches that still grace Oakmont wound up being "perfect" hazards, yet their original purpose was the rudimentary one of carrying nuisance water off the course during heavy rains. They were not for strategy and there is nothing natural about Oakmont's ditches, but today they are revered as a classic element—typifying a time when practicality was in vogue and some things—well, they simply had to be done.

We started out here by noting that natural hazards are favored in golf. At least they are

Fig. 2-10 Representing hazards on hole plans and course layouts has always been a matter of professional style. The late golf architect, William Watson used these symbols on his plans.

---

[2] *Sleeper* is generally thought to be derived from a railroad term meaning a piece of timber (or stone or iron) that supports and keeps the rails in place. But the word predates rail travel and the Industrial Age. In shipbuilding, a *sleeper* is a piece of timber placed longitudinally in a ship's hold, opposite the scarfs of the timbers. And in castle construction, a *sleeper* is the lowest of horizontal timbers. Your authors feel comfortable in representing the view that the term goes all the way back to the 1500s, at least.

today, and this has been the trend ever since golf's popularity took hold across the world. Except for a few isolated periods (let's call them science experiments), golf architecture is a matter of finding natural features or making things look natural. Some fail at the latter, of course. Who has not seen the bunker that looks like a hippie flower? The reality is that nearly all of the built features in golf look artificial to some degree. The trained eye is able to detect the rough-edged bunker or the squirrelly edge of a wetlands that has been sculpted by the shaper in an effort to make it pass as nature's handiwork.

Certainly, there is no right or wrong in choosing between the natural and the artificial. The greatest courses in the world are combinations of both. We suppose that in the strictest sense, only the left-in-place broken ground or completely untouched wilderness area within our golf courses can be 100 percent natural. All other areas in golf are traversed by golfers, continually matted down and changed. Or they are of the created variety, changed for the purpose of carrying out the game and making it more—or less—interesting.

Fig. 2-11 Islands of native grass, Bethpage Black, New York. Islands within formal sand bunkers are considered part of the hazards according to The Rules of Golf (see color insert). (Photo by Larry Lambrecht, courtesy of Rees Jones, Inc.)

Formal vs. Informal

A formal hazard is one defined by the Rules of Golf. A bunker, for example, is defined by the United States Golf Association (USGA) as:

a hazard consisting of a prepared area of ground, often a hollow, from which turf or soil has been removed and replaced with sand or the like.

The USGA has also contemplated islands of turf within a bunker—they are *not* part of the bunker; however, a wall or lip not covered with grass is part of the bunker. Each golf course, however, has ultimate control of determining its own hazards. This is accomplished through local rules and markings that take into account unique conditions and configurations of hazards.

At Pete Dye's Whistling Straits (the Straits Course) in Wisconsin, there are a reported 1,400 bunkers . . . no, wait, the pro-shop staff says "more than 1,500". . . no wait, the yardage book shows only about 1,250 . . . Who knows? Dye doesn't care. They were meant to make golfers think, not become a controversial element associated with the Rules of Golf. At the 2004 PGA Championship, these 1,400 (or so) bunkers did cause a stir when more than one ruling had to be made as to whether a competitor's ball was in or out of them. Stuart Appleby was caught removing a piece of grass and grounding his club within one of these bunkers on hole No. 16 because he "didn't think it was a bunker." Ultimately, this distinction becomes especially important as more and more courses are being developed with rough-edged and natural bunkers that have little hope of offering a black-and-white snapshot of what is part of the bunker and what is not. At the edges of bunkers, especially those near naturally rough terrain, there are interesting gray areas on golf courses. The point at which bunkers end is not always apparent.

The other formal hazard in golf is the water hazard. Again, according to the USGA, a water hazard is

> *any sea, lake, pond, river, ditch, surface drainage ditch or other open water course (whether or not containing water) and anything of a similar nature on the course.*

Golf's ruling body goes on to describe the differences in procedure and markings for water hazards; there are two varieties: water hazards and also lateral water hazards. This is so golfers will know how to proceed when caught by one. Water hazards are typically marked by stakes and/or painted lines; yellow for water hazards and red for lateral water hazards.

Fig. 2-12 A photo of a bunker at Hoylake Golf Club, England, c.1921. On early courses, bunkers would often become "water hazards" after rains, but play was always "as it lies" until the adoption of formal rules permitting a drop and penalty stroke. (Source: Golf Illustrated, April 1921)

Formal vs. informal is a matter of the rules and how any given golf course goes about defining its hazards. These rules are rather recent. Until the Royal & Ancient Golf Club of St. Andrews formalized rules before the turn of the eighteenth century, a golfer only had two rules to follow: (1) Put the ball into play at the tee and do not touch it until removing it from the hole; and (2) Play the course as you find it. Later on, if one found a ball in such trouble that it could not be played, rules helped resolve this. This is exactly how the concept of the formal hazard came into being. Before the mad dash to adopt rules for any and all occurrences in golf, any place on a golf course could be considered a hazard, and it mattered not whether you were in, out, or in between. The player was entitled to ground the club anywhere. The concept of formal vs. informal was not yet defined.

Fig. 2-13 Golf architect, Gil Hanse integrated stacked stone walls into his design of the Boston Golf Club, Massachusetts.

There are, of course, plenty of other hazards in golf besides sand bunkers and water. These are described later in this chapter. Hazards come in a variety of forms, and it is

Fig. 2-14 Under the Rules of Golf, a bunker is "a hazard consisting of a prepared area of ground, often a hollow, from which turf or soil has been removed and replaced with sand or the like." In this restored bunker at the Arizona Biltmore Adobe Course, Arizona (c.1926, William P. "Billy" Bell), Forrest Richardson has left the edges as natural, "hairy" borders (see color insert). (Photograph by Mike Houska, DogLeg Studios)

Fig. 2-15 This natural wash, while sand, is not defined as a formal bunker hazard. The ball, therefore, is played as it lies through the green. Such features are still hazards, just not formal hazards under the Rules of Golf. Phantom Horse Golf Club, Arizona, Forrest Richardson, golf course architect. (Photograph by Craig Wells)

worthwhile to note that not all are physically attached to the ground. Some are the very condition of the ground: is it level or undulating? Some are agronomically induced: is the grass dense and tall, or is it tight and lightning-fast? Some are day-to-day occurrences: is it windy, wet or dry? Obviously each of these examples is well outside the definition of formal.

To be very clear about modern golf: *The only formal hazards are bunkers and water hazards*. The balance of our hazard arsenal in golf architecture is of the informal variety. Without these components, conditions, and elements, we would have a very limited box of crayons with which to color our courses and make them unique works of art and interesting obstacle courses.

Sand Hazards

Sand hazards may be formal or informal. A formal sand hazard is a bunker as described above. Bunkers are typically depressions, although there is no rule stating that they must be. In the case of the bunker, the sand is typically maintained, although there is also no rule requiring this routine. A bunker is not defined with stakes or painted lines. Rather, the edge of the bunker where the grass meets the sand defines its bounds according to the rules of golf.

Informal sand, on the other hand, is any sandy area that is not considered by a particular golf course to be a bunker. Sand dunes, for example, are usually considered *through the green,* a term used to refer to the entirety of a golf course *except* the teeing area, the formal hazards, and the putting surfaces. Informal sand may appear very bunkerlike. But for the purposes of golf and its rules, it may simply be a waste area that is through the green. The primary distinction between a formal and informal hazard is, as mentioned, whether the golfer may ground the club before making a stroke. In any formal hazard, one may not ground the club and may not test the surface conditions. Other distinctions are mostly superfluous. Sand, no matter where it is located or how it is defined, is not where most golfers want to find their ball. It is a hazard, whether one with a set of policies attached to it or one with a simpler existence.

Fig. 2-16 A formal water hazard at Coldwater Golf Club, Arizona. (Photograph by Mike Houska, DogLeg Studios)

Water Hazards

The famous Swilcan Burn at St. Andrews is often reported to be the first artificial water hazard ever created. Here is a ditch that meanders in front of the first green and plays havoc with golfers as they attempt to negotiate their tee shots and approaches. It was originally constructed to help drain the town. Now it helps define The Old Course.

Water hazards are a simple enough concept. There is no point in listing the many nouns associated with bodies of water or water courses. What is helpful to realize,

Fig. 2-17 Rendering for an unusual water hazard at The Links at Las Palomas, Sonora, Mexico. This par-3 drops 30 feet to a green built out into a lagoon. The edge of the green at the lagoon is bordered by stone aqueducts that flow around the green and allow water to cascade into the lagoon (see color insert). Forrest Richardson and Arthur Jack Snyder, golf course architects. (Illustrator: David Smith)

Fig. 2-18 Broken ground is simply rugged ground, usually natural, which forms a hazard, although not in the formal sense. Photo of the 18th hole at Ashdown Forest, England.

however, is that water hazards do not necessarily need to contain water. For example, a dry ravine or barranca may be considered a water hazard, and so may a normally dry ditch. Also, it is of no great consequence for definition's sake whether a water hazard is natural or artificial.

In designing—and playing—golf courses, we must keep in mind the many forms of the water hazard. Numerous types of water hazards are organized in our minds, usually by their appearance. We get visual clues as to how difficult or easy a water hazard may be to avoid from its location and size. These are the overt clues. But we also absorb subtler clues. In an excellent chapter on the psychology of golf course design in *Routing the Golf Course* (John Wiley & Sons, 2002) contributor Dr. Ed Sadalla notes, "The way in which water is incorporated into the scene . . . may increase or decrease its potency." Sadalla cites four factors that add interest and intrigue to water hazards:

1. *Land-water Contrast*—the extent to which the distinction between land and water is visible
2. *Shoreline Complexity*—the variety of shapes that result where land meets water
3. *Size*—the diversity in the sizes of water area, which tends to add interest
4. *Internal Contrast*—the height and texture of vegetation within a water feature

Together these factors send signals to us that are translated by the brain into thoughts such as "danger," "risk," "worth it," "not worth it," and "conquest."

Broken Ground

Player to Caddie: "Why do you keep looking at your watch? I need you to concentrate on finding my ball!" Caddie: "This is not a watch sir, it's a compass."

Fig. 2-19 No. 12 at Addington Golf Club, England. The terrain poses a hazard of its own, falling to the right while the hole twists to the left. (Courtesy of P. Burton)

Fig. 2-20 A natural rock outcrop creates an interesting landing area off the tee at Boston Golf Club, Massachusetts.

Broken ground in golf is defined as any area of unkempt ground. Of course, it is not a formal hazard, or we would call it a sand bunker or a water hazard. Broken ground is usually an open area along a hole or an especially rough area that breaks the line of play. Broken ground comes in many forms. It can be a simple pocket of undulating ground that is rarely mowed, if ever, or an area of wild grasses or a barren, gravelly area. Along the coast it may be sand dunes, while in some regions it may be native desert, woodland meadows, or highland prairie. Such an area of the course need not be natural, as many types of interesting terrain have been created to give golf courses a texture that contrasts with the fairways and areas of improved turf.

The concept of broken ground is also one of efficiency. While these areas are not formal hazards, they can be of great strategic value to a golf hole. At Pine Valley, for example, the great rough and gnarly areas of sandy soil and scrub are the epitome of broken ground. Broken ground requires little maintenance or care. It evolves with nature and gives the unmistakable impression that the golf course was carved from nature. Perhaps this is the essence of broken ground: rather than being a "spot" within a course, such as an individual bunker or pond, it is a common background through which the course itself weaves and flows.

Fig. 2-21 The greens of North Berwick Golf Club, Scotland, are an adventure at every step. (Courtesy of P. Burton)

Bumps, Contours, Undulations & Hollows

"Bumps, Contours, Undulations, and Hollows" sounds suspiciously like the

Bunkers, Pits & Other Hazards

Fig. 2-22 The Dell at Lahinch, a par-3 green setting of tremendous character and mystery (see color insert).

greeting of a receptionist answering the phone at a law firm.

Every golfer has met Mr. Bump, Mr. Contour, Mr. Undulation, and Mr. Hollow. On the ground of linksland, we get to know each one very well. Only the most destructive of individuals would smooth them out to build a golf course. The game is fascinating when *sidehill, downhill,* and *uphill* are used to describe stances and shots. Whether on the fairway or a green, the use of such informal hazards constitutes a ground game of tremendous interest.

Our use of contours in golf has its roots in linksland. As the game moved to inland regions, golfers sought land that would offer many of the same characteristics. In the heathland (which is generally land of scrubby vegetation including heather), the best of sites for golf were those with bumpy, sand-covered terrain and good drainage. In the moorlands (generally rolling land that is considered mostly infertile), golf once again gravitated toward sites with interest and character. This is where golf architecture got its foothold. The earliest golf architects worked diligently, either to find land that would offer linksland ground conditions or, as equipment would allow, to transform parcels of land with many of its qualities. In addition, trees often had to be cleared and new hazards created.

There is also the dramatic effect of uphill and downhill. The most extreme examples are not on linksland or gently rolling land, but on the wild pieces of earth on which we have built golf: alpine courses with hundreds of feet of elevation change, valleys where holes string along the hillside, and canyons where holes dart down and across.

Fig. 2-23 A natural rock edge forms the edge of the green at Carton House Golf Club, Ireland.

Fig. 2-24 The Pit at North Berwick is the odd, but fun, No. 13: a 365-yard, par-4 with an approach over a stone wall set at a diagonal to a putting surface lying directly on the other side. The wall provides an interesting and unusual challenge, to say the least. (Courtesy of P. Burton)

When such drastic contours are put to use, they constitute a challenge—a hazard without sand or, necessarily, roughness. The mere act of selecting a club on a particularly downward or upward shot is, in and of itself, a potential hazard.

Green Hazards

Think of the fact that one half of the game of golf is played upon the surface of the green. At least the concept of par makes this so. On the 18-hole course with a par of 72, we are led down a path to try to reach the green in regulation and then to take no more than two putts per hole after we reach the green. Those who manage this—and few do—have mastered the game. Ideally, then, the game of golf is one-half putting. But even for the high handicapper of 30, putting accounts for more than one-third of the strokes taken on the par-72 layout (36 putts ÷ 102 total strokes = 35%).

A variety of "green hazards" are designed and shaped into greens. The very size of a green can be a challenge to the golfer. The large green requires discipline. One who settles for merely reaching a large green may have left too much work to be done; a long putt or one across complicated slopes can be very tricky. The extremely small green offers a challenge of its own; missing the small green means an extra layer of effort.

Other variables in greens have to do with slope, gradient, and surface. Mr. Undulation, when he is present on a green, requires thinking by the golfer. One must not be too bold or too delicate, for gravity is always a factor. We know these conditions as *speed* and *break*. And when we add slickness to the equation, watch out!

Other factors that can make the green challenging include where the pin is placed and whether we are able to see this area from our angle of approach. While these issues

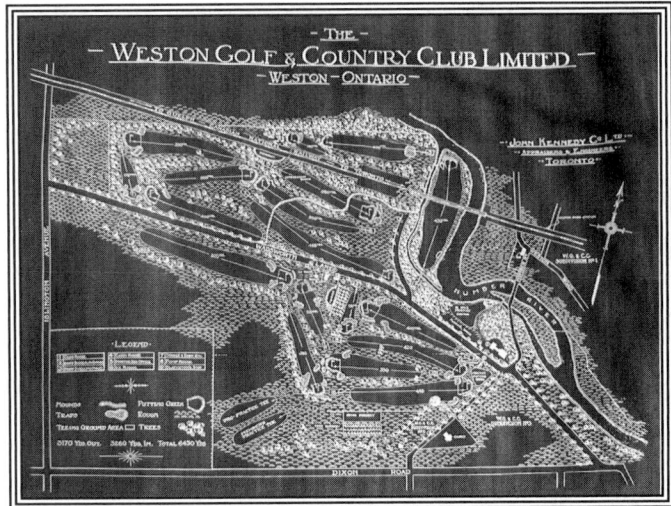

Fig. 2-26 An unusual hazard—the railway line is elevated above the No. 2 hole. (Refer to plan in Fig. 2-25)

Fig. 2-25 An old plan of Weston Golf Club in Ontario, Canada. Note the railway line that runs through the property—in fact, right over the No. 2 hole where golfers must negotiate the elevated rail line and the support pillars. (Refer to Fig. 2-26)

will be covered in depth later on, it is good to think specifically about the setup and visibility of greens as we focus on green surfaces. There may be no better example of a hole that illustrates these two thoughts than the Dell. When we arrive at this par-3, 5th hole at Lahinch in Ireland (see page 30) we might find a hole location by glimpsing a hint of the flagstick. Or we can arrive to find nothing but a massive, grass-covered dune staring us down, begging for a shot to be played over its hairy toupee. In either case, there is an element of hide-and-seek at play. The challenge of the green here is all about the options for setting the cup and the maddening fact that many of the locales where one is able to place a flag prompt a shot of blind faith. (The Lahinch tradition is to place a white stone along the ridge of the fronting dune each day before golfers arrive at the Dell. This is intended to denote where the hole has been set by the greenkeeper. Even this marking poses a challenge, for it must always cause the passing thought in the golfer's mind whether the employee who was supposed to move the stone actually remembered to do so.)

Integral Obstructions

Obstructions are defined in the Rules of Golf for the purposes of giving the player relief in order that the obstruction be avoided. We are interested here in obstructions that, in the language of the Rules of Golf, may include *"any construction declared by the Committee to be an integral part of the course."*

Integral obstructions can be stone walls, fences, buildings, ruins, rock outcroppings, bridges, roads, rail tracks, and so on, that add to the interest and challenge of a golf hole. They can include churches, lighthouses, graveyards, castles, old foundations, and quarry piles. The list is as endless as one's imagination.

We should recall that golf in its most ancient form ran through the streets and not just the open linksland. Such obstructions were not only a part of the game in these times; they *were* the game. Perhaps such structures are now just carryovers from days gone by. However, when one takes into account the great interest that has been brought to golf by these obstacles, it is a wonder that they are not considered more often in the design of modern courses. *Considered* is the key word here. We are not suggesting that modern courses be overdone in this regard. Structure needs to be worked into the routing to make sense, be fun, and be relatively safe. It would not be wise to litter a golf course with integral obstructions to excess, or to make their use monotonous, or to place a golfer at tremendous risk in executing a shot. This latter concern may be partially to blame for the declining use of such structures on golf courses. A golfer, though, should always exercise good judgment. It is the golfer, after all, who has left a shot too close to the huge boulder or the old stone house. What a shame it is to remove or tear down these landmarks when they can often offer such a rich glimpse into the heart of the land that makes up the course. We vote for more hazards in this category, provided they are thoughtful and have a good reason for being.

Trees

William Flynn was among those golden age golf architects who promoted trees and felt they deserved a place on golf courses. He wrote:

> *The old ideas have been discarded and the prevailing belief is that trees, most emphatically, have a fixed place on a golf course. This is true for many reasons: First—Because there are few, if any, sites available that are devoid of trees and it is a costly operation to cut them down and remove them. Second—Trees add beauty to a course, forming picturesque backgrounds and delightful vistas. Third—Their shade is most refreshing on a hot summer day. Fourth—They are of great practical value in segregating the various holes.*

Fig. 2-27 An interesting green that was built around a native desert tree. The tree and stone wall create a one-of-a-kind hazard situation. Phantom Horse Golf Club, Arizona (see color insert). Forrest Richardson, golf course architect.

Fig. 2-28 The term double hazard *is used to describe a situation where a golfer is faced with a second obstacle after finding a first hazard. In this case, a tree may stymie the golfer who has already been bunkered. No. 14 at Moselem Springs Golf Club, Pennsylvania, 442 yards, par-4. George Fazio, golf course architect.*

The original idea in transporting "links golf" to other terrain, including that large tract known as America, was to have golf courses as free from trees as possible. This notion was imported from the seaside courses of Scotland because they were the only prototype known. For the most part, there are few trees on linksland. Ah, but there are the exceptions. Carnoustie is one example of a links course with trees. There are many others throughout England, Scotland, and Ireland. But according to Paul Daley, who has written extensively about linksland and golf, linksland is simply not as conducive to tree growth as it is to the more tolerant grasses, gorses, and so on. Daley points out that, in the early days of St. Andrews, there were even attempts to cultivate trees, but all failed. Why? Daley writes, "The answer lies in the repelling soil and salt, and the stunting nature of the wind."

Yet many legendary golf architects seemed to like the idea of trees. A look at the diagrams in Wethered and Simpson's book, *The Architectural Side of Golf,* will show that Simpson approved of using trees as strategic hazards. Tillinghast wrote about trees and made several suggestions regarding their use in design. Flynn, however, was among their staunchest supporters, reasoning, "It is impossible to conceive that the 'Canny Scots' would have denuded their courses of trees if there had been any there originally. As a race they are entirely too thrifty for any such waste as that."

Trees will be covered in more detail in Chapter 6. For now we will proclaim that the tree—and its pygmy cousin, the shrub—is indeed a "hazard," and perhaps the best of all the integral obstructions that can be incorporated into a golf course. While opinions vary on the acceptable quantity of trees, as well as the placement and degree of penalty a tree may induce, there is little question that trees can serve a purpose on many courses.

CHAPTER 2 | TYPES *of* HAZARDS

Fig. 2-29 A great boundary hole at Talking Stick Golf Club in Arizona. Designers Bill Coore and Ben Crenshaw used an old fence line to route the No. 2 hole on the North Course. Both the tees and green hug the fence at the left, daring the golfer to choose how close the "do or die" OB line is within their comfort zone. (Courtesy of P. Burton)

Fig. 2-30 A variation of the boundary hole where a stone wall flanks the putting surface. Dunbar Golf Links, Scotland (see color insert). (Photograph by Paul Daley, Full Swing Golf Publishing)

There is an urban legend about an architect who is intent on ridding a hole of a particularly large tree. The members of the club lay down the law: "You must preserve that tree at all cost." The architect begrudgingly agrees. The next morning, there is the preserved tree—stacked neatly as a pile of logs next to the dining room fireplace. Many golf purists[3] pooh-pooh trees, saying they have very little place on a golf course. To be fair, a majority of those who share this opinion limit their dislike to the occasion when trees begin to guide a golfer along a single corridor or when trees are so controlling that they take away the variety of shots that a player might consider.

Out-of-Bounds

An area or edge marked out-of-bounds (OB) is the most harsh and rude of all "hazards." If one hits the ball out-of-bounds there is no chance of recovery. The only play is to replay the shot. This means stroke *and* distance. There is no dropping of the ball at the point of entry.

The OB hole often receives mixed reviews. We laud the Road Hole at St. Andrews, but we hate the massive housing community where the back walls of tract housing can come into play. This seems a warranted position. At St. Andrews, we have history and tradition, while at the modern course with breakfast nooks looking out over the course, we have mass-produced housing and often little charm. We should keep the breakfast nook as far away as reasonable; we really do not want it coming into play.

---

[3] We have no definition of a golf purist other than to suggest that this individual has good intentions and a passion for the game. We cannot resist the temptation to also point out that a few will occasionally become so set in their ways that they fail to see the trees through the forest.

Regardless of your opinion on OB, the boundary hole in golf can pose an interesting challenge. The golfer's daring attempt to come as close to the boundary as possible in order to gain a favorable position is what such holes are all about. Such holes are designed to tantalize. The golfer flirts. The relationship begins.

The Elements

Wind is chief among the elements that affect the strategy of golf holes. The golf ball has no real defense against the wind. It is blown wildly as the wind increases, which causes the golfer to make adjustments. This, of course, takes away some of the brain power a golfer might otherwise use to carry out other duties: to plan the attack of the hole, to execute the swing correctly, and to think ahead. It is amazing when you consider all that a golfer must do simultaneously. When the wind is not a factor, it is so much easier.

Old Tom Morris believed firmly that the opening holes of a course should send the golfer in all directions. At Carnoustie this occurs by the fifth hole. At The Old Course the trek is more constant until the eighth, where the golfer must make three quick turns. But these turns at St. Andrews take place in the windiest of all places, at the tip of the cape formed by St. Andrews Bay and the River Eden.

Wind is not alone among the climate hazards. Dampness of the ground is a hazard, and so is dryness. A shot played to a firm and fast fairway or green can be very challenging, more so than playing to ground that will allow a shot to stick without rolling. There is also the harshness of temperature, foggy days, rain, and the influence of altitude. The golf course architect forgets about these too often. The golfer, however, is given no escape route. The hazards that lurk in the air and drop from above are every bit as much a part of the challenge of a golf course.

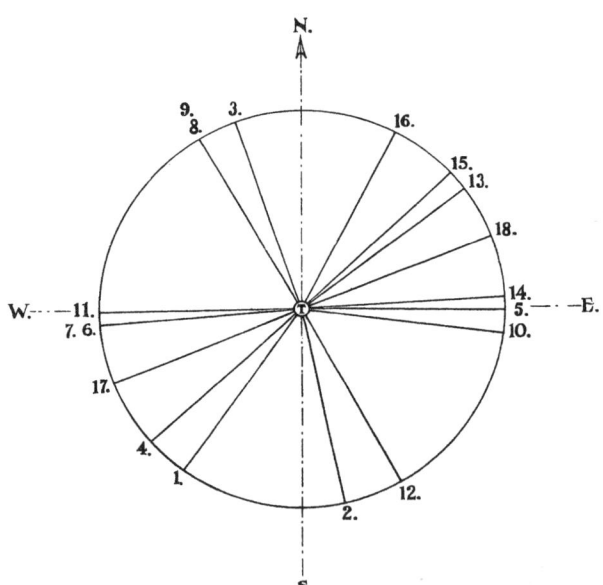

Fig. 2-31 An innovative "wind clock" reprinted from a souvenir booklet (c.1933) about the Carnoustie Golf Links, Scotland. The chart shows the direction of the prevailing wind for each hole, providing a visual diagram. Carnoustie was purposefully routed to dramatically change direction within its opening holes.

Course Conditions

Consider this account of American golf hazards penned in 1902 for *Golf Illustrated,* a rich and opinionated weekly journal of golf:

> *American golfers are not so blest, or curst, as we are with natural hazards, either in degree or number. There is little of the "unfriended wastes and sandy, perilous wilds," which our own best seaside courses possess . . . Our cousins suffer from made bunkers, water hazards, drains, trees, and other things, just as we do, and their "rough" is a thing not to be lightly spoken of. With characteristic American humour it is known as "spinach."*

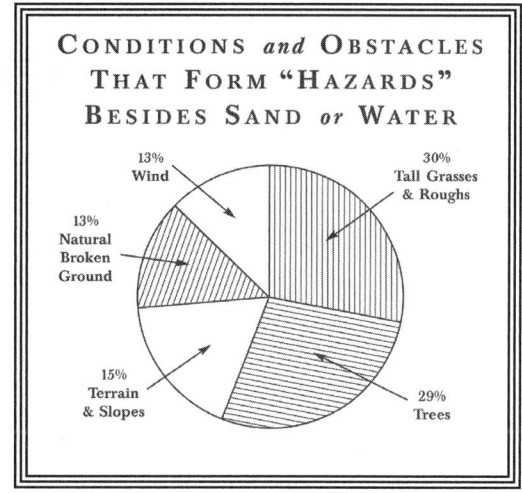

Fig. 2-32 Besides the formal hazards—bunkers and water—tall grasses and roughs are thought of most often as a "hazard" according to our survey.

Course conditions include the height of grass (the rough) and all that is done—or not done—by the greenkeeper. While conditions are more temporary than the constructed and natural hazards of a course, no one can deny that tall rough poses a challenge, or that any number of activities undertaken by a grounds crew can make a course more difficult. Are the bunkers raked? Are the banks leading toward water hazards tightly mowed? Are the fairways narrow? Are the limbs of trees kept high? Are the greens rolled to be as fast as possible? These conditions may change, but they are among the challenges faced by a player. Course conditioning is done by the greenkeepers. They may be under the direction of the golf architect, the owner, or a committee. The way a course is conditioned may be a result of tradition or it may be due to ongoing experimentation. It is a fascinating part of golf—an ever changing variable that adds interest and provides an almost infinite set of possibilities.

Course Setup

Another factor is the placement of tee markers and pin positions throughout the course. The placement of tee markers, not only in terms of length, but also laterally at the tee, will greatly change and affect how a hole plays. This is especially noticeable at the par-3 where the golfer is forced to hit to the putting surface with absolutely no say in the matter.

Fig. 2-33 The greenkeeper often determines a "hazard" through mowing protocols and practices. Long after the golf course architect has left the site, roughs, fairway limits, and mowing around and on greens are continually adjusted. On this reachable par-4, slopes near the green are mowed tight to bring the barranca into play and the attempt a risky gamble. No. 12, The Hideout Golf Club, Utah. Forrest Richardson and Arthur Jack Snyder, golf course architects.

Other setup variables include watering, lack of watering, and daily rolling, which can change green speeds. Rough heights, of course, are determined by how high the cutting blades of mowers are set. Professional staff, the greenkeeper, and members may decide at a meeting how it will be.

Pin positions may be the greatest contribution of the daily setup. Their placement is often determined by whoever arrives at the club before 5:00 A.M. and takes the hole cutter out for its daily round.

Deceiving Tactics

Tricks of depth perception, camouflage, diagonals, and blind or partially blind conditions are examples of deceiving tactics used in the placement and configuration of hazards. Golf courses are full of deceptive features: The short hole that seems a no-brainer, yet is full of trouble; a long par-4 immediately following a very short par-5; the extra par-3 tucked into an 18-hole course. All of these have to do with routing, yet each is a trick, however slight, which can be put into the bin with all of the other formal and informal hazards.

The Purpose of Hazards

One way to classify a hazard is by its purpose. A bunker, for example, may exist to challenge, to confuse, or to prevent. As a prevention device, it might provide a last hope before sending a ball over a cliff, or it may signal that a particular edge is not preferred. All challenging shots in golf are defined by a hazard of one type or another. The five basic shot types and their hazard relationships are:

CHAPTER 2 | TYPES *of* HAZARDS

Fig. 2-34 Hazard placement, green location, and backdrops (or lack thereof) can be deceiving to the eye. Toward expansive, territorial views, the golfer is often "lost" in judging distance. Hole No. 2, Old Head, Ireland (see color insert). (Courtesy of P. Burton)

1. Penal—where the hazard is in the way and requires absolute carry to achieve progress.
2. Heroic—where the hazard offers incremental degrees of risk and reward, the greater risk offering the better outcome when properly executed.
3. Detour—where the hazard sets up multiple choices that are not as simple as pure risk or conservative play.
4. Lay-up—where the hazard demands a throttled back shot, one shorter than the player is capable of making.
5. Open—where the hazard is missing in action.

We shall not concern ourselves too much with open shots, as this is not preferred in golf, especially in a book about hazards. It does deserve mention, however, that an open shot brings with it a certain psychological "hazard." Think how "easy" it is to play a shot when there is nary a hazard to consider. A basketball player can make jump shot after jump shot with defenders all around, but isn't it amazing how many times the basket gets missed at the foul line with no one in the way?

The golf course architect leaves hazards behind as bread crumbs for golfers to find their way. As a golfer puts shots together—heroic, detour, and so on—the results either eliminate hazards or bring new ones into play. Each golfer has an individual relationship with hazards. As a course is played, these obstacles should not be repetitive or seem too laborious. The best hazards create temptation and make the golfer think.

A few hazards serve aesthetic, historical, or drainage purposes. Hell Bunker at The Old Course is partially where it is because gardeners used to dig cockle shells from that spot to tilth into their gardens. Is Hell Bunker, therefore, diabolical, strategic, aesthetic, or historic? Or what about the many "misplaced" bunkers on The Old Course? Those that defined the course in its clockwise routing[4] have no good reason to be there now other than as a link to the past.

And lastly, is there any golf architect who has not placed a hazard simply because it seemed right and he or she wanted to do it? Perhaps it was just a quirky thing to do, or perhaps there were so many reasons that a single one cannot be pinpointed. There are probably many moments when a golfer stands upon a tee and asks why a hazard is the way it is, or is where it is. This brief moment is a "hazard" unto itself, for it has siphoned away some precious time from the golfer. The power of the mental hazard can never be underestimated.

Fig. 2-35 What exactly is the intent of a hazard in golf? "To examine one's game and assess a penalty if it is found wanting," reasons Bill Yates, an expert in positive golf experiences and pace-of-play issues. Perhaps no course embodies this definition more than Cypress Point Club, where the challenge and diversity of hazards are wide ranging (see color insert). (Courtesy of P. Burton)

---

[4] The Old Course used to be played clockwise, and play was altered between the left-hand and right-hand routings until the current layout was adopted in the 1870s.

CHAPTER 3

Twenty Famous Hazards

Are golf hazards truly inanimate? Do we believe that they lie still and have no life, not even a momentary breath? As golfers, when we stand upon the tee and contemplate a hazard in the distance—one that is within our reach—what is it, then, that sets so many things in motion? Who orchestrates the successes and failures of the next few moments? Who is it that ties a knot in the stomach of the golfer? Who nudges the decision to go with one club rather than another? Who—O.K., *what*—causes the grip to become just slightly too tight? Or causes that extra amount of oxygen to be inhaled in the second before swinging?

Could it be the hazard? Ask any golfer to relate a favorite experience on the links and you will hear of a romantic adventure. There will be the chance encounter, the eye contact, the flirting, and perhaps a dangerous love affair. There will, of course, be a longing to return to do it all over again, "if the opportunity ever arises." You will hear of joy and heartache. Many times they are the same story, just told from different perspectives. All golfers have been caught contemplating joy. And all golfers have been caught dwelling on their heartaches. "Expectation is the root of all heartache," reminded Shakespeare. How true in golf.

Our little bunker is not famous. It does not perform in the limelight as do our "Twenty Famous Hazards." Perhaps it lacks strength, size, or maybe it is just too shy. Maybe the links it calls home simply haven't been "discovered" by enough golfers. Boldness, brashness, and the opportunity to allow a golfer to perform are what make a hazard famous. It also does not hurt to be born into royalty. Ask any of the famous hazards at St. Andrews. We include three here, but there are a hundred more. Even the littlest, most isolated bunker probably has a name at St. Andrews. If not an official moniker, then it is surely one bestowed by caddies and golfers who have shared the joy and endured the heartache.

Selecting the Most Famous

This is not the first attempt to select the most famous or best hazards in golf. As early as 1901 *Golf Illustrated* published a series of opinions on the best golf holes. As you can imagine, the discussion often focused on hazards. The same great magazine ran a regular feature on famous hazards, highlighting several every few issues.

More recently, in 1983, writer Mike Bryan put together a panel to pick the top ten toughest bunkers in the world for a series in *Golf Magazine*.

CHAPTER 3 | TWENTY FAMOUS HAZARDS

The panel consisted of professional players, golf writers, and architects. The list they came up with was:

1. The Road Bunker, *St. Andrews*
2. The Devil's Asshole, *Pine Valley*
3. The Church Pews, *Oakmont*
4. Fairway bunker, *8th hole, Royal Melbourne*
5. The Quarry, *16th hole, Merion East*
6. Back bunker, *12th hole, Augusta National*
7. Hell Bunker, *St. Andrews*
8. Fairway bunker, *4th hole, Royal St. Georges*
9. Hell's Half Acre, *Pine Valley*
10. Back bunker, *14th hole, Muirfield Village*

Donald Ross once stated, "The fascination of the most famous hazards in the world lies in the fact that they were not and could not have been constructed." He avoided the use of the word *created,* because he felt a real hazard is and must be a creation of nature. We have taken Ross to heart, but a modern generation of golfers says that even a manufactured hazard—the 17th hole at the Tournament Players Club of Sawgrass is among the greatest examples—can be every bit as exciting.

To choose the following 20 hazards we used two parallel approaches:

1. We invited 100 well traveled and seasoned "golf people" to partake in a survey. Among many other questions about hazards, we asked: IN YOUR OPINION, WHAT ARE THE FIVE MOST FAMOUS HAZARDS IN GOLF? We did not ask about "best" in this question as our intent was to focus on "famous." In the end, we received 75 responses from our pool of 100. Our group included officials from golf organizations across the world (30%), golf architecture enthusiasts and writers (25%), greenkeepers (20%), golf professionals (18%), and golf course architects (7%).

2. We augmented the selections made by the panel with our own take on the most famous hazards in golf. We drafted long lists even before the panelists sent us their surveys, knowing that many of our favorites would be chosen and obviously some would not. We waited. Upon determining that the last response had been received, we went to work adding our own top ten to the ten that had been chosen through the survey.

The result is a hybrid of famous hazards—the panel's and ours. Ten were chosen by consensus and ten others by us. The panel's top ten appear first, in the order they scored. Ours follow in no particular order.

The Island Hole–The 17th Sawgrass

COURSE: The Stadium Course at the Tournament Players Club of Sawgrass
ARCHITECTS: Pete and Alice Dye, 1981

BUNKERS, PITS & OTHER HAZARDS

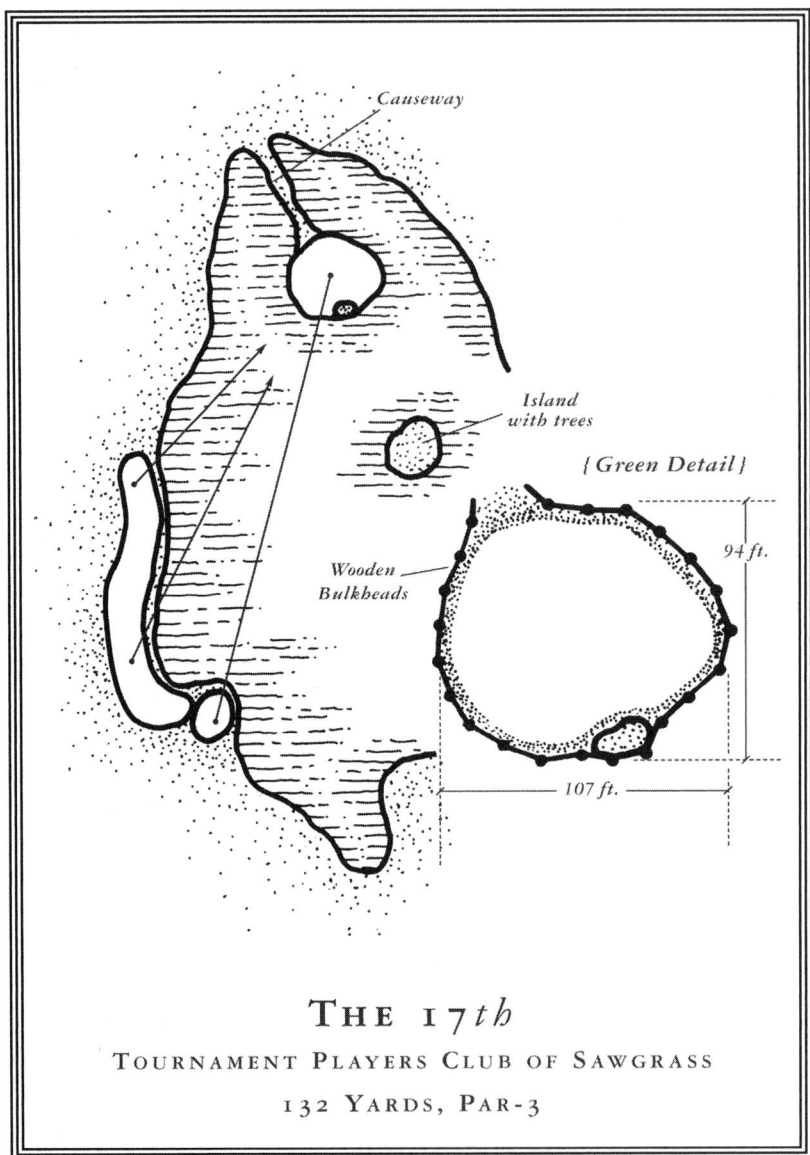

Fig. 3-1

The history of the island green goes back quite a way. Early examples include Hugh Wilson's Cobb Creek, built in 1917. In the same year, Tillinghast created an island green in a wooded setting and went a step further, building an "island within an island" by shaping an abrupt mound of rough grass within the green itself. Later, in 1922, Tillie rebuilt and expanded Baltusrol in New Jersey, getting rid of an island green that had apparently been part of the original course as early as the late 1890s.

CHAPTER 3 | TWENTY FAMOUS HAZARDS

Fig. 3-2 Golf course architect Bobby Weed, who had worked for Pete Dye, rebuilt all of the TPC's greens to USGA specifications. "The 17th hole is the most unchanged of all," he notes. Weed notes a bit of trivia about the wooden bulkhead surrounding the hole, "In 1986 we rebuilt the wall by leaving the original wall in place. The green got just a bit larger—by about 18-inches all around." Imagine the many people who owe Weed a thank-you note and have never known where to send it. Pictured is the island during the original construction. (© 2005 PGA Tour)

Robert Trent Jones, Sr. developed an affinity for island greens beginning in 1936, when he built Pottawatomie Park Golf Course in St. Charles, Illinois, a nine-hole public course on the Fox River. Technically, Jones's "island" was a peninsula, even though accounts from the early days say that golfers reached the green via rowboat. Jones's hole was a par-4 playing about 340 yards, with the green and approach isolated over the watery carry.

All of these designers, we're sure, were responding to a basic human curiosity about islands. An island—and even a peninsula that looks like an island—signals seclusion, isolation, and intrigue to those looking out across the water. From the mainland viewpoint, an island represents the adventure of getting there; the voyage that must be undertaken to reach a distant land. It is no wonder that golfers are fascinated with island greens. Indeed, golfers are also fascinated with island tees and island fairways. Desmond Muirhead's 36-hole McCormick Ranch in Scottsdale, Arizona, has both an island green *and* an island fairway. The 9th of the Palms Course has an island fairway, and the 15th of the Pines Course sports an island green.

The story of the TPC at Sawgrass begins with former PGA commissioner Dean Beaman. His objective was simple: Build a home course for the pros that could serve as a constant site for a "fifth major." Beaman also insisted that the course be conceived from the ground up to serve spectators. For inspiration he looked to Muirfield Village, a creation of Desmond Muirhead working with Jack Nicklaus. Beaman and the PGA settled on a site in Ponte Vedra Beach, Florida, for this undertaking, and Pete Dye was enlisted to bring it to life.

Pete Dye wrote in his book, *Bury Me in a Pot Bunker,* that if he and his wife, Alice, had not been on the scene to supervise construction, there would never have been such a green at the Stadium Course. The area of the 17th proved to contain the best sand on the site. The Dyes excavated this area clean, developing huge piles of sand, which would later serve to cap fairways throughout the project. "The more we dug it out to use on the fairways, the deeper and wider the cavity became," recalls Dye.

Fig. 3-3 Perhaps the most famous hazard in all of golf because of several factors: its extensive coverage on television, access to the public, and the dramatic tee shot with which every golfer can identify (see color insert). (© 2005 PGA Tour)

Many years before, Pete and Alice had played the Ponte Vedra Club, a 1932 design by Herbert Strong. "Such a hole was the farthest thing from my mind when we set the marker for the seventeenth hole," writes Dye. But with massive amounts of sand gone from the area, the Dyes conspired about the possibility of creating their own island green.

With Beaman onboard with the idea, the Dyes went to work figuring out how to completely surround a green with water. Creating access, deciding how much bail-out area there would be, and determining how large a lake to construct were all issues. Originally, the 17th was to have only a small lake to the left of the green. According to Dye, the green was about 26 yards deep and 30 yards wide when they were finished with the shape. A small pot bunker was set at the front of the simple shape.

Pete did not feel the hole would be all that difficult, so he intentionally sloped the green slightly away from the golfer toward the back. Alice, however, vetoed this, feeling that it was difficult enough without the fall-away slope. Pete conceded.

At first the 17th was met with criticism, as were many parts of the Stadium Course. The spectator mounds themselves were the butt of many jokes. Unless you were there as a spectator, the enormous mounds and gallery areas looked like "blights on the landscape." But it was difficult for a professional golfer—in fact, *any* golfer—to find fault with a short iron to a green of about 6,000 square feet. What could be easier then hitting a wedge or 9-iron to a simple green? Sure, the stroke average for the 17th has approached 4.0 during PGA events, but what's the beef? Not only is it a short iron, but you are able to tee your ball for a perfect "lie."

The impact of the 17th is felt even before a golfer arrives at the first tee. For more than three agonizing hours, our golfer is kept waiting in the wings. Finally, upon arriving at the edge of the lake, the tiny island must be faced. Among the ingenious aspects of this hole along with the very fact that it falls one from the last, are the ratio of land to water; the wooden bulkheads that so cleanly distinguish land from water; and the edge of the putting surface, which seems dangerously close to the vertical edge.

The 17th is famous for its history, its intrigue, and its purity in terms of diabolical playfulness with the golfer's mind. There may be no better example of a golf hole where it is hard to distinguish the hazard from the hole—they are one and the same. We cannot, for instance, say that the water is "the" hazard, for it is only one of many hazards at work.

The Dyes took the simplest of concepts and took it to an extreme. There is no namby-pamby bailout, no slopes on which a ball might possibly come to rest, and no hollow to catch a slightly off-line execution. Nothing but a platform of turf, an expanse of still water, and one small bunker for good measure.

Rae's Creek

COURSE: Augusta National Golf Club, Augusta, Georgia, U.S.A.
ARCHITECTS: Alister MacKenzie with Bobby Jones, Jr., 1933

Fig. 3-4 The 13th at Augusta National is now fronted by deeper water than the sandy-bottomed, irregular flowing creek, which used to guard the green. (© Tony Roberts)

Legendary golf writer Herbert Warren Wind is credited with christening the term, "Amen Corner" to the notoriously difficult 11th, 12th, and 13th holes at Augusta. Golfers successfully negotiating the "corner" are said to give thanks, perhaps uttering "Amen." Rae's Creek is at the heart of Amen Corner. During Colonial times, the present-day site of Augusta National was known as Lower Rae's Creek Valley after John Rae, whose plantation and trading post was located at the confluence of the creek and the Savannah River. In 1799, a grist mill was built on the creek in the area that is now the 11th green.

MacKenzie's original routing for what is now known as Amen Corner was played as holes 2, 3, and 4. Bobby Jones, Jr. flopped the nines in 1935, figuring that the new 18th would be a more formidable finish. He may not have realized it at the time, but his decision set in motion what would become one of the most treacherous three-hole series in all of golf's back nines.

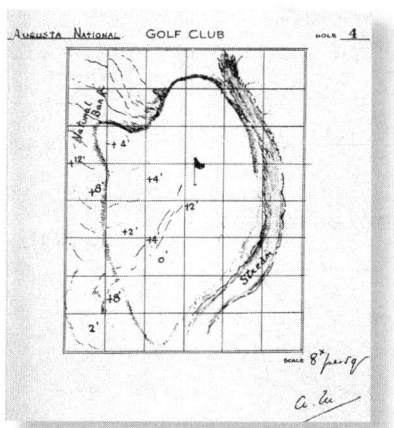

Fig. 3-5 Original green drawing by Alister MacKenzie for what is now the 13th hole, "Azalea."

The outcomes of numerous Masters tournaments have been decided on this stretch of holes. The temptation to flirt with Rae's Creek can lead to disaster or triumph. The 13th—Azalea as it is named—has won the hearts of architects, golfers, and writers from around the world. In his book *Grounds for Golf,* acclaimed writer Geoff Shackelford introduces his thoughts on golf architecture with a blow-by-blow account of the 1996 Masters and how the hole "came to life" to determine the outcome.

Bunkers, Pits & Other Hazards

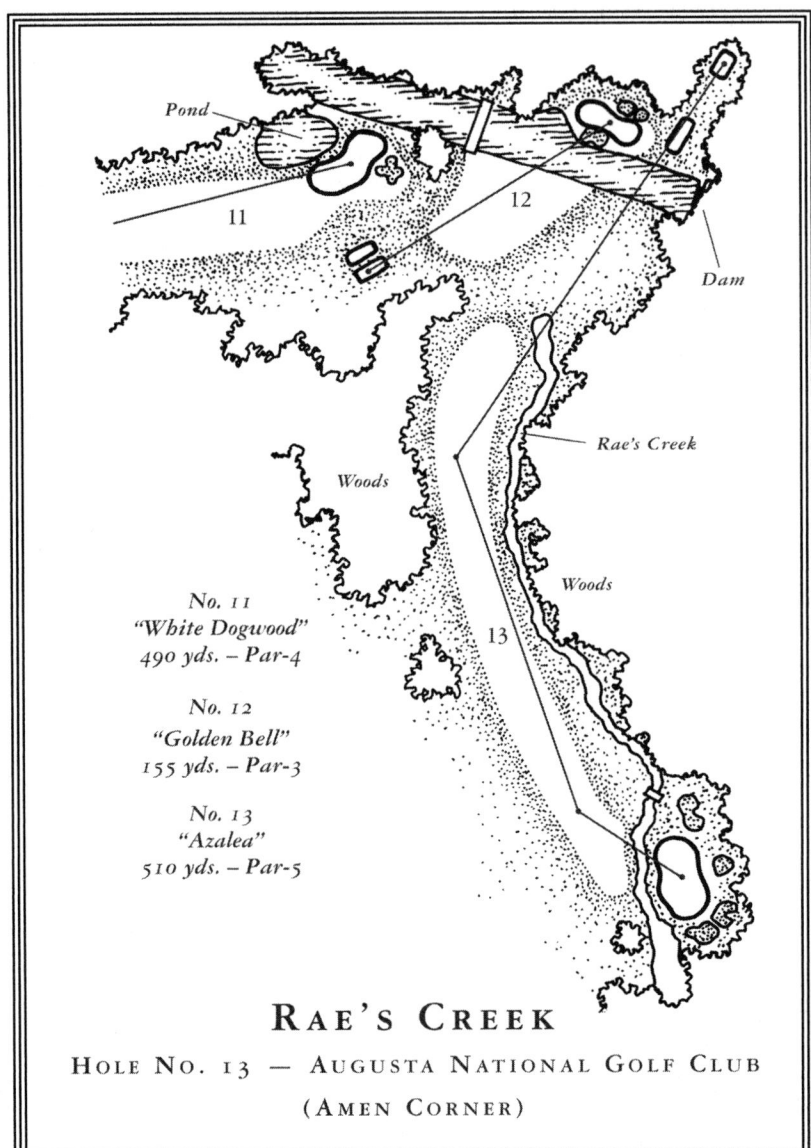

RAE'S CREEK

HOLE NO. 13 — AUGUSTA NATIONAL GOLF CLUB

(AMEN CORNER)

No. 11
"White Dogwood"
490 yds. – Par-4

No. 12
"Golden Bell"
155 yds. – Par-3

No. 13
"Azalea"
510 yds. – Par-5

Fig. 3-6

Changes have unfolded at Augusta. Robert Trent Jones, Sr. had perhaps the largest impact. Jones dammed the creek at No. 16, creating a par-3 of entirely new character. Instead of playing across "just" a creek, the golfer at No. 16 now faces a full carry over a diagonal edge created by the pond. At No. 13, Rae's Creek has also undergone changes, although none as drastic as Jones's work. Over the years, the creek has been adjusted with dams and weirs to control flows and help reduce erosion. Critics have argued that what was once a hazard with possible recovery from sandy, only partially submerged lies beneath a trickle of water, is now a matter of completely lost strokes. These critics claim that the player who might have gone for bust at the second shot to the green will now, too often, lay up. Regardless, Rae's Creek endures at Augusta's famed 13th as a truly remarkable hazard. It articulates to the golf hole and terrain in remarkable ways that simple diagrams, plans, and even television broadcasts cannot describe. If at all possible, one must experience it in person.

The Road Bunker

COURSE: The Old Course, St. Andrews, Scotland

ARCHITECTS: Unknown

There are a lot of misconceptions about the Road Hole. To some it is the most unusual hole in all of golf. The chronology of The Old Course, at best, can only be gleaned from the records available. The first survey of the hole was completed in 1821 (see Fig. 3-10). That work, by A. Martin, refers to what was then called Pilmoor Links, home to the golf course known as St. Andrews. Martin, a landscape and topographical painter, continues to stump scholars today with the distance chart he included in the upper-right-hand corner of his map. Not only do the distances not add up in every instance, but there is no known

Fig. 3-7 The Road Hole green from the right side shows the area, which has been so well equipped to draw balls toward the deep pit. (Courtesy of P. Burton)

Fig. 3-8 From the right side of the green looking across. (Courtesy of P. Burton)

reason for the chart's organization. It is presumed by many that Martin, perhaps not a golfer, was simply responding to the task at hand by providing a surveyor's look at the progression of the golf course. His figures tend to progressively add the distance from beginning to end, and then back.

While Martin's map omits bunkers, it *does* indicate the presence of a golf hole situated along the road where the now-famous 17th green resides. Keep in mind that a hole in the 1821 format of The Old Course would have been an actual hole dug

Bunkers, Pits & Other Hazards

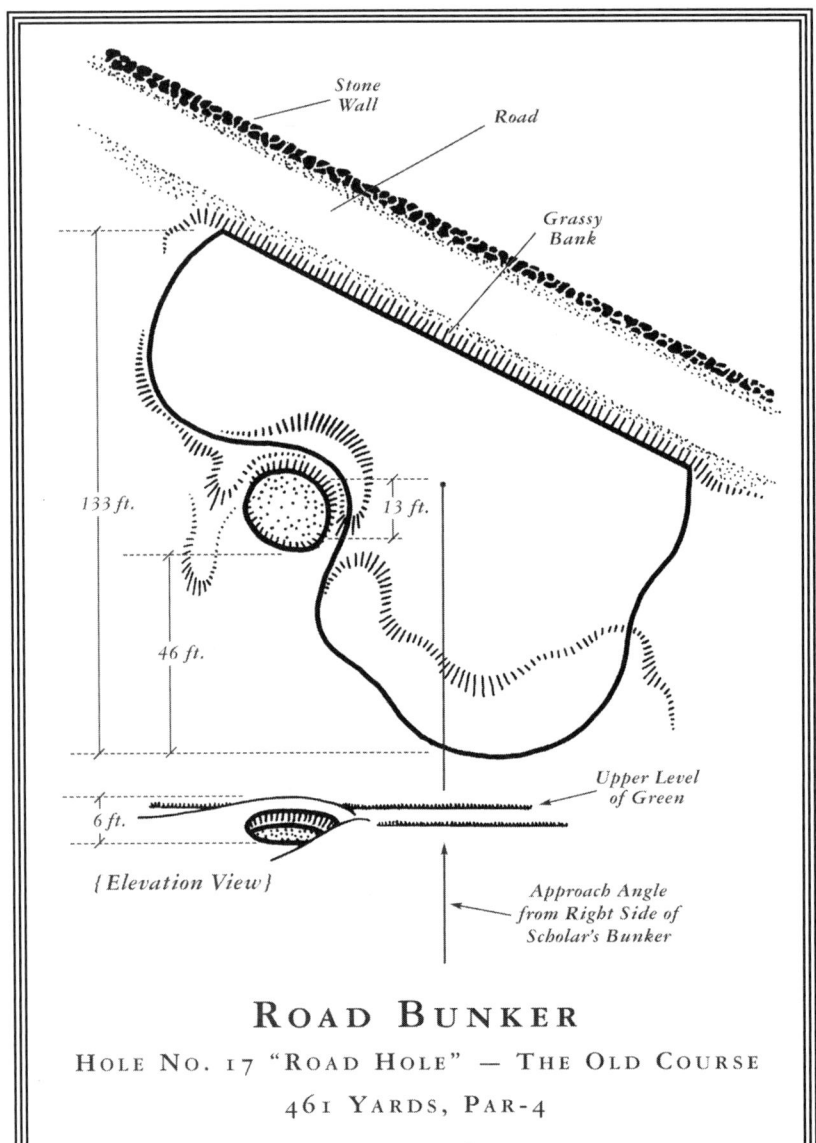

Fig. 3-9

ROAD BUNKER
HOLE NO. 17 "ROAD HOLE" — THE OLD COURSE
461 YARDS, PAR-4

into the ground, a permanent hole to which golfers would play on their way out from the beginning, and then again as they returned. The hole located along the road where the No. 17 green resides today was called the Bridge Hole in 1821, a reference to the stone bridge across Swilcan Burn. The Swilcan Bridge is an enduring landmark that has served the town of St. Andrews for more than 800 years. The Bridge Hole, therefore, was the

CHAPTER 3 | TWENTY FAMOUS HAZARDS

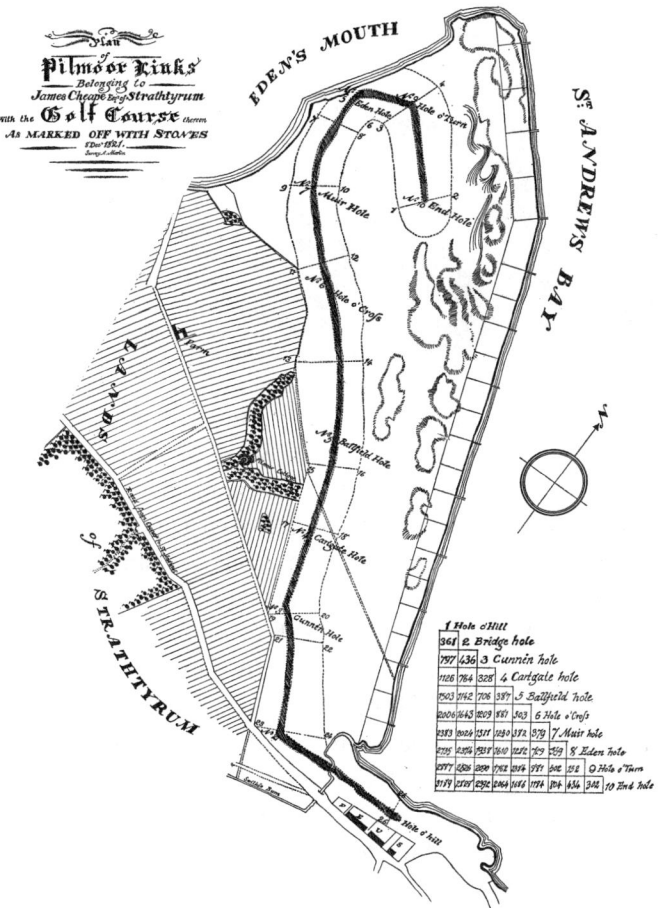

Fig. 3-10 The Plan of Pilmoor Links, a redrawn version of the original 1821 map by A. Martin, a landscape and topographical painter. Martin's map is the oldest recorded of any golf course. The Bridge Hole is shown to be approximately in the location of the present-day 17th green. (Courtesy of Illustrator Jurek Alexander Putter, from the book St. Andrews—Home of Golf.)

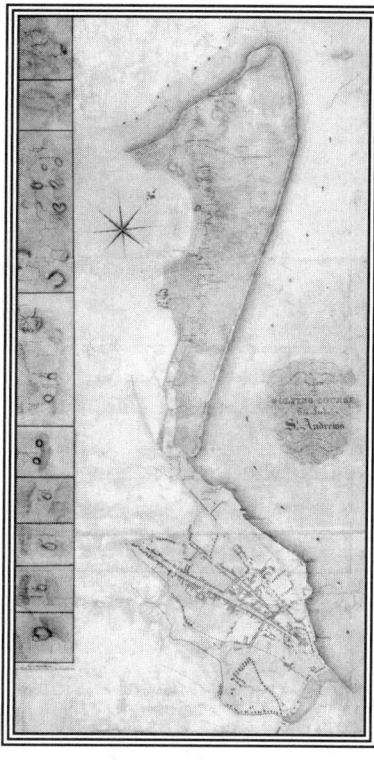

Fig. 3-11 William Chalmers' 1836 map of the "Golfing Course" at St. Andrews is the second oldest map of The Old Course in existence. Is there a bunker in the area of what is now the Road Hole? The Royal and Ancient Golf Club is beginning to use sophisticated techniques to compare the old maps in their collection to try to determine questions such as this (see color insert). (Reproduced by kind permission of the Royal and Ancient Golf Club of St. Andrews)

shared hole for outbound play at what was then No. 1 and No. 17. The hole was along what Martin labeled as the Road from Cupar, a major thoroughfare for the town.

So what do we know specifically about the Road Hole and its famous bunker? Many people think that Allan Robertson or Old Tom Morris was responsible for locating the green where it sits today, and perhaps for locating the Road Bunker itself. Morris *was* responsible for building a new green at what today is No. 1. He also built a new tee for No. 2 at the same time—1870. At the time of Morris's new green work, he was said to have left the formerly expanded Road Hole green where it was.

Fig. 3-12 View of the back of the green, elevated above the road and falling back toward the bunker (see color insert). (Courtesy of P. Burton)

As for Robertson, we know only that he did significant work at St. Andrews in the winters of 1856 and 1857, and continued to be compensated for work up until his death in 1859. The well-documented proposal to expand the greens at the links came in 1832 but was never acted upon at that time. Robertson, by the way, would have been 17 years old in 1832 and was not likely to have been put in charge of anything so precious as changes at the Links at St. Andrews. Some historians take the 1832 proposal and tie it conveniently to Robertson's work throughout his tenure at St. Andrews until his death in 1859.

Robertson is so well known for his work expanding the greens that somehow he has been given credit for building a new green at the Road Hole, and even creating the Road Bunker. But aside from the records of payment to him beginning in 1856, we have little evidence to rely on. Even in 1855 when the High Holes ("going out" and "coming home") were said to have been changed into what looked more like two separate greens than one large one, we can only guess that Robertson was the man behind the work. The enlargement of greens was a progression at St. Andrews. The greens were not expanded one time and then left untouched forever. Rather, they were continually increased in size, first so that two separate holes could be set into the ground adjacent to each other, then so that two holes could be set further apart, and so on until the present state where the holes

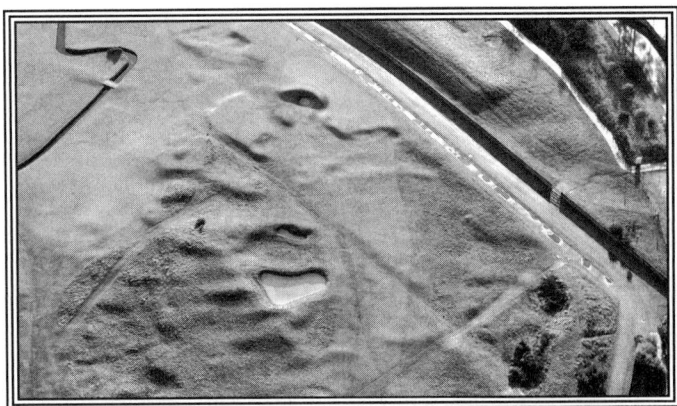

Fig. 3-13 A digital computer model of the Road Hole provides an accurate depiction. Such detailed surveys (if they endure the ages!) will eliminate argument in future generations about where and how the bunker looked in the 21st century (see color insert). (© St. Andrews Links Trust and 3D Eagleview.com)

are acres apart in several instances. Sir Hugh Lyon Playfair, provost of St. Andrews from 1842 to 1861, is said to have driven this idea.

The Road Bunker is simply not documented before the 1875 map (Fig. 3-14) credited to Thomas Hodge, which appears in Robert Clark's *Golf: A Royal and Ancient Game* (1875). Did Robertson, who had been dead for 16 years by this time, create the Road Bunker? No one knows. Robertson could have built the Road Bunker and made changes to the green with the opening of the St. Andrews Branch Railway. There may have been a need to revise the green in order to accommodate the increased traffic along the road going to and from the railway station. Again, it is speculation.

Peter Lewis, secretary of the Royal and Ancient's Golf Heritage Department, points out that "the history of the many changes to the links is shrouded in fog and, I'm afraid, whins." Lewis is currently working to uncover the mystery surrounding

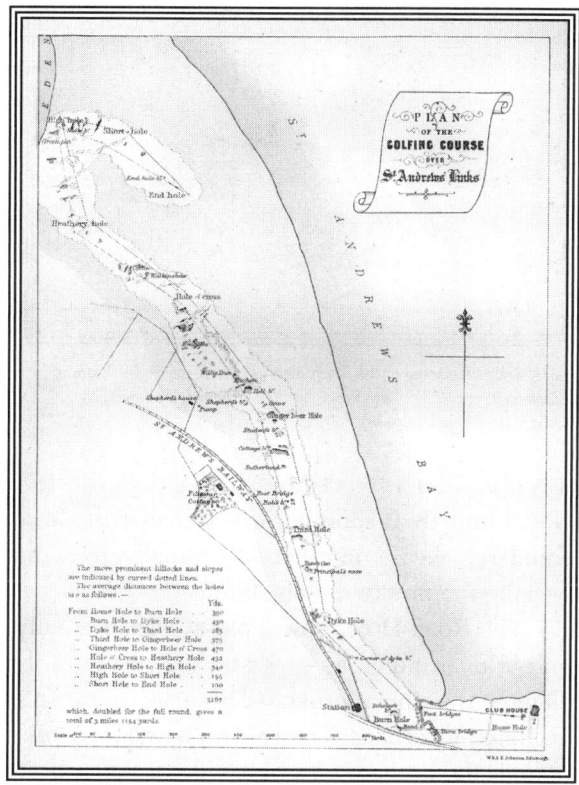

Fig. 3-14 This map, from Robert Clark's Golf: A Royal and Ancient Game (1875), has become known as the "Hodge Map." Thomas Hodge, an R&A member and prolific landscape artist, is credited in Clark's table of contents. However, at the margin of the map is the imprint "W & A. K. Johnston, Edinburgh," well-known mapmakers and engravers of Scotland. One theory is that Hodge may have commissioned the map and provided it to Clark. Regardless, it remains the first map of St. Andrews Links to show the Road Bunker (see color insert). *(Amateur Athletic Foundation Library Archives)*

questions such as the exact location of the Road Hole—and Road Bunker—in these early eras. On the afternoon we spoke with Lewis, he noted the wind was howling at 40 mph. "The course is changing as we speak," he pointed out. "Sand is continually moving around across the links." One needs only to look at old photos and television broadcasts to see the Road Bunker's journey through time.

What we can deduct is (1) in the early out-and-back configuration, at least after 1821, there was a green along the road; (2) Robertson, often called the father of golf architecture, was likely responsible for enlarging the Road Hole green along with the others; and (3) the Road Hole was played as No. 1 and 17 (a shared green) before 1870, when Old Tom Morris created a new green—the first separate green to be built at St. Andrews other than the Home Hole and the End Hole greens.

Bunkers, Pits & Other Hazards

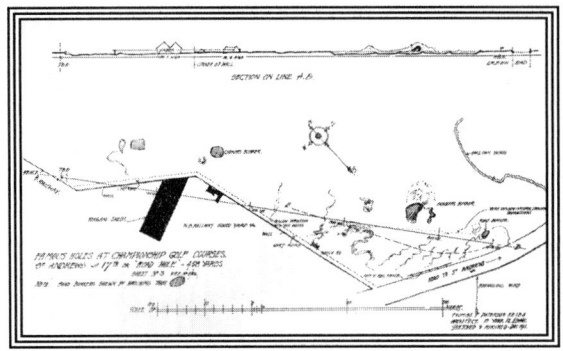

Fig. 3-15 A survey of the Road Hole drawn in 1911 by Thomas Patterson, a Fellow of the Royal Institute of British Architects. (Courtesy of Grant Books)

The Road Bunker, because it is so entwined with the green itself, is a fascinating hazard. Imagine playing to this green as your opening hole before Morris built the new separate green (now the first green). Imagine the terror of having a road and wall to the left, and a narrow passage to the green flanked by a cavernous bunker to the right. And let's not forget the Swilcan Burn. If this were an opening hole, one would need to avoid this at the right. The Old Course was played in its clockwise routing until the 1870 change. This meant crossing shots at Nos. 1 and 18. It soon became a matter of alternate play, clockwise on some days, counterclockwise on others. Eventually, to avoid the crossing shots, counterclockwise became the predominant routing.

The Road Hole, now a par-4, was originally a par-5. The drive usually must be played over old green sheds on the corner of the dogleg in order to gain favorable alignment to the approach. These sheds are facsimiles of the original railway sheds that occupied this space. The Old Course Hotel sits a bit farther to the right now. Out-of-bounds flanks the entire right side of the hole. The Road Bunker, which is best appreciated in person, has probably ruined more rounds than any other hole in the world. In our look at 20 famous hazards, we cannot forget to study each of the hazards for this hole. Each one on its own would not work nearly as well. The OB and sheds set up the approach, the approach brings the Road Bunker into play, the elevated green now takes over, and finally we have that nasty road surface and wall behind the green. None of these hazards is a place to be. Each sets off a domino effect that brings the next into play. Together they work like the mechanism of a great clock. You can hear the gears turning, in both the mind of the golfer and the workings of the hole itself.

The Pacific Ocean—The 18th at Pebble Beach

COURSE: Pebble Beach Golf Links, Pebble Beach, California, U.S.A.
ARCHITECTS: Jack Neville and Douglas Grant (original routing, 1919); Chandler Egan and Robert Hunter (revisions)

The 18th hole at Pebble Beach is a double-heroic hole in that its tee shot and second shot are both risk-reward shots. Off the tee, the golfer is rewarded for playing closer to the ocean. The same may be true of the second shot, depending on the position of the pin on the green.

CHAPTER 3 | TWENTY FAMOUS HAZARDS

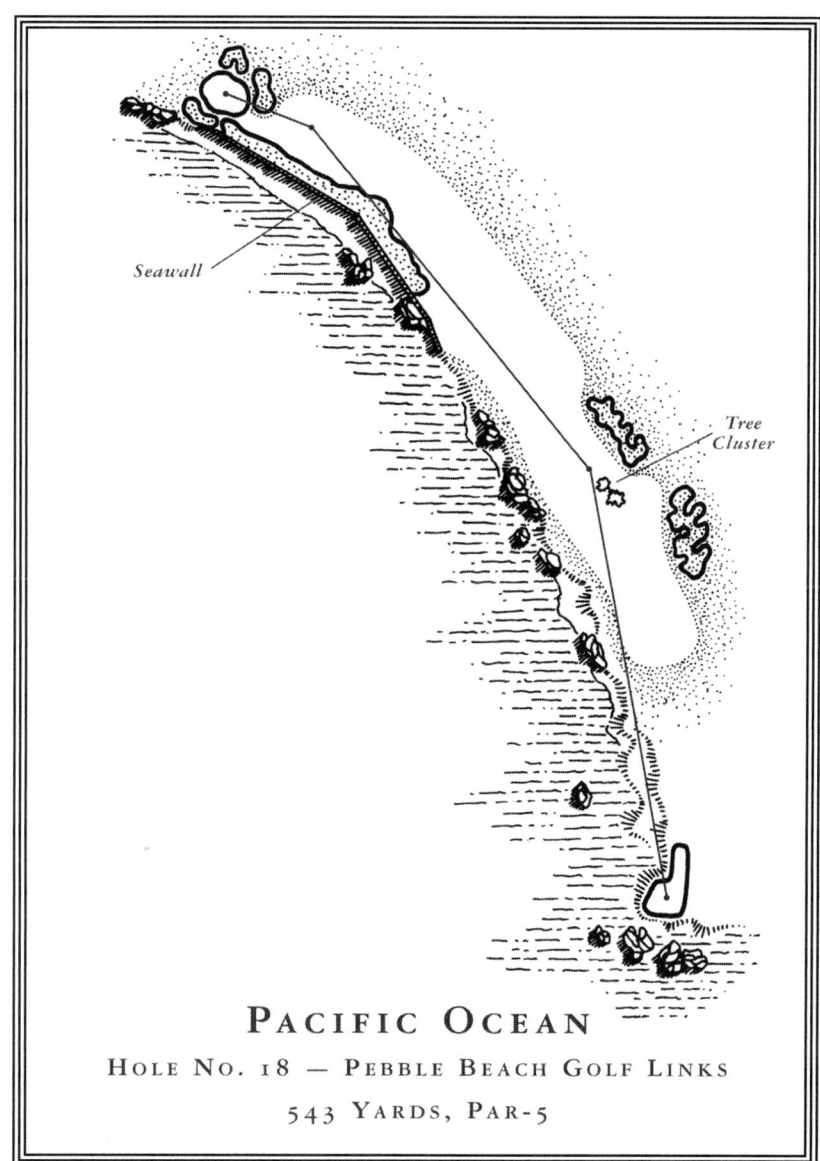

PACIFIC OCEAN
HOLE NO. 18 — PEBBLE BEACH GOLF LINKS
543 YARDS, PAR-5

Fig. 3-16

A cluster of cypress trees provides additional interest off the tee. Recent blights have killed many of these trees throughout the Pebble Beach area, but new trees have been transplanted in an effort to preserve this element of the hole. In 2005, two cypress trees were being planted, one 260 yards from the tee and another at 280 yards. "It gives the golfers a better visual, with the trees as a target," said R. J. Harper of the Pebble Beach Company. "But it also creates more obstacles, because they're definitely in play with the wind."

Fig. 3-17 Perhaps the most famous finishing hole in golf, the 18th at Pebble Beach needs little in the way of explanation in terms of its play. It simply follows the coastline, begging the golfer to take the geodesic route instead of the "out-of-the-way" bend farther right (see color insert). (© Tony Roberts)

Although the hole was originally routed by Jack Neville and Douglas Grant, it was U.S. amateur champion Chandler Egan who lengthened it and transformed it into the risk-reward trek along the rocky beach below. Egan was joined by Robert Hunter in creating many revisions to Pebble Beach. At No. 18, Neville and Grant had left a par-4, described by some as mundane.

In recent years it has become necessary to stabilize and restore a large section of oceanfront at the world-famous 18th hole. Damage from the waves, sand, and pebbles that constantly pound the seawall has finally been kept at bay thanks to fiber-reinforced concrete installed over reinforcing steel. The new seawall, coated with stone veneer to match the natural coastal rock, measures 280 feet long and 20 feet high in places. "We took great measures to preserve the natural beauty," notes Phred Bartholomaei, who oversaw portions of the project from a landscape perspective. Bartholomaei is renowned for his work on golf

Fig. 3-18 The view from the tee at Pebble Beach's 18th. Note the recently constructed seawall toward the right.

course waterscapes. The result has been an award-winning project that stands up to the pounding of the Pacific Ocean and fits beautifully with the environment. Most importantly, it has preserved a treasure to golfers everywhere.

Worth noting is the amazing effect of the wind at No. 18. In 1985, one of your authors hit two woods and was told sternly by a seasoned caddie to hit a third here. The advice was ignored, and the result was a lie in the forward bunker. Five—count them, five—strokes were taken from that bunker, and it took a very long putt to save a nine. The moral, of course, is to listen to your caddie—or choose calmer days on which to play your golf.

The Church Pews

COURSE: Oakmont Country Club, Oakmont, Pennsylvania, U.S.A.
ARCHITECTS: Henry C. Fownes, and William H. Fownes with Emil "Dutch" Loeffler, 1904

The Church Pews gets its name from the grassy ridges that run perpendicular to this nearly 60-yard-long bunker. The "pews" are essentially the gaps between the ridges. It is the expansive, flat-bottomed bunker and the pews together that form this unique hazard.

Fig. 3-19 The famous Church Pews of Oakmont Country Club are defined by the parallel turf ridges, which sit within this huge bunker covering more than 1 acre in size (see color insert).

Although the bunker has been enlarged in recent years (the Office of Tom Fazio added two "pews" toward the 3rd green and two toward the 4th green in 2005), the look is remarkably identical to photos from the early days when the Fownes, creators of Oakmont, established the club's legendary reputation for perilous hazards.

The story of the famous Church Pews begins when Oakmont had more than 350 bunkers, before the 1920s. As hazards became more expensive to maintain, the number was gradually reduced. This was done very methodically by longtime greenkeeper Emil "Dutch" Loeffler and William Fownes. When people griped that Oakmont had too many bunkers, Loeffler cleverly combined some rows of slender bunkers into larger, single traps. Just to make things interesting, he retained strips of turf that had previously separated the bunkers and, thus, created Oakmont's most famous hazard—the Church Pews. Other examples of this effort by Loeffler, although not in play any longer, can still be detected at Oakmont.

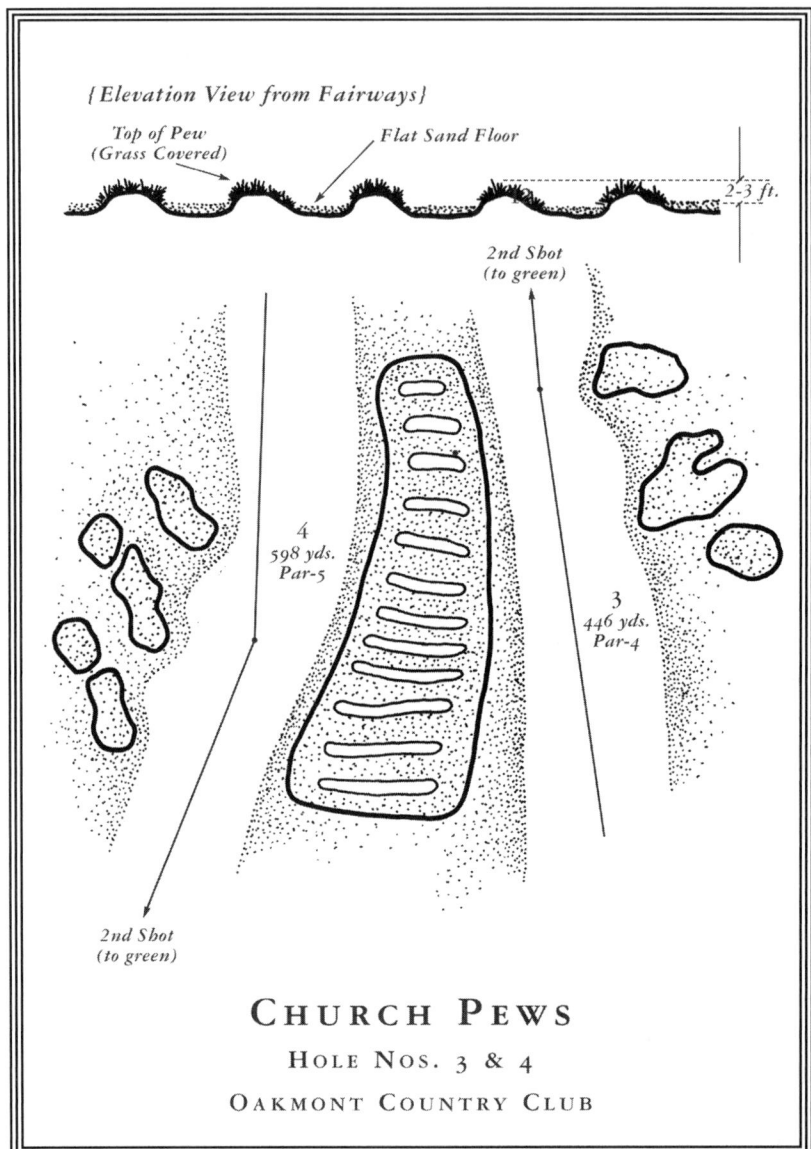

Fig. 3-20

"They look exactly the same as when I was here," said the late Arthur Jack Snyder about the Church Pews when he visited in 1994. Snyder was head superintendent at Oakmont during the 1950s. His love for Oakmont and its traditions was evident when he returned again in 2003, a few years before his passing: "The hazards here were always thought of as *hazards*," he said. "The very idea of them was to create problems for the golfer so the holes would be interesting adventures."

The fact that the famous Church Pews will catch any wayward drives to the left side of the 3rd and 4th holes has come to epitomize the terrors of Oakmont. The bunker itself is almost 40 yards wide at its broadest point and extends along the ideal driving spot for both golf holes. In combination with the 3-foot-high ridges with their tall grass, the pews are to be avoided at all cost.

The Pacific Ocean—The 16th at Cypress Point

COURSE: Cypress Point Club, Pebble Beach, California, U.S.A.
ARCHITECTS: Alister MacKenzie and Robert Hunter, 1928

This is a hole that evokes all of the design strategies into one. It asks us to lay up. It beckons us to be heroic. It gives us a detour. It is open to the left. But it is all the while penal at its core. Even when the play is safe to the left, safety is not guaranteed. There is risk up until the end. The golfer is asked to walk a tightrope made of rock and planted with grass. There is no net.

Here again, the hazard is the Pacific Ocean. But it is MacKenzie and Hunter's expert use of the ocean that makes No. 16 the ideal golf hole. MacKenzie

Fig. 3-21 The rocky shoreline of the Pacific Ocean creates the ultimate hazard (see color insert). (Courtesy P. Burton)

Fig. 3-22 The Pacific Ocean laps at the rocks in this shot taken during the 1986 Pebble Beach Pro-Am Tournament. Cypress Point Club no longer hosts rounds during the tournament. (© Tony Roberts)

Fig. 3-23 An early photograph of a golfer and his caddie on the beach below the green at the famous 16th. (Courtesy of the Western Golf Association Collection)

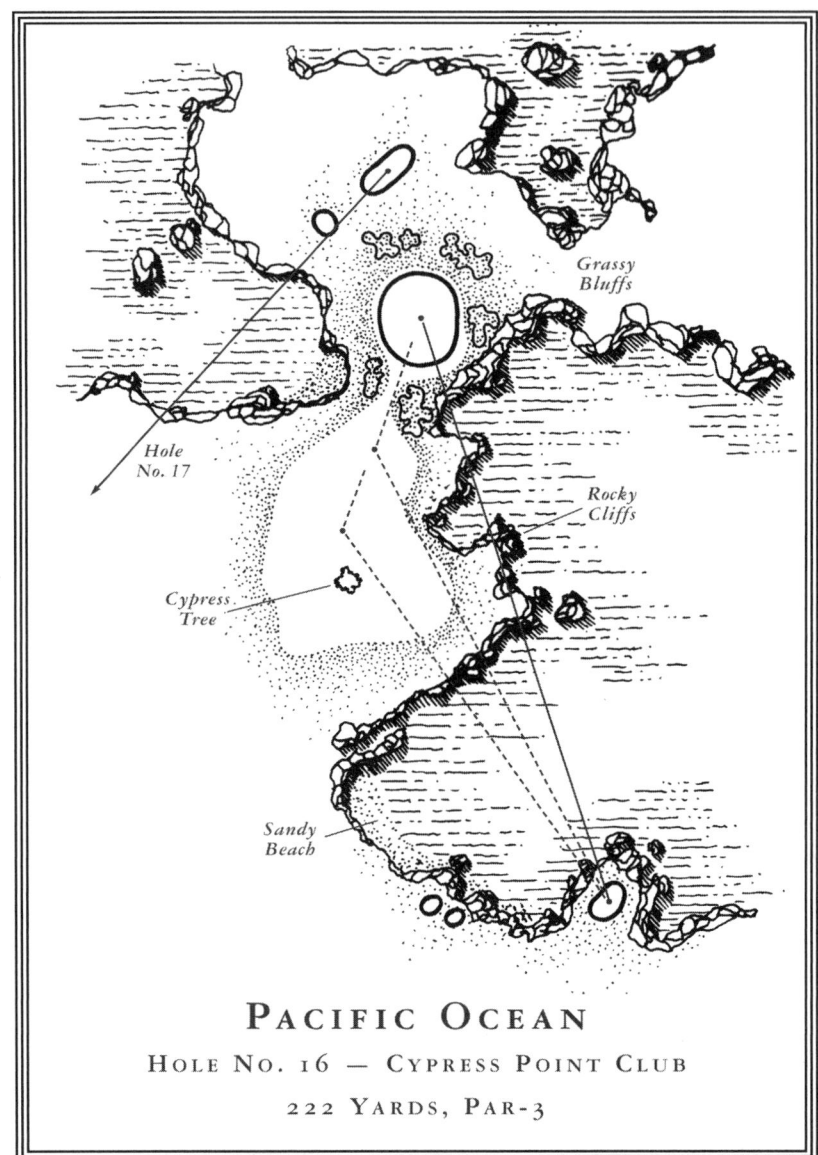

Fig. 3-24

originally felt the hole should be a par-4, agreeing with the late Seth Raynor, who had argued that the carry over this part of the coastline was "too long." But Marion Hollins, a fine amateur golfer who was eventually charged with a large part of Cypress Point's development, had other thoughts. In MacKenzie's own words, "[The design] was largely due to the vision of Miss Marion Hollins. She did not think it was an impossible carry. She then teed up a ball and drove to the middle of the site for the suggested green."

MacKenzie and Hunter have left behind an extraordinary golf hole with breathtaking beauty. While the hazard itself will never be duplicated, we are able to take away plenty of insight from their most fortunate site. They used natural features, they avoided the temptation to try to attain length by staying with the lay of the land, and, finally, they tempted the player to go for it all.

The Devil's Asshole

COURSE: Pine Valley Golf Club, Clementon, New Jersey, U.S.A.
ARCHITECTS: George Crump with H. S. Colt, 1919

We are thankful that our editors did not insist on using an assortment of symbols, such as "the Devil's A**#@%¢," to stand in for the Devil's Asshole. Without any question, the best name ever bestowed to a hazard is that of this nasty, menacing, dirty, unpleasant, foul, mean, horrid, vile, ungracious, loathsome, beastly, and hideous little pit. It is this nasty, menacing, dirty, unpleasant, foul, mean, horrid, vile, ungracious, loathsome, beastly, and hideous quality that makes it so beloved and enjoyed.

Fig. 3-25 The 10th is a shortish par-3 of great character. As repulsive as the bunker sounds, and is, it possesses a quality that seems to lure golfers to test its position (see color insert). (© PDI: Chris John)

The green at Pine Valley's 10th drops off on all sides. From the tee, one cannot help but notice a small tongue of turf that extends down from the green, reaching out toward the golfer as if to offer some solace for all the other edges that drop off sharply

Fig. 3-26 An early photograph showing the 10th hole out in the open compared to its forested setting today. (Source: Golf Illustrated)

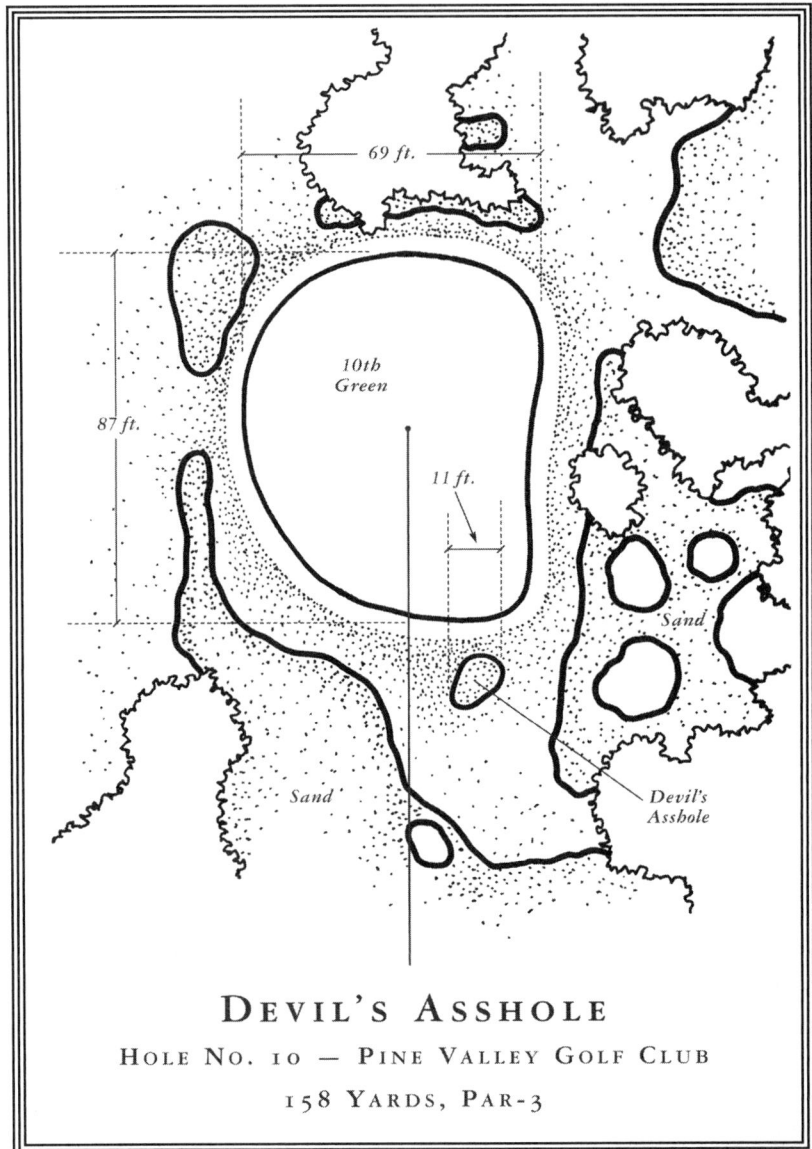

DEVIL'S ASSHOLE
HOLE NO. 10 — PINE VALLEY GOLF CLUB
158 YARDS, PAR-3

Fig. 3-27

into nothing but scrub and sand. And there it sits—the Devil's Asshole. Positioned perfectly to entice the shot that one needs to hit at the front of the green before scooting off toward, or off, the back. The green, this bunker, and the cascading turf that seems to spill outward are all begging for a shot toward the Devil's Asshole. How on earth can it catch so many balls? Is the power of suggestion at play here? Perhaps it is the work of the Devil himself.

Hell's Half Acre

COURSE: Pine Valley Golf Club, Clementon, New Jersey, U.S.A.
ARCHITECTS: George Crump with H. S. Colt, 1919

The Pine Valley story is quite remarkable. A group of Philadelphia-area sportsmen wanted to establish a golf course within easy distance that could be played throughout the winter. Their sights were aimed at the scrub pinelands of southern New Jersey, an area of much milder winters. George Arthur Crump, an accomplished golfer and resident of Merchantville, New Jersey, was among this group. Crump got the assignment of scouting a suitable site, and he ultimately settled on a stretch of sandy terrain amongst the pinelands. Crump was no stranger to the area having made frequent hunting trips for small game.

Fig. 3-28 A less-appreciated "hazard" at Pine Valley's 10th is the sharply elevated green, which falls off on all sides. While the Devil's Asshole basks in the limelight as the famous hazard, the green and its surrounds are very likely the more troublesome obstacle for the golfer.

Soon 184 acres[2] were purchased on which to build a golf course. Crump was appointed chairman of the Greens Committee and it would ultimately be his responsibility to build the Pine Valley golf course. Having never designed a golf course, Crump formulated some key goals. He wanted to avoid parallel holes; he wanted each hole to be secluded; he wanted each hole to move in a new direction; and he wanted the golfer to be forced to use every club in his bag. To see how the famous courses of England and Scotland were laid out, he made extensive trips to visit courses and members at these clubs.

Fig. 3-29 The Devil's Asshole, pictured here as close as one dares, has a similarly named first cousin, located in the middle of the 7th fairway at Lahinch, Ireland.

But Crump knew his limitations. As work began, he solicited the opinions of many noted golfers and golf architects. He brought H. S. Colt onboard to review plans and make suggestions. Colt remained a presence until the completion of the course. Other "regular"

---

[2] Today more than 400 acres of untouched woods and scrub, in addition to the area of the course itself, is owned and preserved by the club.

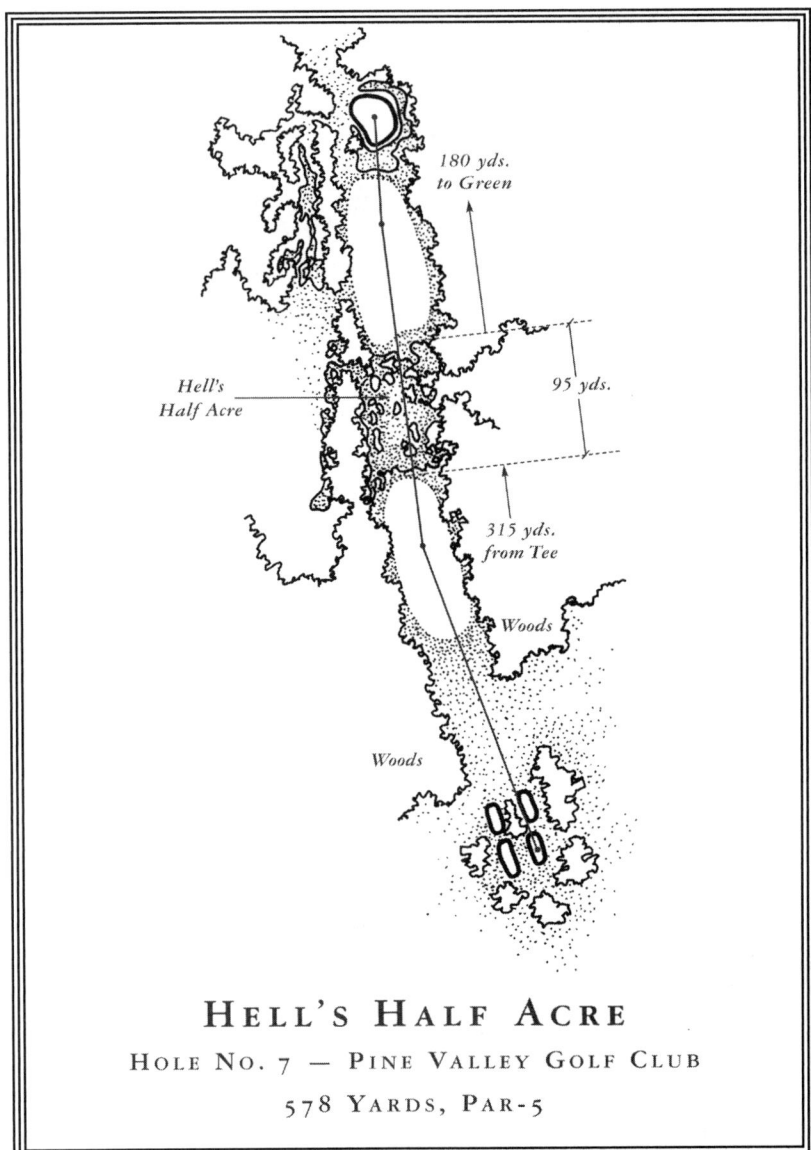

Fig. 3-30

advisers included A. W. Tillinghast and Hugh Wilson. Both men were friends with Crump and are given credit for several of Pine Valley's design traits.

The sandy soils were considered a wasteland to many observers. To create Pine Valley, more than 20,000 tree stumps had to be pulled out with special steam-winches and horse-drawn cables. Dynamite, a proven method in other locales, only blew up the sand around the stump. Marshes had to be drained throughout. Some referred to

Fig. 3-31 This is the look from the fairway across Hell's Half Acre (see color insert). Only the formal bunkers at Pine Valley are treated as "bunkers" under the rules of golf. Here, for example, the area is considered "through the green," and the club may be grounded. The term Hell's Half Acre *is* thought to have originated in the small town of Webberville, Texas, before Texas' statehood. Webberville, known for its lawless and immoral reputation, was dubbed Hell's Half Acre as a result. Eventually, the name became generic for the red-light district in any number of frontier towns. (© Tony Roberts)

the course that was taking shape as Crump's Folly. Skeptics wondered if grass would even grow on the sandy soil. C. B. Macdonald remarked that the course would be among the best ever if only it could support grass.

Crump was so fixated on his creation that he built a small cottage along the 5th hole. From there he oversaw construction and spent much of his personal fortune to see it to its completion. The first areas were seeded in 1913, and the first 11 holes unofficially opened for play in February 1914. Tragically, Crump died in 1918, when just 14 holes were completed. William Flynn, working with Hugh and Alan Wilson, assisted with the remaining construction. Crump, of course, never saw his completed masterpiece, now regarded as one of the best golf courses on American soil.

It may be no small surprise that Crump *did* see the mostly finished results at No. 7 and No. 10, two magnificent holes with equally magnificent hazards. At the 7th—a hole Tillinghast later wrote about—an enormous hazard was created that spanned 100 yards across the fairway. There is no way around this expansive tract of waste and sand. It forces layups at any number of points on the hole. Its position is maddening. It stretches 150 yards in length. As the golfer approaches, the idea is to get close, but not close enough to be bitten. The perfect series of shots is a long drive to a narrowing point, a long second to the left side, and a final approach across the waste area short of the green. A misstep at the tee or second shot—or both—will bring Hell's Half Acre into play. This is sure to cost a stroke, perhaps more.

Tillinghast took some credit for his advice at Pine Valley, saying "I was one of the first to walk the property with him, and that George Crump finally incorporated two of my ideas, the long seventh and the thirteenth, will ever be the source of satisfaction." There have been long and convincing debates over who had the most say at Pine Valley. To the hazard called Hell's Half Acre, it matters not a bit.

Hell Bunker

COURSE: The Old Course, St. Andrews, Scotland
ARCHITECTS: Unknown

To appreciate the bunker named Hell, it is important to study the Long Hole carefully. Hell sits nearly on the straight line to the hole, perhaps only a little left. Its length and width are less important than its steep, banked back. To be in it en route to the 14th green is not at all good. If a ball does fall here, it is always best to allow yourself room away from the bank.

Hell Bunker continues to evolve. While townspeople are no longer permitted to dig its floor for shells to haul back to their gardens, the winds and rains adjust Hell, even if ever so slightly. Is this pit 300 years old, as many believe? Or is it older—or younger? Again, we first find it formally depicted on the Hodge map of 1875.

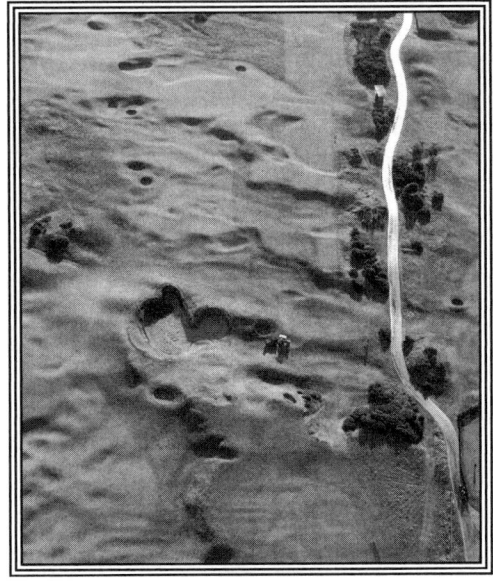

Fig. 3-32 A digital computer model of Hell Bunker from above. (© St. Andrews Links Trust and 3DEagleview.com)

In the first of a series of writings on famous bunkers for *Golf Illustrated* in 1899, Horace Hutchinson shared his thoughts on Hell:

> It is a rather large bunker, on the one side its cliff is rather high and precipitous, but it so happens that that is not the side on which it is necessarily either on the outgoing or the incoming, to attack it. For it is the hazard on the left-hand side going out, which again presents itself as a hazard when the course is on the right for the home coming.
>
> We even remember a golfer of the whimsical, paradox loving kind, coming in from a round of Golf in a season when the lies through the green were not all that they should have been, and gravely telling Old Tom Morris that the only decent lie he had all day was at the bottom of Hell bunker. Whereupon that sage custodian of the green was aroused to drastic action and sent out Hineyman and his satellite with picks and hoes to delve in the bottom of the parlously-named place till no man could possibly boast that he came out of it with a long spoon.

The magic of Hell Bunker lies in the endurance with which it has perplexed golfers. In its original context—a matter of pure estimation and deduction—we envision a bunker

CHAPTER 3 | TWENTY FAMOUS HAZARDS

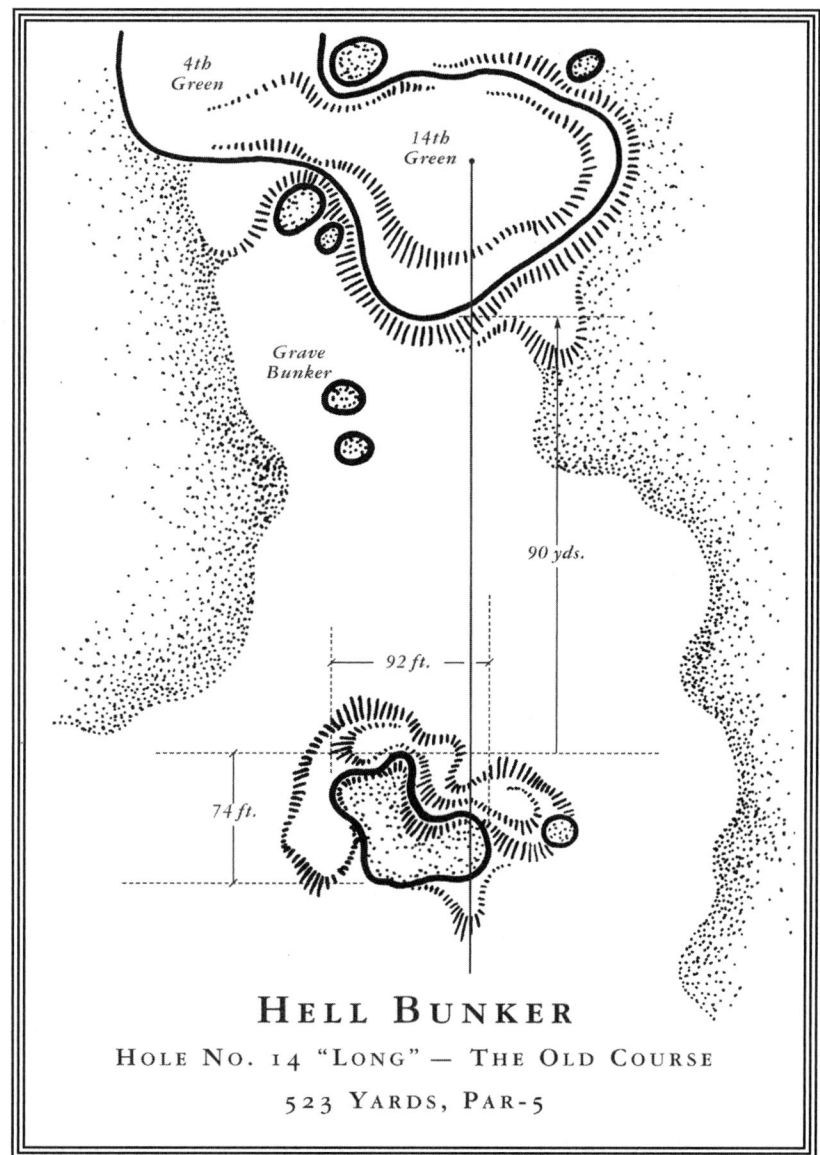

Fig. 3-33

that could not have been avoided without deliberately playing up to its leading edge and then whopping a ball across it hopefully. As Hutchinson put it, "When whins were nearly ubiquitous, instead of reduced, as they are to-day, to the vanishing point, on the St. Andrews green, it was necessary to drive right over it, whereas now it may be evaded on either side, and with comfort on the sea-side."

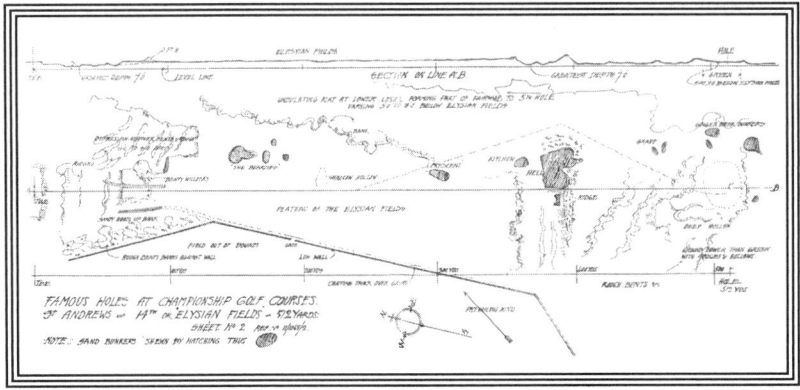

Fig. 3-34 Survey of No. 14, the Long Hole, The Old Course at St. Andrews (Courtesy of Grant Books)

When The Old Course was played in its clockwise routing (opposite from today) the threat of Hell Bunker may have been even more evident. In an opinion written to *Golf Illustrated* in 1901, H. S. U. Everhard commented:

> There used to be a hole which was held in even higher estimation than the eleventh and seventeenth: the old fifth. There was no course to the right; nothing but whingrown wilderness. Hell necessitated a carry of nearly 170 yards, on to a higher level. At the second shot the treacherous "Bairdies" had to be avoided; the third was a long swipe over awful bunkers, much worse than they now are. No hole ever made was a more satisfactory 5, for each shot had to be one of the striker's best, and a hazard had to be avoided with all.

It may be comforting to those who have had problems at the Long Hole, whether they have attempted to play over Hell Bunker or around it, that Mr. Jack Nicklaus, having played this hole during the 1990 Open, was forced to lift a pencil and write two distinct numerals in the tiny space allotted on his scorecard; a 1 and a 0, in that order. We dare not call this score by its more common name. Four of these shots, for reference, were taken to extricate himself from Hell (Bunker).

Fig. 3-35 Hell Bunker, c. early 1900s (Source: Golf Illustrated)

Fig. 3-36 How golfers can wind up in Hell Bunker is a mystery considering the alternative routes around it. As Robert Frost once said, "I hold it to be the inalienable right of anybody to go to hell in his own way." (Courtesy P. Burton)

The Pacific Ocean—The 8th at Pebble Beach

COURSE: Pebble Beach Golf Links, Pebble Beach, California, U.S.A.
ARCHITECTS: Jack Neville and Douglas Grant (original routing, 1919); Chandler Egan and Robert Hunter (revisions)

Fig. 3-37 Pebble Beach's famed No. 8 begins with a tee shot to a plateau high above the crashing waves of the world's largest body of water, the 69.4 million square miles of the Pacific Ocean. The approach is a downhill carry across an inlet of craggy rocks and grassy cliffs (see color insert). (Photograph by Joann Dost)

Few par-4s in the world can equal Pebble Beach's 8th. The hole begins with a shot to a plateau. The golfer is surrounded by ocean and sharp cliffs. This is no run-of-the-mill spot to land a tee shot—it's a perch. The land to our left side is of no concern. The target sits well below, its green hugging its own share of the cliff. The 8th is loved, and made our list, we presume, for its orientation to the ocean and the way the land flows until reaching "the end of the earth."

BUNKERS, PITS & OTHER HAZARDS

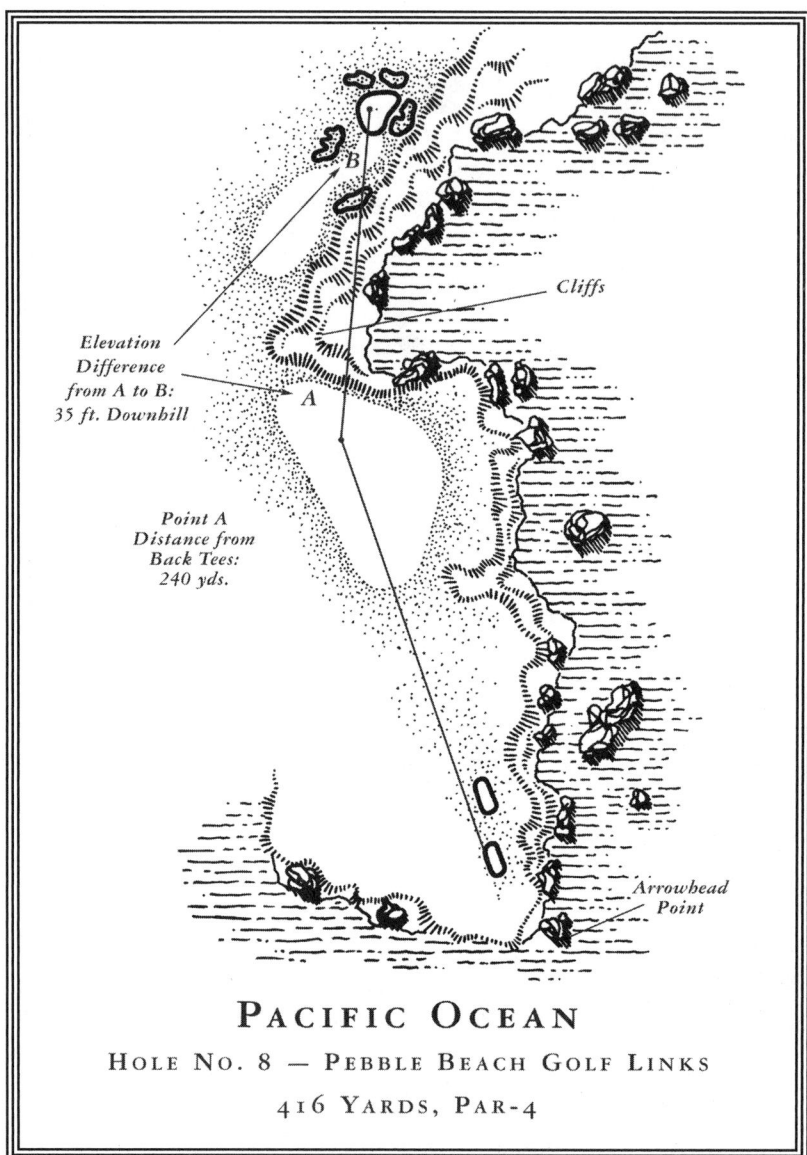

PACIFIC OCEAN
HOLE NO. 8 — PEBBLE BEACH GOLF LINKS
416 YARDS, PAR-4

Fig. 3-38

Nerve. That's what it takes at the 8th. The safe route is well around, and it is not nearly as exciting. The way to the green in two shots is facilitated by playing to the right side off the tee, and then contemplating a second shot for a challenge that may never be equaled.

The three-hole stretch at Pebble's 8th, 9th, and 10th is not only one of the most beautiful combinations of holes in the world, but one of the most testing. It all begins with the uphill blind drive on No. 8. After driving the ball between 230 and 250 yards, you will

Fig. 3-39 View of the 8th green, c.1920s.

find yourself standing over what Jack Nicklaus has called "the finest second shot in golf." There is perhaps no finer view than the one you see watching a shot cross that chasm, giving your ball instructions to "land softly and stop!" One of the authors was recently playing the hole with a good friend. He watched as his buddy sliced his approach shot over the chasm onto the rocks and beach below. Unfazed, he proceeded to drop down a second ball and calmly knocked a 4-iron shot on the green and into the hole for an "all-world" four!

Fig. 3-40 Looking back to the plateau where the approach is played into the green at No. 8.

The Dell—The 5th at Lahinch

COURSE: Lahinch Golf Links, Co. Clare, Ireland
ARCHITECT: Old Tom Morris, 1892

The Old Course at Lahinch boasts one of the most unusual holes in all of golf—slightly unorthodox, but much loved by members and all who play there. The Dell is nearly

Bunkers, Pits & Other Hazards

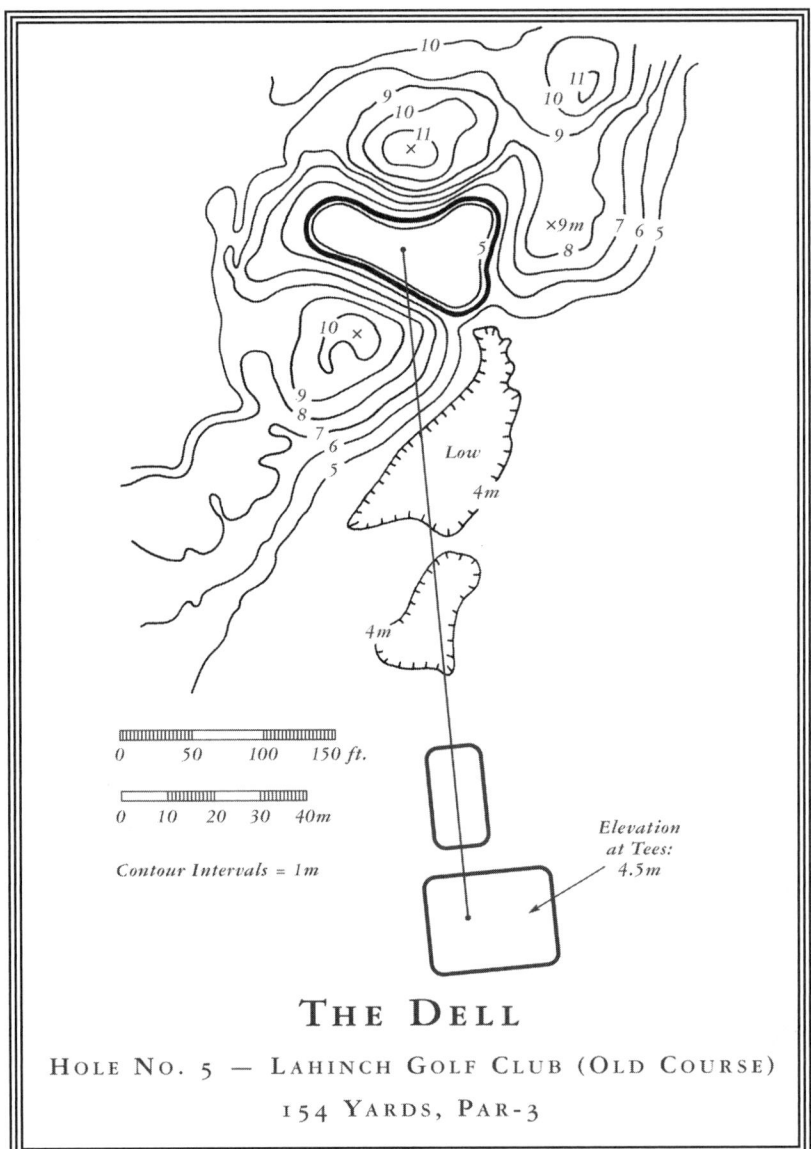

Fig. 3-41

a fully blind one-shotter. From the tee, only a hint of green is allowed by the massive dunes that surround the target. A stone weighing about 8 pounds has been painted white and serves as a marker to let golfers know the position of the pin.

Originally the 6th, now played as the 5th, this interesting test is defined by mystery and the need for blind trust. This, of course, in addition to the dunes themselves. Skill is required to overcome each of these hazards. The player cannot simply outwit the mystery

Fig. 3-43 Zeroing in on one particular hazard at the Dell Hole is a difficult proposition. The Dell is a combination of conditions, all set in motion by the secluded green set amongst the dunes. Judging distance, aiming at a flag you cannot see, and the element of luck are what forms the "hazard" here. (Courtesy of P. Burton)

Fig. 3-42 An enhanced digital image of the famous Dell Hole at Lahinch (see color insert). (© Lahinch and 3D Eagleview.com)

and forget the height and distance needed to keep the ball within the bowl of a green. Nor is it wise to focus totally on the mechanics of the shot—the distance and the alignment over that white painted stone—and fail to concentrate on visualizing what cannot be seen from the teeing ground.

The Cardinal Bunker

COURSE: Prestwick Golf Links, Prestwick, Scotland
ARCHITECT: Old Tom Morris, 1851

Fig. 3-44 The Cardinal Bunker is banked with sleepers, and has been since the first illustrations were made of it in the early 1800s. (Courtesy Ran Morrissett)

BUNKERS, PITS & OTHER HAZARDS

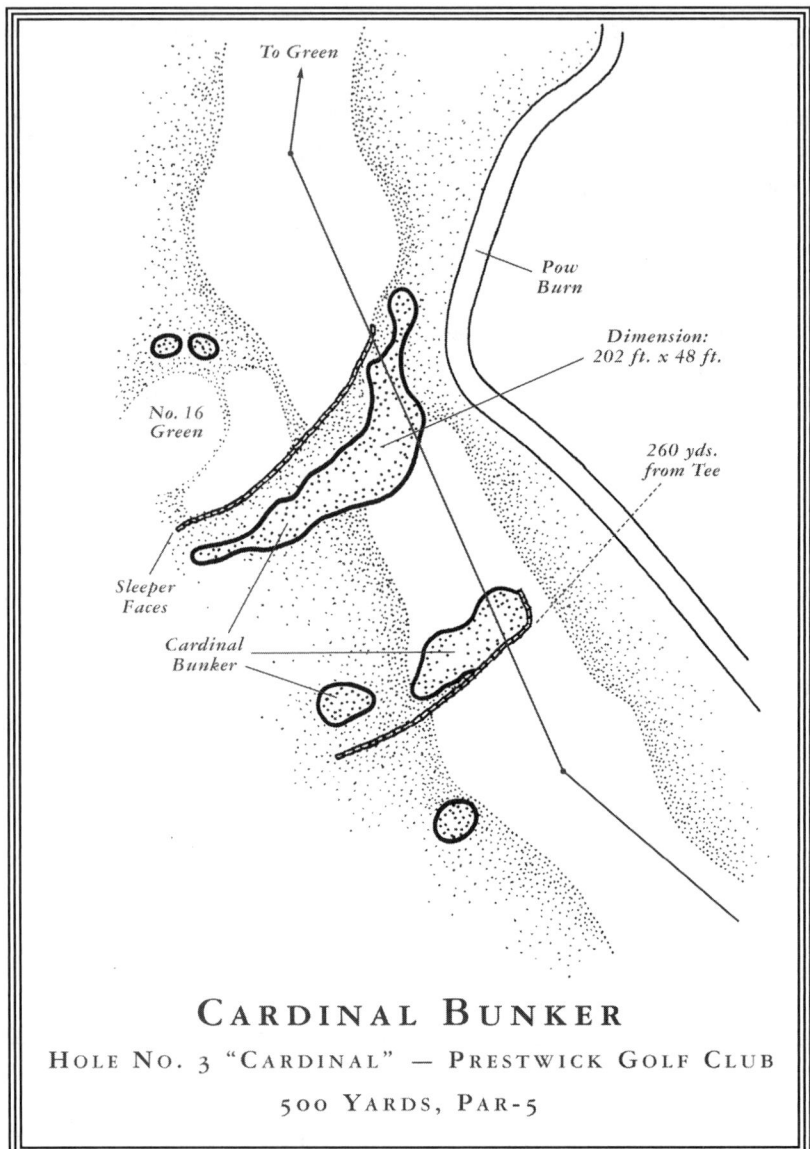

CARDINAL BUNKER
HOLE NO. 3 "CARDINAL" — PRESTWICK GOLF CLUB
500 YARDS, PAR-5

Fig. 3-45

A bit about the names associated with the Cardinal Bunker: The bunker itself is named after the Cardinal's Nob (nob = nose), specifically the nose of a monk of Crossraguel Abbey who engaged in a match to settle a deadly feud against a Lord of Culzean—the wager, his nose. The Zareba is the hollow near the Cardinal under the shoulder of the 16th green.

In 1860, across a 12-hole layout in Prestwick, the Open[3] Championship was born. Many of these holes are still intact today. In 1908, James Braid was stuck in the Cardinal Bunker during the Open. He hit two balls off of the sleepers that fortify the bunker. Each ball ricocheted into the Pow Burn, an evil hazard that guards the right side of the hole. Undaunted, Baird went on to win the championship.

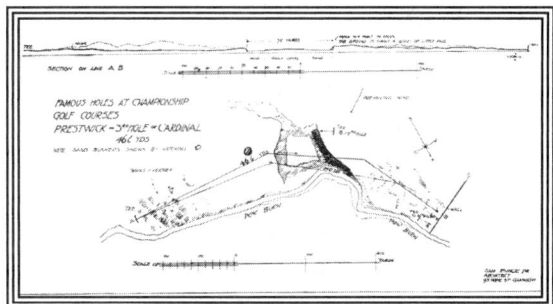

Fig. 3-46 A survey of the 3rd hole, the Cardinal. Drawn by Sam Runcie, Jr. (Courtesy of Grant Books)

> *The third hole at Prestwick is one that stirs the soul of the daredevil golfer, for, after he has dispatched the ball well and safely from the tee, he finds a big, gaping bunker, the famous Cardinal, ahead of him for his second—an ugly brute that gives a sickening feeling to the man who is off his game. Defy this bunker, be on the green with your brassy, put a four on your card and you have done something which should make you happy for the morning.*

These were the words of the great Harry Vardon as printed in the club history, *Prestwick Golf Club*.

Fig. 3-47 An engraving c.1893 showing a familiar Cardinal Bunker, but with considerably more broken ground in its surrounds. (Courtesy Prestwick Golf Links)

Fig. 3-48 The Cardinal Bunker at Prestwick accounts for the No. 3 hole being rated as the toughest hole on the course.

Fig. 3-49 The original name of the Cardinal Bunker was "Cardinal's Nob," a reference to a wager between a monk and a Lord in which the wager involved the loser's nose.

---

[3] While it may not need to be clarified, "the Open" refers to that championship many Americans know as "the *British* Open." In fact, the insertion of this third word is unnecessary. There is only one Open.

BUNKERS, PITS & OTHER HAZARDS

The Redan

COURSE: North Berwick Golf Links, West Links, North Berwick, Scotland
ARCHITECT: David Strath (Greenkeeper), 1876

A *redan* is a well fortified position, a fortification where two parapets meet at a salient[4] angle. The word *redan* is Old French in origin and literally means "jagged notch," as in the angled teeth of a saw. In 1855 the British and French were going at it on the shores of the Black Sea. In the city of Sebastopol a significant battle unfolded. The Russians remained steadfast behind a fortification that became known as the Great Redan. The British initially made two failed attempts at this position, a fortress of jagged parapets protruding toward the enemy and, apparently, quite efficient at thwarting penetration. This is the historical basis for the name *Redan*.

Fig. 3-50 The Redan green from the lower right-hand corner, that small portion to which it is ever so difficult to land a ball and expect it to remain on puttable surface. (Courtesy of P. Burton)

There are three holes for which the West Links at Prestwick is best known: the 13th—the Pit, is a short par-4 with an approach to a sunken green that inconveniently rests behind a stone wall; the 14th—Perfection, requires two perfect shots to hit the green, hence its name; and finally, the 15th—the Redan, a hole that has served as a prototype for many others throughout the world. The Redan is more than a golf hole. It is an idea about golf architecture. While the Redan Bunker is especially notorious, the entire hole is a hazard in itself.

Fig. 3-51 The two bunkers that form the edge of the "redan," a term stemming from the French word to define salient angles that form a fortress against advancing military assault. It is interesting to compare the bunkers with the look in Fig. 3-53. (Courtesy of P. Burton)

---

[4] A *salient* is an outwardly projecting part of a fortification.

CHAPTER 3 | TWENTY FAMOUS HAZARDS

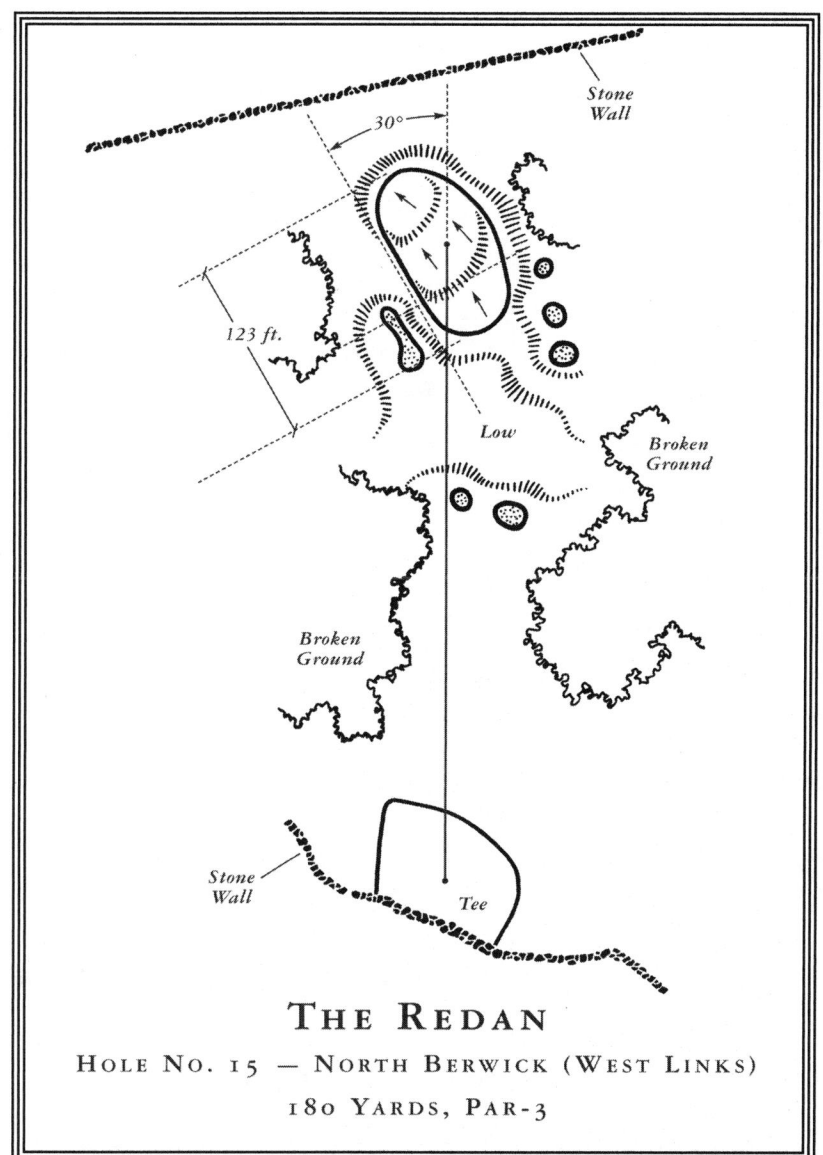

THE REDAN
HOLE NO. 15 — NORTH BERWICK (WEST LINKS)
180 YARDS, PAR-3

Fig. 3-52

The Redan is a deep, steep-faced bunker close to the green, but it is of no great length or breadth. The driven ball may go nicely to the right of it and curl round so as to lie on the green without crossing the great escarpment of the fortification at all. But it has an aspect of no little terror as one faces it from the tee.

—HORACE HUTCHINSON

The strategic principles of the Redan lie in the angle formed by the hazard and the slope of the green falling away from this diagonal line. The angle causes the golfer to think about the shot to the green. On a traditional redan—one with the hazard to the left as Prestwick's original—is the correct play a low and running shot that draws in to the green? Or is the better plan a higher shot, fading in to the flag with enough drop to prevent rolling off the back? If we fail completely, where is it best to find the ball? In the bunker that forms the Redan, or off the back into broken ground?

Fig. 3-53 The Redan from the tee.

If a Redan approach is among the most finicky of shots, then it surely is so in windy conditions. No matter what the golfer tries, it is always a difficult proposition. The angle simply does not agree with the nature of the golf swing and the flight of the ball. When the ball is blown, it brings in another influence, and this is sometimes the golfer's. Only a clever shot, and a well-planned one at that, will reach the Redan and hang on the green.

It is no wonder that, among the celebrated writers in golf who partook in the *Golf Illustrated* discussions on the most famous holes in golf of the early 1900s, the Redan was that single hole listed most often. It is a glorious combination of hazards that both repels and attracts.

Fig. 3-54 An excellent shot of the Redan green and its sleepered edge at the back and right. In this photograph c. early 1900s, the area below the sleepers was largely broken and unkempt.

Fig. 3-55 Perhaps the most replicated one-shotter design of all, the Redan, is shown here in aerial imagery. (Aerial imagery supplied by Bluesky Int. Ltd. which is © Getmapping plc)

Chocolate Drops

COURSE: Myopia Hunt Club, South Hamilton, Massachusetts, U.S.A.
ARCHITECT: Herbert Leeds, 1896 (original nine), 1901 (existing course)

Imagine five club founders, each of whom wears glasses, and the name *Myopia Hunt Club* begins to make sense. *Myopia* (nearsightedness) is the condition of being able to see things up close better than things far away. At Myopia Hunt Club, this becomes a distinct disadvantage.

Fig. 3-56 In many cases, Herbert Leeds dismantled stone walls and had the rocks piled into mounds, then plated these with soil to form interesting hazards, which continue to perplex golfers nearly 100 years later (see color insert). (Courtesy of Ran Morrissett)

The 18-hole masterpiece at Myopia Hunt is the result of dedicated work by Herbert Leeds, a sportsman and well-connected country club member. Leeds developed his love for golf at Brookline Country Club, eventually playing at Myopia's original nine-hole layout, a course devised by the fox hunting crowd who had decided their land was suitable for golf. They were right, but it took the vision and determination of Leeds to take it to the next level.

BUNKERS, PITS & OTHER HAZARDS

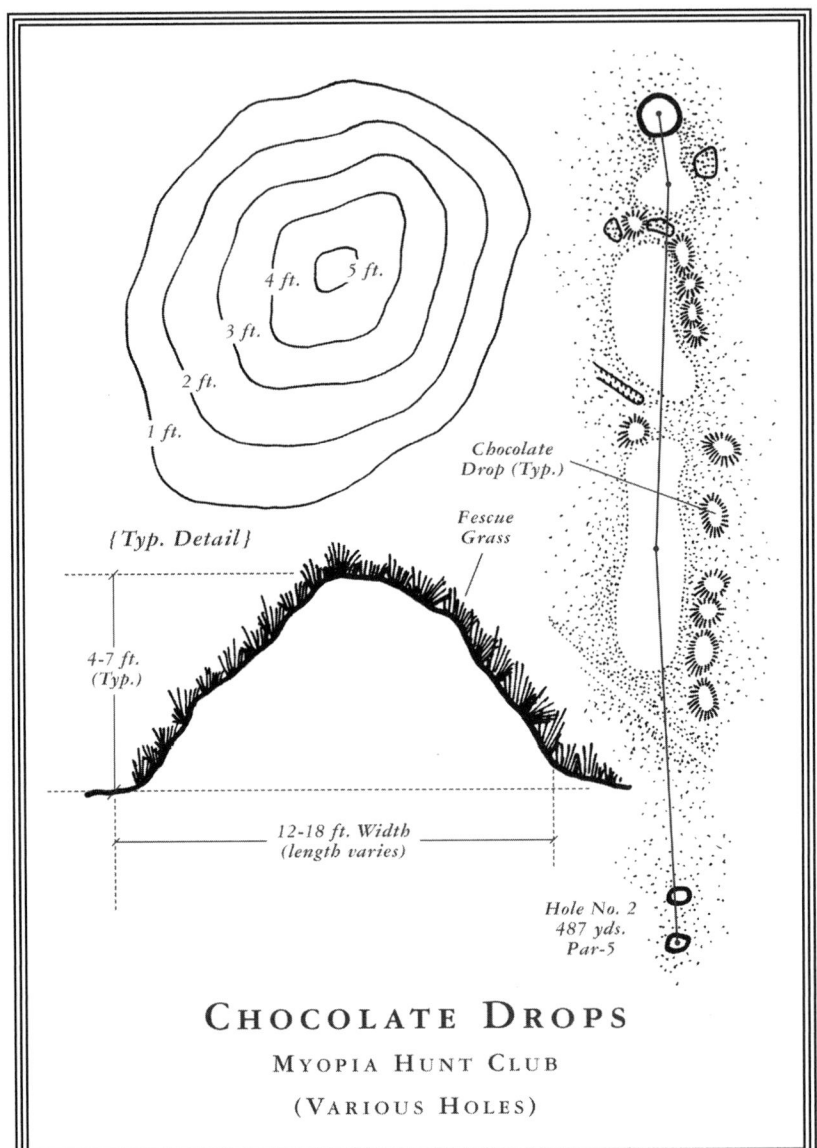

Fig. 3-57

Leeds convinced Myopia's membership to improve their course, and, as in so many cases, he who suggested was given the task. Leeds studied the original course at Shinnecock Hills and visited Scotland, where he gained an appreciation for many aspects of golf courses. In particular, he became enamored with the natural placement of greens and how they work with bunkers, slopes, and approaches.

CHAPTER 3 | TWENTY FAMOUS HAZARDS

Fig. 3-58 Close-up of Myopia's grassy covered mounds.

Fig. 3-59 Myopia Hunt Club's chocolate drop mounds as shown on hole No. 2.

Under Leeds's direction, the original Myopia Hunt Club was rebuilt. The first nine were completed in 1896 and the second nine in 1901. Much was written about the design of Myopia Hunt. The course enjoyed press throughout the United States and across the Atlantic. Leeds was masterful at bunkers, placing them randomly and creatively. At one point, there were nearly 200 bunkers dotted throughout the course.

"There is no other course in the world like Leeds' Myopia—a piece of Scotland smack dab in the North Shore suburbs of Boston," says golf writer Gary Larrabee. How true. On any given day, it is possible for this usually quiet and tranquil heathland to awaken with cries and howls heard across the ridges and valleys. They become louder. Could this be the scream of anguished golfers trying to escape the pits and coffins—bunker traps—that Leeds so adeptly left behind? Or is there a hidden hazard so menacing at Myopia Hunt Club that it leads golfers to cry out in despair? While there is no dispute that Myopia has plenty of menacing hazards, the case of the cries has finally been solved. The Myopia Hunt Club remains connected to its roots—it is still an equestrian club of kennelmen and horsemen. The "cries" we have heard are excited hounds leading a group of riders down a bridle path that eventually crosses the course and empties into the forest a few hundred yards away.

The story of the Chocolate Drops at Myopia begins with the stone boundary walls that traversed the property when Leeds began his work. Although he had seen such walls used at other clubs, Leeds considered them to be second-rate hazards. His method for ridding the site of the walls when they interrupted his routing was simple: He would order the walls dismantled, sometimes only partially, leaving segments that would later be covered with soil. When necessary, he would have the stones piled in strategic locations. In all cases, he made sure that the "drops" would add interest to the hole. With grasses allowed to grow wild on these covered piles, they soon became Myopia trademarks, interesting hazards of an inverted variety, and with not a speck of sand.

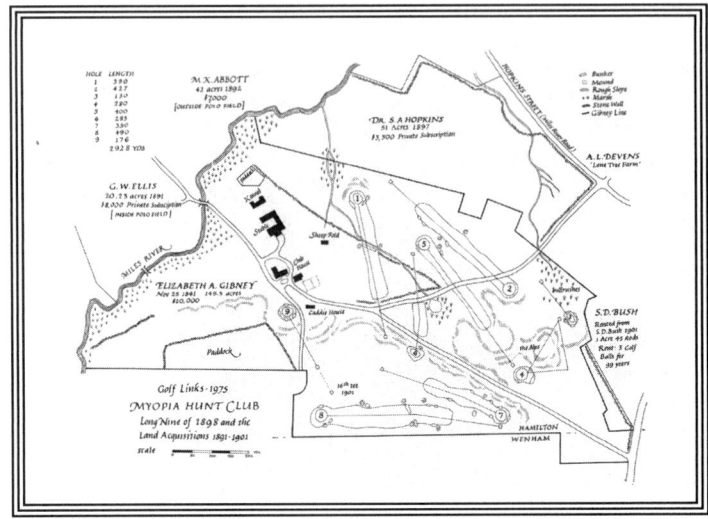

Fig. 3-60 Routing plan of Myopia Hunt Club. (Courtesy of the USGA Library)

Some have mistakenly criticized the Chocolate Drops as excessive and costly, but the truth is that they were carried out in the interest of frugality. One thing for which Leeds developed an appreciation in his tour of courses was the idea of minimal site disturbance. For example, if dirt needed to be moved, it might be better to consider changing the location of the hole so it was more in tune with the natural terrain.[5] The drops served a dual purpose for Leeds: they facilitated removal of the walls without burying or long-distance hauling, and they proved to be very interesting hazards.

Whether the Drops inspired Donald Ross at nearby Essex County Club remains a matter of debate. Herbert Leeds worked on refining Myopia until his death in 1930. At perhaps no other club in America except Oakmont was there a spirit so entrenched in the idea of change and experiment. Like the Fownes at Oakmont, Leeds was constantly adding and subtracting hazards. Leeds also developed an unusual practice. Always carrying small white stones when he was on the course, he would communicate the location for a new bunker by dropping stones to mark its precise location. This ritual would often be performed after witnessing a player get away with a shot that Leeds felt was undeserved. More stones would be dropped and instructions soon sent down the chain of command to deepen, enlarge, or add to the hazard.

---

[5] While Leeds believed in minimal disturbance, he did not always "follow the lay of the land" as we might think of doing so. The first hole at Myopia Hunt Club, for example, is an uphill par-4 ascending steeply up a grade to a sloping and blind fairway with an equally sloping and blind green site. In this instance, the routing takes whatever it is given. If any dirt has ever been moved on this opening fairway, we submit that it must have been only by golfers taking divots.

CHAPTER 3 | TWENTY FAMOUS HAZARDS

Mangrove Lake—The Cape Hole

COURSE: Mid Ocean Golf Club, Hamilton, Bermuda
ARCHITECT: Charles Blair Macdonald, 1924

The idea of a cape hole is a dogleg across a hazard, usually a body of water that invites golfers to bite off as much as they can chew. The bigger the bite, the shorter the distance to the target and also the more favorable the position to the green. It takes a bit of geometry to appreciate the dynamics of a cape. The hole is typified by the green being right on the edge of the hazard. This sets up a condition where shots hit progressively closer to the water will set up an approach to the green that will generally be played at an angle leading farther *away* from

Fig. 3-61 The view from the tee at the Cape Hole. (© Tony Roberts)

the water. Even though the carry across the water may be eminently greater, a ball that does not stop after hitting the green may fall off the back. In the case of playing to the green from a position away from the water's edge, the ball will actually be more parallel or even slightly toward the water as it approaches the green. The advantages when playing a cape must be balanced by the risks. This is the heart of such a hole.

Fig. 3-62 Routing plan of Mid Ocean Golf Club from C. B. Macdonald's *Scotland's Gift—Golf*. (Used with permission from Classics of Golf)

83

BUNKERS, PITS & OTHER HAZARDS

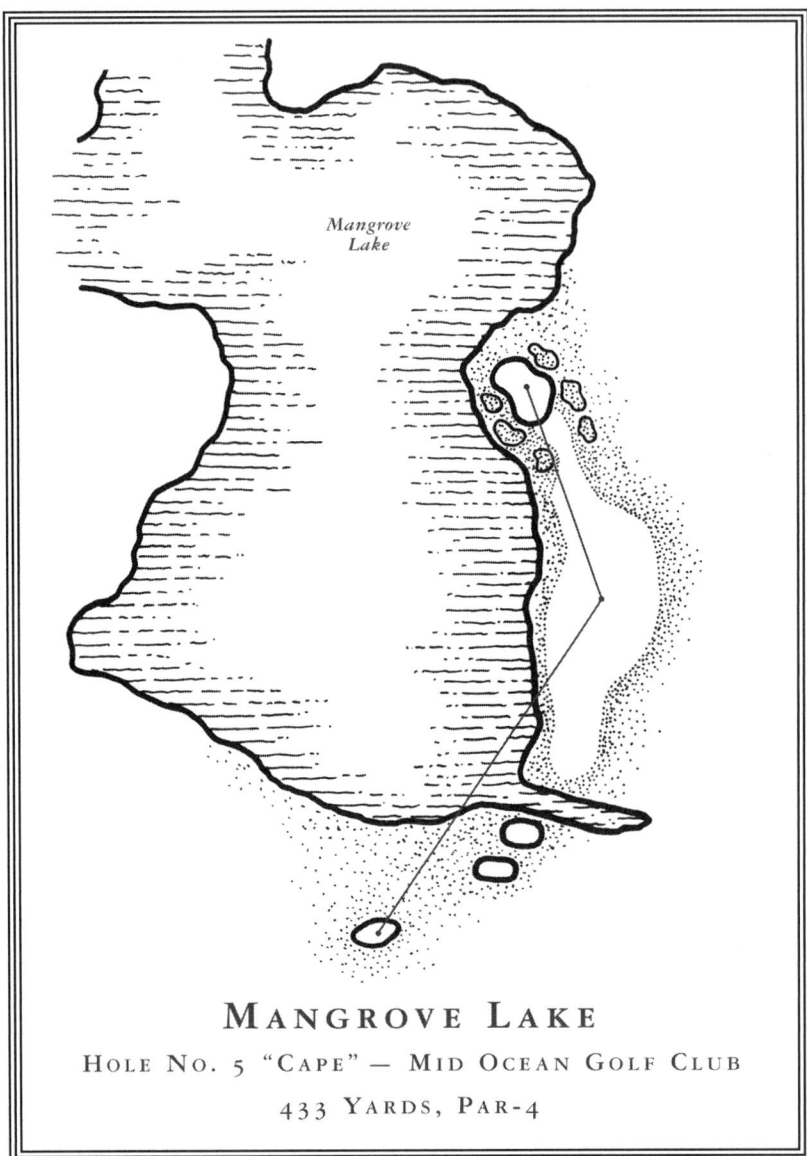

MANGROVE LAKE
HOLE NO. 5 "CAPE" — MID OCEAN GOLF CLUB
433 YARDS, PAR-4

Fig. 3-63

At the famous Cape at Mid Ocean, the tee is notched 100 feet above Mangrove Lake. The fairway stretches all the way to the green along the right side of the lake, tempting golfers to test their courage and play as close to the lake as they dare. The farther left they go with their tee shot, the more carry over water, but also the less overall distance to the green.

Babe Ruth helped make this hole famous when he knocked 11 straight tee shots into Mangrove Lake before giving up. Robert Trent Jones, Jr. calls Mid Ocean's 5th "One of the most truly heroic tee shots ever conceived."

The Himalayas

COURSE: St. Enodoc Golf Club, Cornwall, England
ARCHITECT: James Braid, 1891

A group of locals laid out the early holes at St. Enodoc in 1889, but St. Enodoc Golf Club was not formally instituted until 1891. Early records indicate the course consisted of 27 holes prior to James Braid's design work in 1907, when he transformed the course into an 18-hole layout.

Fig. 3-64 The Himalayas is no place to be. A ball lodged into the top of the sand is an adventure. The trouble lies not so much in hitting the shot, but simply in reaching the ball. Sand is very loose and can cause an avalanche at any given moment. (Courtesy of P. Burton)

The Himalayas on No. 6 at St. Enodoc is believed to be one of the highest sandhills over which golf is played. The bunker on No. 4 at Royal St. George's is comparable in height, but golfers at St. Enodoc are much closer to the Himalayas Bunker so its size appears more daunting. They must get their balls airborne quickly on their approach shots to clear the hazard and reach the blind green set into the hillside.

Just 378 yards long, the 6th is a disaster-in-waiting if the golfer is not disciplined. If your tee shot is not on the extreme left side of the fairway, you will face a bunker of colossal extremes. Many golfers suggest that, because of its proximity to the green (only

Fig. 3-65 The famous sand dune, standing 60 feet in height (see color insert). (© Tony Roberts)

85

BUNKERS, PITS & OTHER HAZARDS

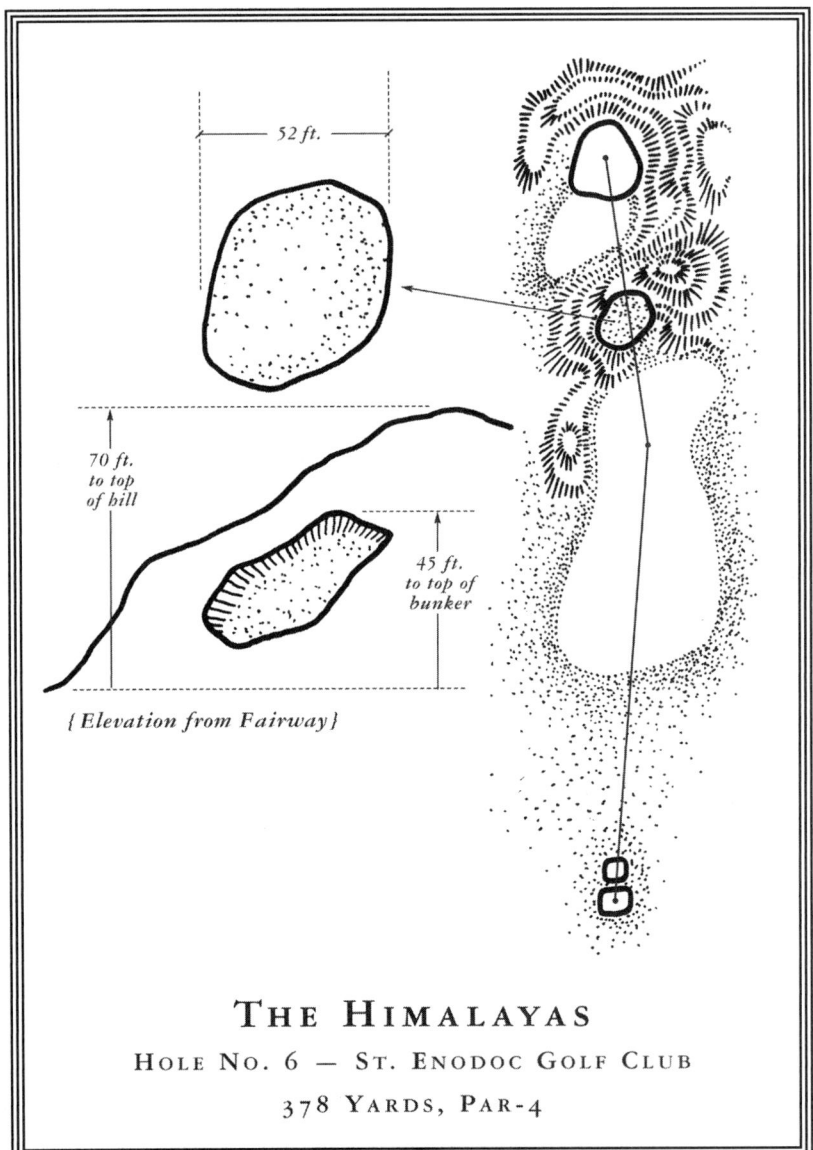

THE HIMALAYAS
HOLE NO. 6 — ST. ENODOC GOLF CLUB
378 YARDS, PAR-4

Fig. 3-66

about 100 yards away), it cannot be ignored. Those who have dealt firsthand with its wrath will never forget the experience. The dune is over 60 feet tall, and, if your ball is near the top, you've got a five-minute hike up the sand just to reach it. No matter how far up the face of the bunker, the smartest option is generally to play out backward. Bernard Darwin called the Himalayas at St. Enodoc "the highest sandhill, to the best of my belief, I have ever seen on a golf course."

CHAPTER 3 | TWENTY FAMOUS HAZARDS

The Green Bunker—The 6th at Riviera

COURSE: Riviera Country Club, Pacific Palisades, California, U.S.A.
ARCHITECTS: George Thomas and William P. "Billy" Bell, 1926

Fig. 3-67 This early photograph of Riviera's No. 6 green captures the lacy-edged bunkers that were so indicative of George Thomas and William P. "Billy" Bell. (Courtesy of Riviera Country Club)

Were it not placed in the center of the green, this little bunker would never have been noticed and the par-3 6th at Riviera would be just another of the great holes in this George Thomas masterpiece. But as with all great hazards, location is everything, and this bunker is located perfectly.

Though it has its critics and many call it unfair, in reality this small bunker simply divides the green into compartments. It is up to the golfer to place his or her tee shot in the correct one to have an unobstructed play to the hole. Even if the player fails and faces a shot with the bunker between the ball and the flag, the contours of the green are ingeniously designed and will at times allow a putt to get somewhere near the hole.

Geoff Shackelford, in his book *The Captain,* describes the strategy: "There is a substantial difference between the left and right pin placements, as those who miss their shot to the left when the pin's cut right have a reasonable chance to hit their putt down the hill close to the pin. When the pin is cut on the left portion, there is virtually no chance to get over the bunker and into the hole in two strokes."

Shackelford claims that the bunker has grown substantially over the years due to golfers excavating sand on their recovery shots. The team of Bill Coore and

Fig. 3-68 The forward pin position is easiest, but there is really no part of the green where one can ignore the lone bunker that interrupts the green so uniquely. (Courtesy of Riviera Country Club)

87

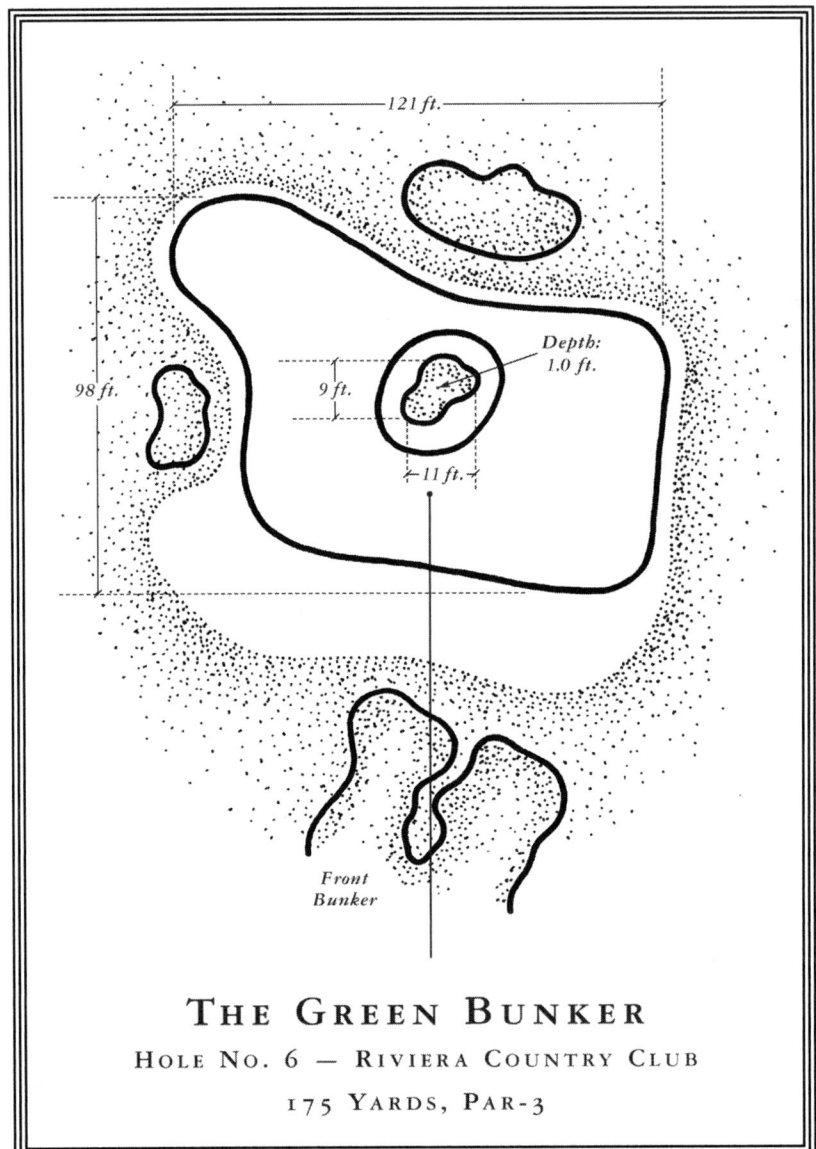

Fig. 3-69

Ben Crenshaw did a gentle restoration of the bunker in 1995, and now the ragged-edged bunkering style of Thomas and Bell has been replaced with a more formal and maintained aesthetic.

CHAPTER 3 | TWENTY FAMOUS HAZARDS

Fig. 3-70 A recent photograph of Riviera's No. 6 green. (Courtesy of Riviera Country Club)

Fig. 3-71 The famous green at No. 6 from behind (see color insert). (© Tony Roberts)

4th Hole Bunker—Royal St. George's

COURSE: Royal St. George's Golf Club, Sandwich, England
ARCHITECT: W. Laidlaw Purves, 1887

The site for Royal St. George's was said to have been determined by a British archeologist, Alexander Pattison Purves, and his brother, Dr. Laidlaw Purves. Accounts are that the two climbed to the top of the St. Clement's Church tower in search of the perfect slice of links land on which to build a golf course. Laidlaw Purves was a physician who first saw the potential of the dunes as a golf course during a visit to Sandwich in 1885. Two years later, the ground that would one day be bestowed royal status became a golf course.

Fig. 3-72 The right bunker, sometimes referred to as the "Himalayas," although this name is not at all how the members refer to it. (Courtesy of P. Burton)

89

BUNKERS, PITS & OTHER HAZARDS

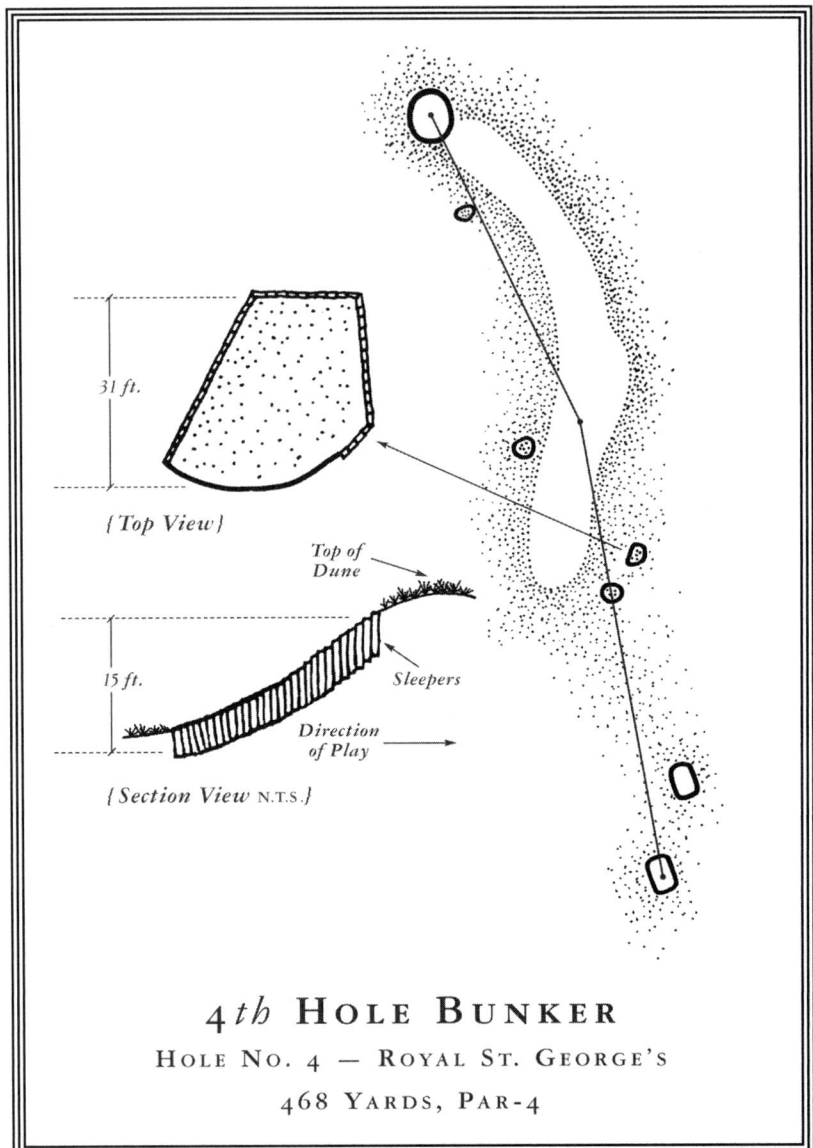

4th Hole Bunker
HOLE NO. 4 — ROYAL ST. GEORGE'S
468 YARDS, PAR-4

Fig. 3-73

The 4th-hole bunker is sometimes referred to on television broadcasts of the Open as the "Himalayas," but no one there calls it by that name. It has become a famous hazard, no doubt, as a result of the many Open Championships played upon the links at Royal St. George's. How discouraging this must be to its larger, taller, and more threatening cousin, the *real* Himalayas of St. Enodoc's 6th, which is located in far away Cornwall. (Refer to page 85.)

The 4th hole at St. George's is the source of a wonderful story. In the 1979 English amateur, Reg Glading, then 54 and the oldest scratch golfer in the country, finished all square with his quarter-finals opponent after 18 holes. They halved the first three extra holes. Then, alas, Glading drove high into the face of the pit on the fourth. He could not come at his ball from above for fear of causing a sandslide that would dislodge it. So he slowly inched his way up from below, club in hand. Gingerly, he took his stance, then set his grip. He swung. At the top of his backswing, the sand suddenly shifted under him, and, in a grotesque reverse cartwheel, he and the club and the ball collapsed down the

Fig. 3-74 Regardless of which bunker comes into play, they both are formidable hazards with vertical sleeper walls. (Courtesy of P. Burton)

slope to finish in a heap at the bottom of the pit. As to how many penalty strokes he may have incurred—testing the sand, grounding his club, moving the ball—neither he nor his opponent would venture a guess. What we do know is that in one inglorious moment, Reg Glading gave new meaning to the term *sudden death*.

What is curious about the 4th-hole bunker at Royal St. George's is that it has not been christened, at least not formally. "We definitely have a name for the bunker at the fourth," says a member of the staff, "but I'm afraid none of the names would be printable."

In recent years, a new back tee at St. George's 4th, some 30 yards beyond, was added by golf architect Donald Steel. The hole has been extended to a par-5 for championships, enticing players to challenge the reinforced bunkers for a better angle to the green. Commenting before the 2003 Open, Steel said, "It has always been one of the most recognizable hazards in Open Championship golf; it was important that it was not seen merely as decoration."

The Principal's Nose

COURSE: The Old Course, St. Andrews, Scotland
ARCHITECTS: Unknown

The 16th hole of The Old Course has recently been extended to 424 yards by way of a new back tee. This brings back the full strategic intent of the Principal's Nose, which had been partly lost due to the increased distance that modern players and equipment have achieved. A drive of 258 yards will now reach the first in a series of three deep and nasty bunkers that make up the Principal's Nose. A drive of 277 yards will fly over all

Bunkers, Pits & Other Hazards

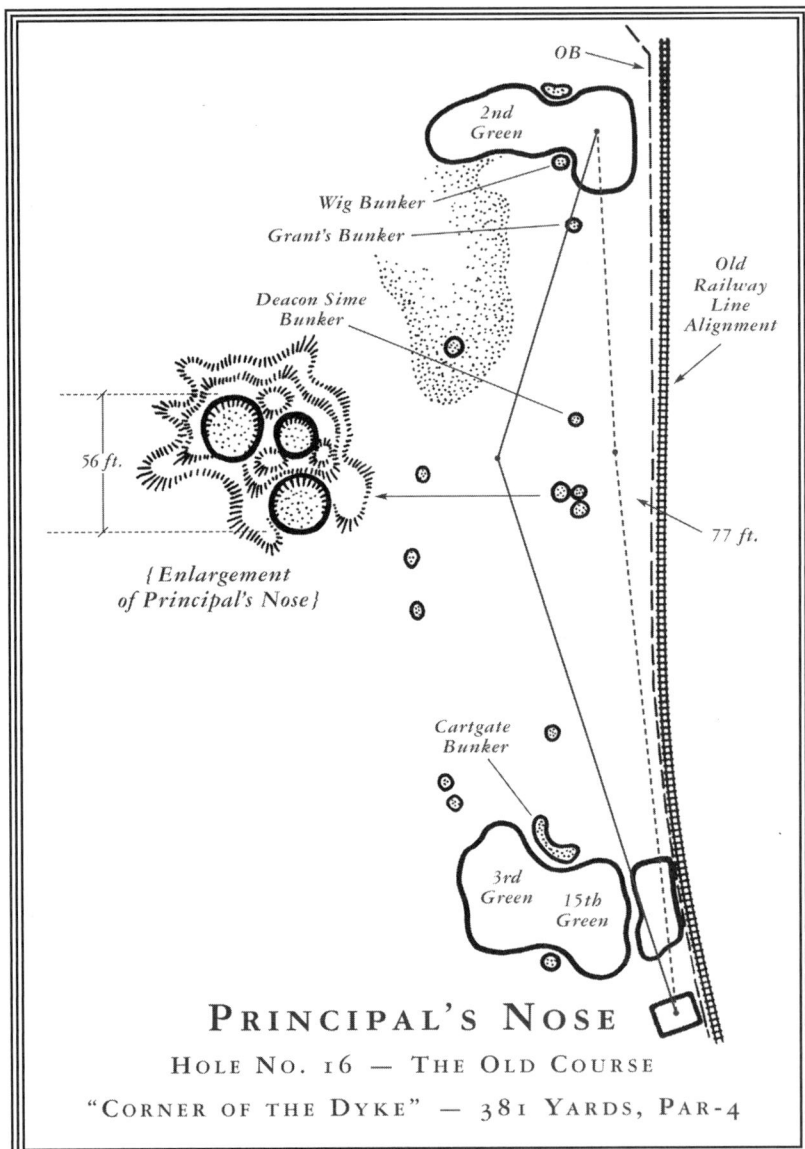

Fig. 3-75

three. The treacherous Deacon Sime, a horribly penal little bunker, lurks some 26 yards beyond this trio, 303 yards off the tee. A narrow strip of fairway separates the bunkers from out-of-bounds, which runs along the entire right side of the hole. Sensible golfers try to place their tee shots to the left of the Principal's Nose, while the more daring attempt to thread this narrow gap. This makes for a much shorter and less difficult second shot.

CHAPTER 3 | TWENTY FAMOUS HAZARDS

Fig. 3-77 The Principal's Nose consists of three bunkers arranged in such a way that they appear as a nose from several angles. (© Tony Roberts)

Fig. 3-76 An enhanced digital image of the 16th hole showing the Principal's Nose. (Courtesy of St. Andrews Links Trust and 3D Eagleview.com)

This line through the gap between the Principal's Nose and the out-of-bounds fence was once famously described by Jack Nicklaus as "strictly for amateurs."

The Principal's Nose may have been so named because of an ugly porch on one of the local school principal's homes. However, it was another local principal who played golf who may have influenced the name—so no firm proof is available. In the narrow fairway between the bunkers and the out-of-bounds fence there used to be something called Tarn's Coo, and even a Calf Bunker. These shallow bunkers, formed by tethered beasts, were filled in during the 1880s.

The preferred and much safer line of play is left of the Principal's Nose, but against the wind this leaves the golfer with Grant's Pot Bunker to clear in front of the green. The Wig Bunker looms a few yards farther on the left.

That Damned Bunker

COURSE: St. George's Hill, Surrey, England
ARCHITECT: Harry Colt, 1912–1913

Located just outside of London, England, That Damned Bunker protects the green at one of the most spectacular par-3s in all of golf. The tee for the short 8th hole sits on a ridge. The shot is played over a valley and over this massive bunker to a slightly domed green positioned on the top of a ridge some 15 feet lower than the tee. In its original form, this enormous bunker measured an amazing 19 feet from its base to its top. At its widest, it spanned 90 feet across and lay 21 feet from the front of the green.

Fig. 3-78 The No. 8 hole at St. George's Hill, Surrey, England as shown in the October 1913 issue of Country Life magazine. The photograph was taken during the opening tournament of the course at which J. H. Taylor and James Braid were among 12 invited professionals. (Courtesy of St. George's Hill Golf Club)

The bunker has been remodeled in recent years, once in 1984 by head greenkeeper John Kendal and again in 2004 by Martin Hawtree. It has been stripped of some of its raw power and intimidation but still remains one of the most memorable hazards in golf. According to James Collier, a prominent member of the club, there are many who would like to see it restored to its former glory. However, there are practical considerations.

Fig. 3-79 A mid-1930s photograph shows the bunker beginning to lose form from its original shape. (Courtesy of St. George's Hill Golf Club)

CHAPTER 3 | TWENTY FAMOUS HAZARDS

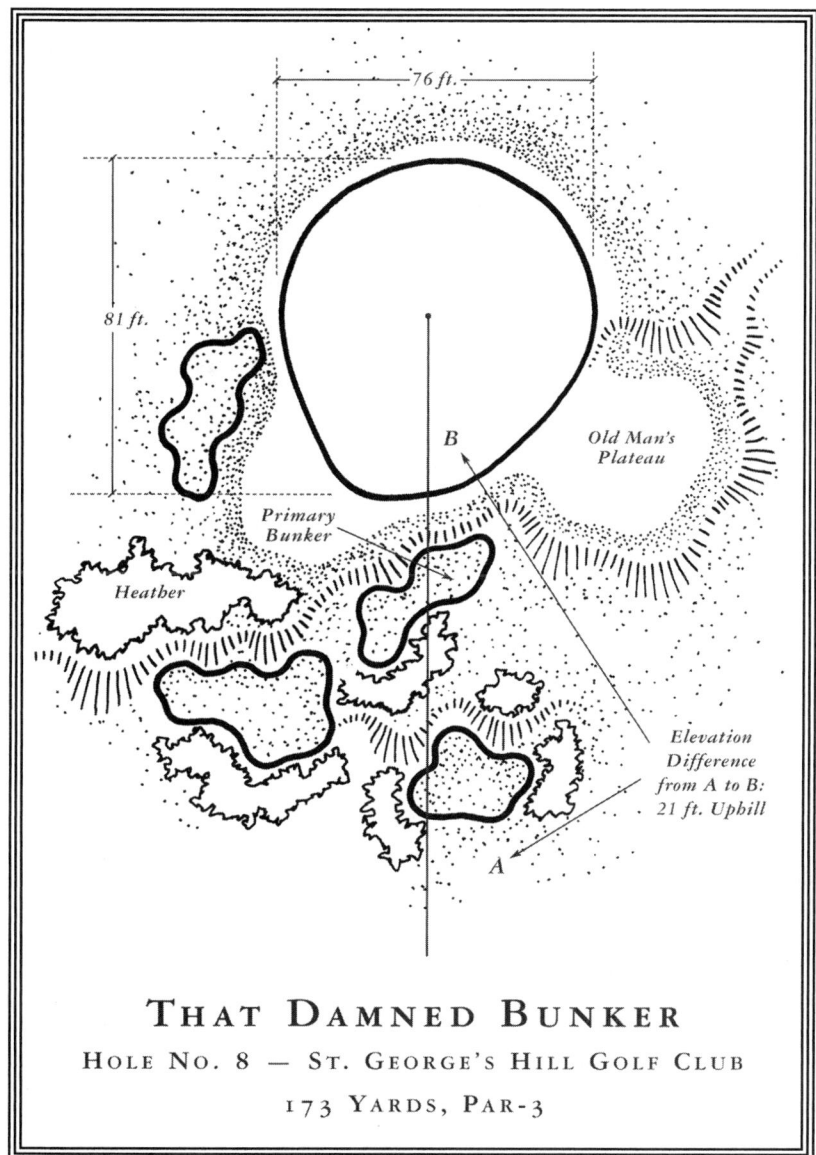

THAT DAMNED BUNKER
HOLE NO. 8 — ST. GEORGE'S HILL GOLF CLUB
173 YARDS, PAR-3

Fig. 3-80

There is no doubt that climate change has had an effect. Over the last decade, the area has experienced higher and heavier rainfall in the spring and winter months, making washouts a recurrent problem. Also, in its original form, a ball would frequently plug in the steep face of the bunker (to which those like James would say, "Tough luck"). When the course was built, all the bunkers were filled with sand from the land itself. In fact, to the left of the 8th hole is a huge pit where the coarse sand was quarried. The type of sand

Fig. 3-81 Heather and gorse, often revered on classic designs, began to consume the bunkers at St. George's Hill. The result was a loss of the long arm of the bunker that flanked the green. In its place, two small pots were created with steps leading to the lower bunker. This shot is from the mid-1980s. (Courtesy of St. George's Hill Golf Club)

used now is much finer than before, more like top dressing so as to prevent excessive wear to the bunker faces and the green surrounds.

The St. George's Hill Club handbook stated that Bernard Darwin included this hole in his description of an ideal 18-hole round. And not surprisingly, considering the Colt influence on both designs, the hole would fit in perfectly at Pine Valley. This bunker is truly special and represents one of the great theatrical scenes of early golf architecture.

Fig. 3-82 Golf architect Martin Hawtree oversaw extensive renovation work to reclaim the looming bunker (see color insert). (Courtesy of St. George's Hill Golf Club)

CHAPTER 4

Philosophies *of* Legendary Architects

The golf course architect is an author of sorts. Curiously, however, the language used by this breed of "writer" is of no use to one's ears. And even on the occasion that it might be neatly laid out on a piece of paper, one will still have little hope of understanding what it means. This language, which takes the form of a golf course and all its parts, is intended to be understood by only one breed of animal: *the golfer.*

Golf architects—dastardly individuals[1]—use a certain code to communicate with the golfer. Their words often change. Their alphabet is many times unclear. There are no pronouns. No rules about dangling participles. And certainly no definite articles. On one day, this code of codes might seem crystal clear to a golfer, while on another it may be like trying to decipher one of those TV evangelists who speaks in tongues.

Even more maddening to discover is that those who design golf courses develop their *own* codes—at least the better designers. What sets golf architects apart is how each of their custom languages is perceived by the golfer. The golfer is the ultimate audience of the work of the golf course architect. Harry Colt started his famous essay on golf architecture, published in Martin Sutton's *The Book of the Links* (1912), by saying, "Golf architecture is a 'somewhat dangerous subject' to write about." He went on to say, "Every golfer has their own opinions about golf course design and to suggest what is 'the right way to do things' will surely not satisfy everybody."

Our little bunker is part of the unusual code that each golf architect sends to us through each shot, hole, and course. This single hazard, wherever it may be in our minds, along with all of its relatives—from siblings to distant cousins—helps to define the message being sent to the golfer. The golfer's role is to learn the signals and interpret the

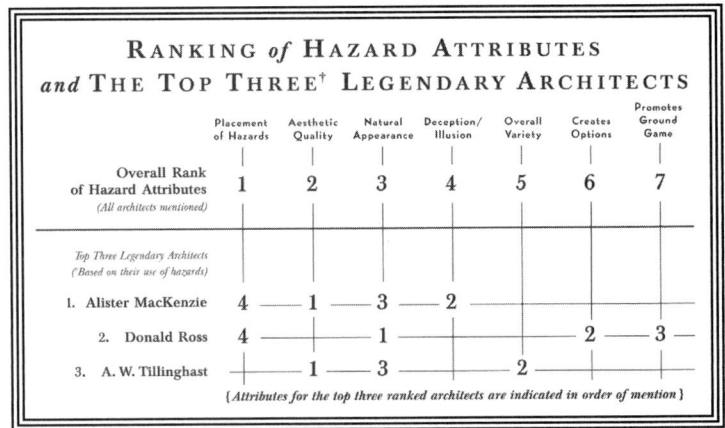

Fig. 4-1 Survey results indicating the three most-respected golf course architects among the legendary (and deceased) architects.

---

[1] While this may seem a self-inflicted insult to your authors, we enjoy the moniker. Anyone who spends his day designing golf courses is bound to take great delight in being referred to as *dastardly*.

clues to better the score. This must be done if any golf hole is to be conquered, assuming the normal allotment of luck[2] is at play.

Our aim in this chapter is to offer in one place a look at some of the philosophies of the legends of our field,[3] those golf architects who have used their language so eloquently and so creatively that their work continues to speak to us—and perplex us—day after day and year after year.

Charles Hugh Alison (1882–1952)

Born in England, Alison was best known for his association with Harry Colt. Few, if any, of Colt's courses in North America were designed without Alison's help. Alison traveled the world extensively and did some of his best solo work in the Far East.

> *Hazards should be visible. In general, they should not penalize to the extent of more than one stroke, provided that the stroke out of them is properly played. They should not be so severe as to discourage bold play. In placing hazards it is vital to keep the course navigable for the duffer. It is perfectly possible to do this, and yet to render it interesting and testing for the first class player.*

— Alison is known for his design of bunkers reminiscent of those at Muirfield—deep and steep-faced especially near the green.
— At courses like Kasumigaseki in Japan, Alison studded the course with deep, cavernous bunkers. Locals called these bunkers "Alisons."

Charles Henry Banks (1883–1931)

Born in New York, Banks was hired by Seth Raynor when Raynor was designing a course at Hotchkiss Preparatory School in Connecticut. Banks ended up spending most of his career carrying on the work of Raynor, as Raynor had far more projects than he could possibly handle. Banks ultimately worked himself to an early death. He did a number of his own designs, such as Forsgate Country Club and Knoll Country Club in New Jersey, but the majority of his work was done building Raynor courses.

— Banks's style (like Raynor's) reflected the tried and proved design concepts of Charles Blair Macdonald. He loved elevated greens with steep shoulders. He believed in moving massive amounts of earth to build gigantic, elevated greens with deep, yawning bunkers. Hog's backs were incorporated into many of the greens he built.

---

[2] The evidence of this, of course, is very sketchy. It has been rumored to be present in some distant and small corners of the world, so we have been told.

[3] It must be pointed out that, for some architects, philosophies on hazards will be discussed at length, while for others only the more obvious traits and tendencies will be covered. This is necessary because many of the figures we have included here recorded few of their thoughts in writing. We are left to draw our own conclusions from the clues and patterns that they left behind in their work.

- He was not afraid to use hidden hazards, and at times an unsuspecting player would walk over a slope only to find his ball in a bunker.
- Unlike Raynor, who relied on an ability to visualize a routing and golf holes in his mind, Banks relied heavily on topographical maps to lay out his routings and design his courses.
- He liked to place his greens on the sides of hills, which often accentuated the depth of greenside bunkers. Some of his bunkers were nearly 30 feet deep. These cavernous bunkers were his main departure from Macdonald and Raynor and became a trademark style.

Max Howell Behr (1884–1955)

Born in New York, Behr was well known as the first editor of *Golf Illustrated* in 1914. Through his writings, he contributed wonderful thoughts on golf architecture, many of which stimulated progress and advancement in the area of design and strategy. As proof, we need only listen to Behr's own words.

> *Unfortunately, hazards have become associated with an idea of penalty. This has resulted in establishing a system of course design in which hazards are used to indicate a fixed idea of what correct play should be. To enforce this requires discipline. Thus hazards, besides being informative of what correct play should be, become agents of discipline necessary to enforce it. And as discipline, if it is to affect obedience, must be definite and self revealing, this system robs golf of all mystery, romance and adventure. Play becomes no more than an examination of skill. The golfer is not required to think, but merely to obey.*
>
> *The direct line to the hole is the line of instinct, and to make a good hole you must break up that line in order to create the line of charm.*
>
> *There is no necessity for artificial barriers. Play does not have to be systematically controlled. An opposite principle is involved. This principle is freedom. And by freedom we compel the golfer to control himself, that is to say, his instincts. If he judges his skill great enough, he will of his own accord go for a strategic hazard to gain an advantage just as the tennis player will go for the sidelines of the court.*

William Parc "Billy" Bell (1886–1953)

Bell was born in Pennsylvania, but he did not know George Thomas or other members of the Philadelphia School of Design. In 1911 he moved to California and became caddiemaster at Annandale Golf Club, and later the greenkeeper at Pasadena Golf Club. He worked briefly for golf architect Willie Watson before setting up his own design practice in 1920.

Bell is probably most famous for his collaboration with George C. Thomas, Jr. Bell and Thomas collaborated on landmark courses such as Los Angeles, Bel-Air, and Riviera country clubs. Known as Billy Bell, he influenced Thomas's trademark lacy-edged bunkers. This style was not present in Thomas's work prior to his association with Bell.

Later, working with his son, William F. Bell, Bell went on to become one of the most prolific architects in the West, designing courses such as Stanford University Golf Course and San Diego Country Club. Bell continued to retain the spirited bunker design style he formulated while working with Thomas.

Fig. 4-2 An advertisement run by William P. "Billy" Bell.

- Bell liked to employ his trademark lacey-edged bunkers, placing them with strategy and temptation in mind. At times, he would leave islands amid his large bunkers. Occasionally, he would place hot-dog-shaped bunkers as backstops to greens. His large multi-bayed bunkers often flowed away from greens, creating a look as if the entire area had been carved from one landform. He was not afraid to place cross-hazards for the tee shot, particularly on par-5s.
- Like Thomas, Bell favored rolling and undulating green surfaces that were strategically linked to pin locations on the green. He designed his approaches to enable a golfer to work the ball onto the green.
- Bell used trees in his designs, but sparingly and mainly to accent the aesthetics of the surrounding area.
- Like many of the classic architects, Bell often used natural drainage paths to drive design decisions. This included the placement of hazards, as well as their size, shape, and design.

Thomas Bendelow (1868–1936)

Tom Bendelow was born in Aberdeen, Scotland. His redesign and addition of nine holes to Van Cortlandt Park was a real milestone in American golf in that it established the feasibility and benefits of municipal (public) golf courses. Bendelow also introduced tee times, regulated play, added caddy rules, and developed instruction and public player associations. All these innovations would help set the standards for the golf operations of the following decades.

Unfortunately, Bendelow is best known for his "18 stakes on a Sunday afternoon" approach to designing golf courses. This description is attributed to Chicago newspaper humorist George Ade. Bendelow did lay out a nine-hole course for Ade at his Indiana home, but it wasn't on Sunday. According to Ade, Bendelow would inspect the ground selected for the course, pick out an appropriate spot for the first tee and put down a stake, then pace off 100 yards and stake out a cross-bunker and plant another stake. Stepping off another 100 yards or so, he would put down a third stake and mark the location of a pit or cop bunker. Another stake would locate the green. He would proceed to do the same for all 18 holes, although some were much shorter than others, and usually one hole per nine was very long. He would always leave instructions to guide the builder of the course.

Bendelow is credited with designing over 600 courses in the United States and Canada, his greatest undoubtedly being Mendinah No. 3. As time passed, he began producing drawings for his designs, indicating that he was putting more time and thought into his course layouts. He also began making clay models for his greens.

- Bendelow liked to build bunkers straight across the fairway (cop-type bunkers).
- He often incorporated chocolate drops (arranged in groups) and flattish square greens, furthering the popular geometric look.
- He suggested that fewer trees and shrubs be planted inside the course.
- He was a big advocate of golf as a public form of recreation, and some believe that more golfers have learned the game on a Bendelow-designed course than any other.

James Braid (1870–1950)

Born in Scotland, Braid was probably more famous for his five Open titles, though his two courses at Gleneagles, Scotland, the King's and Queen's, are among his most noteworthy. Braid also made significant revisions to Narin, Carnoustie, Ballybunion, and Royal Porthcawl. He helped lay out the first American golf club, the St. Andrew's Golf Club in Yonkers, New York, by studying topographical maps created of the land.

- Braid loved to surround a short hole with several pot bunkers, adopting the common practice from Old Tom Morris.
- In the book *Golf Greens and Greenkeeping* (1906), Braid describes raising his bunker banks to make them look as natural as possible. His are some of the first words ever written about creating natural looking hazards.
- In the book *Advanced Golf* (1908), Braid writes about using every natural obstacle he can and always creating a well-guarded green. He goes on to suggest reasons for alternative tees and bunkering courses for what he terms "positional play."

Harry Shapland Colt (1869–1951)

Born in England, Colt was a lawyer-turned–golf architect. His first foray into design was with Doug Rolland at Rye Golf Club in England. A fine golfer all his life, Colt went on to design or remodel hundreds of courses, including many of the best in the world, including Royal Portrush, Wentworth West, Muirfield, St. George's Hill, and Milwaukee

Country Club. His longtime partner, C. H. Alison, worked with him on a majority of these projects.

"I firmly believe that the only means whereby an attractive piece of ground can be turned into a satisfying golf course is to work to the natural features of the site in question."
— THE BOOK OF THE LINKS: A SYMPOSIUM ON GOLF

"The characteristics required of a hazard are that it should be difficult but not impossible to play out of; that it should not be a cause of lost balls; and that strokes played out of it should be calculable as regards strength and direction, and should depend for their success on skill and not on brute force alone."
— SOME ESSAYS ON GOLF COURSE ARCHITECTURE

The diagonal hazard provides sport for everyone and the subsequent scheme of a hole can give advantage to the one who bites off the biggest slice of the hazard.

A bunker stretching right across the course should always be avoided, and, unless there are natural hazards, 'pot' bunkers are preferable to others.

— Colt believed a course should start off with sympathy for the weak and at the same time be as severe as it can be with the first-class player.
— He believed that a course must provide a test of accuracy for tee shots. The player must learn to take a line, and not just blaze away at right angles to the teeing ground. Accuracy off the tee can be enforced by placing the hazards near the green, even when there may be no bunkers off the tee.
— He favored distinctive features that would encourage a golfer to go away remembering each hole individually.
— Colt disliked blind shots, although he realized they are sometimes unavoidable.
— He used diagonals on carry shots to offer safer options and a risk/reward decision.
— He used center hazards with safe paths down the sides.
— Colt believed "a good sprinkling of lateral hazards" is necessary to test accurate driving.
— He avoided overuse of any one type of hazard.
— Two "non hazards" that Colt loved were plateau greens and "hummocky" ground. He felt a narrow plateau for a green or a few hummocks in front of one would very likely cause as much trouble and amusement to a player as a gaping chasm stretching across the line of play.
— He liked turf hollows as well as mounds because they provide for difficult stances and lies.
— Colt advocated variety in the shapes and sizes of bunkers. He hated symmetrical pots, banks, and humps.
— He worked at making artificial hazards look natural.
— On short holes in particular, he supported the use of water hazards if only for the sake of variety.
— His most common natural hazards were sand, heather, long grass, gorse, and water.
— He argued that the reward and penalty for negotiating a hazard should be in proportion to one another.
— He believed deeper, but escapable, bunkers near the green were justified, as these shots are short.

George Arthur Crump (1871–1918)

Born in Philadelphia, Crump never saw his dream course finished. Crump's course, Pine Valley, may have had as much influence on golf architecture as any other classic course in America. Crump died with only 14 holes completed. He was assisted by numerous architects yet abided by his own set of design principles.

Crump's goal with Pine Valley was to build a course that would offer great diversity of play in exacting form, a course that would have no single hole designed with the limitations of ordinary players in mind.

– Crump believed in penalties for bad shots and difficult, if not impossible, recoveries from hazards. A good shot should be rewarded and a bad one severely penalized, he reasoned.
– He abhorred parallelism and desired to keep each hole free of view of any other.
– He was concerned about the wind and wanted no two successive holes to run in the same direction.
– He built larger greens for long shots and smaller greens for short shots, all heavily protected by hazards.
– He loved variety and incorporated forced carries quite frequently.

Tom Dunn (1849–1902)

Born in England, Dunn was one of the most active designers of his day. Like Old Tom Morris, his low-cost approach to designing courses helped introduce many players to the game. Dunn is believed to be the first to use *turf dikes* (dug up earth piled to form a wall). He often placed these about 10 to 30 yards in front of greens, occasionally placing sand at the base. Turf was planted over the dyke. Dunn may have taken the idea for turf dykes from farmers who used such barriers to divide up parcels of property.

Dunn's father was Willie Dunn, Sr., and Tom's brother was Willie Jr. Together Tom and Willie Jr. designed the famous Biarritz course in France. It was Willie Jr., not Tom, who renovated the old 12-hole course at Shinnecock into a full 18 holes.

– Tom Dunn designed most of his courses in England's countryside as parkland courses. He did little to change the topography, relying on the lay of the land.
– Considered by some "the father of penal golf course design," Dunn placed cross-bunkers at frequent intervals throughout the round. It is thought that he followed this practice because it was the easiest and cheapest way to make hazards on a track of gently rolling, wide-open meadowland. These cross-bunkers would often stretch 30 to 40 yards across the fairway.

Devereux Emmet (1861–1934)

Born in New York, Emmet was a golfer and a hunter. A brief exercise for C. B. Macdonald in measuring golf holes may have led to his interest in course design. Teaming up with A. H. Toll, Emmet designed many noteworthy courses in the United States and the Caribbean.

> *I believe in placing hazards in front of some of the tees to compel reasonably good driving. But in the ordinary every-day play a moderately good drive from the tee should not be punished, if straight.*

> *I do not think bunkers should be constructed such that one man's ball will be caught and another's will run through. Every ball that enters a bunker should stop there, and it should only require one good stroke to get it out.*

> *Nothing must be done which will make it impossible for the shorter players and beginners to enjoy the game.*

> *If a course is properly bunkered, the wild player will soon get into trouble and the straight accurate man will inevitably win.*

- Emmet's designs reflected the strategies of the famous holes abroad. He invoked a natural feel and shied away from the overly penal designs that preceded his time.
- He favored the straight, accurate driver and rewarded this golfer accordingly.
- He strongly believed that rough areas should be maintained as rough areas to emphasize the advantage of being on the fairways. He also felt it was worth the loss of a few balls in the rough to preserve one of the features that makes a good golf course.
- He once compared Scottish courses to those in America, stating that there were at least five bunkers and hazards in Scotland to every one in the United States. He suggested that designers be careful in their striving not to lose balls, for doing so would "take all the sting out of our game."

George Fazio (1912–1986)

Born in Pennsylvania, Fazio competed on the PGA Tour against many of the best

Fig. 4-3 George Fazio was known for bunkers with high flashed sand and a variety of shapes.

players in the world. He was the resident professional at Pine Valley, entering the design profession in 1959. Butler National and Jupiter Hills are two of his many prominent designs.

- George Fazio used a variety of shapes in the design of his bunkers. However, he liked to build large ovals and cloverleafs with high, flashed sand. He had one shaper who did the majority of his work. The result was a style of bunker design that stayed with him. He stressed visibility and made sure his bunkers were plain to see from the tee and approaches.
- One of his primary goals was to make his golf courses different from and better than those of Robert Trent Jones, Sr.
- His bunkers are perhaps more penal in nature than strategic. They reward good play, but penalize poor shots.
- According to Tom Fazio, George's nephew, he loved long par-4s and very often elevated his greens, making it difficult to get up and down if one missed to either side. One of the reasons he did this was to save money. He was able to surface-drain these types of greens and avoid expensive underground drainage.
- At the time George was designing golf courses, shaping shots was a major part of golf, and his courses were designed accordingly. He liked angles into his greens and set hazards accordingly.
- George was one of the first to design green sites like amphitheaters for the purpose of holding large galleries during tournament use. He wanted his courses to attract big events and designed certain green sites with this in mind. For this same reason, he focused much of his attention on the last few holes, as that was where he reckoned the TV coverage would be. If budgets were limited, as they often were, he would focus money on creating hazards on the finishing holes.

William S. Flynn (1890–1945)

Born in Massachusetts, Flynn grew up playing golf with Francis Ouimet. He designed his first course at age 19 before moving on to Philadelphia to work with Hugh Wilson at Merion. Flynn went on to design some of the greatest courses in the country, including Shinnecock Hills, Kittansett, Cherry Hills, Cascades, and Lehigh to name a few.

Hazards should be plainly visible. (Flynn abhorred the invisible pot bunker so often encountered on British Courses.)

A concealed bunker has no place on a golf course. When concealed, it does not register on the player's mind as he is about to play the shot and thus loses its value.

The best looking bunkers are those that are gouged out of the faces of slopes, especially when the slope faces the player. They are much more effective in that they stand there like sentinels beckoning the player.

The principal consideration of the architect is to design his course in such a way as to hold the interest of the player from the first tee to the last green, and to present the problems of the various holes in such a way that they register in the player's mind as he stands on the tee or on the fairway for the shot to the green.

By arranging the green bunkers in such a way as to invite play in from one side or the other, you can put a premium on placing the tee shot on a particular side of the fairway. When a test of length off the tee is presented, the best type of hole is the cape or elbow as it takes a really big tee shot to permit reaching the green.

While bunkers are thought by many to be put in as penalizers, they are primarily installed to present a problem or a mode of play. If bunkers were used merely to punish bad shots there would have to be a complete revision of them on most courses.

— When Merion was under construction, and later during revisions to the course, Flynn and Wilson would have bed sheets spread out on the site of a proposed bunker. This allowed one to stand on the tee or the area from which the shot would be played and be certain that the hazard could be plainly seen.
— Flynn felt that the plans first submitted by an architect should cover what might well be termed the *framework of the course,* but should be flexible in the matter of pits and bunkers. Those around the greens and certain traps just off the fairways may be fairly well determined in advance, but the location of the others can be determined better after the course has been completed and played on for a time.
— Flynn promoted the idea that the science of golf architecture is the presenting of problems and the placing of objectives to be reached by the players.
— Flynn was committed to designing a course with 18 interesting holes, each with a variety of play. He believed that a course with such character in its natural state can readily be made even more interesting by the installation of a limited number of man-made hazards.
— Flynn stated that a majority of courses have entirely too many traps that are badly placed and poorly constructed, that cost too much money to maintain, and the removal of which would help

Fig. 4-4 Lehigh Country Club outside Allentown, Pennsylvania, is a prime example of the brilliance of William Flynn. Lehigh uses a variety of sand, water, and contour hazards amongst its innovative routing (see color insert).

the average player, improve appearances, reduce upkeep, and leave the star player practically unaffected.
- Flynn felt that the design for bunkering a course was tremendously important. The architect should spend a great deal of time going over the various holes, determining the exact location of the fairway bunkers.
- An important consideration in the design of bunkers is to make each one surface-drain. In flat country, Flynn achieved this by elevating bunkers above the surface of the surrounding terrain.
- On the majority of Flynn's courses, his bunkers can best be described as ordinary in shape and style. To him, their placement was most important. However, on seaside courses, he made hazards that were brilliant and unique, varying his parkland style of bunker to fit the site. He felt hazards in general need not be numerous, but instead well placed to arouse lively interest.

William Herbert Fowler (1856–1941)

Born in England, Fowler did not play golf until age 35. But he soon became a scratch player, taking on his first and most famous design project, Walton Heath in the early 1900s.

> *One of the most important facts in making a golf course is to find out what the natural drainage is like, and where it is bad or indifferent it is most important to drain thoroughly before sowing the grass seed.*

> *I think it better in making a course in heather land to clear fairly wide and to put in bunkers to act as hazards for wide shots.*

> *There is one test of a good slope from a bank. One should never be able to point to any spot where the slope ends.*

> *There are, to be sure, all kinds of hazards, and most of them are bad: trees, hedges, ditches, and all unsatisfactory, and no doubt the best are sand bunkers, so long as they are properly placed and constructed.*

> *Personally, I think that a slice is certainly a greater fault than a top, and I would, therefore, place the majority of the side hazards on the right and a lesser number on the left of the fairway.*

- Fowler felt that greens were better when guarded on the sides by hazards. He was also in favor of hazards behind the green, but he considered them secondary to those at the flanks. He favored an entrance to the green, with a width dictated by the length of the approach shot. The shorter the shot, the narrower the opening.
- In addition to Walton Heath, Fowler revised such well-known courses as Cruden Bay, Royal North Devon, Royal Lytham & St. Anne's, Ganton, and the Presidio in California.
- Fowler often used the soil dug out from his bunker cavities for mounding. He recommended that all slopes behind the faces of bunkers be as long as the ground would allow.

– He believed that fairway bunkers should be arranged to work with the hazards in close proximity to the green. If a golfer placed his shot well, he should be rewarded with an advantage over the golfer who was wild.

William C. Fownes, Jr. (1878–1950)

Born in Chicago, William Fownes was the son of Henry Clay Fownes. Together they were responsible for the creation of the celebrated Oakmont Country Club near Pittsburgh, their sole contribution to golf architecture. Oakmont was a labor of love, and, along with Oakmont's longtime greenkeeper Emil Loeffler, the three men went with their instincts and boldly created a golf course that was to become "America's toughest."

Drawing on their knowledge (from afar) of the famous links courses of the British Isles, the team stopped at nothing in transforming their Pennsylvania countryside into a work-in-progress that was subject to their continual direction and redesign. William once explained, "The bunkering system is continually being adapted to meet the requirements of longer hitting and more exacting play to the green."

A shot poorly played should be a shot irrevocably lost.

In my opinion, the charm of the game lies in its difficulties. Keep it rugged, baffling, hard to conquer; otherwise we shall soon tire of it and cast it aside.

– The famous Church Pew bunkers at Oakmont were created when Fownes and Loeffler combined a cluster of bunkers into one. Within this single bunker they left rows of piled earth similar to old-style cop bunkers.

Fig. 4-5 Bunkers (sand traps as they were called in Western Pennsylvania) were raked with furrowed rakes prior to 1950. The Fownes felt that it toughened the hazards by creating deep ridges. However, once a player learned how to hit from the furrows, it became second nature.

- Oakmont's bunkers, which at one point numbered over 350, were prepared with special rakes. Each rake was 39 inches wide and had 5-inch teeth spaced 2 inches apart. Emil Loeffler weighted these rakes to make the furrows in the sand even deeper. This effect was meant to add difficulty to his otherwise shallow bunkers, built so because the heavy clay soils prevented digging too deep. Fownes wanted deep pot bunkers but settled for this original idea instead.
- Fownes would add bunkers where most players hit their shots with the sole purpose of making the golf course difficult.
- Oakmont had no water. However, ditches were incorporated in the rough to improve drainage throughout the course, and these became hazards.
- Oakmont was designed to be feared, and though many bunkers have been removed over the years, it still is a great example of penal architecture.

William F. Gordon (1893–1973)

Born in Rhode Island, Gordon was a noted track star and worked as an athletic instructor in the U.S. Navy. Between 1920 and 1923, Gordon built golf courses for architects such as Donald Ross, Devereux Emmet, and Willie Park, Jr. In 1923, he joined the firm of Toomey and Flynn and stayed with them until 1941, when he formed his own design firm, primarily seeding military installations. His most famous designs include Stanwich, Saucon Valley Grace Course, and DuPont Country Club. In 1945, he began building courses for Ross and J. B. McGovern.

- Unlike Flynn, Gordon used bunkering that was fairly formulaic and predictable. His bunkers were also more defensive and penal in nature.
- He was not as artistic or daring as some architects. His bunkers were rather plain at times, guarding both the right and left sides of his greens. He often had openings in front of his greens so golfers could execute run-up shots.
- He left his fairways relatively open with bunkers scattered toward the sides.
- His use of trees varied from site to site, however, he incorporated tree plantings into many of his designs.
- He used water more frequently than many of the golden age golf architects.

Wiles Robert Hunter (1874–1942)

Born in Indiana, Hunter was an assistant to H. Chandler Egan in the remodeling of Pebble Beach and was a right-hand man to Alister MacKenzie in the creation of Cypress Point. Though never really considered a golf architect in his own right, Robert Hunter, as he was known, authored one of the most influential golf architecture books of all time, *The Links*. He is regarded as one of the most thoughtful voices in golf architecture. Each one of his quotes which follow is a gem.

There can be no real golf without hazards, and unless these be varied, plentiful, and adroitly placed there will be no great golfers. Hazards are the decisive influence in the making of golfers.

On Pine Valley: "These superb hazards are a part of nature. Where does art begin?"

All artificial hazards should be made to fit into the ground as if placed there by nature. To accomplish this is a great art. Indeed, when it is really done well it is, I think it may truly be said, a fine art, worthy of the hand of a gifted sculptor.

Without well-placed hazards, golf would fail to arouse and to satisfy man's sporting instincts.

Hazards—how well chosen the name! They are risks, and penalties must come to those who take risks and fail.

Fig. 4-6 Robert Hunter was Alister MacKenzie's right-hand man at Cypress Point Club. Pictured is No. 7, a par-3 (see color insert). (Courtesy of P. Burton)

Hazards make golf dramatic; and the thrills that come to one who ventures wisely and succeeds are truly delectable.

Without hazards golf would be but a dull sport, with the life and soul gone out of it.

Wind and water, hillocks and hollows, mounds and pits, marram grass and bents— these are the hazards of the links; and while they are all difficult to contend with, there is not one of them which cannot be overcome by the skill of the golfer.

The best architects seek, in placing their hazards, to call forth great shots. Some of their best holes reward handsomely fine golf, but have no obvious penalties for bad golf. Such holes are so cunningly laid out that those playing bad shots lose strokes by the position in which they find themselves.

Scores of the most interesting hazards on the seaside courses lie in places where the most foolhardy American architect would never think of putting one of them.

Many hazards punish severely extremely well-played shots—shots often which have so little missed perfection as to make it seem cruel to enforce penalties. And yet even he who pays the penalty knows that were it not for these magnificent hazards, so often placed haphazard—golf on the links would not possess that overpowering fascination which makes the game there sublime.

To make great holes, hazards need not be numerous. A few well placed are quite sufficient to arouse any amount of lively interest and to call forth shots of which the best golfer may well be proud.

Robert Trent Jones, Sr. (1906–2000)

Born in England, Jones moved to the United States in 1911 and studied at Cornell with the intent of becoming a golf course architect. He tutored under the great Stanley Thompson before embarking on his own. Jones designed nearly 500 courses all over the world. Courses such as Valderrama, Spyglass Hill, Peachtree, Bellerive, and Firestone South bear his name. Many consider him one of the most influential golf course designers in history.

> *Collectively all three types of architecture produce every shot known in the realm of golf. Individually each requires shots characteristic to its own school. It would therefore seem logical that the ideal golf course should be a combination of all three.*
> — Canadian Golfer (April 1936), commenting on the distinction between the various types of golf holes[4]—penal, strategic, and heroic

Every hole should be a hard par and an easy bogey.

- The Jones style was a combination of the strategic and penal schools of design often referred to as the *heroic school*. Its dramatic hazards required the player to make thought-provoking decisions with do-or-die consequences.
- Jones favored large rolling greens and huge oval, cloverleaf, and amoeba-shaped sand bunkers.
- He designed man-made ponds and lakes to create heroic carries and other problems for the golfer to contend with.
- He used extraordinarily long tee boxes that seemed to make every hole look more hazardous and its play narrower.
- He designed his courses to be "hard" and of "championship" quality.
- Jones wanted players to have the option of hitting drivers, but with great accuracy and precision. Any shot off its mark would encounter deep grass, sand, or water.
- He anticipated that golf's transformation in America was changing to an aerial game and designed his courses to force high, soft shots to greens heavily protected in the front. Approach shots needed to carry all the way to the green, and anything short found trouble, such as a sloping bunker, a stream, or a pond.

Robert Tyre Jones, Jr. (1902–1971)

Born in Atlanta, "Bobby" Jones was one of the greatest golfers who ever lived. Though he never practiced design himself, Jones's dream golf course, Augusta National, has had profound influence on golf architecture in America and, indeed, across the world. He collaborated on the design of Augusta with Alister MacKenzie after meeting him during a round of golf at the Cypress Point Club.

---

[4] The notion of "penal, strategic and heroic" being the only three types of design "schools" was challenged in Richardson's Routing the Golf Course (John Wiley & Sons, 2002). Richardson suggests the term strategic is too broad, and that all golf holes possess strategy, even in the absence of any hazards at all. His view is that penal, heroic, detour, lay-up and open constitute the five essential types of golf shots that may be executed, and that most golf holes are a combination of these types of shot strategy. The theory is that it is too limiting to always classify a hole as offering only one particular type of design.

Every golfer worthy of the name should have some acquaintance with the principles of golf course design, not only for the betterment of the game, but for his own selfish enjoyment. Let him know a good hole from a bad one and the reasons for a bunker here and another there, and he will be a long way towards pulling his score down to respectable limits. When he has taught himself to study a hole from the point of view of the man who laid it out, he will be much more likely to play it correctly.

There should always be a definite advantage to be gained from an accurate and intelligent placing of the tee shot, or a reward offered for a long, well-directed carry over some obstacle.

There are two ways of widening the gap between a good tee shot and a bad one. One is to inflict a severe and immediate punishment on a bad shot, to place its perpetrator in a bunker or in some other trouble which will demand the sacrifice of a stroke in recovering. The other is to reward the good shot by making the second shot simpler in proportion to the excellence of the first. The reward may be of any nature, but it is more commonly one of four—a better view of the green, an easier angle from which to attack a slope, an open approach past guarding hazards, or even a better run to the tee shot itself. But the elimination of purely punitive hazards provides an opportunity for the player to retrieve his situation by an exceptional second shot.

William Boice Langford (1887–1977)

Born in Texas, Langford suffered from polio as a child but still developed into a fine amateur golfer. He began practicing course design in 1918, using his engineering background to create detailed drawings of cuts and fill for course construction.

Hazards should not be built solely with the idea of penalizing bad play, but with the object of encouraging thoughtful golf and rewarding the player who possesses the ability to play a variety of strokes with each club.

Hazards should be placed so that any player can avoid them if he gauges his ability correctly, so that they will make every man's game more interesting, no matter what class player he is, and offer a reward commensurate with the player's ability.

– Langford was a master at understanding approach angles and used dramatic, steep-sloped bunkers in a style reminiscent of Seth Raynor. He was always concerned about where players would hit the ball and what angles would force them to think.
– He used echelon arrangements of bunkers for tee shots, allowing carries of varying length. Hazards near the green were placed to offer a reward proportionate to the risk taken at the tee.
– He placed hazards to reward accuracy and to challenge the longer hitter to play aggressively but accurately to receive a shorter shot into the green. Lawsonia Golf Club in Wisconsin provides a good example.
– Langford had a distinct predilection for raised greens with sharp edges that fell off precipitously into flat-bottomed deep bunkers.

John L. Low (1869–1929)

Born in Scotland, Low was never a practicing architect, though he did assist Stuart Paton with the remodeling of Woking Golf Club. However, his writing on golf course architecture had a strong influence on the profession. We include him here as more than a courtesy. It would be malpractice to leave his wisdom out.

> *Just as close as he dare: that's golf, and that's a hazard of immortal importance! For golf at its best should be a contest of risks. The fine player should, on his way round the links, be just slipping past the bunkers, gaining every yard he can, conquering by the confidence of his own 'far and sure' play.*
>
> *The true hazard should draw play towards it, should invite the golfer to come as near as he dare to the fire without burning his fingers. The man who can afford to take the risks is the man who should gain the advantage.*
>
> *Bunkers, if they be good bunkers, and bunkers of strong character, refuse to be disregarded and insist on asserting themselves; they do not mind being avoided, but they decline to be ignored.*
>
> *By placing the hazards close in on the fairway, golf becomes a contest of risks, the perfect shot betters the imperfect, and accuracy gets its full reward.*
>
> *On a well laid out golf course, each stroke has to be played in relation to the following one and the hole is mastered by a pre-conceived plan of action.*
>
> *No hazard is unfair wherever it is placed, and this particularly applies if the hazard is visible, as it should be obvious that if a player sees a hazard in front of him and promptly planks his ball into it, he has chosen the wrong spot.*
>
> —Concerning Golf (1903), the first known book on golf architecture

Charles Blair Macdonald (1855–1939)

Born in Canada, Macdonald eventually moved to Chicago. From there he decided to attend the University of St. Andrews in Scotland. It was in Scotland that he fell in love with golf. He brought everything he learned back home and eventually designed the first 18-hole golf course in America, the Chicago Golf Club.

> *I suggest that the construction of bunkers on various courses should have an individuality entirely of their own which arouse the love or hatred of intelligent golfers.*
>
> — Scotland's Gift–Golf

CHAPTER 4 | PHILOSOPHIES *of* LEGENDARY ARCHITECTS

To my mind, an ideal course should have at least six bold bunkers like the Alps at Prestwick, the ninth at Brancaster, Sahara, or Maiden at Sandwich, and the sixteenth at Littlestone. Such bold bunkers should be at the end of a two-shot hole or a very long carry from the tee.

On the National, the first strategic golf course built in America:
The only thing that I do now is to endeavor to make the hazards as natural as possible. I try not to make the course any harder, but to make it more interesting, always striving to give weaker players a way out to negotiate insurmountable difficulties to reach the green, by taking a course much as a yachtsman does against an adverse wind, by tacking.

Glaring artificiality of any kind distracts from the fascination of the game.

More than three blind holes are a defect and they should be at the end of a fine long shot only.

Out of bounds should be avoided if possible.

Trees in the course are a serious defect, and even when in close proximity prove a detriment.

No course can be ideal which is laid out through trees. Trees foreshorten the perspective and the wind has not full play. To get the full exaltation playing the game of golf one should when passing from green to green as he gazes over the horizon have an unlimited sense of eternity, suggesting contemplation and imagination.

On the maintenance of bunkers:
If I had my way there would be a troupe of cavalry horses running through every trap and bunker on the course before a tournament started, where only a niblick could get the ball out and then but only after a few years. I have seen a number of traps and bunkers that afforded better lies and easier strokes than the fairway. This of course is ridiculous.

I do not believe in deep-ditch hazards; they always have long grass, usually very long in the bottom, are generally muddy and frequently have casual water, involving rules not generally understood.

Water hazards should always be well defined. An arm of the sea can be wonderfully utilized, as can also a brook or stream; the former is much to be desired.

[There] should be two holes which have fine large cross bunkers protecting the green.

The object of a bunker or trap is not only to punish a physical mistake, to punish lack of control, but also to punish pride and egotism.

> *I believe the course would be improved by opening the fair green to one side or the other, giving short or timid players an opportunity to play around the hazard if so desired, but, of course, properly penalized by loss of distance for so playing.*

- Macdonald did not like cross-bunkers to be carried from the tee unless built diagonally so that the player has a choice, "to bite off as much as he can chew."
- Macdonald laid out a table of "essential characteristics" of an ideal golf course in his book *Scotland's Gift–Golf,* giving bunkers and other hazards a score of 13 out of 100 total points. In discussing this section, he stated that the subject of bunkers and other hazards creates much dispute and argument. Whether a bunker is well placed has "caused more intensely heated arguments outside the realms of religion," he wrote. He went on to state that a hazard that causes arguments over whether it is fair or properly placed is the kind that has real merit. If everyone believes the hazard is perfect, one usually finds it commonplace. He claimed to know of no classic hole that has not its decriers.
- As for hazards on the sides of courses, he felt that other than bunkers, bent rushes and whins were best.
- Like many others, Macdonald felt long grasses were annoying and caused too many lost balls. He believed that grass should be graduated in height, cut shorter nearer the line to the hole.

Alister MacKenzie (1870–1934)

Born in England, MacKenzie practiced medicine after graduating from Cambridge. He learned the art of camouflage during his military career. In the early 1900s, he got involved in golf course architecture, often collaborating with Harry Colt and C. H. Alison. The "Good Doctor," as he was called, went on to design some of the greatest courses in the world including Cypress Point, Augusta National, and Royal Melbourne.

> *The chief object of every golf course architect or greenkeeper worth his salt is to imitate the beauties of nature so closely as to make his work indistinguishable from nature itself.*
> —GOLF ARCHITECTURE

> *The greatest compliment that can be paid to the architect is for players to think that his artificial work is natural.*

> *The bunkers at St. Andrews are thus placed in positions where players are most likely to go—in fact, in the precise positions which the ordinary Green Committee would suggest should be filled up.*

> *There are few things more monotonous than playing every shot from a dead flat fairway.*

> *The majority of [golfers] simply look upon hazards as a means of punishing a bad shot, when their real objective is to make the game interesting.*

CHAPTER 4 | PHILOSOPHIES *of* LEGENDARY ARCHITECTS

Fig. 4-7 Alister MacKenzie's Pasatiempo, California. Pictured is No. 10, a par-4 (see color insert). (Courtesy of P. Burton)

A hazard placed in the exact position where a player would naturally go is frequently the most interesting situation, as then a special effort is needed to get over or avoid it.

On an inland course the only way (except at enormous expense) of providing hazards as high as sand dunes, is by the use of trees in groups.

Most of the best inland courses owe their popularity to the grouping of trees. Groups of trees are the most effective way of preventing players from reaching the green with their second shots after playing their drives in the wrong direction. No bunkers guarding the green seem to be able to prevent them doing so.

Some of the most spectacular shots I have ever seen have been around, over or through gaps in trees.

Playing down fairways bordered by straight lines of trees is not only unartistic but makes for tedious and uninteresting golf. Many Green Committees ruin one's work by planting trees in rows like soldiers along the borders of the fairways.

Trees should not usually be placed in a direct line with the hole as they block the view too much. They make an excellent corner for a dogleg.

A course should have beautiful surroundings, and all the artificial features should have so natural an appearance that a stranger is unable to distinguish them from nature itself.

The desirability or otherwise of having water hazards depends largely on their spectacular character and beauty.

No hole is a good one unless it has one or more hazards in a direct line of a hole.

117

Bunkers, Pits & Other Hazards

It is an important thing in golf to make holes look much more difficult than they really are. People get more pleasure in doing a hole which looks almost impossible, and yet is not so difficult as it appears.

- MacKenzie believed there should be different avenues to the golf hole and that there was no need for guide posts to direct the way.
- He felt every hole should have a different character and that there should be a minimum of blindness for approach shots.
- MacKenzie felt some hazards should require heroic carries from the tee, but options should exist for the weaker player to play around these hazards.
- He thought long rough was a nuisance and should be kept to a minimum to prevent searching for lost balls. Driving over a stretch of long rough is not the same thrill as driving over a fearsome looking bunker. He once said, "Narrow fairways bordered by long grass make bad golfers. They destroy the harmony of the game and all freedom of play."
- MacKenzie used hillocks but was careful not to make them so high that they blocked the direct view of the hole. He felt hollows were better used in the direct line.
- He had a wider definition of hazards than is given by the Rules of Golf. He included undulating ground, hummocks, hollows, and so on.
- He felt the placing of hazards was much too large a subject to discuss but added that his fundamental principle was that no hazard is unfair wherever it is placed. He argued that the object in placing hazards is to give the player as much pleasurable excitement as possible.
- He believed hazards placed outside the "direct field of vision" were of little interest, acting merely as a source of irritation. Hazards, he maintained, should be placed with an objective, and none should be made that has not some influence on the line of play to the hole.
- MacKenzie felt many courses had too many bunkers, once saying they would be equally interesting if half were turfed over as grassy hollows.
- He believed too many courses (and their hazards) were designed to eliminate the element of luck and argued succeeding at this would only make the game less interesting.
- MacKenzie believed most games of golf were match play and not medal play, and so designed his hazards with this in mind. He said the true test of a hole is its value in a match-play situation.
- He was in favor of using water where it existed as a natural feature, particularly if there was a clean bottom and there was chance of recovering one's ball.
- He liked his greenside hazards tucked right up to the edge of the green. He said a bunker eating into a green is by far the most equitable way of giving a golfer full advantage for accurate play.

Perry Duke Maxwell (1879–1952)

Born in Kentucky, Maxwell took up golf at age 30. Shortly thereafter he laid out a 9-hole course on his family farm. This course became Dornoch Hills. Many of his design philosophies came from a pilgrimage to Scotland around 1920, where he studied many renowned courses. Perry went on to design an estimated 70 courses and remodel 50 or more others.

It is my theory that nature must precede the architect, in the laying out of links. The site of a golf course should be there, not brought there. A featureless site cannot possibly be economically redeemed. Many an acre of magnificent land has been utterly destroyed by the steam shovel, throwing up its billows of earth, biting out traps and bunkers, transposing landmarks that are contemporaries of Genesis. The less of man's handiwork the better a course.

—AMERICAN GOLFER (JANUARY 1935)

- Maxwell felt that 20 to 25 bunkers, plus the natural obstacles, were ample for any course.
- Maxwell would not build a water hazard if one did not exist naturally.
- His undulating greens, dubbed "Maxwell Rolls," were a hazard in themselves.
- He loved elevated greens and elevated tees, and he used them wherever possible.
- He would incorporate mounds into his designs, sometimes placing them in front of greens.
- Maxwell never wrote much on trees, but given his long-term association with MacKenzie, it is probable they shared similar views about them such as using trees in small groups, strategically located.
- Maxwell took the wind into account in all of his designs.
- He incorporated a native grass called *gunsch* into his design at Prairie Dunes. He also used plum thickets, yucca plants, soap weeds, and other flora that thrived just off the fairways.

Fig. 4-8 Examples of Perry Maxwell's bunkers at Dornick Hills, Ardmore, Oklahoma, U.S.A.

Old Tom Morris (1821–1908)

Born in St. Andrews, Scotland, Old Tom Morris learned the business of golf under Allan Robertson at St. Andrews (now The Old Course.) He lived to the age of 87 at *Home of Golf,* and his list of accomplishments touched many of those who went on to create courses during the golden age of golf architecture in the twentieth century.

Despite all the knowledge Morris had to share about making golf courses, he wrote very little. As W. Tulloch wrote in *The Life of Tom Morris,* it is believed that Morris wrote a letter to the editor of a golf magazine sometime in the early 1890s stating his opinions on golf course design. One of the points Morris raised in that letter was: "There is no necessity to have trees on a golf course." He believed it was sufficient to have "large sand-pits dug in the course, called bunkers, or a whin or two to serve as hazards to players."

Morris laid out many courses, including several nine-holers where land and money were scarce. He is credited for modifying St. Andrews to the 18-hole course it is today.

Muirfield, Royal Portrush, Royal County Down, Carnoustie, and Royal Dornoch were all designed or altered by Morris during his design career.

Fig. 4-9 Old Tom Morris (in window) at his shop in St. Andrews, Scotland, c.1899.

— Morris believed bunkers are not places of pleasure, that they are for punishment and repentance.
— One of the most significant contributions to golf was Morris's removal of many of the hazards at St. Andrews that made the original course nearly unplayable for the weaker golfer. He cleared many of the thorny bushes that crowded the narrow corridors of play. The result was a wider, more expansive playing area that gave golfers alternate routes to attack the hole. This was the first real introduction of strategy into the design and alteration of golf holes. Up to this point, most courses were just tees and greens and natural obstacles, whatever and wherever they might be. Morris wanted courses to be fun for the average golfer and decided artificial modifications to the playing ground were quite acceptable and good for the game. He was one of the first to add them, following the lead of Allan Robertson.
— Morris always incorporated the natural features of the site. He really didn't have much choice, as modifying the land was expensive and difficult. He worked during a period when little means were available to build golf courses. The Alps at Prestwick and the Cape Bunker of Westward Ho! are two of his well-known hazards.
— Morris often added bunkers to his rudimentary layouts as the courses aged. Rakes, of course, were not used during his era.
— Morris liked to challenge a golfer with a carry over a quarry or abyss, if one was present on the site.
— Morris used a variety of hazards to protect his greens. These included bunkers, sandhills, grassy hollows, turf dykes, hedges, stone walls, fences, and burns. He would place greens as close as possible to the hazard.
— Morris used every existing hazard available to him on the site to its maximum advantage. Where he felt the course would benefit, and the budget would afford it, he would artificially construct hazards.
— Of all the hazards, his favorite was most likely the bunker. On short holes, he would sometimes surround the green with pot bunkers. He placed tees to play over sandhills and tucked greens behind them. The Dell at Lahinch is a famous example.
— Morris's design of the New Course at St. Andrews had only one blind hole. He may have begun to recognize the golfer's growing disregard for such designs by this time in his life.
— Morris used the grassy holes that were natural depressions on seaside links courses. He would surround some of his plateau greens with these features.
— Morris seldom used ponds as hazards, probably because they were not plentiful on his sites.

Willie Park, Jr. (1864–1925)

Born in Scotland, Park grew up in the famous golfing center of Musselburgh. He was one of the best golfers of his time and a very talented and prolific designer. His most famous designs in England are Sunningdale and Huntercombe. He was most likely the first to demonstrate that a good course could be built on inland property. He designed more than 70 courses in the United States and Canada.

> *A bunker that is not visible to the player is always more or less of a trap.*
>
> *When building artificial bunkers, they should be big enough and deep enough to prevent the possibility of a ball either rolling through or jumping over the bunker.*
>
> *If a bunker is visible to the player, and there is sufficient room to avoid it, it is the player's responsibility to steer clear of it.*

– Park believed there should be no hazard out of which the ball cannot be extricated at the loss of one stroke.
– He believed in punishing poor shots and placing hazards judiciously to do so.
– Park felt all hazards should be visible to the golfer when he stands at his ball before playing a stroke. That said, he laid out a course called Shiskine in 1892 on the Island of Arran where nearly every shot is a blind one. (Architects are notorious for not always following their own rules.)
– He considered sand bunkers the most legitimate hazards.
– Park believed that a hazard should be sharply defined so that players can tell whether or not a ball lies within it.
– He believed that trees were never a fair hazard if located near the line of play, as a well-hit shot might be completely spoiled by catching in the branches.
– He maintained that the presence of an occasional wall, fence, pond, or stream could always be avoided, but he did not recommend the creation of such hazards.
– He considered the placing of hazards a matter of great difficulty and believed their positions should be such that a golfer playing a good game will never visit them.
– He used hazards down the sides of holes to catch pulled and sliced shots.
– During his time, many architects argued that hazards should be in front of all greens. Park felt otherwise, suggesting variety in placement and that any hazard placed in front of a green should allow a well lofted shot to stop near the hole.

Seth J. Raynor (1874–1926)

Born in New York, Raynor obtained a degree in engineering from Princeton. He operated a successful surveying and landscaping business for many years before his introduction to

Charles Blair Macdonald. He ended up working with Macdonald as his design partner until his untimely death at the age of 51.

The mold for Raynor was cast by this relationship with Macdonald. When working on his own courses, Raynor simply carried on with the same styles and philosophy as if he were building courses for Macdonald. In George Bahto's book *The Evangelist of Golf,* Raynor is quoted as saying, "I used to think my ears would grow to be like asses' ears, for I was always stretching them to take in every word that Mr. Macdonald uttered on the subject of golf."

Macdonald hired Raynor for his engineering and surveying skills. Raynor proved to be a quick study, and his responsibilities soon expanded. This ultimately allowed Macdonald to delegate all the details of carrying on his course design and construction business to Raynor. Macdonald designed the National as the prototype and taught Raynor all he knew about golf course architecture. He then left it up to Raynor to carry on duplicating the National's course design philosophies with site-to-site changes. As such, Raynor's bunker styles and techniques were nearly identical to Macdonald's, and they remained that way throughout his career. If there was any difference, it was that Macdonald employed a more strategic use of hazards in the fairway, particularly the cross-hazard. Macdonald loved to present options on tee shots, but Raynor worried more about the greens and their surrounds and less about strategically bunkering tee-shot landing areas. On some of his courses, such as Fisher's Island and Yeamen's Hall, Raynor only used one fairway bunker in the entire 18-hole design. And when he did use fairway hazards, most were set on the sides of the fairway and acted in a more penal manner. Also, according to Bahto, Raynor's interpretation and his design copies of the famous holes such as the Redan and Alps seem to indicate that they were smoother and less defiant in appearance than those of Macdonald.

Fig. 4-10 *The famous Biarritz Hole at Yale, Connecticut, c.1929. Seth Raynor was inspired by the original design at the Biarritz la Phare Course built by Willie Dunn in 1888. (Source: Golf Illustrated, July 1929)*

Unlike Macdonald, who was always given choice land, Raynor took on projects on difficult terrain, yet his eye for visualizing routings led to many wonderful golf courses. Though all his designs incorporated copies many of the famous holes in the British Isles, he never once made the pilgrimage to see the originals.

CHAPTER 4 | PHILOSOPHIES *of* LEGENDARY ARCHITECTS

Allan Robertson (1815–1859)

Born in St. Andrews, Scotland, Robertson is often considered one of the first golf course architects, if not the first. His most famous design was a ten-hole course that ultimately became Carnoustie. He is also credited with building the first "man-made" green site: No. 17 at The Old Course.

Robertson started the modification process at St. Andrews by removing much of the gorse and whins that made the original course nearly unplayable for the weaker golfer. This was the start of the "widening" of the fairways. This trend allowed play around hazards and not just over them. Old Tom Morris continued this clearing process and alteration of the golf holes at The Old Course.

Robertson had too little equipment or resources to modify the land in any significant way. Designers of his era incorporated the natural features of the site. What there was in the way of hazards was put to use to create interesting golf holes.

Donald James Ross (1872–1948)

Born in Dornoch, Scotland, Ross worked as an apprentice at Dornoch Golf Club for John Southerland. He moved on to St. Andrews and learned the game of golf from Old Tom Morris.

In 1899, he moved to the United States. From there, he became quite possibly the most famous golf architect of all time. Though he never saw many of his 400 or so designs, in person, few architects could match his gift for designing unique courses that highlighted every feature of the land. Some of his greatest designs included Pinehurst No. 2, Seminole, Oakland Hills, Scioto, Oak Hill Country Club, Plainfield, Wannamoisett, Salem, and the list goes on.

Fig. 4-11 Donald Ross. *(Courtesy of ASGCA)*

> *Hazards and bunkers are placed so as to force a man to use judgment and to exercise mental control in making the correct shot.*
>
> *Often the very highest recommendation of a bunker is when it is criticized. There is no such thing as a misplaced bunker. Regardless of where a bunker may be, it is the business of the player to avoid it.*
>
> *As beautiful as trees are, we must not lose sight of the fact that there is a limited place for them in golf. If a tree in any way interferes with a properly played stroke, the tree is an unfair hazard and should not be allowed to stand.*
>
> *In bunkering a course, the aim should be to lay them out so there will be both an easy and a difficult way to each hole.*

- Ross ended nearly all of his holes at the back of the green. One of the major hazards on most Ross courses is the netherworld that awaits the ball that is hit long. Ross was a greenkeeper and had no intention of creating improvements beyond the back of the green, as this would mean more area to maintain. According to Michael Fay, author of *Golf As It Was Meant to Be Played; A Celebration of Donald Ross' Vision of the Game,* the number of rear bunkers that were original Ross bunkers "can be counted on one hand."
- Ross greens that were built into a hill with an upslope beyond them usually had a drainage trough immediately beyond the green. This feature means trouble for the player who hits long. Over the years, many have attempted to soften the blow of this condition by adding rear bunkers or chipping areas.
- Ross preferred holes that played up to a boundary line rather than along it.
- Ross was not formulaic and often used the principle of irregular placement for his hazards. He placed bunkers at points left and/or right of the ideal landing area.
- He liked visible bunkers, which were placed in locations to make all classes of players think.
- He believed that a variety of bunkering multiplied the interest of the game.
- Ross used mounds and bunker combinations to divide the line of play on parallel holes.
- He liked the diagonal hazard to vary the length of carry required for different skilled players.
- He loved to create little hummocks and undulations for uneven lies and stances. He used irregular mounds (often buried rocks) as an effective hazard.
- Ross allowed long grasses to grow in front of tees to save mowing expense. He asked that it be maintained such that balls were not continually lost.
- In greens, he incorporated bumps or "pimples" that added character and complexity. Depending on the location of the pin, these could be a real hazard to putt over and/or around.
- Ross rarely incorporated trees as an integral part of the strategy of a golf hole, although he was an advocate of shade at tee boxes.
- Ross went through a number of style changes. Early on, he did what he could with the limitations of the land and equipment he had at his disposal. These early courses had a scruffy look with abrupt mounds built atop piles of rock and rubble gathered from the site. Putting surfaces offered steep contours with sharply graded outslopes rather than smooth flowing lines. As the years went by, Ross hired Walter B. Hatch and J. B. McGovern as associates. The designs transitioned to a more mature, flowing style with features integrated into the terrain. Eventually Ross's designs reflected better engineering support and were built with modernized earth-moving equipment.
- A common Ross design trait on par-3s was to have a dominant hazard on one side of the green, and then to place a hazard on the opposite side for the next par-3.
- Ross mixed mounds, hummocks, and grass hollows with his bunkers to create variety.
- His most common design scheme for greens was an elevated fill pad using pushed-up native soil for contouring and drainage. His bunkers were built low into upslopes. Ross built his greens to accept a number of different approaches, often on the best line of play. His greens tended to accept well-struck shots but repel errant missiles. Nearly all Ross greens slope from back to front and less drastically from one side to the other. Rarely did he build greens that sloped away from the approach shot.

- Ross was not averse to using cross-bunkers, some well short of his greens. His cross-bunkers were more strategic than the penal versions of early design periods.
- His bunkering ranged from flashed sand to flat-bottom grass-faced designs.
- Most of his bunkers were not severe. The depths of greenside bunkers generally reached 3 to 5 feet. In keeping with his belief that there should be a certain proportional relationship of challenge and recovery, he did not build bunkers that were inescapable.
- His fairway bunkers were generally much broader than greenside ones and often only about 2 feet deep. The closer one got to the green, the deeper the bunker and the steeper the greenside wall became.
- Ross would place bunkers in low-lying areas where the ball was likely to run and settle out. This was based on his philosophy that the ground game was an important part of golf.
- He often bunkered the inside of doglegs to allow the player to contemplate the level of risk on the tee shot. He rarely bunkered the outside of a dogleg.
- He liked to set his bunkers into the faces of knolls or slopes.
- He would often sweep the sand up to the top of the faces to make them visible from the tee.
- Ross used water hazards in his designs when the opportunity presented itself. He felt they offered variety and welcomed them as long as they were not overused. He suggested no more than three in the course of a round. If a stream or brook was running through the property, he would incorporate it in different ways by playing along it on one hole and across it on another.
- His routings considered wind direction. But instead of abruptly turning players in different directions, he gently turned holes so the golfer would experience a more subtle difference.

Thomas G. Simpson (1877–1964)

Born in England, Simpson was a lawyer and scratch golfer before he fell in love with the design of courses. He developed that appreciation while observing John Low and Stuart Paton remodel Woking Golf Club. By 1910, he had teamed up with Herbert Fowler in the design business.

Simpson was a prolific writer and authored many essays and articles on golf course design. He also wrote such classics as *Design for Golf* and *The Architectural Side of Golf*. He remodeled Muirfield and many other famous courses, including Ballybunion, Royal Aberdeen, Royal Porthcawl, and Sunningdale.

> *There is one very strong argument against multiplying cross bunkers near the putting green, which is, perhaps, not generally understood, and that is if you have a riband (a stretch of) bunkers across the entrance to a green you concentrate your golfer's mind on the fact that he has got to pitch—this helps him enormously—whereas if you so arrange your hazards that he can run up or pitch, it often happens that he cannot concentrate his mind on the one or the other, with the result that he plays the shot in two minds, and not infrequently falls between two stools.*
>
> — From a 1919 issue of *Canadian Golfer*

> *[The designer] does not want to tell the player plainly what is to be done; in fact, he will be extremely careful to assist with as little information as he can as to where the correct positions of play lie. The best way of giving gratuitous assistance is to erect a profusion of landmarks (or bunkers). All this does is tell the golfer precisely what he needs to do and makes the game dull and less interesting.*
>
> *Bunkers must be used on a course with one purpose or another—either to trap a bad shot or (as we should prefer) to govern the play of the hole.*

- Simpson believed courses had far too many bunkers. He wrote that, "To restrict bunkering, in fact, has a double advantage; it puzzles the proficient and does not diminish the pleasure of the less expert."
- He believed in strategic design vs. penal design, going so far as to state, "If the fairways are properly shaped and the greens and their wing hazards orientated correctly, there is no need whatever for fairway bunkering—unless it be for purely decorative purposes or to meet a conventional demand. In fact, the view we take is that to plaster a fairway or the rough on either side with bunkers merely assists the good player and is only effectual in quite needlessly irritating the long handicap man."
- He believed bunkers should never be a plain circle or oblong and should have lace edges and be irregular in shape to break the hardness of the line.
- Simpson believed that visibility of hazards was essential, but regarded blind shots as admissible in certain cases.
- He argued that many features on golf courses, such as roads, railways, sheds, and gardens, are often criticized, but if taken away would make golf less interesting.
- Simpson believed strongly that in the construction of hills and mounds, the batter of a slope should never be quite smooth but rather have movement and blend in seamlessly with the existing terrain. The same goes for the slopes of hollows and bunkers.
- He suggested arranging fairway bunkers on a diagonal line.

George Clifford Thomas, Jr. (1873–1932)

Born in Philadelphia, Thomas's first love was gardening. He was an authority on roses, writing several books about them. He learned about golf course design working with the leading designers of his time in Philadelphia. Thomas's own career in design did not take off until his move to California and partnership with William P. "Billy" Bell. Together they designed some two dozen courses, including the famed Riviera Country Club and Los Angeles Country Club.

> *The strategy of the golf course is the soul of the game. The spirit of golf is to dare a hazard, and by negotiating it reap a reward, while he who fears or declines the issue of the carry, has a longer or*

harder shot for his second, or his second or third on long holes; yet the player who avoids the unwise effort gains advantage over one who tries for more than in him lies, or who fails under the test.

If one could have a course with sand dunes, with water hazards both as streams and as lakes, with fairways through virgin forests, with long, rolling contours, high plateaus, lovely little valleys to play through and to cross as hazards, one would have the superlative and almost ideal golf country.

The scale on which one makes rolls and mounds depends on the scale of the existing contours, otherwise your creations will not balance with the landscape.

Hazards should be arranged to tempt and to challenge, but laid out such that all classes of players have optional routes to the hole. Hazards should not unduly penalize from which there is little chance of any recovery.

— Thomas believed that trees and shrubbery beautified the course and that natural growth should never be cut down where it was possible to save it; but he also insisted that a tree that spoiled a shot should have no place in golf course construction.
— He did not necessarily subscribe to the popular notion that "no hazard that is visible is unfair." He believed many hazards were unfair because they were unnecessary and not contained in the strategy of the hole.
— Thomas believed that hazards should be of different types depending on the location and conditions of the course. Seaside courses, for example, have firm turf and strong winds, in contrast to many inland courses. However, his belief was that all hazards were ultimately for the same purpose, regardless of what they consisted of. "A variety of hazards teaches a golfer all different types of shots, which is the real essence of the game of golf."
— Thomas liked to vary his sand hazards so they required different kinds of recovery shots.
— He took into consideration the various playing conditions when setting tees and placing any hazards that demanded a forced carry.
— Thomas liked to use rolls and ridges short of greens but only in locations that could handle their maintenance. He hated mounds that dried out from lack of water. He liked grassy hollows, but only if they could be drained easily.
— He felt water hazards were among the best and most thrilling of natural obstacles and even favored artificial water hazards. But he practiced restraint, arguing that any type of hazard in excess was a bad idea.
— Thomas believed all features on a golf course should "melt into the land surrounding them" and appear as if they had always been present.
— He believed in large fairway bunkers to stop a hard-hit ball and argued that all fairway bunkers should give some chance of a recovery.
— He felt trees, mounds, and traps could be used to force play away from congested areas, but was cautious of creating blind conditions.

Stanley Thompson (1894–1952)

Born in Canada, Thompson was eventually nicknamed the Toronto Terror. He was one of the most interesting characters to enter the profession of golf architecture. His dramatic mountain layouts were world-renowned and reflected his flamboyant personality. His courses, including Jasper Park and Banff Springs, were big, bold, and strategic works of art.

> *Nature must always be the architect's model. The golf course should fit the terrain. The lines of the bunkers or greens must not be sharp or harsh, but easy and rolling. Every now and then I get a mean streak and like to fool the boys a little. But, I never hide any danger. It's all out there for the golfer to see and study.*
>
> On his famous course at Banff Springs:
> *The fairways will be doubly wide, there being two distinct routes to each hole. One can stand on the tee and judge which route to follow. For the bold there is a short route, harassed by bunkers, but the reward for such is a birdie. For the short player, the other is a long route, free from bunkers. All classes of golfer will enjoy Banff, for the novice is not discouraged by unfair trapping, nor is the course too easy for the experienced expert.*
>
> *The lines of bunkers and greens must not be sharp or harsh, but easy and rolling. Water not only makes good mental and actual hazards, but the picture which can be created adds greatly to the effect of a course if treated in a natural way. Streams, ponds, and even open ditches, if properly made, give variety, not only to the play, but to the aspect of the course, and through their steady motion of quiet permanence inspire a feeling of restful calm. As soon as a player departs from the straight and narrow path, some penalty should follow. Unless this is so, the game loses some of its enjoyment, for it is only by accomplishing what is difficult that gives satisfaction and pleasure.*
> — FROM THOMPSON'S BOOKLET *GENERAL THOUGHTS ON GOLF COURSE DESIGN* (1923)

- Thompson deployed an extremely wide variety of styles and sizes. He would design a sprawling monster bunker and nearby a small, 2-foot-deep pot.
- He loved to design shared bunkers that sprawled between two holes. These would always have a dramatic effect on both holes.
- He liked to display hazards right out in front of the golfer. His bunkers were placed mostly into natural rises to make them eminently visible. The most impressive features of Thompson bunkers are the numerous capes and bays that create wonderful, ever-changing flashes of sand. In many cases, his bunkers were bold, deep, and "in your face."
- He was not an advocate of cross-bunkers (sometimes called "riband" bunkers) that stretched from one side of the fairway to the other. He felt such hazards were more like fences to be hurdled in a steeplechase, and that they appeared man-made and were more penal than strategic. He designed his courses so they were playable for the average golfer but left options for everyone.
- He felt that blind shots should be minimized and that bunkers around the green should always be visible.

Albert Warren Tillinghast (1874–1942)

Born in Philadelphia, "Tillie," as he was known, considered himself the dean of American golf course architects. He was a playboy in his youth, and became enamoured with the game of golf during a trip to Scotland where he spent time with Old Tom Morris.

Fig. 4-12 One of A. W. Tillinghast's sketches. (Compliments of the Tillinghast Association)

His first course, which he designed at age 32, was in his home state of Pennsylvania at Shawnee. He went on to design some of the greatest courses in America, including Winged Foot East and West, San Francisco Golf Club, Somerset Hills, Bethpage Black, Baltusrol, and Quaker Ridge.

He wrote extensively throughout his career for *Golf Illustrated, The American Golfer,* and the PGA of America.

A controlled shot to a closely guarded green is the surest test of any man's golf.

Instead of relying on hazards which extend directly across the line of play, we are building them diagonally. It is obvious that these diagonal hazard lines present a much longer carry at one end then at the other, and all carry between the two points vary. In brief, every player gets exactly what may be coming to him and it is not necessary for anyone to bite off more then he can swallow. The old-fashioned cross bunker always leers at the player with a 'You must.' The modern diagonal hazard shows even a more ferocious face at one end as it says to the scratch man, 'You should.' But all along the line to the short end it is saying, 'You may.' [5]

A course without notable hazards is a course without distinction!

- Tillinghast's greens were almost always tightly guarded by hazards. He often placed bunkers on the sides and forward portions of his green sites.
- He felt the relationship between a properly placed shot to the fairway and the following one to the green was one of the most important considerations in the design of a hole.
- Tillinghast had a flare for strong, intimidating hazards that would dictate and direct the line of play.

[5] It should be noted that, despite this quote from Tillinghast, he enjoyed taking credit for the famous Hell's Half Acre at Pine Valley. He used this notorious hazard concept at a number of his courses early in his career.

- He believed that shallow traps were of little value either as hazards or design features.
- His artistic bunker styles ranged all over the map from grass-faced, flat-bottomed to dramatic, flashed, sand-faced designs. Almost all had a rugged, less tended look.
- As Tillinghast progressed in his career, he evaluated courses together with the PGA. This led to many recommendations to remove bunkers at dozens of courses around the United States, including many of his own designs. The driving force was to reduce "unnecessary maintenance costs and make the game more fun and appealing to golfers." His once famous cross-bunkers were something he no longer approved of in his later years.
- Tillinghast was a strong advocate of risk/reward options. He encouraged courageous play that awarded a very distinct advantage if one successfully negotiated a carefully placed hazard.
- His fairways were wide, but there was almost always a preferred side. He liked diagonal hazards and used a wide assortment of bunkers, mounds, rough, swales, and so on. to challenge golfers and reward their successful efforts with a better angle of approach, including the option of playing a run-up shot.
- He advocated clearing brush and debris a considerable distance off the fairway to allow the chance of a recovery shot.
- His opinions on roughs were similar to others of his time. He believed rough should be a prominent feature on every golf course to extract a penalty, but not to cause a lost ball.
- Tillinghast had a love for trees and often incorporated them into his design schemes. He felt trees added beauty and could contribute to the distinction and charm of a golf hole. He would use trees to help mark the true line of play—in his words, "to chart the channel of the hole"—and to make the judgment of distances more difficult for the golfer. However, he believed that trees placed too close to the proper line of play, particularly in front of greens, could not be condoned. Recognizing that trees offer comfort from the sun on a hot summer day, Tillinghast often directed the efforts of his construction crew from the shade of a tree "with bottle in hand," another of his design "traits."
- Tillinghast felt water was used too frequently as a hazard, but he also appreciated that golfers enjoyed water as a landscape feature. He worked to make ponds look as natural as possible whenever he felt the need for a water hazard. Tillinghast felt water used as a diagonal hazard was best, as it gave players the option to play it safe or to bite off as much as they could chew. The "make the carry or get wet concept" went against his philosophy.
- He loved the forced "three shot hole," coining the term *double dogleg*. Although he didn't like to force a player's hand often, he did feel there were situations when the architect should be able to dictate play.

Walter J. Travis (1862–1927)

Born in Australia, Travis moved to the United States in 1885. He was an outstanding golfer, a prolific writer, and a superb golf architect.

The primary idea of a hazard is to punish, to the extent of one stroke, a poorly played shot, and to make the recovery exceedingly difficult, and even by the virtue of the following shot being extraordinarily good. If this end is not attained, the existing hazard fails to fill its functions.

Travis liked to: *compel a player to extract the full value from each and every club in his bag during the round, and on one or two of the holes to play certain testing shots with such nicety and keen judgment as to make even the best player pause before attempting their execution.*

Golf cultivates patience and endurance under adversity, yet keeps alive the fires of hope.

- Walter Travis was falsely accused of working in the penal style because of the depth and difficulty found in many of his bunkers. What the critics missed was his belief in rewarding shot making and management. His belief was that negotiating hazards and other difficulties was an integral part of the game. He felt that the majority of hazards should be arranged to compel one to drive "far and sure," but give weaker players a chance to avoid being bunkered.
- He loved wide fairways with hazards in play dictating alternate routes.
- He used a variety of bunker types. One of his most common techniques for creating a bunker was to excavate the soil from the interior and use it to create mounds around the hazard. Often, these mounds were in a predictable triangular pattern.
- He loved hazards that you had to carry and wasn't afraid to make a hazard ugly or invisible.
- Travis would place deep bunkers flanking the green while still allowing a run-up option.
- He designed wild greens and sometimes used mounds rather than bunkers to add variety.

Dick Wilson (1904–1965)

Born in Philadelphia, Wilson worked early on at Merion with William Flynn as a construction superintendent before becoming a design associate. Wilson and Flynn stayed together for many years, though they never were the best of friends.

Wilson formed his own golf course design company in 1945. His design of the NCR Country Club established him as a prominent designer of his time. Architects Joe Lee and Robert von Hagge trained under Wilson.

Wilson seemed to blend the penal and strategic schools of design similar to the work of Robert Trent Jones, Sr. Wilson is credited by some as one of the early designers who helped usher in the aerial game in golf.

You can put a beautiful woman in an expensive dress, but if the dress doesn't fit, neither the woman nor the dress is going to look any good at all. It's the same with building a golf course. You got to cut the course to fit the property.

— *Sports Illustrated* vol. 17, no. 1, July 2, 1962

— Wilson placed bunkers with strategy in mind. His bunkers were often big and sprawling and many times required an aerial shot to avoid them. Their appearance varied according to the terrain; however, Wilson liked to use huge flashed bunkers sometimes in the shape of cloverleafs.
— He created ponds and lakes on a routine basis.
— Wilson used trees more than many of his predecessors for separation and strategy.

Hugh Irvine Wilson (1879–1925)

Born in Philadelphia, Wilson was a Princeton graduate and captain of his college golf team. A member of Merion Cricket Club, he was selected to make a study of the great golf courses of the British Isles in order to develop ideas for a new course at Merion. After spending seven months abroad gathering field notes, sketches, and maps of great holes and features, he returned to design Merion's famous East Course, which opened for play in 1912. He would later design the West Course there as well.

During construction of the East Course, Wilson met William Flynn. A lifelong friendship ensued. Wilson and Flynn saw eye to eye on golf course design and agreed on many of the same principles, such as the style and visibility of hazards. Both believed that "a concealed bunker has no place on a golf course." Wilson had a great influence on Flynn, and the two had planned to form a design partnership before Wilson's declining health made that impossible.

Wilson once said that he was fortunate to get a good start and gives much of the credit for his success to Charles B. Macdonald. Before traveling to Britain, Wilson spent two days with Macdonald at the National Golf Links, where he claimed to have absorbed more ideas on golf course construction than he had learned in all his years playing. Wilson commented, "Every course I observed in England and Scotland confirmed Macdonald's teachings."

— Wilson focused his efforts on understanding the principles of great design and hazard placement, setting out to build courses that utilized these ideals but fit into the natural conditions.
— He suggested one of the best ways to study the design of bunkers was to go to the seacoast and walk among the dunes.
— He believed that bunkers should not be so steep that players of all skill levels would be forced to hit the same kind of recovery shot.
— Wilson was heavily influenced by Pine Valley and maintained that it contained many of the finest holes in the country. With the help of his brother Alan, and Flynn, Wilson was commissioned to oversee completion of the final four holes, Nos. 12 through 15, when Pine Valley's original designer, George Crump, passed away in 1918.

COLOR PLATES

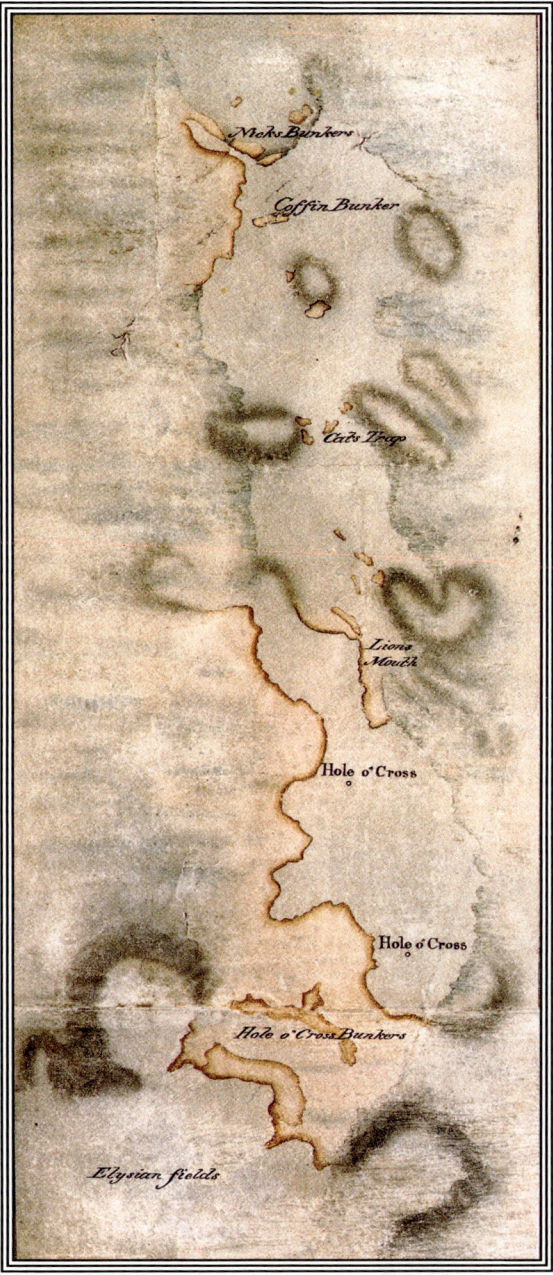

Fig. 1-10 *William Chalmers' 1836 map of the "Golfing Course" at St. Andrews (see page 51) contains nine details of the holes and bunkers. Shown here is the detailed area of the Hole o' Cross holes, Holes 5 and 13 of what we now refer to as The Old Course. (Reproduced by kind permission of the Royal and Ancient Golf Club of St. Andrews)*

Fig. 1-14 There may be no more beautiful linksland than the terrain of Royal Dornoch in the north of Scotland with its dense gorse and undulating terrain. (Courtesy of P. Burton)

Fig. 1-19 Sand Hills Golf Club in Mullen, Nebraska is an example of a modern course with an approach to hazards that is reminiscent of natural links courses. Bill Coore and Ben Crenshaw, golf course architects.

COLOR PLATES

Fig. 2-7 *The late Desmond Muirhead began his work as a golf course architect creating innovative, but still classic, designs. His work during the 1960s and 1970s was no indication of what was to come in the 1990s when Muirhead turned to symbolism in golf design. Pictured is the 7th hole, Clashing Rocks, from his famous, Stone Harbor Golf Club, New Jersey. The hole is based on the Greek mythology of Jason and the Argonauts, in which Jason is sent on a journey through a narrow sea guarded by two "clashing rocks." The green (60 feet wide by 125 feet long) represents Jason's boat; the two water-born traps on either side emulate the clashing rocks. (© Paul Barton)*

Bunkers, Pits & Other Hazards

Fig. 2-11 Islands of native grass, Bethpage Black, New York. Islands within formal sand bunkers are not considered part of the hazards according to The Rules of Golf. (Photo by Larry Lambrecht, courtesy of Rees Jones, Inc.)

Fig. 2-14 A restored bunker at hole No. 9 of the Arizona Biltmore Adobe Course, Arizona (c. 1926, William P. "Billy" Bell). Renovation by Forrest Richardson and Patrick Burton, golf course architects. Photograph by Mike Houska, DogLeg Studios)

Fig. 2-17 Rendering for an unusual water hazard at The Links at Las Palomas, Sonora, Mexico. This par-3 drops 30 feet to a green built out into a lagoon. The edge of the green at the lagoon is bordered by stone aqueducts that flow around the green and allow water to cascade into the lagoon. Forrest Richardson and Arthur Jack Snyder, golf course architects. (Illustrator: David Smith)

Bunkers, Pits & Other Hazards

Fig. 2-22 The Dell (hole No. 5) at Lahinch Golf Club, Ireland is a par-3 green setting of tremendous character and mystery.

Fig. 2-27 An interesting green that was built around a native desert tree. The tree and stone wall create a one-of-a-kind hazard situation. Phantom Horse Golf Club, Arizona. Forrest Richardson, golf course architect.

COLOR PLATES

Fig. 2-30 A variation of the boundary hole where a stone wall flanks the putting surface. Dunbar Golf Links, Scotland. (Photograph by Paul Daley, Full Swing Golf Publishing)

Fig. 2-34 Hole No. 2 at Old Head Golf Links, Ireland. Hazard placement, green location, and backdrops (or lack thereof) can be deceiving to the eye. Toward expansive, territorial views, the golfer is often "lost" in judging distance. (Courtesy of P. Burton)

Bunkers, Pits & Other Hazards

Fig. 2-35 Hole No. 8 at Cypress Point Club, California. (Courtesy of P. Burton)

Fig. 3-3 Hole No. 17 at The Tournament Player's Club of Sawgrass, Florida. Perhaps the most famous hazard in all of golf because of several factors: its extensive coverage on television, access to the public, and the dramatic tee shot with which every golfer can identify. Pete Dye, golf course architect. (© 2005 PGA Tour)

Bunkers, Pits & Other Hazards

Fig. 3-11 *William Chalmers' 1836 map of the "Golfing Course" at St. Andrews (see Fig. 1-10 for enlarged detail) is the second oldest map of The Old Course in existence. (Reproduced by kind permission of the Royal and Ancient Golf Club of St. Andrews)*

Fig. 3-12 *Hole No. 17, the Road Hole, at The Old Course, St. Andrews, Scotland. This view shows the back of the green, elevated above the road and falling back toward the bunker. (Courtesy of P. Burton)*

Fig. 3-13 *A digital computer model of the Road Hole provides an accurate depiction. (© St. Andrews Links Trust and 3D Eagleview.com)*

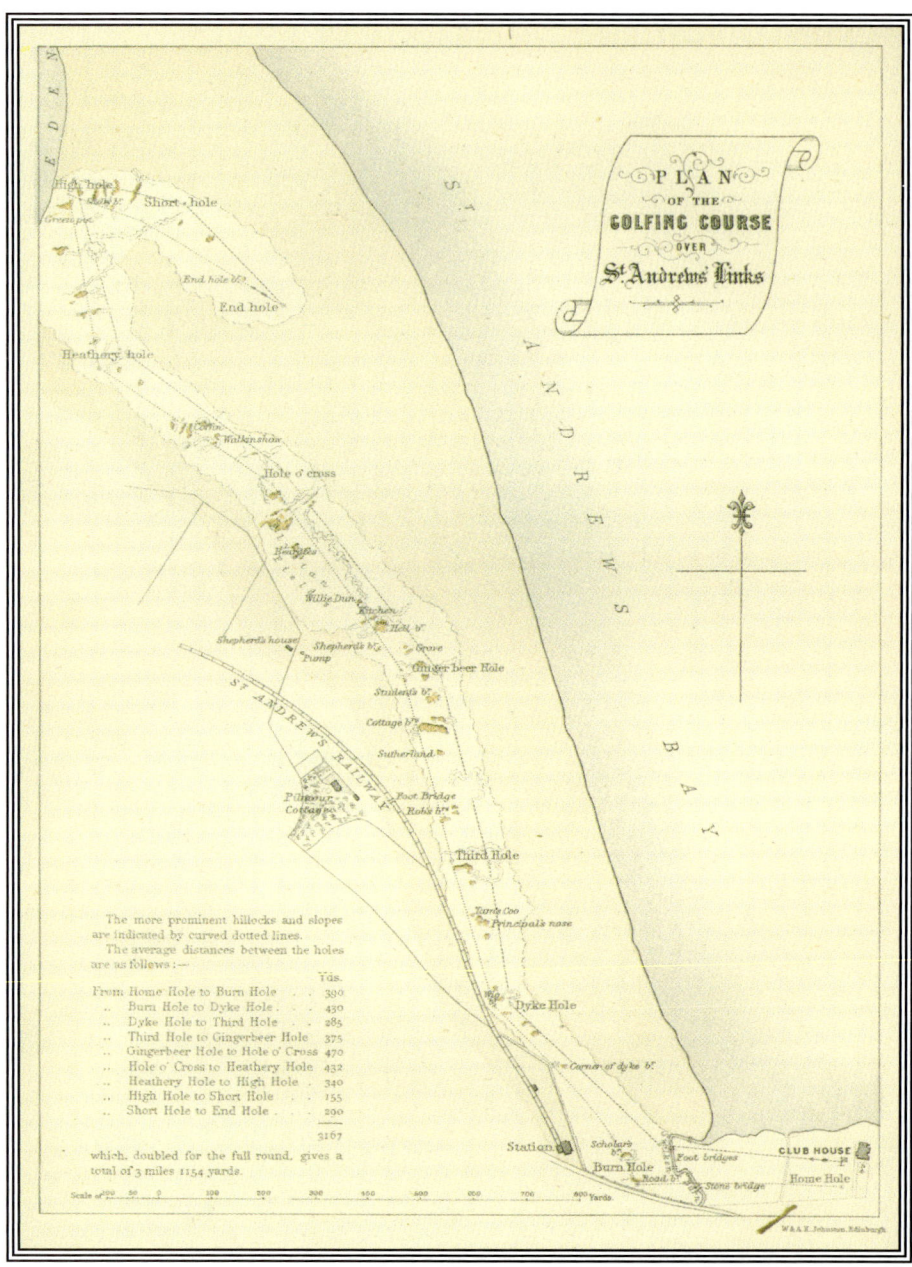

Fig. 3-14 This map, from Robert Clark's *Golf: A Royal and Ancient Game* (1875), has become known as the "Hodge Map." Thomas Hodge, an R&A member and prolific landscape artist, is credited in Clark's table of contents. However, at the margin of the map is the imprint "W & A. K. Johnston, Edinburgh," well-known mapmakers and engravers of Scotland. One theory is that Hodge may have commissioned the map and provided it to Clark. Regardless, it remains the first map of St. Andrews Links to show the Road Bunker. (Amateur Athletic Foundation Library Archives)

COLOR PLATES

Fig. 3-17 *Perhaps the most famous finishing hole in golf, the 18th at Pebble Beach needs little in the way of explanation in terms of its play. It simply follows the coastline, begging the golfer to take the geodesic route instead of the "out-of-the-way" bend farther right. (© Tony Roberts)*

Fig. 3-19 *The famous Church Pews of Oakmont Country Club are defined by the parallel turf ridges, which sit within this huge bunker covering more than one acre in size.*

BUNKERS, PITS & OTHER HAZARDS

Fig. 3-21 Hole No. 17 at Cypress Point Club, California. The rocky shoreline of the Pacific Ocean creates the ultimate hazard. (Courtesy P. Burton)

Fig. 3-25 Hole No. 10, Pine Valley Golf Club, New Jersey. This shortish par-3 features the famous Devil's Asshole bunker (to the front and right.) As repulsive as the bunker sounds, and is, it possesses a quality that seems to lure golfers to test its position. (© PDI: Chris John)

COLOR PLATES

Fig. 3-31 This is the look from the fairway across Hell's Half Acre at Pine Valley Golf Club's hole No. 7. Only the formal bunkers at Pine Valley are treated as "bunkers" under the rules of golf. Here, for example, the area is considered "through the green," and the club may be grounded. The term Hell's Half Acre is thought to have originated in the small town of Webberville, Texas, before Texas' statehood. Webberville, known for its lawless and immoral reputation, was dubbed Hell's Half Acre as a result. Eventually, the name became generic for the red-light district in any number of frontier towns. (© Tony Roberts)

Fig. 3-37 Pebble Beach's famed No. 8 begins with a tee shot to a plateau high above the crashing waves of the world's largest body of water, the 69.4 million square miles of the Pacific Ocean. The approach is a downhill carry across an inlet of craggy rocks and grassy cliffs. (Photograph by Joann Dost)

Bunkers, Pits & Other Hazards

Fig. 3-42 *An enhanced digital image of the famous Dell Hole (hole No. 5) at Lahinch. (© Lahinch and 3D Eagleview.com)*

COLOR PLATES

Fig. 3-56 The notorious Chocolate Drops of Mypoia Hunt Club, Massachusettes. In many cases, Herbert Leeds dismantled stone walls and had the rocks piled into mounds, then plated these with soil to form interesting hazards, which continue to perplex golfers nearly 100 years later. (Courtesy of Ran Morrissett)

Fig. 3-65 The famous sand dune known as Himalayas at hole No. 6 of the St. Enodoc Golf Club, England. The top of the dune is 70 feet above the fairway. (© Tony Roberts)

Fig. 3-71 The famous No. 6 green at Riviera Country Club as shown from behind. (© Tony Roberts)

Fig. 3-82 Hole No. 8 of St. George's Hill Golf Club, England. Golf course architect Martin Hawtree oversaw extensive renovation work to reclaim the looming bunker, known as "That Damned Bunker." (Courtesy of St. George's Hill Golf Club)

Fig. 4-4 Lehigh Country Club outside Allentown, Pennsylvania, is a prime example of the brilliance of William Flynn. Lehigh uses a variety of sand, water, and contour hazards amongst its innovative routing. Pictured is hole No. 10.

BUNKERS, PITS & OTHER HAZARDS

Fig. 4-6 Robert Hunter was Alister MacKenzie's right-hand man at Cypress Point Club. Pictured is No. 7, a par-3. (Courtesy of P. Burton)

Fig. 4-7 Alister MacKenzie's Pasatiempo, California. Pictured is No. 10, a par-4. (Courtesy of P. Burton)

COLOR PLATES

Fig. 5-11 The 486 yard, par-4 17th at the Kapalua Plantation Course, Hawaii. The golfer cannot help but think about the deep canyon that lies between the fairway and the green. The thought alone makes the hazard seem and play more difficult. Bill Coore and Ben Crenshaw, golf course architects. (Mike Klemme, Photographer)

Fig. 5-13 The famous "Sahara" bunker at the "Alps" Hole (No. 17) at Prestwick (also referred to as the "Alps" bunker.) Interestingly, this hazard is completely hidden from the fairway by the massive alps feature that rises up to conceal the entire green. This shot was either taken from a very bad lie atop the alps, or perhaps as reference for the next round. (Courtesy of P. Burton)

Bunkers, Pits & Other Hazards

Fig. 5-14 *Hole No. 16 at Sutton Bay, South Dakota. Graham Marsh, golf course architect.*

COLOR PLATES

Fig. 6-9 A restored bunker and green at hole No. 10 of the Arizona Biltmore Adobe Course, Arizona (c.1926, William P. "Billy" Bell). Renovation by Forrest Richardson and Patrick Burton, golf course architects. (Photograph by Mike Houska, DogLeg Studios)

Fig. 6-10 Bunker at The Honourable Company of Edinburgh Golfers (Muirfield), Scotland. (Courtesy of P. Burton)

Bunkers, Pits & Other Hazards

Fig. 7-25 *Hole No. 12, aptly named Jailhouse Steps, of Phantom Horse Golf Club, Arizona. Even with its elevated and guarded green, this par-5 lures golfers to attempt the green on their second shots because of its deceivingly short length. Forrest Richardson, golf course architect. (Photo Courtesy of Destination Resorts)*

COLOR PLATES

Fig. 6-20 A par-3 of just over 130 yards provides a "hazard" through slopes and banks without any sand or water. Hole No. 3 of The Hideout Golf Club, Utah. Forrest Richardson and Arthur Jack Snyder, golf course architects. (Photograph by Mike Houska, DogLeg Studios)

Fig. 7-11 Steep faced bunkers at Doonbeg Golf Club, Ireland. Greg Norman, golf course architect. (Courtesy of Doonbeg Golf Club)

COLOR PLATES

17th Hole Cherry Hills Golf Club

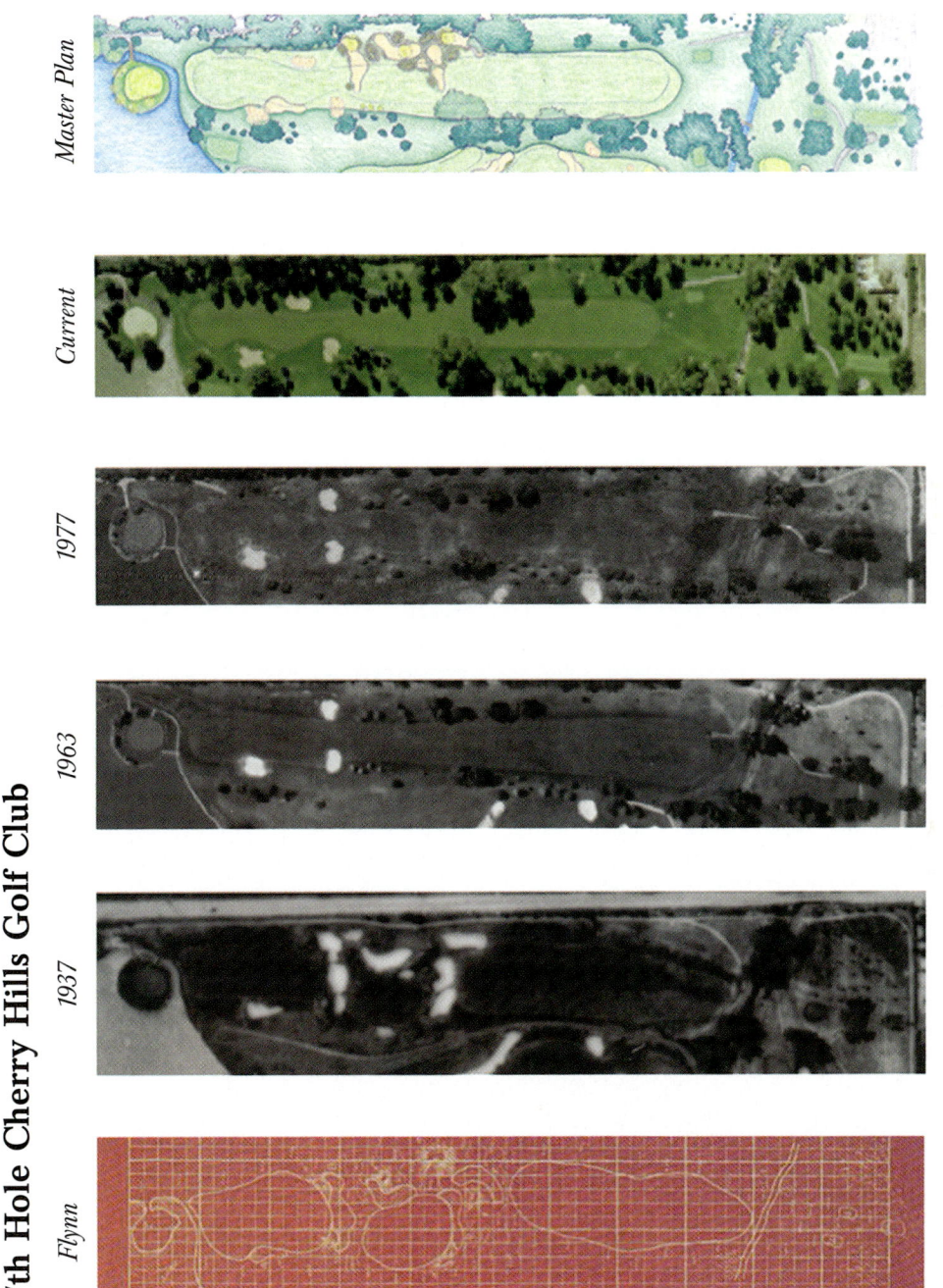

Fig. 8-13 A hole-by-hole analysis of hole No. 17 at Cherry Hills Country Club, Colorado. This presentation was prepared as part of a master plan for each hole showing how the original design had changed over the years. The culmination of the work is the recommended change at the far right. It is evident that William Flynn's original strategy was all but lost when the bunkers were filled in and pushed toward the edges of the fairway. Mark Fine, golf course architect.

Fig. 9-4   Hole No. 13 of the Tobacco Road Golf Club. Mike Strantz, golf course architect.

COLOR PLATES

BUNKERS, PITS & OTHER HAZARDS

Fig. 9-7 *Rustic Canyon Golf Club. Gil Hanse, golf course architect. Geoff Shackleford, design consultant.*

Fig. 9-8 *Ventana Canyon Golf Club, Mountain Course. Tom Fazio, golf course architect.*

COLOR PLATES

Fig. 9-11 Fiddler's Creek Golf Club, Florida. Arthur Hills, golf course architect.

Fig. 9-12 French Creek Golf Club, Pennsylvania, Gil Hanse, golf course architect.

Fig. 9-14 *Hole No. 9 of Sutton Bay, South Dakota. Graham Marsh, golf course architect.*

Fig. 9-16 *Devil's Paintbrush Course of the Devil's Pulpit Golf Association, Canada. Mike Hurdzan, golf course architect.*

CHAPTER 5

Psychological Effects *of* Hazards

by
Dr. Edward Sadalla, Ph.D.

He had walked the narrow path hundreds of time before. It was always the same. The grass seemed to know just how to bend and lay over to avoid being trampled. Brian tried to focus his thoughts on the grass, the path, and the next tee, but the last hole kept getting in the way.

How could he possibly have let things go so badly? What had caused him to put the iron back in the bag? Was there some sort of defect in his brain that allowed him to believe a driver was the right choice? Why this day? A driver had never been an option on that hole. Maybe twice he had taken a driver there. "No," he thought, "three times. Yes, I remember using a driver there three times. Or maybe four?" He had been up two and things were going well. Then, all of a sudden, the match was bloody even. "How can you drop two holes in a row? Yes, it was four. I've hit a driver there four times. Why today," he kept repeating to himself.

Back to the path. It seemed to be taking forever to reach the tee. "What's the hold-up?" One part of his mind seemed to be carrying on a conversation with another part. He was just overhearing this banter. And what's up with this slowness? "Can't you walk any faster?" He nearly caught himself opening his mouth to actually ask the question out loud. But the thoughts and comments racing through his mind were quiet. Too quiet. He tried to think louder. This helped. It seemed to drown out the voices. The images of the last two holes faded more and more the louder he thought.

Then, as if someone had opened a huge curtain in front of him, light began pouring into his eyes. With two longer and more confident strides, Brian arrived onstage. For a brief moment, everything was completely quiet.

The back of the tee was a good place to stand. A person can think when he stands at the back of a group. When you stand out in front, or in the middle, you need to keep watching your back. Brian didn't need to worry about his back. He was the back. From where he stood, it was possible to be a part of the match but also a spectator. Yes, a spectator. That's exactly what he felt like.

"It's a beautiful sight today. I've never seen it so clear." Even though no one could see him, Brian rolled his eyes in disgust upon hearing this. "It's no more beautiful than any other day," he muttered to himself. Brian looked down into his golf bag. In the bright light, he could almost see the bottom. "What is that down there?" It was very bright. "Why the hell am I looking into the bottom of my golf bag?" he wondered. It sounded like one of the same voices that had been talking in his head as he had walked up the path. He cut it off. "No more talking—I've got to play golf."

Maybe it was a beautiful day. His reaction to the innocent comment was probably unfounded. Even though no one had seen his face or heard his muttering, he took on

CHAPTER 5 | PSYCHOLOGICAL EFFECTS *of* HAZARDS

Fig. 5-1 A cartoon from the November 17, 1905 issue of Golf Illustrated. The caption read, "Our artist is of the opinion that the architects of the links have not yet realized all the subtleties of resource that can be demanded of the bunkered player."

a look of remorse. As the others readied for play and tapped their clubs on the grass, Brian stared out toward the sea. Yes, it was beautiful. The sunlight was coming at just the right angle. The bay was shining, but not glaring. Each bump and knob in front of the group had its own highlight. Everything was just about as perfect as he had ever seen it. They were right. He had been wrong to roll his eyes. How could anyone disagree with the beauty?

Why is it that people you play golf with—otherwise the greatest of friends—can sometimes be so irritating? Why is it that the most innocent of comments can sometimes grate at your ears? He had nothing against this bunch of regulars. But how could they possibly be thinking of the beauty of the hole when there was still such golf to be had? If he were in their shoes, his thoughts would certainly be of the remarkable comeback. Of gaining back the holes. Two in a row.

It was taking forever. The wait was frustrating. Just like the walk. Brian wanted to hit the ball soon. It would help to take out some frustration. But he had to wait his turn. And he would be last.

Finally the moment came. As he eyed the shot, the very few thoughts he had been thinking just a few seconds before somehow transformed themselves into dozens of thoughts. Now, instead of just seeing a hole with a drop-off along the left, and one small bunker to the right, he saw much more. That tall grass well right of the bunker. That patch of gorse—"I've never noticed it there before"—the low area extending across the fairway. . . more gorse. . . more tall grass what about that other bunker, the one farther down—"Is it within reach today?" He hesitated. "How deep is the first bunker?" he thought. Brian had been in the little bunker dozens of times. Why today, all of a sudden, did he need to know its depth? As he focused on the bunker, one final thought rushed through his head before he addressed the ball. "The fairway—is it wider than usual?" Perhaps it was the light. That's it. The light. The fairway wasn't any wider. What an absurd idea.

Introduction to Chapter 5

It is not good for golf course architects to write about psychology. While there may be no law against it, it simply isn't the right thing to do. We know of golf and golf courses, how to design them and how to get them built or renovated. We think we know about the psychology of the game, but then we meet someone who really does.

Early on in our work on hazards we arranged a meeting with Dr. Sadalla, an environmental psychologist and avid golfer. We discussed the framework for our writing and what we would be covering in the chapters. At this first meeting we assumed that the psychological aspects of hazards might be interwoven throughout the chapters, but this assumption proved to be a bad idea for several reasons. First among them was that, despite our most earnest effort to seem authoritative on the psychological aspects of hazards, we failed. It also became apparent that the topic of psychological effects deserved its own section. Arnold Haultain, writing in one of our favorite books, *The Mystery of Golf,* aptly reminds us in the preface to the second edition (1912): "Besides, Mr. Practical Golfer, whether it improves your game or not, Golf has a Psychology, and a Psychology interesting enough to be written down."

So we met Sadalla again about our work. But this time we convinced him to serve as a guest author, to bypass trying to enlighten us, and to enlighten you directly. It was the right decision. We are grateful for his insights.

Psychological Effects of Hazards—*by Edward Sadalla, Ph.D.*

> *"Hazards make golf dramatic; and the thrills that come to one who ventures wisely and succeeds are truly delectable. Without hazards golf would be but a dull sport, with the life and soul gone out of it. No longer would it attract the lusty and the adventurous, but would be left to those who favor some form of insipid perambulation, suited to the effeminate and senile."*
> —Robert Hunter

This chapter reviews some of the psychological reactions that are likely to be produced by the presence of a hazard on the golf course. It is easy to see that the reaction to a hazard is highly situational, depending upon the state of mind of the golfer, the context of the game (it is a tournament, whether wagers are at stake, etc.), and the nature of the hazard. Hazards produce a variety of psychological reactions, but the impact of the hazard is almost invariably related to the degree of confidence and control perceived by the golfer. If a golfer has sufficient confidence and a good command of his or her game, hazards on the course provide an interesting diversion, adding interest to a course in the same way that spices may add interest to a recipe. However, because of the intrinsic unpredictability of the golf swing, hazards more commonly introduce an element of fear into the golfer's experience.

Hazards Are Tests

Hazards test us through varying degrees of difficulty. The relationship between the difficulty of a hazard, the competence (skill) of the golfer, and the golfer's experience of fear, stress, or anxiety can be seen in Fig. 5-2.

An interesting study was conducted some years ago that illustrates the relationship between the amount of stress produced by a task and the skill or competency of the subject. Researchers studying the experience of stress fitted a skilled cardiac surgeon with a heart-rate monitor on the day the surgeon was to perform an open-heart coronary bypass operation. The heart-rate monitor revealed that the surgeon was not unduly stressed by his job. On the morning of the operation, the surgeon's pulse rate was a normal 70 to 80 beats per minute while driving to the hospital and just before the beginning of the operation. As he began the operation, his pulse increased very slightly, reflecting the increased workload and concentration demanded by the situation, but did not exceed 90 beats per minute. Peak heart rate, around 100 beats per minute, occurred at the most dramatic moment of the operation, when the patient's heart, which had been stopped during the procedure, was restarted. This was literally a life-or-death moment. Overall, the heart-rate data indicated that the skilled surgeon experienced relatively little physical arousal during the procedure, even though failure would have had real consequences for his professional reputation. The lack of physiological arousal was most likely due to the fact that the surgeon's competencies were equal to the difficult task.

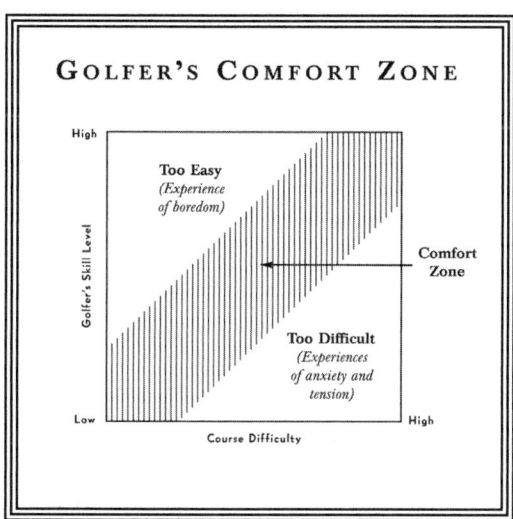

Fig. 5-2 Chart correlating the difficulty of hazards with their interest.

The following day, the same surgeon was scheduled to play in the pro-am day of a PGA tournament. He was paired with a professional, and there were spectators on the course who had come to watch the professionals. The surgeon, who was merely an average golfer, was again fitted with a heart-rate monitor. The resulting data indicated that the surgeon's pulse rate averaged 110 beats per minute while he was driving to the event. This rate was higher than any rate that had occurred the day before or during surgery. As our golfer stood on the first tee, preparing to hit his first drive of the day, his pulse was 140 beats per minute. The monitor showed that, during the entire round, his pulse rate fluctuated between 125 and 145 beats per minute, indicating a high level of

Fig. 5-3 The level of stress brought about by a situation is a factor of the task and the skill or competency of the subject.

physiological activation, most likely produced by fear. This occurred despite the fact that the surgeon's performance occurred during a game that had no consequences whatsoever for either his finances or his professional life. The explanation here is that the surgeon was in a situation where the environmental demands were high relative to his merely average competencies.

The diagram in Fig. 5-2 indicates that the most psychologically interesting hazards on a golf course are those that challenge the golfer's competence level. A course design that is too easy leads to boredom, while designs that are too difficult lead to excessive stress. There is, however, an interesting exception to this diagram that is peculiar to athletic competition. When the difficulty of the task becomes extremely high, stress and fear begin to disappear. If an athlete begins to feel that the task is impossible for virtually anyone, then there is no shame or threat involved in failure. Few golfers, for example, would expect to actually make a 50-yard pitch shot or even a 50-foot putt. Situations that require that a golfer actually execute such a feat generally do not elicit fear. On the other hand, a 4-foot putt that must be made might paralyze the same golfer with fear and tension.

There is a well-known line of psychological research in which subjects are allowed to choose the difficulty of an athletic task, such as throwing a ball into a basket. In these studies, subjects with low self-confidence in their physical ability tend to prefer either very difficult or very easy tasks. They will choose a distance very close to the basket, where it is almost impossible to miss, or they will choose a distance quite far from the

Fig. 5-4 An old photo of the Corsets Bunkers at Sandwich Golf Club, England. The psychological aspect of hazards are studied from two main perspectives: the experiences of the golfer in pre-shot and post-shot times. (Source: Golf Illustrated)

CHAPTER 5 | PSYCHOLOGICAL EFFECTS *of* HAZARDS

basket, where it is almost impossible to be successful. When they make these choices, their own personal skill level and, by extension, their self-esteem, are taken out of the equation. Subjects with high levels of self-confidence in their ability tend to choose intermediate distances in these studies. They pick a distance that will give some experience of success and failure and that will provide some indication of their skill at throwing the ball.

In the same way, golf course hazards that are too easy or too difficult to overcome can become psychologically irrelevant. Imagine, for example, a hard,

Fig. 5-5 Hazards, even those that are especially difficult, can be aesthetically appealing. Such a characteristic can conceal the difficulty, giving the golfer an impression that the hazard may be "pleasant." These fairway bunkers at Swinley Forest Golf Club, England, are surrounded in heather. (Courtesy of P. Burton)

fast green with a mound, on top of which the hole has been placed. In this hypothetical example, balls going past the hole in any direction with any speed tend to end up 10 to 15 feet away. Approach shots rarely end close to the hole. This level of hazard difficulty is likely to destroy interest in the hole, even among advanced golfers, because outcomes do not sensitively reflect the accuracy of the shot or the skill of the golfer.

In contrast to a practice range, a golf course may be regarded (in tournaments, in betting situations, or even in solitary rounds) as a test of skill. What are the characteristics of a good test? Most experts on testing agree that a good test measures the smallest possible differences in ability between test takers. A test that blurs differences—that is, a test in which people of different ability levels achieve the same outcome—is inferior to one that distinguishes between all ability levels. Hazards on a golf course are a way of making the course more difficult. The challenge for the architect is to construct the optimal level of difficulty. Overly simple hazards and overly difficult hazards do not distinguish between different golfers' ability, and perhaps more importantly do not pose an emotional challenge to golfers. Since this book is primarily about real hazards that

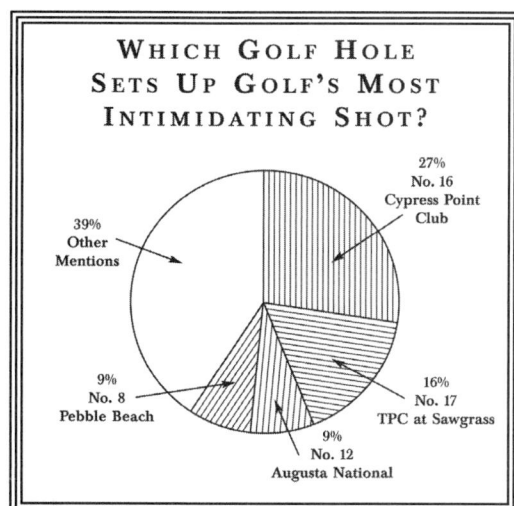

Fig. 5-6 Results of our survey indicating the most intimidating shot in all of golf. Of interest is that the 17th at the Tournament Players Club, Florida, was the only modern design mentioned among the responses.

139

Fig. 5-7 Hazards are contemplated by golfers at many stages. Location, distance, difficulty and the importance of the shot in the context of the match are all factors that will affect the stress level.

Fig. 5-8 As any golfer will attest, the presence of an audience, such as at the first tee, can add to the anxiety of a golf shot. In essence, this creates a "hazard" of its own. Photo c.1899 of Donaghadee Golf Club, Ireland, a seaside and meadowland course. (Source: Golf Illustrated, September 1899)

occur on real courses, it is by definition about conditions of greater-than-average difficulty. For the average golfer, the psychology of golf course hazards is primarily concerned with cognitive processes (decisions that are made with respect to hazards), and the emotional experiences that accompany them. We can distinguish preshot experiences from postshot experiences. If the hazard poses a difficult problem, the preshot experience typically involves emotions that can variously be labeled as *stress, tension,* and *fear.* In the following paragraphs, I will review what is known about the effect of such emotions on performance. Of course, there could well be positive preshot experiences as well. The hazard may be beautiful as well as dangerous. The hazard may evoke feelings of confidence, as well as excitement about the challenge that is posed.

Do Hazards Affect the Golf Swing?

> *"What happens immediately before the ball is struck is an altogether different equation involving motor-neurone skills, brain synapses, physical fitness, anatomy, ironmongery, sociology, human behavior and psychology, amongst millions of other variables."*
>
> —JEREMY PERN

What do we know about the effects of fear, stress, and anxiety on golfing performance? Although little research has been specifically focused on golfers, a large body of research, conducted mainly in the laboratory, has yielded consistent findings. If we think of a hazard on the course as being analogous to a stressor in a laboratory situation, we can draw the following conclusions.

1. The experience of stress depends upon subjective feelings of control. In a now classic laboratory study, subjects were placed in a room and given tasks that required some degree of concentration, such as proofreading a chapter for typographical errors, or doing long-division problems by hand. While doing these tasks, they were subjected to loud, intermittent noise, a stressor that has repeatedly been shown to interfere with performance on tasks that require concentration. One group of subjects simply had to endure the noise and try to complete the tasks as best they could. A second group of subjects was giving a device with a large red button and was told: "If you press this button, the noise will immediately stop. We hope you will not press it, because we want to study the effect of noise on your performance, but if the experience becomes too unpleasant, go ahead and press the button." This second group of subjects thus had control over the noise. Interestingly, in this study none of the subjects pressed the button.

Fig. 5-9 Hazards, which add modest stress to a shot, will tend to increase performance. However, hazards with perilous obstacles—such as this wild dune and bunker at Hayling Golf Club, England—will tend to increase the incidence of error in execution. (Source: Golf Illustrated)

Fig. 5-10 A 1927 cartoon from Golf Illustrated.

When the experimenters examined the results, they found that the group that had perceived control over the aversive noise performed much better on the proofreading and the long-division tasks. They were exposed to exactly the same objective stress as the group that had no control over the noise, but the stress did not have the same effect on their performance. This experiment has been repeated many times, with many different stressors, and the same pattern of results typically occurs.

If we apply these findings to the issue of golf course hazards, we see that the same hazard is not the same for different golfers. Is the hazard to the left or the right of the target? Does the golfer typically slice or hook the ball? How confident is the golfer feeling? How important is the shot to the golfer? All of these subjective considerations influence the psychological reaction to the physical hazard that the designer has placed on the course.

Fig. 5-11 The 486-yard, par-4 17th at the Kapalua Plantation Course, Hawaii (see color insert). The golfer cannot help but think about the deep canyon that lies between the fairway and the green. The thought alone makes the hazard seem and play more difficult. (Mike Klemme, Photographer)

2. *Stressors increase physiological activation.* Under conditions of stress, heart rate increases, respiration becomes shallower and more rapid, and perspiration increases. These bodily changes may pose distractions for the golfer. Additionally, under stress, there is increased muscular tension throughout the body. Grip pressure is increased. The muscles of the neck and back become tighter. It becomes more difficult to turn away from the ball freely. Tension in the forearms and wrists inhibits a free setting of the club at the top of the backswing, a free release through the shot, and a free turn through to the follow-through. Additionally, the golfer finds that, because of the increase in bodily tension, feedback from the muscles feels different from usual. Tension tends to interfere with body awareness and with the ability to make rhythmical movements. The body feels different and the swing feels different. Normal habits are disrupted. Unless the golfer has considerable practice playing under stressful conditions, the golf swing tends to deteriorate.

Fig. 5-12 A common hazard type, in psychological terms, is the "all or nothing" situation. Here, at the aptly named "Death or Glory" 10th Hole of Northwood Golf Club, England, the approach to the par-4 green is either in the sleeper banked bunker or on the green. (Source: Golf Illustrated, April 1903)

3. *Stress increases error rate.* We generally think of stress as simply increasing mistakes, but laboratory studies indicate that the relationship between stress and performance is curvilinear. Simply put, this means that adding a little fear or a little stress tends to improve performance by improving concentration. Adding a little more stress, however, will typically cause an increase in errors.

Because of this effect, hazards put the golfer in double jeopardy. A hazard that the golfer could avoid if an average shot were played becomes dangerous because it prevents the golfer from playing in a relaxed fashion. Imagine a golfer who typically plays on a

CHAPTER 5 | PSYCHOLOGICAL EFFECTS *of* HAZARDS

Fig. 5-13 The famous Sahara bunker at the Alps Hole at Prestwick (also referred to as the Alps bunker.) Interestingly, this hazard is completely hidden from the fairway by the massive alps feature that rises up to conceal the entire green. This shot was either taken from a very bad lie atop the alps, or perhaps as reference for the next round (see color insert). (Courtesy of P. Burton)

course with wide fairways. Imagine further that the golfer tends to hit the ball relatively straight off the tee. Laboratory research would lead us to expect that on a course with narrower fairways, the golfer's accuracy would decrease, especially because conditions demand that his tee shots either stay the same or improve. A hazard on the course may not require exceptional play; it can cause trouble if it simply demands that a golfer hit his or her average shot.

4. *Stress narrows the field of attention.* Attention tends to be focused on central information, while peripheral information is neglected. The result is a kind of tunnel vision. The golfer focuses excessively on immediate threats. The hazard exerts a magnetic pull on the golfer's mind.

Fig. 5-14 Nearly every hole at Sutton Bay, South Dakota, offers a masterful view of water and shoreline. The water, however, never comes into play. Once the golfer realizes this, the threat diminishes and the focus is diverted to the bunkers and other hazards that lurk at every hole (see color insert). Graham Marsh, golf course architect.

Golfers are frequently told to try not to focus on a hazard. For example, if there is a water hazard that runs along the right side of a fairway, a golfer would be well advised to focus on the center or left-center of the fairway, to think positively, and to ignore the hazard. Many golfers will find however, that their minds are consumed by the idea "don't hit it to the right." The swing becomes disrupted, because this is not the normal swing key, and erratic shots occur. The ball is more likely to go to the right. Stress, in the form of a hazard, will disrupt the normal attentional processes that guide the golf swing.

5. *Stress reduces creativity.* Under stressful conditions there is a decreased ability to be creative, to entertain different ideas or thoughts about how a problem might be avoided. One idea comes to mind, and under conditions of great anxiety, tends to become fixed in the mind. If a problem solver (golfer) is relaxed and confident, a number of ways around a problem

may be visualized. When the task difficulty is very high, however, the first thought in the golfer's mind tends to perseverate.

6. *Stress produces a sense of time pressure.* Under stress, people tend to behave as though there is time pressure when in fact there is none. The golfer will tend to rush a difficult shot, perhaps in an attempt to quell the anxiety or the doubts produced by the situation.

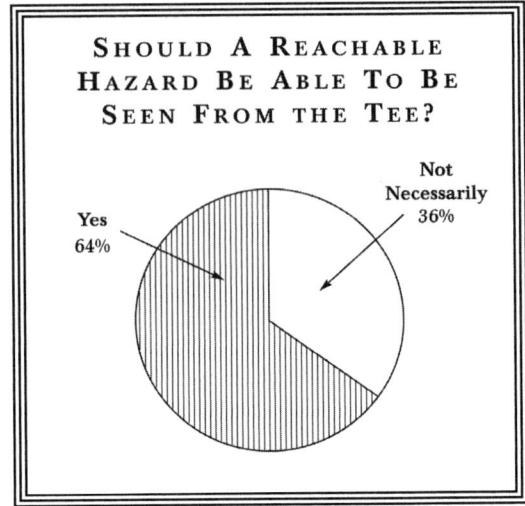

Fig. 5-15 The opinion about being able to see a hazard is decidedly against such holes at the Sahara Bunker at the Alps Hole of Prestwick. (Fig. 5-13)

It is also worth noting in this regard that some hazards are more time-consuming than others. If a ball is hit in a lateral water hazard, the golfer realizes it, drops a new ball, and plays the next shot without much delay. However, if a ball is hit into long rough, time is spent searching. Not only does this delay the round, but the error is likely to produce a sense of time urgency in both the golfer and in playing partners. What began as a leisurely round of golf becomes subjectively more urgent because of the pressure to keep up with the group ahead. This sense of time urgency has negative effects on the golf swing, because the best golf tends to be played when the golfer is moving and thinking in a relaxed, leisurely fashion.

7. *Decision processes are changed, often for the worse.* Laboratory studies have shown that when subjects are threatened, they reduce their search for additional information and jump to premature conclusions. Further, under stress subjects shift decision criteria from complicated or subtle strategies to simple strategies.

Resilience

After the golfer has either succumbed to or successfully negotiated the hazard, emotions associated with success or failure are experienced. Successful experiences breed confidence; the golfer relaxes, and the rhythm of the swing improves. Failure to negotiate a hazard penalizes the golfer, and, depending upon the magnitude of the penalty, the golfer may experience some level of disappointment. Disappointment may in turn engender self-doubt, tension, and experimentation with technique. If a golfer makes a big score on a hole, he or she may find it difficult to recover. Failure can lead to a lack of confidence, which in turn leads to further failure. A common lament following a round is "I played great until the _____ hole, then the wheels came off." Typically, a bad hole is followed by others.

Ideally a golfer should be focused only on the shot at hand, with no thought given to previous successes or failures, but the human mind rarely works that way. The difficulty of remaining in the moment, with no thought of previous shots, is one of the great challenges of the game. Golfers who can stay focused on the shot at hand, with no memory of the past, may be said to be resilient to stress. However, this is a rare skill. In general failure experiences have a lasting effect; course architects know this intuitively, so the greatest challenges on the course rarely come early in the round.

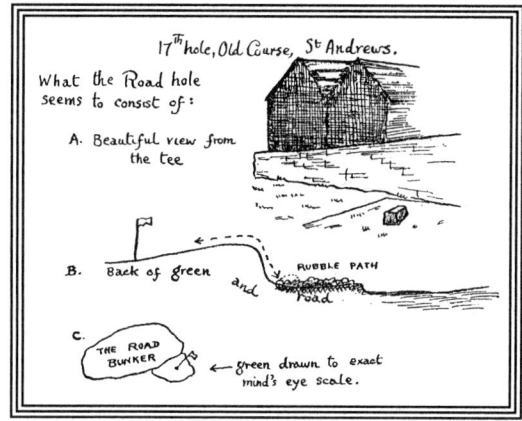

Fig. 5-16 The late Patric Dickenson, former Poetry Editor of the British Broadcasting Company, authored A Round of Golf Courses, a Selection of the Best 18. *His insightful diagrams accompanied his wit and poetry. This look at the Road Hole at The Old Course, St. Andrews, strikes a chord with anyone who has been there and challenged the mighty hole. Note the "mind's eye scale" of the Road Bunker itself.*

Hazard Perception: Perceived vs. Actual Difficulty

It is important to note that the difficulty of a hazard and the fear, excitement, or arousal that is produced by a hazard do not always go hand in hand. Many of the difficulties in golf are mental, not physical, and subjective not objective. Tom Doak puts it this way:

Hazards on golf courses exist in two dimensions—physically on the ground, and in the player's mind. Of the two, I am convinced that the latter has far more effect on the play of the average golfer. Take a simple pond immediately in front of a tee—how often would we top the ball if the hazard were not there? And how often do we, because we have worried about embarrassing ourselves?

One may distinguish between the actual difficulty of a hazard and the perceived difficulty of the hazard. Hazards with high perceived difficulty catch the golfer's attention, stimulate the imagination, and produce an emotional response. Water is an example of a hazard with high perceived difficulty, even on holes where it is easily avoided. Water seems to compel fantasies of failure in the average golfer. Peter Dobrineiner, a British writer, put it succinctly: "Water creates a neurosis in golfers, the very thought of this harmless fluid robs them of their normal powers of thought, turns their legs to jelly and produces a palsy of the upper limbs." On many occasions, however, hazards with high actual difficulty have low perceived difficulty. For example, deep rough is a more difficult problem for most players than is a shallow sand trap. However, a green with prominent bunkers will tend to attract more attention and will elicit more apprehension than will a green

Fig. 5-17 Bunkers at Prairie Dunes Golf Club, Kansas, designed by Perry and Press Maxwell. The vegetation within the bunker makes the hazard stand out, sending a clear message to the golfer. (Courtesy of P. Burton)

surrounded by rough. The former will be more visually interesting, will be more exciting, and will tend to be perceived as more hazardous, although the green surrounded by deep rough is likely to add relatively more strokes to the scorecard.

Generally, golfers are likely to notice and emotionally respond to any hazard that a human would have difficulty walking through. Water, sand, trees, shrubs, and desert all constitute a challenge to human movement, and hence are visually salient. Subtle difficulties on the course, such as those that cause an uneven stance, or those that cause a ball to roll off the fairway, may not catch the attention of the recreational golfer, but will surely add to the difficulty of the course. The recreational golfer will benefit from fairway landing areas that are relatively flat. If the fairway is canted to one side, the high side should be to the right, because the average golfer is right-handed and tends to slice the ball. While golfers are likely to notice prominent hazards to the right of the fairway, subtle tilting of the landing area is unlikely to be noticed. In such cases, the hazard penalizes the golfer and slows play without adding much excitement or interest to the round.

It is also important to recognize that as the skill level of a player progresses, the perceptual effect of different types of hazards changes. For the average golfer, hazards should be well placed and salient. Driving over rough is not as exciting as driving over a bunker. The better golfer is more likely to notice hazards with high actual difficulty is and to play to avoid them. Further, more-advanced players tend to focus on the target while less advanced players tend to focus their attention on hazards. For the advanced player, hazards may function as landmarks, allowing more-precise distance estimation and more-precise calculation about where to land the ball.

Fig. 5-18 An ominous graveyard confronts the golfer off the No. 1 tee at Ballybunion's Old Course. (Courtesy of P. Burton)

CHAPTER 6

Design & Strategy *of* Hazards

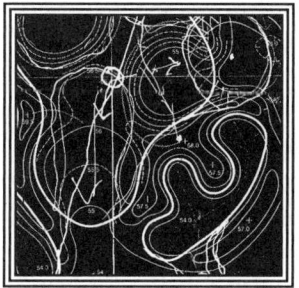

Bunkers, Pits & Other Hazards

Handwritten, torn, and tattered. In a hallway rarely used by golfers, it sat behind glass as long as anyone could recall. The initials "C. H." were all that identified the author. Who penned these words? Who's lovely prose was it that summarized our golfing spirit to a tee? Could it be that our little bunker inspired the thought? What caused these lines to flow from someone's mind? The answers to these questions we may never know.

> *This ancient game—unrivaled quite, in which so many take delight,*
> *Holds lore profound, life's but a round!—*
> *Thus think and go a-golfing.*
>
> *When on the tee the ball you place, learn how unsure our mortal race;*
> *To oft on sand, our hopes do stand!—*
> *Thus think and go a-golfing.*
>
> *The club wherewith the ball you smite, is tipped with metal hard and bright;*
> *So iron Fate, doth rule our state!—*
> *Thus think and go a-golfing.*
>
> *The ball a distant goal that sought, is in a bunker often caught,*
> *So worldly care the soul doth snare!—*
> *Thus think and go a-golfing.*
>
> *And when we win the green at last to rest with every hazard past,*
> *A tap—and lo, below we go!—*
> *Thus think and go a-golfing.*

It is, without any doubt, the act of holing a ball after trials and tribulations across a golf hole that so makes us want to come back for more. How incredibly unfulfilling it would be to strike a shot from the tee, almost blindly, find your ball easily with no worries, and then go about another shot with nary a bump, pit, or obstacle in the pathway. To design such a lame golf experience would be as if Steinbeck were to author a book without verbs. Or Picasso to use a straight edge to create his lines.

The design of hazards is what golf architects bring to the table. It is their legacy. If they fail to design, then they have failed to carry out their duties as authors. The golf architect has a dramatic play to write. As Arnold Haultain so aptly wrote in *The Mystery of Golf,* "There is Act I, the Drive... There is Act II, the Approach... the lie, the hazard, the wind, the character of the ground—all become of increasing importance. There is Act III, the Putt. . . the irregularities of the green, the peculiarities of the turf. . . . Eighteen dramas, some tragical, some farcical, in every round." Haultain goes on to proclaim, "No wonder the ardent golfer does not tire of his links, any more than the ardent musician tires of his notes."

The strategy of golf holes—courses, too—is the order and the nonorder of things. The word *strategy* comes from the Greek *strategos,* meaning "general." It was the *strategoi* (more than one general) who commanded troops during the Roman Empire. The *strategoi* of golf are the golf course architects. They organize and plan what often looks unorganized. In fact, the very impression of chaos is often a goal, just as it is in war. Through purposeful confusion and trickery they tempt, lure, and bait. Only the smart and skillful warrior will come through unscathed.

Reasons for Hazards

The hazard lives primarily for intrigue, to create strategy, to penalize, and to suggest to the golfer, however subtle or strong, that he think about choosing a different route. These are the core reasons for hazards. But recently, as golf courses have become big business, the driving force behind hazards has grown. We now hear of bunkers being placed "as an aid in aiming," water and sand created for "aesthetic qualities," hazards conceived to direct balls away from adjacent land uses, and even grass bunkers whose sole purpose is to stop balls from entering a— what?—a deep and perilous—you guessed it—hazard.

Fig. 6-1 The design of hazards is both simple and complex. The simple part requires an understanding of the basic purpose of a hazard—to test and dare the player. The complex part lies in the nearly endless combination of forms and features that work together to create any given hazard. The rolls and ground game at Gullane Golf Club, Scotland, are just as much a "hazard" as the deep bunkers that seem to have a hunger for golf balls. (Courtesy of P. Burton)

There is another tier of hazard rationales. The aesthetically minded designer might use a hazard to offer a contrasting texture. This is a by-product of landscape architecture, a relatively new profession in our built environment. In terms of civil engineering, lakes, ponds, and ditches are often required for drainage, whether they are natural or not.

A hazard may be the perfect way to convey water across a golf course. This is a topic we never tire of. Golf architecture should preserve these natural features wherever possible and practical.[1] Perhaps the very best hazards are natural features preserved during the clever routing and design of the course.

---

[1] Even a natural feature that seems impractical can make a great hazard. There was probably nothing practical about building the Cypress Point Club's 15th, 16th, and 17th smack along the ocean. Undoubtedly it would have been easier and less hassle to maintain if built on farmland somewhere near Gilroy, California.

We know a golf architect who was on-site building a course when the vice president of marketing for the owner showed up and became livid at the relationship of the entry road to the golf course that was taking shape. A most amazing series of bunkers dribbled into the left portion of the fairway. They created an interesting game of do or dare. But the vice president was unhappy despite the design and execution. "They have to be seen from the road," she barked. In the end she got her way.

A second series of bunkers was added at about 120-yards from the main tee. They

Fig. 6-2 One of the well-known illustrations of Charles Crombie as it appeared in the April 29, 1904, issue of Golf Illustrated. In the design of hazards, there is an approach that suggests that it may be generally better to develop hazards in which a golfer can not only find his ball, but also have a chance of recovery upon a well-executed shot.

serve no purpose but to offer "eye candy" to those arriving at the club. Is this good for golf? Well, the addition of the bunkers *does* serve a purpose. That cannot be denied.

The Old Course at St. Andrews may not have been subjected to this need for "curb appeal" during its formative evolution, but it most certainly is subjected to it now. The Old Course is big business for golf. The driving force to "preserve at all cost" the famous bunkers at St. Andrews is done partly to attract customers. Preservation, until the last few decades, was of no concern at the Home of Golf.[2] The very essence of the links was its continual improvement, change, trials, and adjustments. Now, we sit writing and reading several centuries after golf was first played there and it is obviously impossible to ask any of the early regular players about this. But the facts are plain. Holes changed, the course changed, new things were tried, and new ideas came to life. Today, the marketing angle of the Links Trust is one of keeping. . . The Old Course "the way it always was." Of course, this is in the eye of the beholder—of those here in the twenty-first century.

Whatever the newfound motivations for creating hazards—curb appeal included—their fundamental purpose has to do with the playing of the game of golf. One of our favorite haunts is an online discussion group called Golf Club Atlas, about golf courses and golf course architecture. A regular contributor, Pat Mucci, could not have said it any better than with this eloquent post from cyberspace: "Golf courses are nothing more than fields of play for a game called golf. That game has principles and rules for play. The object is: A golfer must get from point A to point B in as few strokes as possible, and it is the architect's function to impede and frustrate that attempt which creates the interest and the challenge in the endeavor."

---

[2] St. Andrews is called the Home of Golf because there is no better or more suitable place. As home to the Royal and Ancient Golf Club of St. Andrews, it holds this title and it is unlikely anyone attempting to move this "home" will ever be successful.

An Obstacle Course—*The Hunt*

We have learned that humans evolved on the savannas of Africa, and modern humans have inherited an attraction to savannalike environments—expanses of grass dotted with trees. Of the entire span of time humans have inhabited the Earth, just 5 percent has *not* been spent hunting and gathering in order to survive. When they were not hunting, our ancient ancestors spent time refining their tools and practicing the skills that would help them survive. Dr. Ed Sadalla writes, "The games of ancestral humans, like the games of contemporary hunter-gatherers, probably involved demonstrations of skills that were central to hunting. These skills remain the most common elements in modern sports."

We might compare golf—a hunt of sorts—to the steeplechase. The first steeplechase took place in Ireland in 1752. A wager was set between two horsemen to run a "course" of roughly 4 1/2 miles. Thus the sport of steeple*hunting*, as it was often called, was established. Of interest is that jumping prowess and stamina were judged more important than pure speed. This is much like golf. Replace jumping prowess with *accuracy;* and replace stamina with *length*. Both endeavors encourage skill, and it is not necessarily brute strength that wins. This concept is so dear to golf that it forms the key to understanding the design and strategy of golf holes.

Fig. 6-3 Golf is a form of hunting involving human skills similar to throwing. The game is an obstacle course across land devised to emulate the hunt. In this historic photo of golfers from Golf Greens & Greenkeeping by Horace G. Hutchinson, a golfer and his caddie are negotiating what Hutchinson describes as "Floral Hazards."

Accuracy, Carry & Length

Some golfers might feel that a flat fairway with nothing in their way but manicured green grass leading right up to the green is challenging enough. But they would eventually grow tired of such a featureless design, and the game would become boring. Though hazard features need to vary in quantity and difficulty from course to course, all courses need hazards to add strategy and enjoyment to the game. Designs with optional routes of play allowing safer passage around, over, or along different types of hazards provide challenge and interest to the greatest number of golfers. It is, in fact, a core principle of golf to challenge and test the golfer.

Perhaps no designer of golf courses has ever stated it more clearly than William Flynn when he wrote in 1927, "The problems which should be developed on the various holes in the order of their importance are first—accuracy; second—carry; and third—length." We highlight Flynn's great wisdom because it is so germane to the task of designing hazards. The idea of balancing accuracy and length is a fundamental of golf course design and vital to planning hazards. There are about six immensely important ideas that we would like every reader to take away from this book. If you only take four, make sure Flynn's words are among them. If you take more than six, please double-check your shopping bag to make sure that Flynn's comments have made it out with you.

Fig. 6-4 A bunker sits guard at the front of a green at Sand Hills Golf Club, Nebraska. Its location, almost centered, creates a significantly more interesting "line of charm" than if the bunker were positioned off to one side or the other. The line that the player feels is the best and most advantageous—and within his limits—becomes the player's own personal "line of charm." Bill Coore and Ben Crenshaw, golf course architects.

The Line of Charm

Golf relies on the quality of its playing grounds. The more interesting and exciting the golf course, the more pleasurable and gratifying the game. Think about playing tennis without a net or skiing with no contours in the slopes. What fun would most sports be if there were no challenges or obstacles to face?

Two terms are often confused: *Line of play* and *line of charm*. Let us resolve this once and for all. The line of play is thought of in two ways: First, it is that line that a player ultimately *takes*. Second, to the golf architect, it is a line drawn on a plan (or multiple lines showing alternative paths) that a golfer would ideally follow to get from A to B. Whether a golfer follows through with this is another matter.

The Line of Charm is a provocative path. It is the line that *attracts* the golfer. It is often an instinctive route that shaves off distance and cuts the corner. It almost always falls close to hazards. It thwarts the line of play that the golf architect has in mind and puts the golfer in charge. The golf course architect's role is to create exciting possibilities that pit these two lines against one another. The goal is to use hazards to suggest a line of play, but to entice players toward a line of charm that will catch their fancy.

Accuracy, of course, is at the heart of the idea of the line of charm. Also involved are carry and length. The interest of a golf hole is in sending a shot accurately. Risks and rewards are always most appreciated when they are left up to the golfer.

Unfortunately, hazards have become associated with penalization. This penal approach uses hazards to mandate the correct and only way to play a hole. The adventure and intrigue of golf are diminished with this approach. The golfer must obey, or else.

Nick Faldo had a great comment about The Old Course: "If a good straight drive up the middle finds a nasty hidden little pot bunker, then clearly the drive shouldn't have been aimed toward the middle of the fairway. This puzzles some people, but golf would surely be a monotonous game if the center of the fairway was always the optimum line, and at St. Andrews it usually isn't."

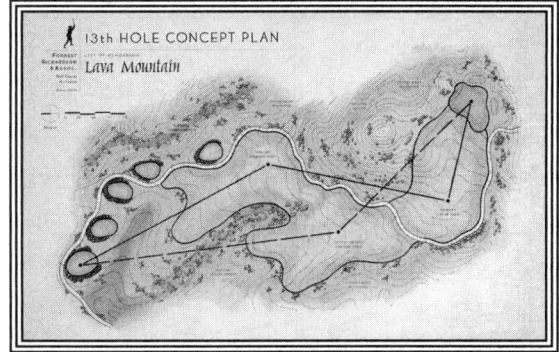

Fig. 6-5 The design of a golf hole must consider the various levels of playing skill. In this example, an uphill par-4 may be attacked in a variety of ways. The natural terrain forms hazards at every step.

Hazard Placement

Robert Hunter, writing in his acclaimed book *The Links*,[3] told us, "The hazards which distinguish the best golf courses are those which make every hole a new and interesting problem." What more do we really need to know?

A great way to think about hazard placement is by visualizing the *x, y,* and *z* axes. Hazards get placed[4] either far away from the origin of a shot or closer to it—the *x* axis. They are then positioned left or right—the *y* axis. And, finally, their relationship to the golfer is either level, up, or down—the *z* axis. All of the many attributes of hazards can be

Fig. 6-6 A cluster of bunkers at the Boston Golf Club, Massachusetts. Golf architect Gil Hanse has worked the bunkers into the natural flow of the hole.

---

[3] *The Links*, by Robert Hunter, is likely the best book ever written about golf architecture as a whole. Even though it was written nearly a century ago, it embraces the spirit of design that is so dearly required to properly design or even play a golf course.

[4] The placement of hazards, of course, is a combination of the placement of individual built features and the routing of holes around, across, and through natural features. Certainly golf course architects do not move natural features, so "placing" natural features is a misnomer. Placement, however, is the most suitable term for the act of designing and arranging a hole to take advantage of natural features in addition to those added by the designer.

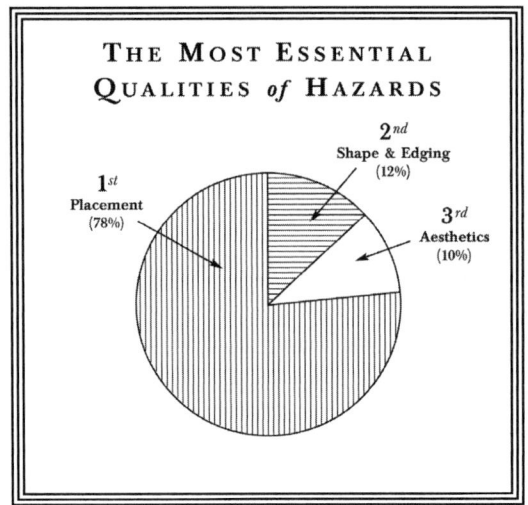

Fig. 6-7 Results of our survey indicating the most important aspects of hazards.

thought of in the context of this spatial system. The golf architect uses accurate surveys and measurements to determine placement for a variety of considerations. It may not be assumed that strategy is all that matters. Drainage, visibility, aesthetics, and so on are all factors that must be carefully weighed in the final assessment and plan.

In terms of strategy, hazard placement is driven by the following primary influences:

Player type. The decent design considers various playing abilities and the type of play expected at a course. Hazards are placed to provide interest and not to unnecessarily hinder one particular type of player.

Shot type. A hazard may promote a high shot or allow for a running shot in order to gain advantage toward a target. Hazards continually falling on the right side of holes will likely affect the lesser player more, as these golfers slice more frequently. The 18th at Pebble would not be so enjoyable if the Pacific Ocean were on the right. Look at the routing closely. The figure-8 that begins clockwise would not be as enjoyable in the opposite direction.

Target proximity. Hazards are set by the designer in relation to the target. Tillinghast wrote extensively about the "tucking" of hazards into greens. The proximity of hazards to targets, landing areas, and approaches are vital to interest and the entire idea of making golf exciting.

Setup of play. Hazards may be placed with a particular event in mind. Perhaps the event is the club championship, when back tees and difficult pin positions are used. A particular tee may be used, or side of a tee, which will cause a particular hazard to become more involved in the play of a hole. No. 6 at Riviera is one example. A small bunker sits within the middle of the putting surface, and although it is always a concern, the line of charm to a pin set in front of or behind this sand pit brings it considerably more into one's thought process.

Format of play. Stroke play may mean that hazards need to be softer on the players. For in match play we can concede the hole after ruining ourselves in a deep bunker where we have tried the unlikely shot two, three, four times without success. We move on in match play. In stroke play, we keep at it come hell or high water.

CHAPTER 6 | DESIGN & STRATEGY of HAZARDS

Conditions. At a course near the ocean that one of us recently completed, it became necessary to think of hazard placement on the par-5 holes in order to provide interest in various wind conditions. There are fairway bunkers that may never be noticed on a calm day because they are set well beyond the normal hitting area off the tee. But when the wind howls, and even an average length drive will go "forever," these bunkers come into play.

Natural features of the site. Oftentimes, a hazard is located in a particular spot because that is where nature placed it. A meandering stream, an abyss, a rock outcropping, and a natural ridge are just a few examples. Golf architects should do their best to incorporate these features into their routing plans, ultimately creating hazard opportunities.

Before undertaking the writing of this book, we asked golf architects, golf historians, and others associated with the business end of golf what priority they would place on size, shape, and placement of hazards. The results did not necessarily surprise us. The placement of a hazard was considered most essential, by a whopping 78 percent of those who were kind enough to partake in our survey. Shape and the edge treatment placed next, and aesthetics last.

The placement issues we have covered here are not the only ones to be considered, for sure. Golf course design is full of "rules," although we avoid this term. Granted, when we protect tees of adjoining holes, other fairways, and entry drives by situating hazards, we are following a set of guidelines that many may consider rules. But these are not rules. Many are common sense to the golf architect. Their importance is dependent on each individual situation. If we are to consider them rules, it is also essential that we must consider these rules of hazard placement are meant to be broken. As Robert Hunter put it, "Many a dull schoolmaster can lay down his laws of writing and reduce Shakespeare's methods to a few simple rules and regulations; and some golfers can lay down the law for the placement of hazards in a manner no less pedantic."

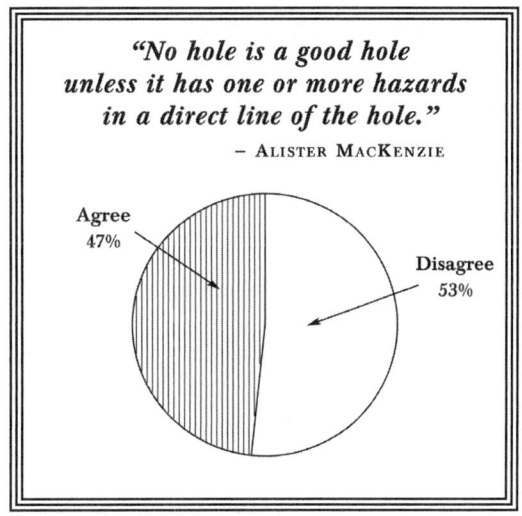

Fig. 6-8 More survey results. As evidenced by the results, there is a division on the matter of hazard placement on the "direct line of the hole." Perhaps this question is dependent on too many factors to develop a firm conclusion. If nothing else, the results demonstrate the controversial nature of hazards as they come closer to the line of play toward the target.

Fig. 6-9 Rhythm, frequency, and variation of hazards are integrated to the course routing. How a course unfolds to the golfer is much like that of a book. Arizona Biltmore Adobe Course, Arizona, c.1926, William P. "Billy" Bell (see color insert). Restoration by Forrest Richardson, golf course architect. (Photograph by Mike Houska, DogLeg Studios)

Rhythm, Frequency & Variation

Donald Ross once said, "Variety is the spice of golf, just as it is of life." No one type of hazard should be overused during design of a golf course. When possible, the type and location of each hazard should be a function of what naturally occurs on the site at hand.

Rhythm is the dishing out of hazards across a routing. When we speak of rhythm in golf, we rarely mean cadence or a continual beat. Instead, we are suggesting the changes of pace, the surprises, and the built-in moments of quiet when we wait to hear what comes next. The absence of rhythm is sometimes the answer.

Frequency is the quantity of hazards we must face on a given shot, approach, hole, or course. On a bad day, quantity might well be determined by the golfer himself. It is good to recall that the original design of Augusta National had just 22 sand bunkers. The number of hazards is a function of course type, player type, and what the land suggests. It should not be about more for the sake of more. The other *Q* word, *quality* is of tremendous importance. The advice for us all should be to side with quality in favor of hazards set by pure numbers.

Variation is the key. In Chapter 2, we covered hazards of many varieties from stone walls to undulations in the green. But many hazards get left behind. Discussions and writings most always focus on sand and water, with only a mention of the many other hazards that come into play, or can come into play. These other hazards are rather permanent and, when a course is "finished," there are probably ten times the number this book could possibly cover. We hope very much that a young person reading these pages will be inspired to write down other possibilities. It would make an excellent assignment for anyone interested in golf architecture, and it would probably lead to some wonderful concepts. To say golf has seen it all is surely a bald-faced lie.

Hazards come in many shapes, sizes, and configurations. They are musical notes waiting to be arranged, shaped, and played. Desmond Muirhead, the great golf course architect and visionary, was passionate about the idea of rhythm, frequency, and variation. "It surprises me how many don't understand this concept," he once said. "A golf course is much like a river. It must ebb and flow. That is what creates the interest."

The Size & Shape of Hazards

Size will affect depth perception, orientation, and, of course, such considerations as maintenance, budget, and playability.

Fig. 6-10 An interestingly shaped bunker at the Honourable Company of Edinburgh Golfers (Muirfield), Scotland (see color insert). (Courtesy of P. Burton)

In their 1929 work *The Architectural Side of Golf,* Weathered and Simpson advised against designing round or oval bunkers. They came right out and said to use only "lace-edged" shapes. This may have been a trend. There is no right or wrong, *is there?*

Size and scale are important attributes of hazards. The great Canadian architect Stanley Thompson, for example, was well known for making the scale of his hazards match with the existing terrain. If there were breathtaking mountains in the backdrop, or his holes played through expansive valleys, his hazards were of complementary scale and size. A small pot bunker just didn't fit with a massive mountain or river nearby. Dimensioning hazards "appropriately" makes for aesthetically pleasing golf courses.

The Aesthetics of Hazards

Just look at the many images we have brought together on these pages. The aesthetics are a potpourri. What makes them pleasing is that they provide mystery, interest, and sometimes beauty. It has been said that a hazard can be a "thing of beauty," though it might be ugly anywhere else but on a golf hole. As George Thomas wrote in *Golf Architecture in America:*

> *Place the golf course on a level plane; have no traps of any kind; let every fairway be flat; the green unprotected and without rolls; let there be no rough; nothing between the tee and the green but perfect fairway, and the green itself absolutely level; and what would be the result?—a thing without interest or beauty, on which there is no thrill of accomplishment which is worthwhile; a situation untrue to tradition, and apart from the spirit of golf as it was given birth among the rolling sand dunes of Scotland.*

BUNKERS, PITS & OTHER HAZARDS

Severity of Hazards

Recoverability is the essential topic here. While Old Tom Morris left us with the quote, "Bunkers are not places of pleasure; they are for punishment and repentance," we cannot unilaterally accept his thought as some kind of doctrine to be taken and turned into a cult following. We would like to believe that Old Tom would embrace the idea of recoverability and did not mean to have young golf architects growing up yelling at the excavator operators, "Deeper! Deeper! Deeper!"

Opinions vary on hazard severity. Walter Travis wrote an article subtitled, "The guiding principal should be at arranging the hazards to penalize by one stroke only." Horace Hutchinson thought the bunkers at Muirfield were awful because the faces were perpendicular. Willie Park was responsible for what could have been the first man-made water hazard on a created course when he had a small pond (unrecoverable, of course) constructed at Sunningdale's Old Course— in 1900.

In Chapter 2, we delved into hazard types quite extensively. The severity of hazards is driven by the type combined with the way they have been placed, designed, and built. Let us not forget maintenance, as it can surely affect severity. And what about the double-hazard condition, when we find a tree behind or within a sand bunker? Both hazard types and relationships need to be discussed.

Fig. 6-11 A 1908 cartoon from Golf Illustrated. Deep grass too close to the line of play is often considered one of the most severe hazards in golf. Tall grass is not only a difficult condition, but often leads to a lost ball, a time-consuming situation that is full of uncertainties and frustrations that go beyond the striking of the ball.

The Concept of Fairness

The modern pursuit of fairness and equity has not necessarily been good for the game of golf. A pastime that once had only two rules, golf has now evolved to where a typed booklet of over 150 pages is required to explain the game. Ever since it was decided that "play it as it lies" and "the rub of the green" needed to be tweaked, the game seems to have suffered. Far too much time, too much money, and too much attention is now directed toward making sure every good shot is rewarded and that perfect playing conditions leave no one with an "unfair" disadvantage. This mindset has led to expensive maintenance practices and less creative and more sterile playing grounds. Heaven forbid that two similar shots could potentially result in two distinct outcomes—one good and one bad. That would just not be fair—or would it?

CHAPTER 6 | DESIGN & STRATEGY of HAZARDS

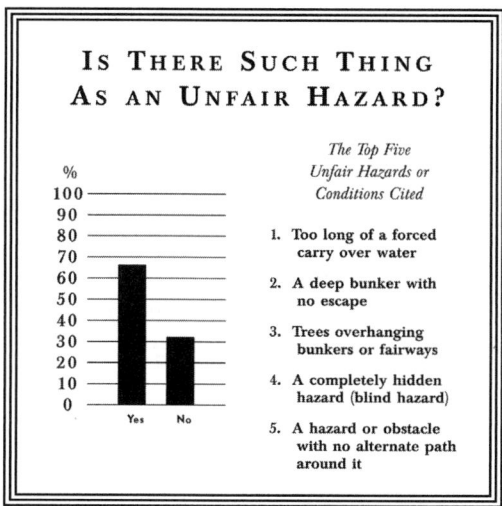

Fig. 6-12 Survey findings show that there is a definite threshold of fairness in hazard design and harshness.

Have golf architects, and the clients they work with, forgotten what golf is really all about? The game was never meant to emulate physics, where every action equates to an equal and opposite reaction. As with life, golf is expected to have ups and downs. Some days a golfer might do everything right, and yet the result still turns out badly. Other times, a lucky bounce or carom might lead to good fortune even when the swing and all its results should have led to an awful mess. Golf can teach us many lessons about life, but only if we allow skill, luck, and fate all to remain part of the game.

If all the uncertainty and unpredictable outcomes are conditioned away, what tests and challenges will remain? Aren't those bumps in the road of life just like the hazards of golf? In many ways, it is the triumph of overcoming setbacks that keeps us energized. Were it not for ordeals, it would only be a matter of time until we would become complacent and our lives (or rounds) filled with boredom.

When we think of "fairness," we are reminded of a situation that occurred at The Old Course at St. Andrews. Walking up the 18th fairway after hitting our final tee shots, one member of our group cringed at the site of his ball lying in the middle of Grannie Clark's Wynd, a macadam road that crosses the 1st and 18th fairways. The thought crossed his mind, "Here we are playing the grandest of all golf courses, and this perfectly struck drive on the final hole has found a lone stretch of rockhard road in the center of the fairway. What a bad break. What poor luck to deserve such an unfair fate." You see, in Scotland, and especially on The Old Course, you still play it as it lies, and this little macadam path is considered an integral part of the golf course. There is no free drop to gain relief. No automatic allowance that says you can place the ball back on

Fig. 6-13 In this 1905 cartoon that appeared in Golf Illustrated, John L. Low, a prolific golf writer, opines on the question of fairness.

forgiving turf to play your next stroke. No, you are stuck with the situation, and you deal with it the best you can.

As the golfer prepared to play his shot from the tightest of lies, one couldn't help but notice the spectators watching his misfortune from the fence rail along the hole. As his club swept toward the ball and picked it cleanly off the hard, dark surface, there was a sense of elation as it rose quickly and somehow managed to scurry up onto the green surface, coming to rest about 30 feet from the flagstick.

The golfer's walk to the green was one neither he nor his playing partners would ever forget. Every one of the onlookers had applauded the shot. Two putts later, the golfer scored one of the greatest pars, and most memorable moments, of his golfing career. And all thanks to what looked like a dire and "unfair" circumstance.

But that is golf. Many of the elements that add so much richness to the game may be lost in our pursuit of "fairness." There is too much at stake. The concept of fairness must be tempered at all cost.

Shot Values

You have heard golf tournament announcers use this ubiquitous term, and now here we are throwing it in your face: *shot values*. Shot values describe the various types of shots that golfers are asked to execute. Hazards define most shot values. And if you consider length itself a type of quasi-hazard, then all shot values are defined by hazards. Golfers, of course, will change the nature of shot values depending on their skill. Mother Nature will change shot values depending on her mood. And a $5, £5, or 500¥ bet is always bound to change shot values!

As we have discussed, golf holes are commonly classified in terms of their play as penal, strategic, or heroic. Yet all golf holes are really strategic—it is just that some involve more strategy than others. Strategy is a constant even in penal holes. It is not really a type of design as much as it is design. Strategy is part of the game regardless of what lies ahead of the golfer. The term was picked up long ago to suggest a movement away from penal mentality.

The conclusion is that the traditional classification—penal, strategic, or heroic—is better replaced by terms used to classify golf strokes: penal, heroic, detour, layup, and

THE REPORT CARD of SHOT VALUES

		Penal Design	Heroic Design	Detour Design	Lay-up Design	Open Design
Par-3	Tee Shot	B	A	B	D	F
Par-4	Tee Shot	B	A	A	C	D
	2nd Shot	C	B	A	C	F
Par-5	Tee Shot	D	A	A	C	D
	2nd Shot	D	A	A	B	D
	3rd Shot	B	C	A	F	F

A = Ideal   B = Good   C = Acceptable   D = Ill Advised   F = Unacceptable

Fig. 6-14 The five fundamental shot types (penal, heroic, detour, layup and open) are shown relative to the six basic non-hazard locations from which golfers play shots. The grades given for each of the 30 combinations are: A, B, C, D, and F, just like in school.

open. By combining the five types of golf shots demanded by par-3, par-4, and par-5 holes, hundreds of variations on hole "strategy" may be created. A tee shot may be heroic in nature, an approach may present a detour, and so on. Infinite possibilities come into play when all the other variables are added to the equation, from alignment, to length, to hazards placement. And we have yet to consider that every golfer holds a unique perspective and ability. What may be a heroic shot to one golfer may well be thought of as penal by another.

Penal Hazards— *"Go Here"*

The forced carry is the most common penal design feature. It is a matter of "do or die" when a hazard is so much in the way and of such great mass that it cannot be overcome by going around it or deciding on an easier, perhaps less advantageous route. Regimented hazard placement can also be penal. Bunkers placed strictly left and right, for example, may be penal in that they restrict the golfer to one path, and one path only. A penal hazard allows no one the opportunity to challenge the design with a risk-taking or alternative path. It is a do-or-die situation if one attempts to carry the hazard.

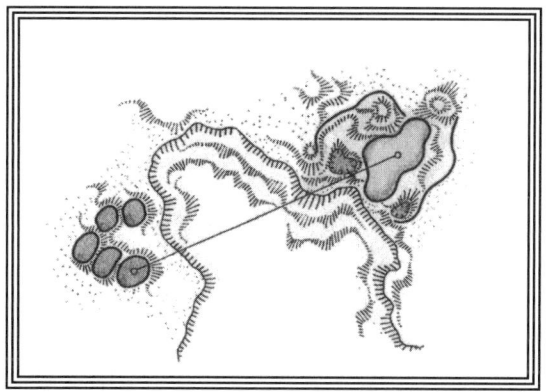

Fig. 6-15 Example of a par-3 requiring a penal shot over a deep canyon. Although penal, the shot required is only 60 to 70 yards from the regular tees and may be played to the left if the slightly longer carry directly to the center of the green is too much for the golfer. The worst of penal shots are those for which the required carry is in excess of 70 yards from a tee point, or any penal condition beyond the tee shot, as the spot from which a golfer will need to play this shot cannot be predicted. The player who hits just 170 yards off the tee, when faced with a penal shot to the green of a 330-yard par-4, will face a shot he likely will be unable to negotiate.

A penal shot, therefore, is a golf shot that presents no alternative route to avoid a hazard or feature. The word *penal* comes from the Latin *poena,* which means "fine" or "penalty." Penal golf design was a standard of the years when it first became fashionable to build golf courses rather than simply discovering them. Almost all courses built in America until 1910 were penal in nature. Certainly the links courses of the British Isles were penal in places, but they almost always offered detour routes to the hole. Golfers devised their own routes to the hole and, in the process, invented what has become known as strategic and heroic design—or, in our vernacular, detour, layup, and heroic design.

Penal shots are not in favor in today's world. An obstacle that requires playing across is not as appealing as one where the golfer has the choice of playing around it and where playing across becomes a matter of risk.

Penal hazards, nonetheless, provide a change of pace during the golf round. The most workable condition for penal hazards is when the design will not overly penalize the higher-handicap golfer. Penal design is also an excellent choice where there is no choice—that is, when a natural hazard presents itself such that routing must get across it and the opportunity for drama cannot be ignored. A gorge 150 feet across is a good example. The hole might just lead to the shot of a lifetime, and for most golfers, a carry of this length is a doable feat.

The classic example of a penal shot is the very short par-3, where a range of tees can create a forced carry over water, wasteland, or sand. The actual carry is perhaps no more than 50 or 60 yards for the golfer who plays from the forward tees. It is presumed that nearly all golfers can negotiate a 60-yard carry. This is significantly more palatable than the same forced carry designed short of the green on a par-4. In this instance, the higher-handicap golfer may attempt a long iron or fairway wood to reach the green by virtue of his position off the tee. To necessitate a penal approach in this instance is reason for criticism of the penal school of design.

Heroic Design— *"How Dare You!"*

Jack Nicklaus says, "What I like to do is make [the golfer] decide between the glory of the long ball and the practicality of another alternative." Heroic is penal design with an optional route. It is the ultimate in terms of risk and reward. If you make the shot, you are well rewarded. If you play a safer route, the hole is longer.

On heroic shots, golfers can incrementally adjust their shot to aim either more over the obstacle or more away from it, depending on the level of excitement desired. The hero is the guy who clears the hazard or obstacle most dramatically. The classic example of heroic design is the shot over a diagonal hazard that extends into the golf hole. The expression "bite off as much as you can chew" is often associated with heroically designed holes and shots.

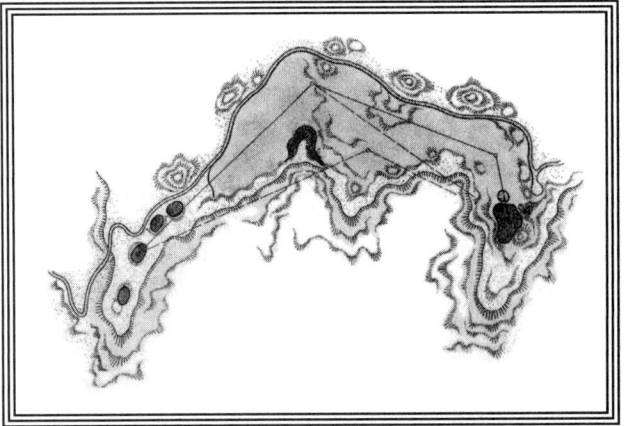

Fig. 6-16 The heroic shots occur here at the tee and at the second shot, depending on where the tee shot is placed. The entire side of the hole is defined by a steep cliff that meanders from the tee to the green. The green sits out on a point. The successful heroic shot at the tee will put the golfer in position to reach the green in two with a relatively short approach. For the tee shot that is played conservatively, a heroic shot opportunity is afforded at the second shot to reach the green. The conservative shot here sets up a short third-shot approach when played away from the hazard. Many golf holes, especially par-5s, are not generally all heroic or all detour in makeup. Rather, most par-4 and par-5 holes require a combination of strategies that change depending on the ability of the individual golfer.

Detour Design— *"Your Choice"*

Detour shots, unlike heroic shots, offer distinct pathways around obstacles. The choice is to deal with the obstacle or hazard or not. This is not to say that heroic and detour design principles cannot be blended; in many instances, they are. If, for example, a lake presents a heroic opportunity, there may also be a wide and slightly longer fairway route to the hole along which the lake is taken almost completely out of play. In this case, the golfer faces both heroic and detour shot options.

Detour shots are shots around. Split fairways and isolated hazards sitting almost in the middle ground of a hole create detour options from which the golfer must choose—and the more the merrier. In golf, detours are good. They prompt thinking and problem solving. They bring out the best in golfers without requiring reliance on length.

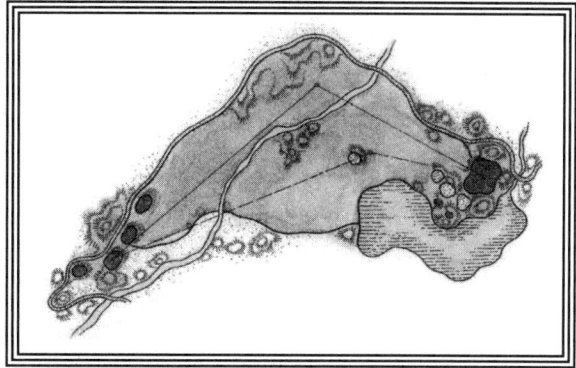

Fig. 6-17 *The detour shot is played from the tee along one of two routes: well right of the stream that bisects the hole, or to the left. The small pot bunker to the left further defines the options—detours that may be taken when playing in that direction. A player may elect to play closer to the wetlands, shortening the approach, or toward the stream, slightly lengthening the approach. This is a classic detour hole in that its shots are clearly optional in nature without approaching the heroic.*

Layup Design— *"Hold Back"*

A layup shot is up to the golfer and may be invoked at any moment in the round, even on penal, heroic, and detour shots. The hallmark of the true layup is that it is forced. The design condition that forces a shot to be played well short of a full shot cannot be considered either heroic or a detour. The layup shot is not always liked or appreciated, but it is nonetheless a part of the game. It can be brought about by playing conditions or through the use of a particular set of tees. That extremely penal lake fronting the green can require a layup shot when the wind is howling and the tees are back, but

Fig. 6-18 *This par-4 requires a layup off the tee for all but the very long player, who may try the Hail Mary shot to the well-guarded green. Options are presented to control the direction and length of the layup shot as shown in the wide fairway. The rough ground beyond the landing area is in turf but not an ideal place to position a tee shot. The best layup holes require thought beyond just hitting shorter. Without some degree of choice and decision, the forced layup shot can be a letdown.*

this is only a temporary condition. The lake fronting the green is meant to be carried and is therefore penal in nature on any other day.

The reason that layup design is not well liked is that it takes the element of gamble out of the golfer's arsenal. If a shot is forced to be hit short, there is no real decision, only restraint. Aside from the possibility of a heroic shot by a skilled golfer to clear the obstacle that has caused the layup condition, the element of choice is all but eliminated.

A layup design is probably best deployed on shortish par-4s at the tee shot. This interruption of brute force, when used sparingly, can be an interesting diversion. The best layup shot is one that involves a degree of heroic and/or detour playing. Layup design in this case, brings even more decision making into the picture. Obviously, layup design has little use at par-3 holes, but great examples of par-3s where a layup area has been provided do exist. Merely having a layup area, however, does not necessarily constitute layup design. The layup area is provided as an option, not as a primary landing point. The most famous example of a par-3 embracing this design is the 16th at Cypress Point Club, a MacKenzie masterpiece. In reality, the 16th at Cypress is heroic, detour, and layup all wrapped into one.

Open Design— *"We Goofed"*

Maybe it is a bit brash to suggest that the purveyor of open design has "goofed." Open design is typically boring, with nothing-to-it fairways that are not encumbered by hazards, twists, obstacles, or anything else. The object is just to get there. That such shots and holes exist in golf is no reason to design more of them. To create abundant shot requirements that are completely open in their design is to go against the origins of golf and its point. Open design strategy should be reserved for appropriate points in a routing. Examples include leading up to a particularly difficult penal shot on a hole or for starting holes of a round. Even then, there should always be *some* obstacle and choice.

Play does not always have to be controlled. Even in the absence of hazards, the golfer must exert self-control and judgment. "It looks so open and wide" and bam, the shot is topped no more than 60 yards. A boundary hole, usually an open hole that begs the golfer

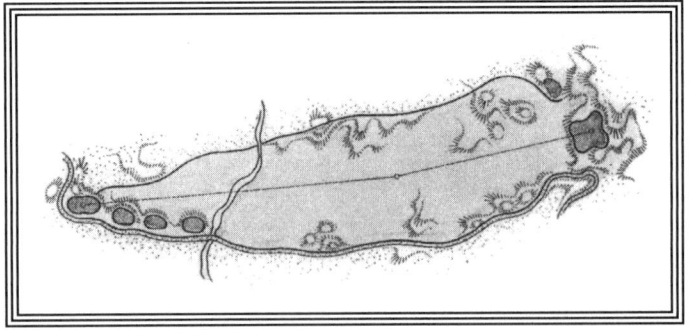

Fig. 6-19 *Both the tee shot and the second shot are relatively open in this example of open design strategy. Although not condoned in a vast majority of instances, open design can be tolerated at the beginning hole of most courses providing it does not become a trend. Truly "open" designs are hard to achieve, as even the subtle movement of the fairway provides interest to an otherwise open shot.*

to hit along a perilous edge, is an example of open shot values being presented. If the area to the left is vast and the peril is along the right, we might say this is partially a situation of open design. It is surely also a disaster waiting to happen.

Hazards at the Par-3

The par-3 represents a unique condition in golf. The hole is intended to be negotiated in one tee stroke and two putts. It is the only place in golf where we put golfers within a set area of ground intending to have them hit a green. We mandate that they do not venture any farther than this teeing ground. This is great power for the golf architect. When the hole is planned, the hazards can be set to follow the lead of the design as the architect sees fit.

Fig. 6-20 A par-3 of just over 130 yards provides a "hazard" through slopes and banks without any sand or water. Perhaps the most eloquent quote on par-3s was penned by John L. Low when he wrote, "The short hole should not be long." While length can be a hazard of its own, the par-3 is so much more about accuracy. After all, we have a chance to score an ace. Pictured is the Hideout Golf Club, Utah, Forrest Richardson and Arthur Jack Snyder, golf course architects (see color insert). (Photograph by Mike Houska, DogLeg Studios)

A review of Chapter 3 will reveal how many of the great hazards in golf are at one-shot holes: the Redan, the Biarritz, the Dell, and so on. These holes have become defined by hazards that have been assigned the duty of interrupting the lines of play and giving the holes exciting lines of charm.

Hazards at the Par-4

The par-4 offers hazards off the tee, from this point to the green, and finally at the green itself. When thinking of hazards on par-4s the designer uses length, width, terrain, and all of the devices at his or her disposal to develop the hole-hazard relationship.

While there are many variables, some of the more enjoyable par-4s are the short risk/reward holes. It is these short 4s that have required the least amount of "Tiger-proofing" over the years. That is because the challenge of the short hole has always come from exacting and strategic characteristics, unlike the demands of long-ball striking.

Hazards at the Par-5

The par-5—the three-shotter—offers hazards off the tee, from this point to the ideal area of the second shot, from here to the green, and finally at the green itself. Here we have more elbow room; indeed the hole has more opportunity to, in fact, *elbow* than other holes. The variations of alignment at the par-5 can be all in one constant direction, such as in a cape hole. Or one can consider a button-hook hole, where only that last shot to the green is angled, or the double dogleg, where the hole bends in two opposite directions.

Hole Orientation

Orientation of par-4 and par-5[5] golf holes involves such variables as direction, dogleg, wind, light, background, relationship to adjoining holes, and any other condition brought about by where it heads. A skyline green, for example, is quite dependent on orientation, for it may be rather ordinary in terms of background if it is not located just at the correct spot, with just the right incoming angle.

Hazards can be enhanced through orientation. When a finishing hole goes perpendicular to the setting sun, the shadows cast by rises at bunkers may extend across the fairway. How lovely is this? Think about the finishing holes you have enjoyed. How many of the truly extraordinary examples would have been such if they had headed in some other direction?

A common orientation is the dogleg, a curious term. It must sound entertaining even to nongolfers. It will often come up in conversation when a golf architect is speaking about the design of courses: "Oh, so you decide where to put the *doglegs?*" We do not believe that it can be said that the dogleg hole was created by a golf architect. More than a few golfers of the 1600s must have "doglegged" around a large dune or an old church, and they accomplished this before books about golf design, golf hazards, or how to calculate "slope."

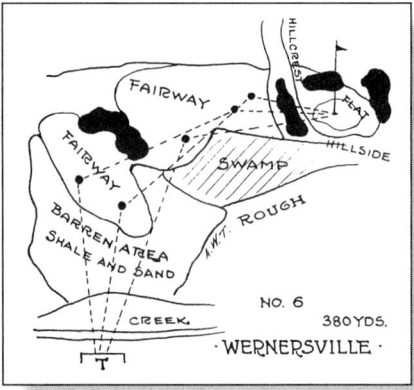

Fig. 6-21 *A drawing by A.W. Tillinghast, which accompanied a series he wrote titled, "Modern Golf Chats" in* The Golf Course, *April and May of 1916. Tillinghast, as usual, was opinionated in his views. Among his conclusions was that designs involving doglegs, elbows, and other twists would help eliminate the dreaded disease of "parallelitis." (Compliments of the Tillinghast Association)*

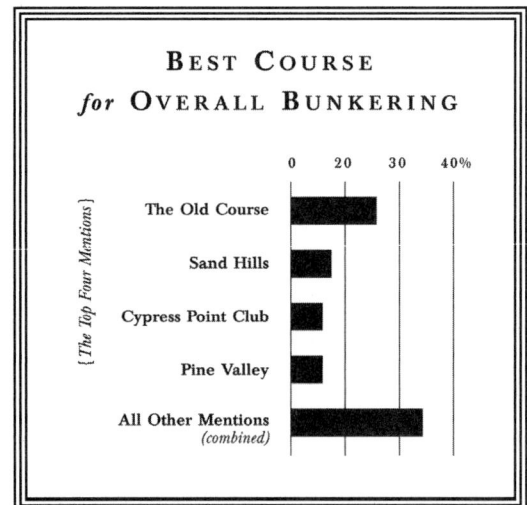

Fig. 6-22 *Whether subjective or objective, the overwhelming results show that The Old Course is highest regarded when it comes to bunkering.*

---

[5] The par-6 or greater is not itemized, although it does exist. There is no "International Agency of Par." Par is simply an idea influenced by play and is usually very dependent on the length of a given hole. The USGA published guidelines about par relative to length, including those par values beyond the par-5.

CHAPTER 6 | DESIGN & STRATEGY *of* HAZARDS

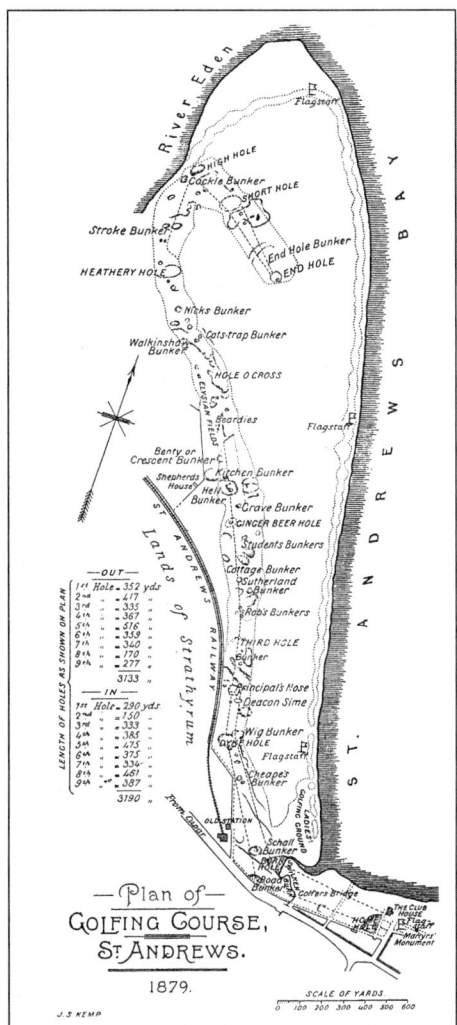

Fig. 6-23 The Old Course, St. Andrews, is perhaps the most extreme example of parallelism. But it is this very condition that makes the relationship of holes and hazards so unique. A study of the hazards and hole alignments is a must for anyone with an interest in golf holes and hazards. (From Harper's New Monthly Magazine)

Tillinghast was specific in his writing about doglegs. He used the terms *elbow* and *cape hole,* somewhat distinguishing them from doglegs. One of his points was that a dogleg amounted to a bend with a hazard that prevented the golfer from driving over it. Trees, for example, that were too tall to drive over on the inside of the bend made the hole a true dogleg. To Tillinghast, an elbow or cape hole offered options. Not only did the hole have an orientation, but golfers were able to overlay their own idea of orientation to the direction of play before each turn.

Dogleg holes, in addition to their amusing name, are amusing in their requirement that we turn as they do and must add the element of a change in direction to our list of things to remember at each shot before the green. Dogleg holes require greater width than straight holes of the same length, at least in most instances. It is efficient to fill the inside of a dogleg with a permanent feature or hazard. Doglegs can get tiresome to the golfer, especially when used too frequently, too severely, or too often in the same direction. Very few holes are perfectly straight; almost all have slight bends.

Parallelism is another form of orientation in golf. The Old Course is among the most extreme examples. The intermingling of hazards—orientation—makes the holes work in special ways. It should be a requirement that golf architects, club committees, course developers, and greenkeepers make careful study of The Old Course. There is no better example of the magic of hazards. The Old Course clings to golf architecture, golf architects, and golfers.
It will not let go of us for fear that we will forget how the holes unfold, how the hazards needle, and how everything comes together in one great symphony. As we know, even the greens are shared at St. Andrews. The holes were once played in reverse, as they still are once per year in homage to the original counterclockwise routing.

It is odd that we find parallel holes so dreadful in modern times. Certainly the dunes played a role in early links layouts, with their linear orientation, but even courses laid out over linksland as golf began growing in the 1900s seemed to avoid the out-and-back routing. In America, the notion of having holes return along one another became more than unpopular—it was taboo to the early architects. Triangulation became the fashionable way to route golf courses. Even across the sea, where golf architects did not need to go far to study St. Andrews, it was trendy to lay out courses with varying orientations of tee shots.

Hazard Visibility

Is a hidden hazard acceptable? When a visitor to The Old Course complains about the surprise of finding a hazard hiding amongst the holes, caddies often reply that the hazards have been there for 500 years. "How can anyone consider them hidden?" they ask. "A hazard will only be blind once," is another common response.

Fig. 6-24 A tall aiming pole at Royal Portrush, Northern Ireland, eliminates, at least to some degree, the complaints associated with a blind approach. (Courtesy of P. Burton)

The notion that all hazards must be visible is an interesting point for debate. The argument for complete visibility is stronger when the scenario is that of a shot played from a tee, but even so, where does one draw the line in deciding how far or how off to one side a hazard can be? If there is peril along an edge, why can't there be more peril on down? Do we have to see it? An argument for keeping hazards visible is that this makes them part of the show. Of course, the interesting thing about golf is that each player—except from the tee—defines where the next shots will be played to a hole. The architect, the greenkeeper, and the playing partners are not a part of this decision. The golfer is alone in this trek. It is quite impossible to make hazards everywhere visible for the poor chap who has hit wide right and is exiled behind a thicket. He is on his own; we cannot deal with him. The real debate comes through the green. Is visibility of hazards a requirement? Certainly not by any rule or mandate. Perhaps it is preferred, but exceptions will always be made, and a good case is often presented when they are.

A hazard or feature may be fully blind, partially blind, or temporarily blind. The Dell Hole at Lahinch is an excellent specimen to dissect. Here we have a green set behind a dune and surrounded by other dunes. It might be said that on most days the cup is fully blind. But this is temporary, because the cup can also be set far to the right where it is possible to see, sometimes, the upper part of the flagstick. In this case, it is said that the hole is partially blind. One might say that the former pin position directly behind the dune was "temporarily blind." We mentioned earlier that the position of the cup each day is marked by a white stone. You might also guess that yardage booklets and caddies are of great assistance—it is their duty to explain the hole and our duty to pay attention. One thing we can tell you about the Dell is that, when the pin is set so far right that it is no longer the mystery it was in the fully blind locations deep behind the grassy dune, the visitor who has traveled thousands of miles and endured the swill served by airlines[6] feels terribly cheated. Maybe this answers our question about blindness.

Camouflage & Deception

Hazards are not simply meant to penalize bad golf shots. If that were the case, almost every golf course ever built would have to be revamped. Some of the greatest hazards are designed to conceal and to disguise. They may scare a golfer away from a preferred angle of attack or a less arduous way to the hole. They may prevent a golfer from calculating the correct yardage to a hole or lure one into a false sense of security.

Fig. 6-25 Alister MacKenzie was brilliant at injecting camouflage and deception into his designs. A graduate of Cambridge, he was trained in medicine and served as a field surgeon during the Boar War. Among his assignments was to observe camouflage techniques of Boar soldiers, gaining understanding of their tremendous ability to conceal themselves in treeless landscapes. Pictured is the approach to No. 11 at Cypress Point Club, California. The combination of bunker size, location, and position from the green work to make the green seem closer to the golfer.

Hazards & Pace of Play

We asked Bill Yates, an expert on pace-of-play issues in golf, about the effect of hazards on pace. Bill was kind enough to share with us the following notes, listed here in order of priority:

1. *Hide and Go Seek.* Tall grass can be the worst offender, and the worst place for tall grass is on the inside of doglegs. Trees and underbrush in landing zones off the tee can cause time to be wasted looking for lost balls. Leaves in the fall can be a big problem—anywhere. A blind tee

---

[6] It is, of course, not food at all. Airlines call it this because it resembles food and will occasionally smell the part. In reality it is something to do that occupies your time and prevents people from packing homemade lasagnas, curries, and their own wok to make stir-fry.

Bunkers, Pits & Other Hazards

shot will often cause trouble, as will a close out-of-bounds line that comes into play off the tee. Tee-marker placement is critical, making certain that forced carries are not too long and alignment is well planned on tees. On confusing holes, pace can be improved by giving players signs with yardages, much the way a caddie would alert a player to a carry or other important feature.

2. *Water, water everywhere.* Water hazards do not delay play if banks are kept free from especially tall and dense grasses which can lead players to hunt for balls, rather than simply giving them up as unplayable. Relatively sharp drop-offs at the shoreline prevent "fishing" for balls, another delay factor. Drop areas can speed play.

3. *Bunkers.* Sand play can be the fastest shot around greens. The player knows what club is to be used—the sand wedge, typically—and the shot is played. Other shots around greens can lead to several options for club selection and potential indecision and, thus, a delay. Fairway bunkers can be used by designers as targets for the best line to the hole or to keep balls from running out-of-bounds or down a steep hill into heavy grass or underbrush. This helps the pace of play.

4. *Green speed.* Ultrafast greens (10 and higher) can cause play to slow for both amateur and championship play. This is not to say that greens should not be fast. It is simply a recommendation to know when and where to crank up the speed of the greens. After all, players "love" smooth fast greens. On the other hand, they can love slow greens, too. Green speeds should be kept in line with the traditions of the course.

Fig. 6-26 *A cartoon with the title: "The St. Andrews Bunker Chair, Designed to relieve golfers of the necessity of walking round bunkers." Drawn by Heath Robinson and appearing in* Golf Illustrated, *February 1924.*

When it comes to speed of play, two things come to mind regarding the architect's role. For one, players don't like or want to be tricked. Blind landing areas with heavy grasses or lakes that cannot be seen will not only slow play but may make players angry. Anything that can keep players from searching for balls will go a very long way to improving the pace of play and their appreciation of the design. Secondly, hazards—no matter whether they are water or sand—in and of themselves need not add undue time to play the hole. The golf architect simply needs to make sure the players can see them. Their ability to negotiate these hazards is precisely the point of the game.

Hazard Logistics & Routing

Hazards can align play to one side or the other. Placing a hazard on one side of a fairway may cause play to favor the opposite side. The opposite may also happen; a hazard may attract play toward it if the golfer contemplates taking a shorter, riskier route. Hazards can also affect otherwise efficient routing, especially when they cannot be accessed quickly and when recovery may take multiple shots by the average or below-average player. In planning hazards, the designer must consider the benefit of a hazard and its potential to undermine both a good time and good routing. Exciting and intriguing are good; guaranteed frustration and failure are bad.

It should be kept in mind that especially large hazards must be carefully weighed for their benefit, suitability, and efficiency. They can reduce maintenance costs if the space would otherwise be occupied by improved turf, but then there is the annual cost of maintaining the hazard itself. If a wetlands, perhaps it can live on its own with no care at all. But if it is a huge bunker to be raked, beware. Hazards can also preserve. Retaining natural areas is an excellent way to integrate golf with environmentally sensitive areas. Access must be appropriate; golf uses need to be true complements to the environment and not a detraction. One of the world's richest collections of wetlands resides within golf courses. Golf has been responsible for reclaiming wetlands, creating wetland habitats, and preserving wetlands.

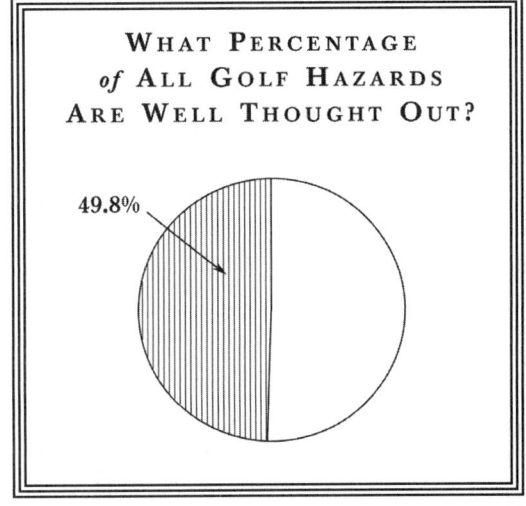

Fig. 6-27 Results of our survey showing the opinion that only half of all hazards in golf are well thought out.

Methods of Design

In the early stages, the golf architect goes about designing mostly with paper and pencil. This, of course, is after the site has been evaluated, studied, and contemplated in person. It is almost always the case that detailed surveys of the property and topographical data—contour lines—are taken along in the field so notes can be made and distances accurately measured. Aerial photos may be used. Armed with these rolled up reference materials, the designer identifies natural features that will become hazards. Ideas for other hazards are being jelled as well. Sketches might be made, in plan view or perspective view. Usually the golf course architect will take notes and wrinkled plans smeared with mud and swatted bugs back to the office, where more-precise evaluations can be made. Photos from the site are also common at this stage.

It is essential to appreciate that almost every golf course project will take shape—at least in broad vision—upon a plot of paper that contains the accurate lay of the land. The most common scale is 1 inch = 200 feet (in metric, usually 1:2500.) There is no substitute for this accurate mapping of a site. While many believe that good results may be obtained by pounding stakes wherever it might look good to set tees, fairways, hazards, and greens, this is not usually the case. Some type of measurement is needed. There is no better or more appropriate perspective than the single map that will tell you about the x, y, and z of a site. How much room is there? What is the exact elevation difference? The geometry of a site does not lie when it has been professionally surveyed.

Fig. 6-28 Thankfully, some natural features dictate routing. Boulders Golf Club, Arizona, Jay Morrish, golf course architect. (Courtesy of P. Burton)

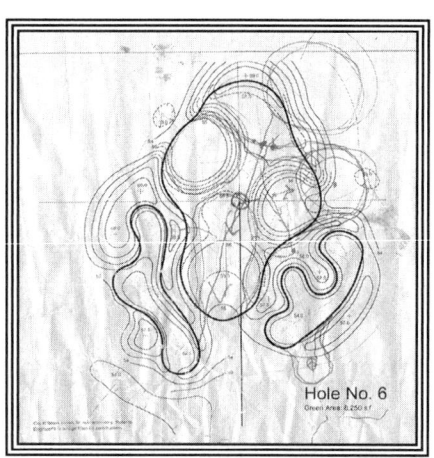

Fig. 6-29 Detail plan of a green and bunkers that has been marked up with notes drawn in the field. While plans form the basis for the design, there is no substitute for on-site visits by the golf course architect to meet with the shaping crew. In this case, the green was expanded to the right around the bunker, creating a lower area of the green that falls off to a hollow. The plan is of the No. 6 green at Buenaventura Golf Course, California.

A golf course architect learns about a site from being there and from studying plans of the site once he leaves it. A designer cannot take every ridge, drainageway, or valley in mind, photo, or notebook. This is what the survey (mapping) is for. It is invaluable in giving those responsible for the design a "model" of the site. It is sometimes difficult to explain how a flat piece of paper can be so useful. People who meet golf course architects are often interested in how they go about their task. Some may believe that somehow golf course architects can magically walk into thick brush and emerge with proven designs. Surely that approach has been taken, but it is not a standard.

There are exciting new tools at the disposal of the golf architect working today. Computer aided drafting (CAD) and global information systems (GIS) allow sophisticated surveys that combine all sorts of data into layers; not just

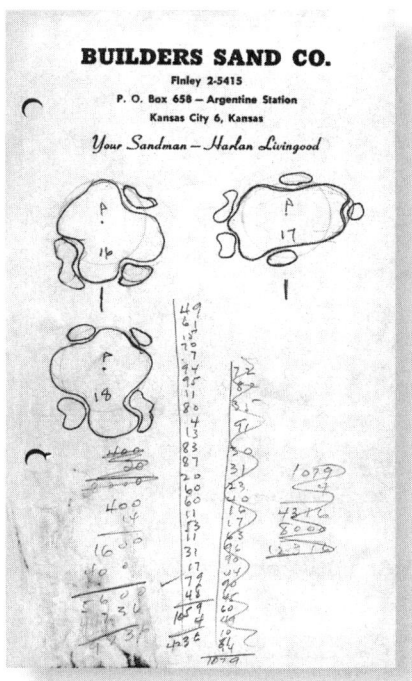

Fig. 6-30 A small sketch on notepaper by golf architect, Floyd Farley. During his career Farley would typically make small green sketches and then refine them onto larger pages when he had worked out bunkering and sizes. These greens are for an unidentified course.

Fig. 6-31 A design is only as good as the people in the field who will bring it to life. Here, the construction superintendent, shaper, and golf architect meet to review the intent of a golf hole being constructed among natural sand dunes at The Links at Las Palomas, Sonora, Mexico.

contour lines, but soil data, vegetation, precipitation, ground temperatures, slope analysis, drainage, ground water, and more. This data can also be manipulated to create terrain models of a site—very accurate perspectives of the lay of the land. Routing plans, hole layouts, hazards, features, and green concepts can eventually be integrated as a layer of their own. The result is a virtual tour of the design. Does this computing take the place of anything? A few things, yes. But as Ray Bradbury remarked once, "Put me in a room with a pad and a pencil and set me up against 100 people with 100 computers. I'll out-create everyone in the room."

The process involves field work, continually fine-tuning the vision and bringing the best to the surface. Once a course is under construction, the golf architect will not stop. The best designers will spend time on-site, send their assistants, and make sure the shaper doing the work is "one" with the vision. Occasionally, clubs and balls will be taken to the site so shots can be hit, even on bare ground. Hazards are always getting shifted for one reason or another, test-shot results being just one of them.

As a hazard is coming to life, the architect's design work goes beyond paper and plan. The golf architect is a sculptor; the canvas is three-dimensional. As details of shape, edging, and texture emerge, the golf architect must ensure that these are brought full-circle with the intent and concept of the design. Hazards are often the focus of the golf architect's work, whether of the formal or informal variety. Everything on a golf course is eventually planned, sketched, adjusted in the field, discussed, or hammered out by actually pushing soil and excavating on the spot.

The Character of Hazards

Hazards attain their character through many influences. It may be that the type of course will set the tone for the hazards. The type of play can influence how hazards are designed and worked into the strategy. We have seen courses that are nearly brands. In these cases, the hazards follow form—maybe the form of a particular architect, a region, or even a developer of courses who becomes known for a particular style. In the design of chain stores, we call this kind of style and "trade dress." The term is used to describe the articulation of a brand.

What do we call this character in golf? Do we dare say that an architect who decides to embrace a classic style, let's say, is following a fad or a trend? As much as we might

Fig. 6-32 Gil Hanse is among a handful of golf architects who take to machinery to actually bring their designs to fruition. This shot was taken at Boston Golf Club, Massachusetts, in 2004.

Fig. 6-33 The bunkers at Royal County Down, Ireland, are highly distinctive. The combination of the natural forms etched into the dunes, flowering grasses, and rugged edges set them apart. Here, one of your authors is doing some "field study" and has his hands full with a recovery shot.

want to avoid sticking any such label on a project, designer or course, it is often unavoidable. The best courses are originals. They may take their lead from courses that have come before, but they define their own sense of character, independent of any trend or fad. Sure, a hole may be Redan-ish or Cape-ish, but hopefully the course and its hazards have brought originality to the dance.

The Naming of Hazards

Here is a brief but entertaining list of hazards around the world that have been bestowed names:

Mrs. Simpson Bunker	The Coffins	Bruce's Billabong
Road Bunker	Himalayas	Swilcan Burn
Hell Bunker	The Scabs	Barry Burn
Strath Bunker	The Taft Bunker	Pow Burn
Cheape's	Church Pews	Wee Burn
The Beardies	Sahara Desert	Scoonie Burn
Cottage	The Kitchen	Rae's Creek
Purgatory	The Cardinal Bunker	The Maiden
The Devil's Asshole	Scotch & Soda	Old Man's Plateau
Hell's Half Acre	Eleanor's Teeth	Valley of Sin
Tip O'Neil Bunker	Gumbleys	
The Spectacles	Soup Bowl	

Naming should be reserved for special hazards. The hazards cited above have a soul, a heart of their own. They have become loved and hated, feared and conquered, and, as if that were not enough, people talk about them behind their backs. This may be the real test of whether a hazard is special: Is it so recognizable and at the forefront of golfers' minds that it needs no introduction? If so, it may need a name. There is, after all, a wonderful feeling that is passed on when we name holes, so why not hazards?

When the Arizona Biltmore Golf Club in Phoenix decided to restore their 1928 William P. "Billy" Bell design, the Adobe Course, a charity event kicked off the work. Club members and guests could sign up for a day-long gathering called "The Bunkered Weekend." Those attending would help probe the original bunker sand, work with the golf architects and shapers, and ultimately don shovels to help reconstruct the lost bunker buried under years of neglect and destructive mechanical raking. At the end of the marathon day, the 25 participants gathered for a celebration dinner, and the talk was all about the bunker they had brought back to life during the daylight hours. By evening's end it was given a name: *Scotch & Soda*. Forever more the left greenside bunker at the Adobe's 9th Hole will be known by this pet name, for this otherwise insignificant bunker, which had been lost under the sands of time, was now "back." What could be more fitting?

Memorability

It is often the hazards that golfers remember most when they reflect back on the design of a golf course. Many of the best golf holes offer at least one unique feature that makes it memorable. If there is nothing distinctive about a hole, it is likely to be forgotten. Poor and boring hazards are usually the cause.

Differentiation is critical to the success of almost any golf course. Every property needs to generate interest and attract golfers to come play there. Unique hazards do just that. An island green, a cavernous bunker, or a natural rock outcropping, although these have been done before, definitely are interesting. Hazards that offer striking natural beauty or significant challenge are but two simplistic ways of thinking of the marketing potential that a hazard can bring to a course. How many times have we all been bitten by a single photo of a golf hole? In nearly all of these cases, what has it been that has sparked our interest? A hazard, of course. As golfers we long to experience the thrill over and over again.

Fig. 6-34 Expressing what will be different or unique about a golf hole requires a combination of artistic talent and good communication skills. While hazards can be described and drawn in plan view, many people will find this difficult to visualize. In this rendering, artist Bruce Kimball captures the essence of a par-3 by focusing on the bottleneck opening to the green and the majestic view toward the mountain backdrop. Conceptual plan for the Phoenician Golf Club, Arizona, Forrest Richardson, golf course architect.

CHAPTER 7

Constructing Hazards

"Tell me then, who is the potter, pray, and who the pot?" questioned Omar Khayyam, the eleventh-century mathematician, scientist, astronomer, philosopher, and poet. A work of art that has been sculpted is special. We cannot separate the craft from the crafter, for each has evolved from the other.

As we take long looks across our golf courses, we rarely take time to consider that much of the view has been sculpted by someone other than nature. This thought is far down on our list of priorities. After all, there is a game to be played. Who has time for such thinking? But deep down in every golfer there is a realization that this is not all by accident, that the golf course—even one so naturally perfect—has been brought to life by the handiwork of individuals. That lone bunker, for example, has been discussed, cussed, adjusted, and contemplated on many occasions. While it is but one of several hazards and obstacles dotting the course, it has been given its personality through a remarkable combination of artists and influences.

The artist begins with a mission. This mission is made possible by an opportunity. In golf architecture, the opportunity is a site, a project, and an objective. The golf architect begins to sculpt the opportunity, but rarely alone. A shaper is brought in to do the heavy lifting. This shaper is joined by other shapers, tools, and equipment. Finally, influences such as weather, germination of grass, and age move into the picture. The mission is never completed, for it will outlive the artist, the shapers, and the tools. Our little bunker is a prime example of this. Here it sat in the 1600s, and here it sits today. It will never be finished, for it rides along with the game of golf and changes with time.

The Nature of Constructing Hazards

As we have touched on, the first hazards to be found on what would turn out to be the original playing fields for golf were created by animals seeking shelter from the prevailing winds along the sea. The sheep and goats would find areas on the leeward side of mounds and dunes and scrape away at the turf to expose the sand below. Over time, these areas would expand and develop into the first natural "bunkers." It is understandable that many architects state that "the most natural looking bunkers are those gouged out of the side of a hill or slope." In the same fashion, natural hollows and depressions were used by animals for resting places and became the pot bunkers that are common on the famous seaside links courses. This is a glimpse of the DNA of hazard construction. From this beginning, we now have progressed to the point where we rely on bulldozers instead of sheep. We thumb our noses at the wind—bunkers can now be built anywhere we need them. If we have no sand, we order it.

"Every golf course that has ever been built is a collaboration between the architect, his staff, the client, the superintendent, the engineers, the contractor, and last but not least, the property itself," says Tom Doak, one of the most influential golf course architects of our modern time. Doak's statement is worth a second read. It drives home the point that there is not one single person who creates the course or its hazards. While the golf architect is the conductor, the music still must be played by an orchestra.

There are various styles, opinions, methods, and approaches to constructing hazards. This chapter is meant to present the fundamental considerations in constructing hazards. Hazards are inherently different depending on where they reside. Specifications cannot be the same in Florida as in an arid region of Australia. Methods are nearly as unique as every individual golf course. This is because every site has slightly unique soils, conditions, and drainage requirements. Add to this the very common desire of the club and the golf architect to create something new—to be different than that other golf course—and you can see why there is no absolute standard.

Hazard construction may be looked at in terms of new construction, remodeling, restoring, and renovation. In this chapter, we will focus on the new construction of hazards, which is sure to have applications when one is making changes and improvements to existing hazards. A look at restoration is contained within Chapter 8, Maintenance & Restoration of Hazards.

Fig. 7-1 The best possible hazards are those which do not need to be constructed at all. For example, this tremendous setting at Tenby Golf Club in Wales has made for an interesting skyline green amongst natural rock outcroppings and rugged dunes escarpments. When natural features are present, they should be preserved at all cost. (Source: Golf Illustrated, April 1903)

Fig. 7-2 At Black Rock Golf Club in Idaho, Jim Engh made preservation of natural features a priority. The preservation of site features is the first step in construction.

Preservation of Natural Hazards

So who is it that takes responsibility for building golf hazards? It might be good to begin with the individual who selects the site upon which to build a golf course in the first place. The late Jack Neville, an acclaimed amateur player who routed and co-designed Pebble Beach with Douglas Grant, was not responsible for the selection of land upon which those magic golf holes still reside. "We simply were given a great piece of land to work with," he said to one of your authors in the 1970s. One can deduct that, besides Neville's use of the land, much of the credit for this celebrated course should go to Samuel Morse, a driving force in promoting the idea of Pebble Beach to his directors at Del Monte Properties.

Even before a pencil is laid to paper, and long before a mark is made on the ground, the formation of hazards begins. In the case of sites with natural features, it must begin very early. Only with vision and careful planning can natural features be preserved and put to good use. It would have been a crime if the Pacific Ocean at Pebble Beach were not used so thoughtfully. The routing of the holes, in the case of Pebble Beach, defines the ocean as a hazard. One cannot appreciate the hazards there without acknowledging the masterful routing and foresight of Neville and his client.

Fig. 7-3 Natural features on this Colorado property are identified by the golf course architect. For this project, special features such as these future bunkers were verified with GPS equipment and transferred to survey maps for use in routing and design.

The first step is to assess a site; to ask what it offers and find ways to integrate features as hazards. This is often a thankless task. The golf architect endures the elements, the thickets, stickers, bogs, and critters. On a site in Italy, golf architect Bill Amick was either chased by a porcupine or gave chase, the story is unclear. Regardless, during the chase Amick swallowed an airborne bug of unknown specimen. Amick's advice is "never to give up trying to save and preserve natural hazards, and also to go about your site work and always keep your mouth shut." No matter the trials and tribulations, the goal remains to identify and locate natural features, and ultimately to preserve them as hazards and challenges for the future golfer. It takes perseverance and creativity to accomplish this. Donald Ross wrote it best: "Man cannot do in a few days what nature took years to accomplish."

The Three Methods for Bunker Shaping

Not all sites, admittedly, have much in the way of natural features that will make good hazards. This is a reality of golf course development driven by several factors. Among them are a demand for golf in specific areas, integration of golf into housing communities, restrictive environmental hurdles, and the golf developer who is simply asleep at the wheel. To avoid a Boredom Links outcome, and to make the game interesting and fun, golf architects have begun creating features and hazards on otherwise lame sites. Even on sites with moderate interest, we have come to accept that augmentation is worth the effort. Bunker shaping is at the core of such augmentation. Except for the rare, completely natural bunker, bunkers are constructed features.

While there are hundreds of individual approaches to shaping a bunker, and certainly many hundreds of styles and looks that can be created, there are just three basic methods for beginning the process. (Refer to Fig. 7-4.)

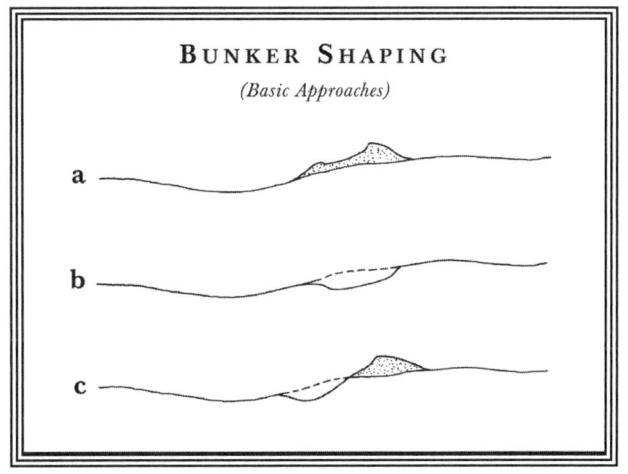

Fig. 7-4 The three primary methods of shaping a bunker are shown. (a) Material is brought in to create a landform. (b) Material is dug and hauled away, leaving a bunker or hollow behind. (c) Material is dug out and used in and around the area, balancing the material excavated and filled.

(a) *The Export Method.* An area is dug out to form the bunker, with material taken away to other areas. In essence, this is the quintessential pit that has been carved out. Most pot bunkers are built by this method. It results in a depression, while leaving the surrounding area alone. The residual material must be dealt with. It is often needed nearby for another purpose.

(b) *The Import Method.* Fill material is brought in and used to create a hillock or rise. A depressed area is left, and this becomes the bunker. Planning must ensure that there is ample material available to be brought in; if it is to be robbed from somewhere else, this must be part of the plan.

(c) *The Balance Method.* The bunker is formed by digging out the lower portion and using excavated material to create rises behind or around the resulting low areas. On sites with minimal earthmoving and areas that are to be left undisturbed, this method is preferred. All in all, it is the most efficient if the design can accept this localized approach of borrowing and exchanging material.

BUNKERS, PITS & OTHER HAZARDS

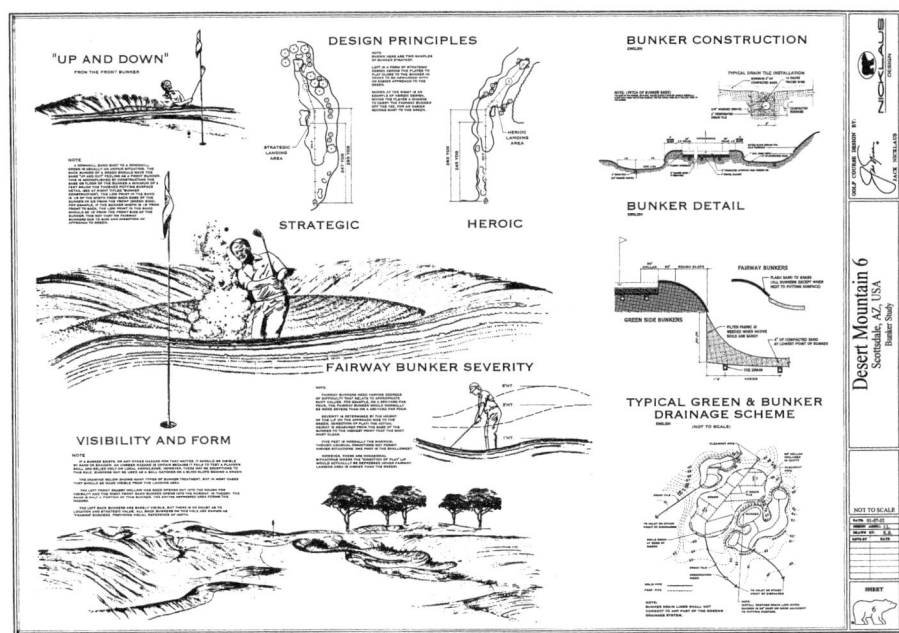

Fig. 7-5 Sheet for the plans for bunker style and construction for the Outlaw Course at Desert Mountain, Arizona. Jack Nicklaus, golf course architect. (© 2005 Nicklaus Design, Inc. All Rights Reserved)

Some may argue that there are other methods. Keep in mind that we have purposefully not listed the "found" bunker, that 100 percent natural depression or rivulet in the earth that is so perfect as it is that one must only touch it up slightly and then add a bit of sand. That example is not a method as much as it is a blessing. We also have not listed anomalies such as beach bunkers along lakes. For the purposes of simplification and clarity, any sand-filled or grassy bunker that is built is constructed by one of the three basic methods listed above.

A bunker, here, is defined as an area filled with sand that is usually a depression, although it may also comprise sand splashed onto a rise or bank. In the case of sand being used to replicate sand dunes and not really in defined depressions, we might use the term *dune bunker,* as such a hazard is mimicking a natural dune. Remember that the word *bunker* dates back very far in the Scots language. It can also mean a chest or a pile of sod on which a seat could be fashioned on the open land. In golf, however, a bunker is a pit, a sand trap, or a hollow, whether filled with sand or not. We qualify this by pointing out that the Rules of Golf define the bunker as only the area within the edges, but to the art of golf design the meaning is slightly less restrictive. The bunker is thought of as not only the sand-filled depression, but also the noses, capes, and bays that create its shape and shadows. Included are the bumps and forms that create these. When it is looked at from this angle, a bunker is the entire neighborhood of the bunker, whether you are in it or not.

In summary, our three methods of roughly shaping a bunker can be looked at from the viewpoint of convenience and efficiency. In an area where the terrain allows for the simple excavation and establishment of a bunker, method (*a*) works nicely. For a flatter area, or one where there may need to be a more prominent form, method (*b*) is called for. And where it makes sense to spread the excavated material nearby—and not hassle with bringing in or carting away soil—method (*c*) is an excellent choice. The method will be site-specific, and it will be a matter for the golf architect to determine. There will always be a preferred method, and a single hole may involve multiple methods.

The Sequence of Bunker Construction

When we build a bunker a sequence of events unfolds. It is not without variation, but it mostly follows these nine steps:

1. *Strategy Determination.* A routing plan will drive design, and this will eventually drive the location, shape, size, and style of the bunker. Such aspects as severity, recoverability, and intimidation should be in mind at this point. In a nutshell, at this stage the bunker is being brought to life by the golf architect, even though its design may still be fluid.

Fig. 7-6 In the field work with the shapers for a series of tiered bunkers, the golf course architect has used orange paint to mark the edges of the bunkers so the shaper can fine-tune work completed. (Refer to Fig. 7-25 for completed bunker.)

2. *Specifications.* A bunker should be appropriate for its locale. Drainage, soil types, and play intensity will all affect how it needs to be built. At some point in the development of the plans for the golf course, the specifications will be solidified and there will be more detailed plans or even renderings for the style of the bunker. The specifications and plans will spell out how the bunker is to be constructed. Ultimately, this will determine the quantity of materials, costs, and resources required. The golf architect thinks about this for each and every bunker, for it is a sure bet that the golf course contractor will do so.

3. *Field Verification.* Once a project is approved for construction,[1] it is customary that the location of the bunker be identified in the field, as are all of the other features: tees, clearing limits, greens, and so on. This may be done with wooden lath stakes, small flags, or outlines painted on the ground by the golf architect or his representative. Reference points are taken from plans and located on the ground. Occasionally, this is accomplished with GPS survey equipment. In the case of a mass graded site, the process of actually marking the bunker

---

[1] The process of attaining approval is often very complicated. Apologies are in order here for those reading who are in the midst of an approval process at any stage of a project. Certainly, we are aware that the sentence written makes it sound painfully simple when it is, in fact, usually not.

Fig. 7-7 As bunkers are finished, edging and raking is typically performed by hand. This photo shows a finished bunker in the foreground with drainage installed. The area to the back is being filled with sand.

may wait until earthwork (grading) is complete, at least to a point at which the location of the bunker can be better defined. Regardless, a certain level of field verification is always done before equipment begins to transform a golf hole. (When a golf hole is built, it is common for the centerline of the hole to be established by bulldozers once the tee, angle point[s], and green are staked. This allows the golf course architect to walk the hole and fine-tune the limits of clearing, decide which trees and vegetation might remain, and adjust the locations of features and hazards that have been designed into the hole.)

4. *Clearing and Grubbing.* The bunker work cannot continue on a wooded or covered site until the area to be worked has been cleared and grubbed. Clearing is the removal of vegetation and debris from the surface. Grubbing is the removal of roots and stones from a defined area below the surface. This defined area will vary depending on the soils and preferences. In some cases, of course, there may be no need to clear or grub—the natural land might fit perfectly to the golf hole.

5. *Rough Shaping.* By this time, the golf architect has been joined by plenty of assistants. A shaper has been entrusted to transform the lay of the land. This may be an enhancement of what was already there, or it may be something created by drawing contour lines and assigning target elevations for the heights of landforms, mounds, and low areas. However it is communicated to the shaper, the area of the bunker and the bunker itself have now come to life. If we assume that the bunker described here is a depression with a slightly raised back, then we can envision a useful trick described by Robert Trent Jones, Jr. in his book *Golf by Design:* "Sometimes we place white bed sheets in the bunkers to test their visual qualities." Jones is referring to

Fig. 7-8 A common method of stabilizing edges is to install plywood to form a barrier against edges. The plywood is kept in place until well after the bunker is finished and turf has rooted to hold soils together around the edges.

how the bunker reads from the tee or origin of the various shots that might be played around, over, or into it. Jones's tip has been passed down by generations of golf architects, and it works rather well. The key at this stage is approval of the bunker. The balance of work to be done should not be contemplated until the basic formation, relationships of grades, and general shape is accepted by the golf architect. Visibility is often a priority.

6. *Drainage and Irrigation.* The plumbing is next in our sequence. Drainage is installed by a variety of means, with the sole purpose of removing water from the bunker. The most prevalent source of water intrusion in bunkers are irrigation sprinklers and, of course, rainfall. Irrigation is installed around the bunker wherever turfgrass is to be established. Ideally, it is diverted away from the bunker as much as possible. This infrastructure (the drainage and irrigation) is often destructive to the progress that has been made in forming and shaping the bunker. Although it does not sit well with irrigation workers, a favorite term for irrigation trenching, pipe laying, and equipment traversing is the *irritation phase*.

Fig. 7-9 A typical method of sand placement is to form a dam with the perimeter of the sand. This forms a low area where silts and contaminants are collected and isolated from the sand. Silts can be easily shoveled out once the grow-in or turf around the bunker is complete.

7. *Finishing, Edging, and Stabilization.* After the plumbing is installed, it is up to the finish shaper to restore the desired shaping and finalize the bunker (that is, to "finish" the bunker). In many cases, this is done by hand with crews working to trim edges, build noses and intricate shapes, and rake areas to the subsurface that will form the floor of the bunker below the sand. In terms of stabilization, the bottom and slopes of our bunker may need to be held in place by any number of means; extra compaction or special fabrics and spray-applied coatings. These efforts can help prevent sloughing of soils and erosion. Fabrics and coatings can also help reduce sand erosion on steeper slopes by forming a base on which sand is more apt to stay put.

8. *Sand Placement.* After everything is finished and approved, it is time to place the sand. There are different ways to accomplish this. The most common method is to place the sand in a pile within the bunker, protecting it from the edges, where silt may intrude into the depressed area during the establishment of grass in the surrounding area. Very often, the pile of sand will be covered to keep it free from dust, which may be present across the construction site.

Bunkers, Pits & Other Hazards

9. *Final Edging*. The detail work of establishing the edge of the bunker is completed. It may have been done even prior to Step 8, but on occasion there will be more detail work to be performed. Sod or native grasses might be laid by hand around the edges or in back of the bunker. The tie-in of fairway and rough areas may still need to be raked and floated up to the edge of the bunker.

Fig. 7-10 Sod is laid around a newly constructed bunker to keep the shape intact while turf is grown in after finish shaping is complete. (Courtesy of S. Witcombe)

Equipment for Bunker Construction

There are no hard and fast rules on what type or class of equipment is used to build bunkers. There are as many ways to build a bunker as there are bunkers. On the whole, golf architects are a creative bunch, and they are continually coming up with new ideas that are bound to involve new construction approaches.

In the light-duty category, a small bunker can be created by a small excavator with a backhoe bucket. An excavator is a track-driven machine. For bunkers, the best arm is not only able to reach, but also turn at angles. This small machine is ideal for its maneuverability and agility. A skilled operator can dig a bunker in hours, creating terrific shapes and intricate edge detail.

On flatter sites where mass amounts of dirt must be moved, bulldozers usually shape landforms and can shape bunkers. Again, a skilled operator using a small bulldozer[2] can form a bunker quite well. The equipment is only as good as the shaper. Make sure that your shaper has the equipment he or she is most comfortable using.

Bunkers are also built using common backhoes or loaders. Generally, these are rubber-tired machines with backhoe buckets or larger loader-type buckets. The loader bucket end may be used to excavate a bunker in its rough stage, while the backhoe bucket may be used to create the detail and smaller areas of bunkers.

Compaction is an important aspect of bunker construction. Adequate compaction will result in a bunker that is stable and less likely to erode or collapse over time. When soil is moved, it becomes loose compared to its natural state before being disturbed. The most essential ingredient for reestablishing a compacted state is water. During construction, water must be applied to the ground as soils are moved and shaped. The weight of equipment and the added water will usually recompact soils adequately.

---

[2] Bulldozers are commonly sized using the models manufactured by Caterpillar, Inc., which begin with the small D3 and continue up to an impressive D11. Golf course construction typically utilizes D8s or smaller, favoring machines that are easily maneuvered. A bulldozer used for bunker construction is usually a D5 or smaller machine.

CHAPTER 7 | CONSTRUCTING HAZARDS

Fig. 7-11 Small bunkers with intricate or steep edges are usually built with small excavators. These steep-faced bunkers at Doonbeg Golf Club in Ireland were dug with this method. Sod walls were then formed to finish the edges (see color insert). (Courtesy of Doonbeg Golf Club © 2004)

Water is applied from water trucks or by hand watering from hoses or tanks. Occasionally, soils will be naturally moist; too much saturation will make shaping eminently more laborious.

The floor and edges of bunkers will often require even greater compaction. After stones and debris are raked away, the shaper and designer achieve the desired subgrade. The subgrade is the bare ground that will form the bunker before sand is installed and turf established. Additional compaction, when necessary, is achieved by hand-operated vibrating compactors or hand tampers. A hand tamper is an extremely heavy, flat-bottomed tool at the end of a long handle. The user mashes the soil by thrusting the flat end at the edges and surrounds of a bunker, usually concentrating on noses and other features that have been formed from loose soil. Trust us, it is hard work.

Of course, shovels, spades, and rakes are used in shaping bunkers. For edges, a floor scraper (a long-handled tool with a straight, flat blade) is often used. The process of trimming, shaping, and raking is always completed by hand. Even during this process water is applied to help bond the soil and attain stabilization. The golf course architect will typically paint or mark the edges of the bunker before this work. Hand crews can appear like ants during this process, shifting little bits of soil from here to there, eventually bringing a work of art to fruition. Slowly, the area begins to look like someone's idea of a bunker.

Bunker Drainage

Making sure a bunker drains after a rain or daily irrigation is necessary when building golf courses where soils do not drain as well as they do upon the natural sand-based ground of links courses. Even on sand-based linksland, the silting of the top layer of a bunker floor can lead to clogged conditions that will turn the bunker into a pond. Unfortunately, golf in the twenty-first century is more and more a matter of trying to attain "perfection." How could we possibly allow standing water—in any amount—to remain in a bunker? The Rules of Golf have this covered quite well: casual water in a bunker entitles the golfer to relief without penalty. This is a far cry from the "play it as it lies" spirit of early golf. A hazard then was truly a hazard, be it wet, muddy, or strewn with rocks. "Watery filth" was a hazard.[3] Nowadays each of these conditions is apologized for, and the golfer gets a stay of execution.

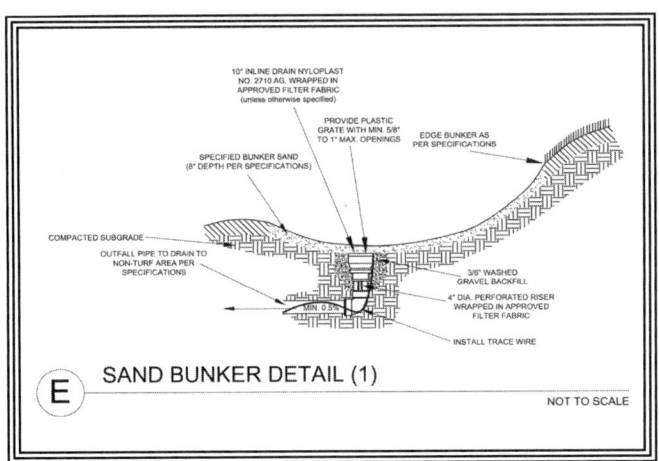

Fig. 7-12 Detail section from a set of construction plans. The information to be communicated must cover compaction requirements of the soil, edge details, depth of sand, drainage, and outfall pipe criteria.

Jeremy Pern, an English golf course architect based in France, writes, "To golfers, the aesthetics of design and the playing characteristics of a golf course are subjective, where as construction details remain more of an objective science. Water will always flow downhill just as grass always needs food, water and air. The science of golf course architecture resides in finding solutions to technical problems related to geology, agronomy, botany, civil engineering and the physics of the game itself." Pern could not have said it better. The golfer owes it to the game to appreciate the science of our courses. Water does run downhill, and that fact is never more important than when we are constructing a green, a fairway, a bunker, or any other hazard.

As we have noted, the first step to bunker drainage is to prevent water from entering the bunker in the first place. The late Arthur Jack Snyder, who began his design career as a superintendent and then went on to design more than 50 golf courses, created a pleasant little 9-hole course near Phoenix in the early 1960s. A golf professional got involved with the developer and eventually began *re*directing the shaping work at the greens and greenside bunkers. Snyder became discouraged and walked off the site, letting the developer know that he could not go along with the golf pro's advice. Snyder pointed out that many of the greens, which his shaper had shaped very well, were now sloping

---

[3] *Watery filth* is a term taken from the earliest surviving written Rules of Golf, compiled by the Gentlemen Golfers of Leith, later the Honourable Company of Edinburgh Golfers, drafted on 7th March 1744. It is contained within Rule 5, "If your Ball comes among watter, or any wattery filth, you are at liberty to take out your Ball & bringing it behind the hazard and Teeing it, you may play it with any Club and allow your Adversary a Stroke for so getting out your Ball." In other words, you play it as it lies or lose a stroke in exchange for removing your ball.

into bunkers.[4] What was more, areas surrounding bunkers were no longer draining away from the bunker edges, but were actually diverting runoff from the area around greens into the bunkers. Aside from its routing, which is very clever, this otherwise pleasant course has ever since been plagued by drainage problems around the bunkers and greens. Snyder was happy to disclaim the course as his own design.

The second step to draining a bunker is forming the floor so that any water collected inside the bunker—a likelihood even when care is taken to prevent it—will be collected toward a single point, or a few points if the bunker is very large. As long as these two general rules are adhered to, the bunker can be drained.

There are three basic methods of draining a bunker. They are:

1. *Naturally Draining*. Occasionally native soils, usually sand, will permit adequate drainage downward without any artificial drainage. Nearly all of the bunkers on linksland courses are drained in this way. No heroic measures are taken except the basics of keeping a large flood of water from entering the bunker after a rain. One can imagine that a regular occurrence of flooding would begin to deposit silts and clippings in the bunker, and this would clog the permeable material below the sand layer of the bunker. On most courses located on land that is not linksland, this method is only a terrific dream that gets interrupted by the realities of every soil type other than 100 percent pure sand.

2. *Sump Drains*. A sump is a hole drilled or dug into the ground that ideally reaches a depth where a suitable—again, permeable—layer of natural soil is evident. This suitable layer is often gravelly, sandy, or even rocky in makeup. The sump itself, perhaps 18 inches in diameter if drilled with an auger, is filled with gravel and begins its duty of transmitting water downward from the floor of the bunker. A small bunker may be equipped with a single sump; a large bunker may have several. If the floor of the bunker is formed of compacted soils that are stable enough, water

Fig. 7-13 Drainage lines being installed in a bunker. These lines consist of a 4" diameter perforated pipe in an 8" x 8" trench. The trench is backfilled with pea-sized gravel. Water seeping down to the low points (valleys) will enter the trench and migrate into the perforated pipe. In this particular bunker, the trenches terminate to a common drain point. From the common drain point, non-perforated pipe carries water to a master drainage system that serves the entire golf course. (Courtesy of E. Easley)

---

[4] Anyone familiar with Snyder will know that, in his words, the term *bunker* would never have been used. *Sand trap* was the correct word in the dialect of the golfer born in western Pennsylvania. In a film tribute to Snyder produced in 2005, a clip is included where he laments, "I call them sand traps and always will. That's what they were known as in western Pennsylvania, and I have a running feud with the USGA over this."

moving downward through the layer of bunker sand will reach the floor and make its way to the sump(s). If the soils are less than ideal, it may be necessary to install drainage trenches with gravel and/or perforated pipe, which will eliminate the need for water to find its own way to the sump. The trenches, in this case, are laid out in a pattern that follows the low valleys of the bunker. The perforated pipe allows water to seep into it from the gravel trench and be taken to the low point where it finds the sump waiting to complete the job. There are even variations of trenching and pipe. In some cases, a main trunk line will not be perforated, whereas the shorter trenches and pipe will be.

Fig. 7-14 A bunker foreman puts the finishing touches on a special type of drain called a "Horizontal Drain Box." This drain works like an air filter with filtration fabric inserts that prevent silts from entering the drainage system through the bunker sand. The "box" can be cleaned out periodically to remove silt and contaminants such as clippings. (Courtesy of E. Easley)

3. *Carry-away Trenches and Pipe.* Bunkers may be drained with a network of trenches and pipe that carries water to low points, where it intersects with other pipe and is eventually carried out underground to areas of the course such as ponds, wetlands, or out-of-play areas.

It may also connect to a master drainage system that may move water by gravity to drainage ways located entirely off property. There are many variations of the "carry-away" method. Typically, trenches and perforated pipe follow the low valleys, where they terminate to a catchment drain; a main trunk-line may not be perforated. The trenches and pipe allow water to drain to the catchment drain location(s) where the pipe will change to smooth-walled (nonperforated) pipe and no longer be surrounded by gravel. At this point, the drainage system becomes its own small sewer utility. The goal from here is simply to find a place for the water to go.

You will see other drainage-oriented measures, devices, and designs. Some may seem like snake oil, for in the quest to make sure our bunkers are drained properly there is no shortage of ideas and patents being developed. A few deserve mention here for their merit and proven track record.

Certainly the flush-out is a common practice. This amounts to a continuation of the drain pipes within the bunker to a higher edge of the bunker, where the pipe is fitted with a 90-degree elbow and trimmed flush with the sod around it. Periodically, water can be forced into the flush-out to clean silt and debris from the pipe, keeping it running clear to handle day-to-day drainage.

A top-edge drain line may be installed, with the intent of catching as much water at the upper edges of bunkers as possible. This is thought to reduce erosion by handling water before it destroys the higher levels of steeper banks.

An oversized catchment "box" may be installed at the low point of the bunker. One such device, the Horizontal Drain Box, is a plastic tray measuring 1 by 4 feet and is just over 1 foot in depth. Two grates rest on top of the tray. The lower grate is inserted into a fabric envelope that traps silt and prevents sand from entering the tray. Water is able to pass through. The idea of this design is much like an air filter—the small silts and particles are trapped before they enter and disrupt the drainage system at the low point of the bunker.

Our last example is an inventive pipe system called EZ-Flow. Imagine a 4-inch diameter perforated plastic pipe surrounded by a 10-inch diameter layer of Styrofoam "peanuts" similar to those common in packing and shipping. The Styrofoam is held in place with netting, allowing 20-foot lengths of the pipe and Styrofoam to be handled with ease by a single worker. The benefit is in not having to transport heavy gravel across courses to bunker locations. And the tedious process of backfilling perforated pipe in trenches is eliminated by simply dropping the lengths into the trenches and covering them with suitable barrier fabric that will prevent sand from getting into the pipe and its foam-based surround.

Sand-Bunker Stabilization

There are a host of products on the golf market for stabilizing the slopes of sand bunkers. These range from fabrics, blankets, and netting to applied materials such as sprays and coatings. We shall not attempt to list any brand names here, as they are sure to be replaced by the latest-and greatest "new" products by the time you get to reading this chapter.

Fig. 7-15 Bunker fabric may be installed to help stabilize sand on steeper slopes or to form a barrier between the sand and the soils under the bunker floor. In this example, fabrics (sometimes called blankets) are placed along the slopes to help hold the sand layer in place. (Courtesy of P. Burton)

Besides compaction, which we have covered already, the most obvious strategy for stabilization is simply not to attempt to construct bunkers with steeper slopes than can be reasonably held in place given the conditions of a particular course. These conditions include rain frequency and intensity, wind, soil and sand types, and the wear and tear exerted by golfers. Steep banks can be kept in check when there are few golfers using a course and when there is more than adequate maintenance staff to rake and repair deteriorating banks. You can deduce that there are courses where conditions make slope stabilization difficult. Yet it seems commonplace for bunkers to get built under such adverse conditions. Despite all of the measures one might inject into a design, gravity rules—always. Sand particles are heavier than air, they will migrate downhill unless conditions are right, and someone must rake the sand back onto the slopes every so often.

You *can* force a square peg into a round hole. The problem is that this takes its toll on the peg, not to mention the poor chap doing the hammering. It's simply not natural. One rationale for having steep slopes to bunkers is visibility—so we can see the bunker, or at least the back upward slope of it. Another rationale is difficulty. Perhaps the style of the course is to have steep banks. Maybe this is intended to make the bunker more difficult and challenging—to send the message *"Avoid this bunker!"* No matter why a bunker slope is steep, an effort will be required when this steepness exceeds what the environment and other conditions can accommodate. It is surprising to us that more prototype bunkers are not built in the months before a golf course construction project begins. What a worth-while investment it is to construct a bunker, even if it is to be removed later on, enabling a test of several conditions, styles, and approaches to construction.

Fig. 7-16   A sod-walled bunker at Doonbeg Golf Club, Ireland.

The Bunker Wall

A bunker may also be fortified by nearly vertical walls. Layers of sod have been used for this purpose for ages, most notably on the older courses of England and Scotland. Stacked sod needs no further explanation other than that it is strips of sod layered on top of one another. This "wall" is then backfilled with soil, and—voila—the

Fig. 7-17   To construct a sod wall, sod is layered in stacks at the desired angle. Once the height is set, soil is backfilled and the other edges raked and finished. (Courtesy of P. Burton)

CHAPTER 7 | CONSTRUCTING HAZARDS

Fig. 7-18 Progression of a sod wall bunker after soil has been backfilled. (Courtesy of P. Burton)

bunker looks like the Road Hole Bunker (page 49), one of the most famous in all of golf.

Sod may also be installed traditionally and pinned to a steep bank or edge. At Fox Chapel Golf Club in Pennsylvania, a Seth Raynor design, many of the edges of bunkers are way too steep to traverse. Some are more than 10 feet in height. It is a wonder that grass can even grow at this angle, or that the banks can be maintained. But they are, and Fox Chapel sports an incredible look that we are certain Raynor would be pleased to see preserved.

Wooden railroad ties (sleepers) and timbers have also been used to form walls of bunkers. Pete Dye was among the first of the modern-age architects to use this treatment, at least on a widespread basis. The use of sleepers, bulkheads, and sod walls was rampant in Dye's work, especially in the 1970s and 1980s. According to Dye, it was on a trip to Scotland during 1963 that he discovered railroad ties and their historic relationship to bunkers.

Fig. 7-19 The formation of steep banks, such as this bunker at Fox Chapel Golf Club in Pennsylvania, are sometimes as difficult to build as they are to maintain. It is sometimes necessary to retain soils by initially installing sleeper walls and then pinning sod to the walls while root growth is established. Openings in the walls, which can be made of wood or heavy geo-grid panels, allow for turf to root into soils behind the wall.

Sand-Bunker Edges

The edges of bunkers were historically ragged and anything but crisp and precise. Even the sod-walled banks were left ragged. There was no maintenance to speak of before the 1900s. Aside from the occasional rehabilitation of a bunker, it is doubtful that anyone much cared whether it was tidy or not.

Today there has been a return to a more ragged look. Whether this is a passing fad we will not know for many years. If golf is ever to be grounded in its past, however, then this should be seen as a definite pilgrimage back to the core value of golf and hazards. After decades of nail-clipper precision on the entire golf course, the game is beginning to enjoy a more natural look and feel. There is certainly no better place to start than within a bunker, for it is here that we mean to provide a hazard—*why not allow it to look the part as well?*

A common construction technique for creating natural edges is to leave them ragged and rough, with ample compaction where called for, and then to seed the edges and areas surrounding. This might be done by hydroseeding[5] with native grasses, fescues, and so on. After a period of growth that allows the seed to take hold, crews go in and reshape the edges, removing stray grass from within the bunker and then tweaking the edges for the right degree of randomness and ruggedness. This is just one technique. At Sutton Bay Golf Club in South Dakota, a design by Graham Marsh, an innovative solution was devised. Well-known course builder Bill Kubly used a mechanical tree spade to plunk large chunks of native plants and grasses out of areas along the course and plopped these along the edges of bunkers to create "instant" rugged bunker edges— already planted and growing. "It was not only extremely efficient, but it was fun," reports Kubly, who oversaw much of this work himself.

Of course, we have dwelled on the rugged edge, but this is not our only choice. We can venture to the walled edge, as previously discussed, or we can choose from a variety of other edge treatments. We can also combine these looks, depending on the desired result. At Riviera, the bunker grass is allowed and trained to grow over the 8- to

Fig. 7-20 Railroad ties (sleepers) can be used in a variety of ways. At this bunker, the ties are laid back at a gradual slope and spaced apart. Coldwater Golf Club in Arizona, Forrest Richardson, golf course architect.

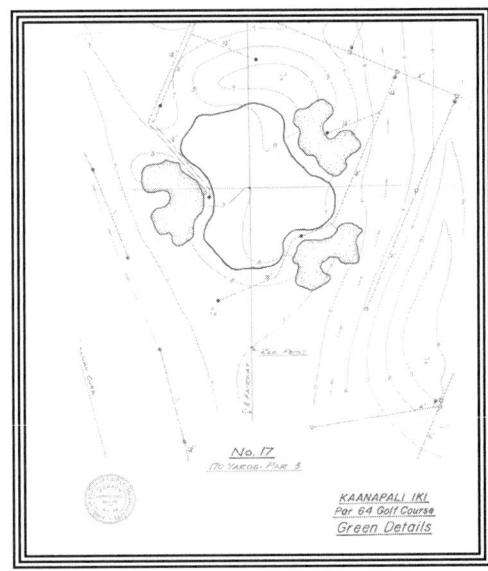

Fig. 7-21 Plan for a green and bunkers. The "lacey" and unsmooth edge is a design trend that has come and gone, and come again. This plan was prepared by Arthur Jack Snyder for Kaanapali Golf Course on Maui, Hawaii.

---

[5] Hydroseeding is the process of mixing seed with mulch, water, fiber (wood pulp and even old newspaper), and tackifiers. The result is a slurry that sticks quite well, even to steep slopes.

CHAPTER 7 | CONSTRUCTING HAZARDS

Fig. 7-22 Example of a rough and random bunker edge on a bunker that blends into natural dunes areas. Pacific Dunes Course at Bandon Dunes, Oregon, Tom Doak, golf course architect. (Courtesy of P. Burton)

12-inch bunker edges (sometimes referred to as "lips"). Another method is to maintain the lip of the bunker without turf. In this case, the soil beneath the surrounding turf is exposed above the sand around the edge of the bunker. Adequate compaction in this case is essential for obvious reasons. There is also the method of having virtually no lip. The level of the finished sand in the bunker comes up to the surrounding turf in this case.

Grass selection for bunker edges and surrounds is an important decision that can easily be overlooked. In most cases, the golf architect will specify a certain grass for either the intended look or for a particular objective. Whatever the reason, the following questions should be asked when determining grass type for your bunker surrounds:

1. Is the grass native to your area and climate?
2. Will the grass require irrigation to thrive?
3. Does it handle traffic well?
4. How will it affect playability (pace of play, golfer expectation, wear and tear)?
5. Will sand accumulation affect its growth habit?
6. Does it fit the architect's design philosophy?
7. What does the grass require for maintenance?

Fig. 7-23 At Bel-Air Golf Club, California, bunker edges are kept thick and hairy, forming a vertical edge of grass. (Courtesy of P. Burton)

Once the proper grass is selected, the question that usually remains is: Do we seed or sod the bunker surrounds? Though there is higher up-front expense, the benefits from sodding the bunker surrounds far out weigh the expense. Depending on the grass species, sod can reduce establishment time up to 80 percent.

195

When designing bunker edges, it is a good idea to consider the need for steps or stairs on occasion. There is nothing so frustrating as a bunker that the golfer cannot extricate himself from without losing composure. Thankfully, the Taft Bunker at Myopia Hunt Club near Boston is equipped with a seven-step stair/ladder which provides access as well as a means of escape, at least for the golfer. This 8-foot-deep cross-bunker was made incrementally deeper by member-turned-designer Herbert Leeds, who had a running battle with then U.S. President William Taft. Each time Taft, who was a very big man, would get into the bunker, Leeds was said to have deepened it ever so slightly in the following days. Caddies were seen on occasion with ropes hoisting the exceedingly large president out of the bunker.

Fig. 7-24 The famous Taft Bunker at Myopia Hunt Club, Massachusetts. The stairway has been installed since the days when U.S. President Taft had trouble extricating himself from the bunker after hitting his shot. The Secret Service was said to have used ropes to hoist Taft up and out of the bunker on many occasions.

Bunker Sand

The variables of (new) bunker sand are particle size, particle shape, particle composition (hardness), color, initial compaction, and finished depth within the bunker. In terms of playability, these are the primary considerations before pollutants (dust, silt, etc.) and dampness might intrude on the bunker. Another consideration is how well the sand will crust and how fast it will percolate water to the floor of the bunker, where our tidy drainage system has been installed. Color is more a personal preference, although it comes into play in making bunkers contrast more or less to their surroundings. And as anyone playing golf along the equator at noon will tell you, bright white sand in a dish-shaped bunker can act like an oven, quickly baking the legs of any golfer wearing shorts.

Although it remains an efficient "Scottish" philosophy, the idea of getting bunker sand from the closest source is not always followed. In modern course construction it is customary to find sand being trucked in from miles away to obtain just the "right" consistency or color. This can often be an expensive proposition. Several courses have had thousands of tons of beach-white silica sand delivered by flatbed truck, in convenient 100-lb. sacks as if ready to mix into cement.

One should make sure that sand used in bunkers will not adversely affect greens. In fact, there is good reason to use the same sand in bunkers as that used to construct the greens. As many bunkers are of the greenside variety, significant quantities of sand reach the greens through the act of hitting sand wedges from bunkers. As sand accumulates on greens, it works its way down and mixes with the sand that was used to form the green as well as the sand used to topdress it. Of course, it is not always possible to use the same sand in both greens and bunkers. Some greens (especially old greens) are built on native soils, and the only sand in their profile is that which has been added to the top. In addition, the sand used on greens is not always ideal for bunker use due to the playing conditions sought by golfers.

In general, the particle size, shape, and composition of bunker sand should work together to form a well compacted surface that will allow a flying golf ball to dent it, but ideally not embed to the point of the dreaded "fried egg" lie. This is primarily dependent on the particle shape of the sand and the peak height and descent angle of the approaching golf ball. The playability of a bunker will be affected by all of these considerations, including the depth of sand installed and maintained in the bunker and the wetness of the sand. The use of a sand penetrometer can determine the likelihood of having a fried egg lie in a sand trap. A penetrometer is pressed down onto a golf ball with a line drawn around its equator until the ball reaches the line. The result is measured in a pressure reading of kilograms per square centimeter (kg/cm^2). A reading of anything less than 2.2 kg/cm^2 will produce a moderate or more likely chance of getting a fried-egg condition. Generally, unless you want your bunkers very tough, a higher reading is advised.

Sand particles between 0.25 and 1 millimeter are recommended for bunkers. Larger sands can be too gravel-like, while smaller particle sizes will tend to form continual crusts. Smaller sizes will also silt up more quickly and not drain as well.

The angular quality of sand particles can have a great influence on compaction and the ability of the sand to stay put on slopes. Angularity will also greatly affect the reading of the sand penetrometer. Rounded sand particles will tend to displace and act as ball bearings. Angular particles will interlock and remain less mobile as gravity or other influences affect the sand. However, too much angularity is likely to produce

Fig. 7-25 Bunker sand is held in place naturally by the angularity of the sand particles. At these steep-faced bunkers at Phantom Horse Golf Club, Arizona, special coatings were sprayed on the bunker floor that assisted in stabilizing the soils and giving the sand a better subsurface (see color insert). Forrest Richardson, golf course architect. (Photo Courtesy of Destination Resorts)

extremely firm bunkers. Fortunately, most sands consist of a mixture of particle shapes and sizes. Angularity is ascertained by examining particles under a microscope, which can be done by a testing lab.

The composition of individual sand particles affects hardness. Calcareous sand particles will deteriorate with weathering and will break down. This is because they are high in calcium carbonate and not harder elements. Bunker sand is subject to wear. Even raking causes sand to break down. Crusting of the top layer of sand in a bunker will be related to the percentage of silt and clay in the sand. As silt and clay increase, the crusting increases. Laboratories have developed a crusting test for bunker sand that is a bit like a fourth-grade science experiment. It involves wetting the sand, waiting overnight, and then using a spatula to try to remove a layer of crust.

Initial compaction is necessary to settle the sand and make it firm from opening day. The depth of sand will also have an effect on the general quality of a bunker. Too little sand can cause soil areas to be exposed. Too much sand can cause fluffy lies. It is probably never possible to please everyone. In an attempt to do so, golf architects sometimes call for less sand on upward slopes (faces) of bunkers and slightly more depth on flatter floors. It has also been specified that greenside bunkers receive more sand by depth than fairway bunkers. As you can see, there is almost no end to the variables that one can consider with the simplest of materials—sand.

Fig. 7-26 This wetlands water feature was formed by damming a small creek in front of a green. Natural stone was stacked to form a retaining wall at the leading edge of the green. The Hideout Golf Club, Utah. Forrest Richardson and Arthur Jack Snyder, golf course architects.

Artificial Lakes & Ponds

Since we do not construct natural water courses, we shall not cover them beyond mentioning how important they are to the game of golf. We should preserve and integrate them where possible and practical. Anyone who stands up as a purist and says that the true golf course is devoid of water features has not experienced the swirling winds above the High Hole at St. Andrews, with the beach of the River Eden lurking just behind the green. If that is not the most natural of all water hazards, then what, pray tell, is it?

The nonstrategic reasons for constructing an artificial water hazard include storing water, accommodating drainage, and creating an aesthetic. Each may be essential to the design of a golf course. Some water hazards serve all three purposes.

Fig. 7-27 Shorelines can take many forms. This stacked stone wall at Headwaters Golf Club, Idaho, creates a formal hazard line, which makes the carry to the target "all or nothing" in nature. (Courtesy of Alliance Golf)

A water hazard that begins its life for the purposes of storing water is referred to as a *reservoir*. Water for irrigation, especially in arid climates, may need to be stored so it can accumulate from its source and then be available quickly to be pumped to all areas of the golf course, usually during the night. Another reason for reservoirs is to store *effluent*, a nice name for the water produced after treating sewage. Often, it is a requirement that a golf course accept millions of gallons of effluent water per day because the golf course is a tremendously convenient place to use this reclaimed water and discharge it back into the ground, where it eventually replenishes water that has been pumped for agricultural and other uses.

Constructed bodies of water are able to accept drainage from areas off of the golf course as well as areas within it. One of the best uses of a pond, lagoon, or lake is to serve as a basin into which other areas of the golf course get drained. The surface of the water hazard is typically regulated by some sort of spillway that prevents the water from rising too high. In many cases, the water hazard has what is called a *retention capacity*. This is the capacity above the normal water level within which flood waters and excessive drainage can be temporarily stored until it is carried away, evaporates, or is otherwise depleted.

Aesthetic reasons for creating a water hazard may have to do with any variety of considerations. Golf designer Ted Robinson, Sr. authored a very convincing paper many years ago about the value of aesthetic water features on golf courses in residential communities. His conclusion was that residential lot values looking out upon artificial lakes, waterfalls, and streams were very high, even compared to golf fronting lots without any views of water. Such aesthetic value should not be relegated to residential communities alone. Surely one would find that Augusta National's Rae's Creek is just as aesthetically pleasing as it is a good drainage conveyance. While Alister MacKenzie must have "been forced" to integrate Augusta with Rae's Creek, he was also responding to the aesthetics.

Beyond all of this, MacKenzie sought great strategy in his use of Rae's Creek. Strategy is given little weight in this chapter about building and creating hazards, but it should never be forgotten. If the truth were to be told, we would place strategy at the very front of the pack, for without it your water hazard will never seem quite right on the golf course. The golfer is not stupid and will know you have another motive up your sleeve if you fail to use water in a way that makes it seem natural and a part of the overall design of the holes.

Constructing Water Hazards

Unlike the bunker, the water hazard—or feature—is of so many varieties that it would be nearly impossible to cover the many types, conditions, and construction options there are. Having stated this, there is a short list of concerns that must always be addressed in the creation of water hazards on a golf course, no matter what the design or precise construction method.

1. *Lining*. The mechanisms for keeping the water from seeping into the ground are plentiful. This is not to say that it is always preferable to keep water from seeping downward, but it is always a point to consider. Ground water might also want to move upward into a water feature. The pressures between ground water and water in an artificial pond or lake are very complex issues, especially if tidal waters of the ocean are involved. Trust an engineer—preferably a good one. When a lining is preferred, methods for lining ponds and lakes

Fig. 7-28 Water is kept moving in this artificial stream at Iron Bridge Golf Club, Colorado. Arthur Hills/Steve Forrest, golf course architects. (Courtesy of Alliance Golf)

include soil-sealing additives that are blended with soils to form a barrier, impregnated fabrics that bond with soil to form a liner, plastic sheeting, and concrete.

2. *Volume.* Ponds and lakes may require a specific volume, depending on their purpose. If they are for storage purposes, they need to be engineered to house enough water to sustain the course and hold whatever incoming water may be required. This is a matter for irrigation consultants, civil engineers, and water-feature designers to work out in the process of design. Another consideration is "draw-down." This is the fluctuation of the water surface resulting from the continual adding and subtracting of water in the water hazard. Draw-down, if underestimated, can increase shoreline erosion and may leave a water feature looking unsightly until it is once again filled.

3. *Shoreline.* The edges of ponds and lakes should be stabilized to prevent unwanted erosion and unstable conditions. Concrete edges, stone walls, bulkheads, and other solutions are used for this purpose. Turf is also an excellent edge treatment, providing it will hold up to the action of small waves caused by wind and the movement of the water. Streams must also take into account their edges. The continual flow of water will erode edges unless they are planted or lined with stone or other solid surfaces.

4. *Slopes.* Slopes to water features are generally kept relatively gradual, but not always. Slopes within water features will vary. In a lake design, there will sometimes be a gradual shelf that extends out for 10 or more feet before the slope drops off more sharply. This is supposedly to make the lake safer should someone fall in. The theory is that someone caught out in the lake would be able to move toward the edge, where the shallow shelf area provides an easier escape than if the sides were all a continuously steep slope. There are different schools of thought on this, however. One may argue that it is impossible to make a lake or pond entirely safe, and that while one is trying to mimic nature, the integration of a shelf may give the appearance that the pond does not even have any deep areas.

5. *Water Quality.* Certainly the overall quality of the water is paramount in any water feature. No club desires a smelly or unpleasant body of water. Besides the obvious consideration of the source of the water, treatments for water can include *aeration* (forcing air into the water, just like an aquarium air pump); keeping the water moving; introducing appropriate fish varieties to maintain a stable ecosystem; and planting aquatic plants along the shoreline. Of special interest in recent years has been the potential for the water to attract mosquitoes. Ideally, water should be kept moving, stocked with fish, or otherwise managed to prevent mosquito infestations.

The reality of modern water hazards is that there are now specialists to work out the design nuances of water features. Phred Bartholomaei, a landscape architect who specializes in aquatic waterscapes, gets into such minute details as what species of fish are added to the water once it is built. "A lot of people consider the lake or pond finished once it gets filled with water," notes Bartholomaei, "but it is a living ecosystem full of plants, animals, and microorganisms, and one which needs to be managed over the long term."

Constructing Other Hazards

There is really no great secret to constructing hazards that are closely related to sand bunkers. We are referring to waste areas and the like. They, of course, need to be drained as conditions warrant. This can be accomplished in much the same way as bunkers are drained. If the tolerance is lower, it might be acceptable to allow them to drain on the surface if a low spot is fitted with a simple drain or sump. At the wild and intricate Tobacco Road Golf Club near Pinehurst, South Carolina, we find a course where you are hard pressed to tell where the bunkers end and the waste bunkers begin. The late Mike Strantz, one of the most innovative modern-age designers, amassed an entire zoo of waste bunkers, waste areas, and dune-like hillocks, with a few sand bunkers mixed in between. It is among the most fun golf courses anyone will ever play, to be sure. The solution to drainage is simple: drains are where the low spots are, and water is efficiently carried away to out-of-play areas, usually from waste bunkers that should be "out-of-play" anyway. Strantz used a variety of equipment to shape his homage to dunes, hillocks, and sand.

The list of constructed hazards is long. Dry water hazards can consist of low waste areas, meandering ditches, and artificial ravines. The shaping and drainage is much the same as any area on a golf course—water still runs downhill. Bumps, hummocks, and grass hollows are shaped in a variety of ways, by small excavators, loaders, or small bulldozers. Some shapers are handy at creating small mounds and bumps with a small loader, such as a Bobcat.

Irrigation & Hazards

Irrigation around sand bunkers is an art. The irrigation designer must use a variety of methods to avoid introducing too much water to the bunker itself. This is difficult while still delivering an adequate volume of water to grassed areas immediately surrounding the bunker. For water hazards, while it may not matter how much water is sprayed into the hazard, it is certainly a waste of resources to "water the water." There are also situations where irrigation water may need to be isolated from water features. An example might be the course irrigated with treated effluent. Irrigation control is the key to resolving all situations involving irrigation adjacent to water features.

The goal for many years has been to find ways to attain the control offered by hand watering, but through an automatic system. Good progress was made with computerized

Fig. 7-29 Irrigation around bunkers must be carefully planned and integrated with the final shape and edge of the hazard. (Courtesy of Bryant Taylor Gordon)

irrigation systems that could control individual heads. The heads themselves, however, were mostly static when placed in the ground. Aside from replacing them with smaller heads or making them spray in a different pattern, one had little control over the heads but to turn them on or off. One solution for bunkers was to plan more small heads into the overall design and place them along the perimeter of the bunker. Irrigation lines are usually looped around bunkers, so this is easily accomplished. It is costly, however. This approach results in more heads, which leads to more maintenance and replacement.

Now a new breed of irrigation head has offered increased control. Instead of relying on the rate of water delivered, which is controlled by the timing of the head (on or off), sprinkler heads have been designed that allow water to be applied as a full-circle sprinkler or, at the touch of a button, as an adjustable part-circle sprinkler. Heads are also being equipped with both rear and forward nozzles that have multiple adjustments. By adjusting rates and trajectory of one or both nozzles, one can control a single sprinkler in several ways—in addition to the timing afforded by the computer program that runs the entire system. Even newer designs are programmable with various speeds. The net effect of these new products is similar to that gained by hand watering, which, by the way, is still an excellent solution for maintaining areas around complex hazards. Using either method—a state-of-the-art irrigation system or hand labor—a superintendent is able to make subtle adjustments around bunkers, reducing the amount of water that gets into the bunker.

There may be solutions in other ideas, too. Drip irrigation can be used to keep native grasses along bunkers thriving. This is a cost-efficient method and uses very little water. For greenside bunkers, the designer will take great care in planning the heads so there is maximum control to allow for a separate rate of water to be delivered to the green while limiting the water to areas between greens and bunkers. The same concept also applies to approaches, tees, and fairways that may be located near hazards. Hazards and areas around them are not uniform in slope and size, and many may have extreme changes, from gentle slopes to extreme slopes.

CHAPTER 8

Restoration & Maintenance *of* Hazards

Of all the statements that one can make about golf, none is more true than that our courses are all different. Even two golf holes that appear alike will be very different once you get to know them better. As golfers, we also know that from one day to the next there will be differences on the very same hole. And it is all too true that a short gust of wind can make one player's tee shot very different from his opponent's just seconds before. Golf is like nothing else in this respect. The conditions, the setup of the courses, and the courses themselves are always being reinvented—if not by the discovery of some new approach to a hole, then surely by a clever superintendent who begins mowing some tight lies around the green, or maybe by nature herself who sees fit to send us a dry and hot summer every few years.

"Our dilemma is that we hate change and love it at the same time; what we really want is for things to remain the same but get better," says author Sydney J. Harris. It is likely than none of us will ever meet the golfer, greenkeeper, or golf architect who truly wishes to see a hole or course remain exactly the same. "Exactly" may be the loophole in this case. There is nothing perfect about any one golf hole or course. Perfect is for tennis courts, the height of basketball hoops, and the mechanisms of crossbows. A golf hole is nature reconditioned, but still nature. It lives and breathes. To say it must or should stay the same is blasphemy against the heart and soul of the game.

As early as 1896, Willie Park, Jr. reminded us about the ever-changing state of our golf courses. He said it is a mistake to assume that our older golf courses in their present condition are the same as when they were first fashioned. Park's comment reminds us that the original formation of our cherished older courses has been lost in past centuries; that changes have frequently been made, and that these changes have been the result of ages of experience; that all golf courses evolve in the course of time, some for the better and some for the worse.

This evolution will continue as sure as our little bunker is not the same as it was back in Chapter 1. It has aged by now—with wrinkles, many adjustments, new sand, and perhaps a new role to play. Is the fairway wider toward its opening? Does this little bunker still serve to catch a bounding shot along the right side? Should it be abandoned entirely? Or now, with the advent of new equipment and hotter golf balls, does it beckon the bold player with an advertisement that reads, "HIT IT OVER HERE — JUST A SHORT IRON TO THE GREEN WITH EVERY WINNER."

The Idea of Change

Golf course design is an art, not a science. Whether constructing a new course or performing renovation work on an existing course, we are never dealing with standardized design features. Each bunker and hazard is unique and must be treated as such. In the case of remodeling, the quality of the finished product is often a direct result of the amount of time the golf architect spends in the field with the golf course builder. The cooperation between designer and builder should not be underestimated. Detailed construction drawings are frequently a help, but frankly, there is no substitute for in-the-field communication between parties who have come to know and trust one another. Communication and trust are at the heart of making changes to a golf course, even when the change might seem insignificant. A new mowing pattern or a change in bunker edging, for example, is best when all parties get together and discuss the change, its impact on the design, and any long-term consequences.

Fig. 8-1 The idea of change is a double-edged sword. Progress and improvement are necessary, but so is preservation. At Fox Chapel Golf Club, Pennsylvania, golf architect Brian Silva restored the work of Seth Raynor while also making necessary improvements.

Change through Maintenance

Everyone connected with a golf course should appreciate the fact that golf courses are changing all the time. Besides renovation, remodeling, and restoring, we see change take place as a result of weathering, use, and maintenance practices. In the day-to-day routines of maintaining a golf course, it is possible to make changes purposefully—such as by adjusting mowing limits—or inadvertently through habits that lead to change over time. The latter will occur whether there is good control over maintenance practices or not. Owners who desire to retain the design of their course must take notice of how hazards are being maintained and what degree of change might be occurring through their maintenance programs.

Change through Restoration

The word *restoration* communicates very clearly that a golf course is being returned to an earlier condition. *Restoration,* therefore, should not be thrown around lightly when we talk in golf course lingo. Maybe the real task at hand is a "renovation," perhaps a "remodel." Could it be a "rebuilding," or do we mean a "faithful restoration"? For the purposes of clarity, it may be helpful to all of us—superintendents, green committees, architects, course owners, and golfers—to come to some consensus about these terms.

Renovation. A gentle term. In the business of golf courses, we have come to expect it to mean that all or part of a course is being "improved." The word *renovation* implies that we are not making widespread changes and we are probably doing nothing that is going to cause the golf architecture police[1] to come running. But many "renovations" bring with them significant changes to golf courses. Beware the word *renovation.* If it is just the tee surfaces and bunkers that you expect to see rebuilt, then why not call it "existing tee and bunker renovation work."

Fig. 8-2 A bunker is re-edged and rebuilt at Pebble Beach Golf Links. Under careful direction, the grounds crew carried out the work.

Remodel. Perhaps the most common of our nomenclature. A test: In the 1940s, did Robert Trent Jones, Sr. (a) restore, (b) renovate, or (c) remodel, the 16th hole at Augusta National by damming up Rae's Creek at critical points to create the pond that now defines Augusta's finish? Hint: The answer is certainly not (a) or (b). In fact, Jones *changed* Augusta and forever altered what Alister MacKenzie had left in the way of a 16th hole. Remodeling a hole or course usually will mean changing it, not just putting it back in shape or improving a subtle condition here or there.

Rebuilding. A rebuilding may as well be new construction. Here we move into territory beyond any of our other *re-* terms. Admittedly this can get confusing when we decide it is best to "rebuild" the course in order to "restore" the hazards.

Faithful Restoration. Hmm. Extremely clever. This term can be taken to mean anything from restoration to rebuilding, but in the context of a particular era or style. In all seriousness, a "faithful restoration" may be exactly what a club needs most. In many cases, there are

---

[1] We would like to think that one or more readers of this book will accept the challenge of actually forming the golf architecture police. Wouldn't it be convenient to have a brigade of uniformed officials to control, corral, and levy fines upon golf architects, course owners, and others throughout the world who flagrantly abuse and disregard the laws of golf course architecture?

elements of good within the design, but these qualities may not be widespread or entirely evident. Perhaps there has been much tinkering with the golf course. The time may be right to bring the positive bits to the surface and give them some meaning.

For the purposes of our topic here, we will focus on the process of changing golf courses and not the nearly new construction associated with rebuilding. When we tear down a course and rebuild it, we are dealing with new construction techniques, and these have been covered in the previous chapter. The topics at hand are associated with improving or changing individual hazards, features, or areas of holes and courses. In these instances, we are mostly working in confined areas, leaving major portions of the course intact.

Fig. 8-3 Through the study of old aerial photography prints and photographs, it is possible to piece together a lost hazard. Another method is to probe areas around bunkers, excavating areas of old layers of sand to find the limits of original bunkers. Both were used on this project. The golf course architect takes time out from writing this book to mark the edges of the soon-to-be-restored bunker.

Investigation & Research

Ideally, every golf course should have its own golf course architect. It amazes us how often we find this not to be the case. If there ever were a type of facility within our built environment that truly needs and deserves the continual advice of a design professional, it is the golf course.

We encourage clubs, committees, and greenkeepers to develop an ongoing relationship with a qualified golf course architect. You would be surprised how easy it is to find a dedicated individual who will take the time to come by every so often. The idea is not to have a golf architect "always on the clock," but to have access to someone you trust who is capable of offering recommendations and encouragement every so often.

Golf course architects have a vast understanding of the game. Their training gives them a perspective into history, strategy, construction, budgeting, and turf matters. Ideally, "your" golf course architect would be the one responsible for the original design. But with so many modern courses reaching the 50-year mark, many of their designers have long since retired or have gone on to that great golf course in the sky.

Fig. 8-4 Club members and staff meet on-site to be a part of reclaiming a bunker lost to time. The flagged outline represents the portion of this William P. "Billy" Bell bunker that was able to be put back. A good portion of the original bunker is now located beneath the clubhouse addition, further to the left.

The first step in restoration work, or any undertaking to change a golf course, should be a thorough evaluation of what has gone on in the past. Through a series of research steps, any club should be able to piece together information that can, at the least, prove helpful to understanding its golf course. Many green committee members and superintendents have taken this project on themselves, handing over their findings to the golf course architect after they have finished.

Common resources that may shed light on a golf course's past include:

The Original Designer. Determining the original designer of the golf course is an excellent initial step. The authority in this area is the now out-of-print book *The Architects of Golf* by Geoffrey Cornish and Ron Whitten. Although copies are becoming scarce and newer courses are not covered, this remains as invaluable to those interested in the work of golf architects as it is to collectors of golf architecture books. Other resources include online directories of golf courses, but beware, as the information they provide is very often inaccurate.

Original and Old Plans. There may be original plans hanging around the golf course. These are often in the hands of the greenkeeper or in a storage closet known only to a retired manager. Occasionally, an irrigation consultant who has worked on the course will have a set of plans. The obvious source of plans is the original golf course architect. Keep in mind that even when a club is very old and the architect has passed away, plans (if they were created in the first place) may well have been passed down to a younger architect who now has an office of his or her own. Although many changes and adjustments might have been made in the building of the golf course, original plans are helpful for understanding the intent of the designer. A tremendous find is the occasional set of "as-built" plans. On more than one occasion, we have come across a set of plans labeled as such. As-built plans are usually a marked-up set of original plans clearly showing what was built and where adjustments were implemented by the architect during construction.

Topographical Maps. Most counties and municipalities have files of topographical surveys and aerial photos. These go back several years and may sometimes be the same maps used in the original design and plans for the course. Equally interesting are surveys of the course *after* it was built. With a few of these, one is able to piece together snapshots of the golf course as it matured and underwent changes throughout the years. It occasionally helps to research whether an engineer was involved in the original work. If so, and if the engineer is still in business, he may have files of old maps—and even plans. Aerial-survey companies in the area of the course are also rich sources of information. It is surprising how often just a few simple phone calls to local aerial-survey companies will yield information on who may have been in business at the time the course was constructed. This can lead to a company that may have

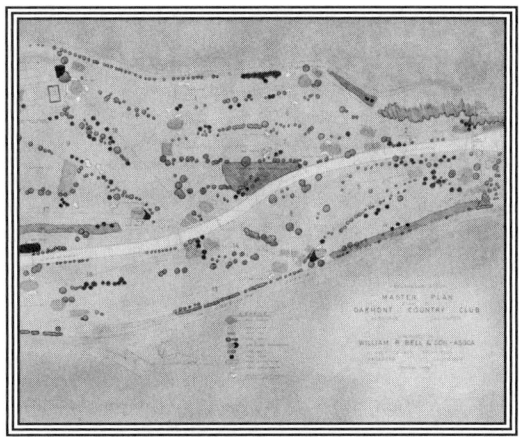

Fig. 8-5 Old blueprint from a drawing by William F. Bell of Oakmont Country Club, California. This particular drawing was tucked away in the back of the maintenance building and had not been unrolled for several years. Such legacies of clubs are best archived or framed as a record of the club's history.

Fig. 8-6 Topographical surveys can show the exact location of hazards from days gone by. The enlarged area here shows where bunkers had been shaped.

done the original work and may still have old maps and aerial photographs. Old topographical surveys can be helpful in showing how the land was configured *before* the course was built.

Public Submissions. Permits may have been issued for plans submitted to public agencies. These became popular during the 1970s and are increasingly common after that period.

Aerial Photography. Aerial photos offer excellent two-dimensional views of the golf course at intervals. Aerial-survey companies, public agencies, libraries, and aerial archival services are good resources. With practice, it is possible to detect shadows and other topographic features from aerials, but they are not as reliable as accurate topographical surveys or close-up photos of hazards and other features.

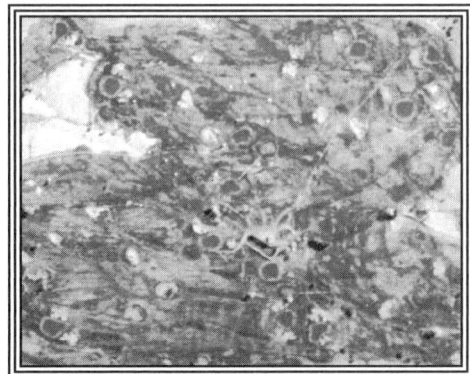

Fig. 8-7 Aerial photo c.1936 of the Arizona Biltmore Adobe Course. The dark circles are greens and the large white areas are enormous William P. "Billy" Bell bunkers, some larger than the greens themselves. (This aerial was used as reference in the restoration shown in Fig. 8-3 and Fig. 8-4.)

Club Histories, Articles, and Photos. Everything from old scorecards to albums and photos from regular players can be helpful. It is amazing how one thing can lead to another in researching a course. A single member or retired employee may hold the keys to a wealth of information, including old newspaper articles, photos, event programs, and so on.

Fig. 8-8 Oblique aerial shots can be useful in ascertaining depths of bunkers and to give a view under trees. Note the bunkers at the lower portion of the photograph. (This aerial was used as reference in the restoration shown in Fig. 8-3 and Fig. 8-4.)

Interviews. One-on-one interviews can be very helpful. When a former superintendent or golf professional is taken around a course, it often jogs his or her memory and all sorts of useful clues to the past can be gleaned.

On-site Probing. Very often, the answer is right under one's nose. The Sherlock Holmes part of a golf architect's brain is able to see hazards and features of a golf course that have been lost over time. By locating points on the course and comparing them to available aerial photos, surveys, and plans, it is possible to uncover old hazards and features. When there is doubt, it is often a matter of probing areas where old bunkers may have resided and ascertaining the presence of old sand layers beneath the upper layer of turfgrass.

Once armed with all of the findings gathered during research, what ultimately does a course do with it? This is where committees, owners, superintendents, and golf architects make the transition from being enamored with the fruits of their research to doing something with it. If a course has maneuvered through this work without a golf course architect, it is now time to choose one in order to move to the next step. A course that has been working with a designer is one step ahead.

Selecting a Golf Course Architect

A common question is "When should we hire a golf course architect?" Maintaining a relationship with a golf course architect, as we have recommended, provides a head start whenever changes to a course are being considered. The course superintendent—it is assumed that all courses have one—may be the most logical individual to maintain an ongoing dialogue with a golf course architect. Use your superintendent as a resource wherever it makes sense. Other individuals who may serve as the liaison between the course and a golf architect are the green chairman, general manager, or, in the case of a privately owned course, the owner. The question of "when" can be answered by looking at the many projects that have, unfortunately, gotten off to rocky beginnings and have headed for trouble. Many times a course has waited far too long before engaging professional assistance, or has gone down a path assuming that it could be completed without a golf course architect.

Fig. 8-9 Close-up of a bunker that has been stripped of sand so an investigation can be made to determine where the original edge had extended. Once found, the edge is revised to match the original shape and size.

There are several ways to go about engaging a golf course architect. The "right" golf architect will either come as a result of a recommendation, or it will become obvious that a particular individual is "right" because of past experience with similar projects or familiarity with courses by the original architect or courses of the same era.

Occasionally, there is a need to consider a few individuals or firms and make a selection from among them. In this case, the credentials of each golf course architect are secured and finalists are invited to an interview. If the travel distance is significant, travel expenses are often provided for these finalists. Only rarely are golf architects asked to prepare reports, plans, or approaches before being contracted. If they are, certainly the course should make

Fig. 8-10 An example of classic shaping and forms. Owners, members, and committees should take care to match the needs of a project to a golf course architect who has the skills, experience, and knowledge for their specific golf course. (Source: Golf Illustrated)

some arrangement to pay for this effort. Soliciting speculative work without compensation may seem to be a valid and cost-efficient way to go about getting ideas. But only with significant time and effort will a dedicated professional be able to bring meaningful and useful ideas to the table for consideration. Through interviews, references, and a review of past accomplishments, a selection panel should be able to ascertain who would be best to work with on a project.

The Role of the Golf Course Architect

The fees paid to a golf course architect are nearly always the least costly part of any remodeling effort. Having a golf course architect on your team should ultimately save the time, expenditure, and hassle of having to do things over. The golf architect can provide many services, depending on the nature of change that will be made to the golf course. Indeed, it is in defining the extent of change needed that an architect can prove invaluable. No other individual is really capable of seeing all of the many perspectives of a golf course.

Fig. 8-11 The golf course architect (foreground) makes a final inspection before a bunker is readied for sand to be placed.

The role of the golf course architect includes:

1. Assistance in evaluating needs and determining the feasibility for remodeling or change.
2. Historical review and interpretation of old plans, and aerial photography and "forensic" research into old bunkers and other features and areas of a course.
3. Preparation of master plans for the golf course, including the factors of strategy, playability, maintenance, turfgrass improvement, drainage, irrigation, and aesthetics.
4. Assistance in determining options based on evaluation and master plans.
5. Preparation of cost estimates throughout the planning and design process.
6. Agronomic consultation and coordination.
7. Observation of construction progress and compliance with specifications and plans.
8. Consultation with course superintendents, green committees, management, and owners on priorities and the ongoing aging and improvement of their golf course.

One of the most valuable assets of the golf course architect is an ability to communicate with members of a club, player groups, and local authorities who may need to approve plans and permits for work. An oft-overlooked phase of remodeling is taking the time necessary to address all the constituents of a project.

The Master Plan

Just as all golf courses should have a golf course architect to rely upon, all courses should have a *master plan.* For new courses, the master plan may well be the original plan created for the course. In this case, it is likely that hazards, features, and other details will have been updated in some form to show changes made during construction. (We noted previously that this was typically referred to as an "as-built.")

For older courses, a master plan becomes the key to any and all potential changes. It is often referred to as a roadmap. Literally each and every time a component of the course is considered for a change—even a maintenance adjustment—the master plan, when properly devised, will help those in charge weigh the benefits and detriments of the proposed change.

There can be no better investment by a golf course than a well-thought-out master plan. It is far less costly than nearly any of the physical work done to a golf course, and it will last for many, many years. Among the most beneficial attributes of a master plan is its ability to express a long-range vision. How many times do we see effort being expended on a course that has a cloud of suspicion hanging over it? There is usually no bad intention at work in these cases. Everyone is "doing his job." The sad part of this situation is that money and resources are being spent, often with no regard for the bigger picture. A master plan prevents this. Everyone is forced to look at it and uphold the approved vision that it embodies.

The life span of a master plan will depend on such variables as how often a green committee changes. This can be one of the most frustrating roller coasters a course endures.

It is discouraging to go through all of the time and effort of research, the sharing of design philosophies, and the planning only to repeat the process once a new green chairman comes into power. Taking a serious and hard look at earlier efforts to develop a master plan is always worth the time. Most master plans are not created to appease any one person or single interest. Certainly no decent master plan is created for such a limited audience. Take cover when you hear that a master plan is being changed again and again. A combination of things may be going wrong in these cases; those involved may be too transient, or perhaps there are too many people trying to get their voices heard. Of utmost importance is having a "champion," someone to stay with the master planning process and see to it that communication is held in high regard. Regular meetings, input, and disclosure are absolutely essential in nearly all instances.

Each master plan is inherently different in focus, but all follow a basic outline similar to the one below. This happens to be for a 1920s-era club that underwent a comprehensive master planning process to prepare for major restoration work. It uses seven sections to adequately address the elements that are fundamental in almost any master plan, regardless of the age of the course:

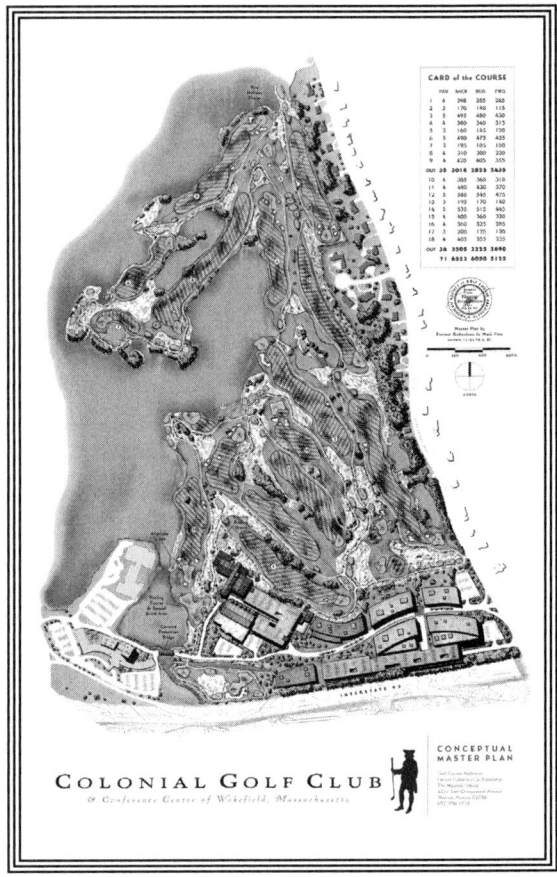

Fig. 8-12 *A master plan is an essential tool for all golf courses. Even relatively new courses should have a roadmap for future improvements and additions. This master plan is for a 1950s-era course that had been neglected before being brought under new ownership. The master plan was created by careful on-site research, planning, and design. The approach for this course was to rebuild the entire course using about 50 percent of the existing routing. The club-house will relocate and a new 3-hole short course will be added. Forrest Richardson and Mark Fine, golf course architects.*

I. *Course History.* This opening section looks at the golf course and its early development. The original philosophy of the strategy and design is covered, as are any of the known architectural intents expressed in the original design. The history concludes with an account of the course's evolution; how has the course changed over the years to get to its present state? Within this section may be plans, maps, surveys, and aerials supporting the original design and the evolution.

CHAPTER 8 | RESTORATION & MAINTENANCE *of* HAZARDS

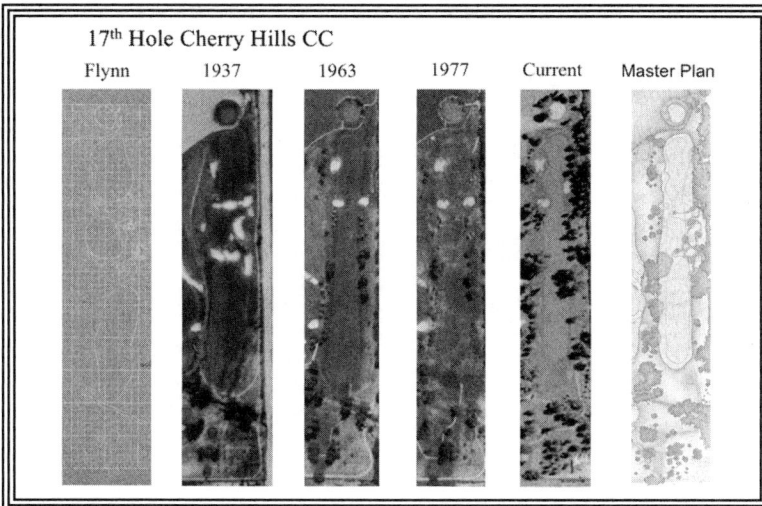

Fig. 8-13 A hole-by-hole analysis is very helpful for historical perspective. For Cherry Hills Country Club, Colorado, a presentation was prepared for each hole showing how the original design had changed over the years. The culmination of the work is the recommended change at the far right. It is evident that William Flynn's original strategy was all but lost when the bunkers were filled in and pushed toward the edges of the fairway (see color insert). Mark Fine, golf course architect, and historian.

II. *Hole-by-Hole Analysis.* Each hole as it exists in its present-day state is detailed in written form with itemized concerns and challenges. This narrative may be accompanied by drawings or aerials showing current conditions and configurations of each hole.

III. *General Features.* An appraisal of the course as it exists currently is provided. The routing is studied from the perspective of interest, pace-of-play, yardage, and safety. The course is then looked at with regard to individual groups of features: tees, greens, bunkers, water hazards, fairways, approaches, roughs, contouring, and trees. Infrastructure, including irrigation and drainage, are evaluated. This section will typically cover conditions, deficiencies, and goals associated with each area covered.

IV. *Ongoing Maintenance.* An assessment of maintenance practices and conditions associated with maintenance is made.

V. *Profile of the Original Architect.* A master plan benefits from incorporating the research of those responsible for the original design, as well as subsequent remodeling/design efforts undertaken throughout the years.

VI. *Recommendations.* The conclusions of a master plan should be presented in a form that is clear and easy to understand. The written portions need to correspond to a visual exhibit. The recommendations should address the extent of work that may be considered. This will allow for budgets and priorities to be determined. Of course, the heart of a master plan will be the architectural rendering itself. This view of the work will become the centerpiece of the recommendations. It must visually communicate the ideas and extent of the work to a variety of audiences.

Fig. 8-14 The Duel Hole at San Francisco Golf Club, California, c. 1927. (Source: Golf Illustrated, October 1927)

Fig. 8-15 Photograph of the Duel Hole (from Fig. 8-14) taken recently. Note the difference in trees between the two images. Trees, while tremendous assets to many golf courses can stifle the design intent if left to overtake fairways and holes. (Courtesy of P. Burton)

VII. *Budgeting and Prioritization.* The final chapter in a master plan begins the process of assigning budgets and grouping work into phases that can be carried out over time. Of course, it is always possible to complete all of the work at one time and under one contract. Generally, though, a master plan is a vision of the future to be implemented over time. Consideration of future needs is an essential ingredient of the plan.

Implementing Change

Psychologist and author Kurt Lewin hit the mark when he said, "If you want truly to understand something, try to change it." There is nothing quite as eye-opening as the process of changing a golf course. Even the mere suggestion of changing a course can be quite enlightening. People have a very difficult time visualizing change across a golf course. A golf course is a large-scale object, whereas the diagrams and sketches for a golf course are done at a very tiny scale compared to the real thing. Many people are simply unsure if they want change, and when people are unsure there is bound to be a challenge.

It is assumed that not all golf courses will be able to develop a master plan in advance of the need to make changes. We hope that our reiteration of the importance of master plans is beginning to sink in—we are genuine in our belief that they are invaluable. Whether you have a master plan or not, heed the advice that communication will be your best asset once you embark on implementing change. Open houses, forums, and meetings with key employees and others will go a long way toward making people feel a part of the plans and decisions. It will also help to explain plans and the change associated with them.

Adding, Subtracting & Shifting Hazards

Very often hazards are added or subtracted. This is a simple concept. Golf courses may change, or need to change, in terms of length or the type of play carried out over the

CHAPTER 8 | RESTORATION & MAINTENANCE of HAZARDS

course. As a private club ages, for example, more tee options may need to be added to allow hazards to come into play for aging members. On the other hand, a public-access layout that is taken private may need to add back tees where possible to provide extra length for an increase in low handicappers who might be playing the course. The great Bobby Jones, Jr. had an interesting take on this trend: "We can move all of our tees forward, if we wish, without investing more money in costly land, but we cannot keep on moving them backward." Jones, by the way, made this comment long before massive titanium-head drivers and golf balls designed by sophisticated computer modeling.

What needs to be kept in mind in looking at hazards is that more or less is not always the best answer. It is often better to consider the relocation of hazards. By sliding the bunker right, left, forward, or backward, we can create options and breathe new life into a golf hole. This, of course, implies that shifting a bunker or other feature will be possible and fits well with the terrain. In reality, all adjustments wind up being site-specific "custom" work that can only be worked out with great concentration on the golf hole at hand.

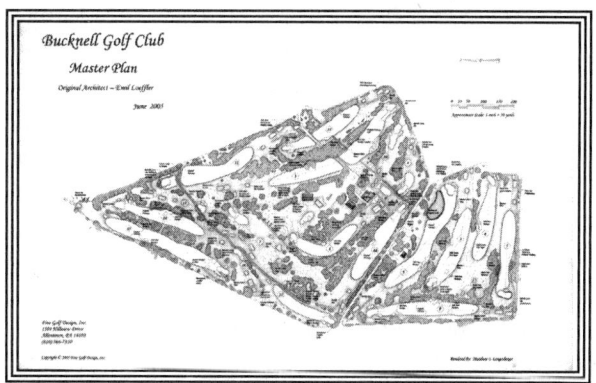

Fig. 8-16 Final master plan rendering that features the proposed changes to Bucknell Golf Club. The original 9-hole course was designed in 1930 by Emil Loeffler, the famed greenskeeper of Oakmont Country Club. Ed Ault added nine additional holes in 1963. The objective for this project was to utilize a combination of restoration on the Loeffler holes and renovation/redesign of the Ault holes to Loeffler's style adding harmony to the combined 18-hole design. The end result will be a standing legacy to Emil Loeffler and an example of some of his greatest design/hazard philosophies.

Maintenance & Preservation of Hazards

Hazard maintenance is an interesting topic. Hazards, as we know, came into the world of golf as ragged, natural areas—certainly the last thing they were was *maintained*.

Today, however, we focus on hazards in the maintenance of our golf courses. As course managers invest in keeping the conditions of their courses in tip-top shape, the hazards come along for this ride. Hazards are now ranked high among the areas to be maintained at courses. While the extent of maintenance depends on the type of course, it is still a widespread reality especially at many American courses.

Even the tough and threatening Oakmont Country Club is focused on hazard maintenance. Superintendent, John Zimmer is continually expending energy on hazard care at Oakmont. "A lot of work goes into maintaining our hazards, but much of it falls under preservation," he says. At Oakmont about 25 percent of the entire budget for taking care of the course is for hazard maintenance and preservation." The need to

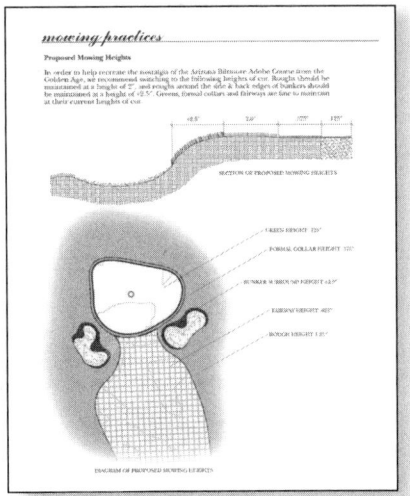

Fig. 8-17 Golf courses, unfortunately, do not come with owner's manuals. This is a page from a booklet entitled "Bunker Protocols." It was prepared for a club as part of a major restoration effort. It leaves a permanent record of the intent of the golf course design and strategy. Patrick Burton, golf course architect.

preserve hazards, especially bunkers, is among the hotter topics at courses these days. Our advice to those who wish to preserve any hazard is to begin by accurately surveying the golf course in adequate detail. Methods for recording the precise topographical relationship of grades in and around a bunker, for example, have come a long way in recent years. Through GPS and digital aerial mapping, it is possible to develop extremely accurate records of individual bunkers. New technology, such as LIDAR (light detection and ranging) is becoming increasingly available to golf courses for this purpose. With LIDAR, signals from millions of beams of laser light, typically sent from a helicopter, are rebounded from the ground, which permits millions of individual measurements to be computed into a digital model of the terrain below. The result is astonishing. The model allows the area to be looked at from virtually any angle or perspective. The resolution may be set to record individual blades of grass, but this is hardly necessary. What seems very promising is that a club wishing to preserve the integrity and accuracy of a bunker, for example, can create a super-accurate snapshot of this hazard, essentially preventing any and all arguments about how deep, how big, the overhang of the lip, and so on.

One must begin somewhere, however. The club that goes through the cost and trouble to so accurately record for prosperity an individual bunker is only preserving whatever the condition and configuration of the bunker amounts to at the point in time of this super-accurate survey. At the controversial Road Hole Bunker, for example, if tomorrow we conducted such an accurate survey, we would have no hope of knowing exactly how the bunker was in 1870—perhaps the most interesting time in its life.

Bunker Maintenance

Taking care of bunkers is the first step to preservation and all of the other attributes we hear about when it comes to our sand hazards: decent sand, aesthetics, good drainage, and so on. We asked John Chassard, director of grounds at Lehigh Country Club, to help us survey fellow superintendents and report on the top ten factors that enable—or hinder—proper maintenance of sand bunkers:

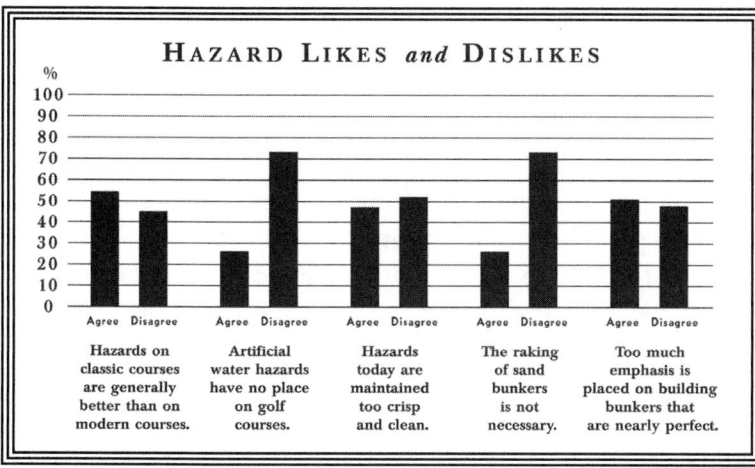

Fig. 8-18 Results of our survey concerning some interesting questions about golf architecture.

1. *Design.* The size, shape, type, and quantity of bunkers obviously influence bunker care on a course.
2. *Construction.* The quality of the original construction, including drainage, erosion control, and surrounding grass type, contributes to the condition of a bunker as it ages.
3. *Budget.* No matter how good the design and construction of the bunkers, the size of the budget directly correlates with their long-term quality and upkeep. When a course's budget for bunker care is small, yet the player's expectations are high for bunker maintenance, it leads to problems. Appropriate budgets, along with clear communication of priorities, is important.
4. *Sand Type.* Particle size, particle shape, hardness, color, and consistency are essential considerations for replacement sand as bunkers are maintained.
5. *Contamination.* Crusting, freeze/thaw factors, the presence of dust/pollution, and infiltration rates all enable or lead to contamination that impacts maintenance.
6. *Raking Methods.* The methods for raking bunkers can vary from course to course and can have a pronounced affect on bunker quality.
7. *Edging and Weed Control.* Grass and weed encroachment can dramatically change the size and design intent of a bunker.
8. *Irrigation of Surrounds.* Irrigation has become an integral part of bunker maintenance.
9. *Mowing Methods.* Maintenance of the grass around bunkers will determine the severity of the surrounds, even to the point of creating a more penal condition than the sand itself.
10. *Education.* All parties need to understand expectations for bunkers—players, members, management, and crews.

Bunkers are usually one of the biggest line items in the maintenance budget for a golf course. Some courses commit as much as 25 percent of their budget to bunker maintenance. Standards and maintenance guidelines should be established to meet golfer expectations. How often do you rake bunkers—daily, every other day, or weekly? Are the bunkers hand-raked, machined-raked, or a combination of both? How often are the bunkers edged or weeded? What kind of labor is required to mow and trim the bunker surrounds? Are the slopes steep or can they be mowed with a riding trim mower? Expectations should be carefully evaluated to determine if they are realistic and affordable. Budgets should then be determined to meet those standards. Courses have been known to easily spend $300,000 a year to provide "championship" hazard conditions. The average course, however, chooses to spend in the area of $85,000 per year for labor relating to bunker maintenance. It may seem shocking, but it is not uncommon to find courses spending more in labor dollars on bunkers than on green maintenance. In reality, bunkers have become playing surfaces similar to greens, tees, and fairways.

We have discussed sand type, quality, and all of the details of particle size, and so on, in the previous chapter. It is good to be aware of this science of bunker sand when planning bunker maintenance, as the condition of the sand itself is the most critical aspect in determining the playability of any given bunker. Routine maintenance will affect sand condition. Maintenance practices may harm the condition of bunker sand.

Since particle shape and size play a roll in the firmness of the sand and how it will perform over time, clubs

Fig. 8-19 Bunker raking is a rather recent phenomenon. As golf rules developed and the idea of counting strokes became popular (in lieu of match play) hazards became more and more maintained. When he went to create the 16th hole at Littlestone Golf Club, England, Laidlaw Purvis, we are sure, had no concept that, many years in the future, things called "bunkers" would be raked and maintained with mechanical equipment.

are encouraged to get their existing sand tested at a qualified laboratory. The suppliers of bunker sand should be able to provide a sand analysis on demand. If they cannot, it will give cause to question whether their sand is consistent at all. If you are seeking a supplier for bunker sand, ask for a tip from a nearby course where the sand is acceptable. You should also query the supplier for course references. The important thing to realize is that the analysis of the sand in your bunkers will almost always be different from the fresh sand that is being sold to your course. Only in the case of very new courses will the sand prove to be identical.

There are three primary factors related to conditions and maintenance that can be destructive to bunker sand. This is not counting the unfortunate course that simply has the wrong sand type to begin with, or has not replaced its bunker sand in many years.

Sand will deteriorate over time. It is not permanent. The three factors that can render bunker sand less-than-adequate include:

Fig. 8-20 A bunker that needs drainage. . . in the worst way.

1. *Poor drainage and wet conditions.* Continually moist sand usually means that silts and organic particles are being introduced to the sand. This translates into contaminated sand, which over time loses its purity and becomes a concoction of not just sand, but tiny silt particles along with bits and pieces of grass clippings, minerals, and so on.

2. *Blowing dust.* Even with great drainage, a course that experiences blowing dust or airborne pollutants will eventually see bunkers become crusted with an off-colored layer of this foreign matter.

3. *Harsh raking or use.* Both affect sand in the same way. Mechanical raking, such as with small riding tractors fitted with sand rakes, can exert extreme pressure on particles, grinding them up into smaller and smaller particles.

Especially firm conditions can cause a perception that there is too little sand in the bunker. When the golfer cannot easily penetrate the sand surface with the club, this is where the blame is directed. But drainage problems can also contribute to firmness. The continually wet bunker, when it does dry, will often leave behind a crust of minerals and silts. Some are brought into the bunker by the water itself. Other particles, silts especially, migrate across the surface as water runs into a bunker from turf and adjacent areas. This contaminated surface layer compacts and becomes harder and harder, and eventually thicker and thicker.

Freezing and thawing is another influence creating firm bunker sand. The freezing and thawing cycle will cause stone and rock to work itself through the soil floor of a bunker and up into the sand layer. When this occurs, soils and silts are brought with the rock and the result is contamination of the bunker sand. Moisture or water within a bunker exasperates the negative impact of freezing and thawing. Keeping the soil at the floor of a bunker as dry as possible greatly reduces the contamination that is associated with freezing and thawing.

Erosion control around bunkers is a must. Runoff from rains and irrigation needs to be directed away from bunkers. Interceptor drains can be a solution where it is not practical to change grades around a bunker. Many people do not appreciate that 100 percent drainage perfection is never achieved on golf courses. By nature, a golf course is made up of imperfect conditions. This is especially true around hazards. Slopes and the intricacies of the area will often be subject to erosion and damage from heavy rains. Repairs are part of the game, and certainly so when it comes to maintaining bunkers. While good drainage measures prevent damage, nothing can be totally perfect.

Raking Sand Bunkers

Philip Truett, an authority on the history of golf, writes in an essay included in the 1993 edition of *Hazards,* by Alex Bauer, "When you are next in a bunker and that bunker has no sand in it, or too much, or your ball is beneath some wicked lip, or you are forced to play out sideways or backwards, or, perish the thought, your ball is on the wrong side of a rake mark, you are in a hazard and must put up with all the unfairness that only nature can provide. After all, you shouldn't be there in the first place! Bunkers are not intended to be pleasure grounds but places of repentance."

Fig. 8-21 A ride-on, or mechanical, bunker rake. (Courtesy of the Toro Company)

"If I had my way there would be a troupe of cavalry horses running through every trap and bunker on the course before a tournament started, where only a niblick could get the ball out and then but only after a few years. I have seen a number of traps and bunkers that have afforded better lies and easier strokes than the fairway. This, of course, is ridiculous."

—C. B. MACDONALD

Sound design, proper construction techniques, and appropriate sand play critical roles in how a bunker will perform. However, the maintenance program and the skill and knowledge of the maintenance staff may have the greatest influence on sustaining the original integrity of a bunker. An ongoing bunker-maintenance program needs to be developed to meet each course's standards and the goals for playability. The maintenance staff needs to be properly trained in specific techniques to achieve whatever standards are put forth.

Raking methods vary from course to course. What works well at one course may not work well at another. Labor is the factor most often recognized when it comes to determining methods for raking bunkers.

Hand raking is recognized as a means of achieving a high standard of bunker maintenance. In most cases, hand raking is the best way to protect the original integrity of the bunker. Hand raking is simply more gentle than the alternative mechanical raking.[2] Mechanical bunker rakes are far more likely to be misused. It is easy to imagine the extent of damage that could be done with a ride-on tractor equipped with rake tines. Typically, the operator faces forward and the rake attachment is behind. Maybe this is the problem. It seems easy to gouge the edges of a bunker or exert too much pressure when one is riding happily along in a gas-powered vehicle.

The notion that mechanical rakes are necessary when it comes to bunker maintenance is not entirely an accurate assessment. When misused, mechanical rakes can contribute to many inconsistencies, and their use can wind up costing significantly. If used properly, they *do* offer convenience, occasionally reduce labor cost, and can give a smooth finish to a bunker floor. Mechanical rakes with cultivation attachments are the best tool for "fluffing" up the sand when silt contamination is present. There are many different styles of mechanical rakes with cultivation attachments. Superintendents should demo and evaluate the different rake and attachment options to decide which is right for their course and its style of bunkers.

There are a number of tricks to successfully using a mechanical bunker rake. These should be obvious, but they are often overlooked:

1. Enter and exit the bunker at different points each time to reduce wear on one particular area of the bunker. When exiting the bunker with the machine, lift the rake a few feet from the edge to avoid dragging sand out over the lip. The remaining area should then be raked by hand.

2. One of the more blatant abuses is riding the machine too high on the banks of the bunker and causing sand to be pulled off the faces and redistributed to lower areas. The machine should remain on the flattest part of the bunker floor with the rakes at the proper depth to either fluff up, or smooth out the sand to achieve a firmer surface. The depth must be determined by the operator. He or she should be trained to meet the standards set for playability.

3. The creation of a series of ridges or speed bumps within a bunker is the result of an operator traveling too fast while raking. This is especially common in larger bunkers when an operator is hurrying to complete his or her task. At faster speeds, sand is also pulled around and distributed disproportionately. Over a period of time, a bunker with a consistent 4-in. sand depth could result in a 2-in. depth in some areas and 6 in. in other areas. For best results the operator should rake at a slow, consistent speed, making wide, gentle turns.

---

[2] Aside from no maintenance at all, the way bunkers were once "maintained."

4. Operating the machine too close to the edge is another common error. An operator may try to rake up to the edge or lip of a bunker to avoid having to rake the perimeter by hand. This often results in either pushing too much sand against the lip or dragging sand away from the lip. The rake can also catch the edge or dig into the soil subsurface of the slope leading to the edge, causing soil and rock contamination. Depending on the bunker, the operator should remain at least 3 feet from the lip with the mechanical rake. The remaining perimeter can then be raked by hand.

In many cases where damage has occurred, an operator has likely tried to accomplish too much with a mechanical rake. If given the choice to sit and ride or stand and walk, most will take the easy way out. This is human nature and looms as the largest problem with these machines. A combination of both hand and machine raking may be the most reasonable solution if mechanical rakes are to be used. Use of the mechanical rake strictly on the floors of the bunker and hand raking the banks is common policy at most golf courses. Regardless of how you utilize a mechanical rake, education of the maintenance staff is critical for the proper operation of the machine and to protect the integrity of the bunker.

Hand raking is a common method at most of the top courses in the country. While hand raking is labor-intensive, it has numerous advantages over using a mechanical rake. Many bunkers are too small to allow a mechanical rake to be

Fig. 8-22 Large bunkers and waste areas are sometimes maintained only periodically. This bunker at The Ocean Course at Kiawah Island Resort, South Carolina, extends from tee to green and melts away into broken ground. Pete Dye, golf course architect. (Photographer, Michael Romney)

Fig. 8-23 Photograph from an early 1900s article on bunker maintenance. The rake being used is referred to as a "furrow rake," although it is significantly different from those used at Oakmont Country Club, Pennsylvania, where the furrow rake was made popular. The article points out that the raking with furrows provides "a uniform surface to all players." The opinions expressed may well have marked the beginning of an era of hazard maintenance.

maneuvered properly without causing damage. High-faced bunkers require hand raking, as it is impossible to properly rake a steep slope with a mechanical rake. A bunker may be designed with severe features that can only be raked by hand. If bunker sand is too fluffy and needs to settle in, hand raking can give the desired effect with minimal surface disturbance. Like mechanical raking, hand raking is a task that requires properly trained personnel. The most difficult aspect of hand raking may be raking the bunker face. Depending on the bunker and conditions, sand is either raked up toward the lip or pulled down toward the floor. Continual raking down the face causes sand to migrate to the floor of the bunker, leaving a thin covering on the face and an excess of sand at the bottom. Care should be given not to pull too much sand up toward the edge of the lip, leaving an excess of sand accumulation near the lip or even over the turf edge. Some courses prefer leaving an even, well-defined edge; others prefer the sand surface nearly level with the turf edge. Raking patterns can be achieved by hand that are not possible with a mechanical rake. Hand raking bunkers has produced the most desirable playing conditions on a very consistent basis.

Though bunker maintenance is often viewed as a low-skilled job on the course, each maintenance worker helps determine how bunkers will play and retain their design integrity over time. Proper bunker maintenance is an art that requires a skillful, patient, and conscientious laborer. As in all areas of the course, proper training can't be emphasized enough.

Bunker Edging

Edging will influence how a bunker may change over time. We edge bunkers to create aesthetic appeal, to fulfill design intent, and to add difficulty to the hole. When grass encroaches into the bunker from the surrounds, edging is sometimes called for. If ignored, grass can cause a bunker to become smaller. Repeated and severe edging can increase a bunker's size. Both situations will change the hazard, perhaps not for the better.

Fig. 8-24 A sod-wall bunker at Bandon Dunes, Oregon, David McLay Kidd, golf architect. Small irrigation sprinklers have been installed to help keep the turf growing on the steep slopes. In contrast, at Royal Dornoch, Scotland, the grass-covered bunker walls are periodically set on fire so they will not become too lush. (Courtesy of P. Burton)

Bunker faces and the edges of sand lines can also become higher as sand is blasted onto the face of greenward slopes. This can cause grass to die, and when this is edged the bunker lip gets higher and higher. Design features such as tongues and capes might disappear over time as a result of these practices. This is especially true on classic courses.

Many golfers seem to like the aesthetic of a sharp vertical edge at the lip of the bunker. This look is highly manicured and it is an easy path to the problems we have noted. A more natural look is achieved by allowing the grass to encroach into the sand. Regardless of the style of edging, the superintendent must work to find the look and level of practicality appropriate. This is a balancing act between perception, design integrity, and the realities of things that cannot easily be changed, such as turf, soil, growing conditions, and weather.

Proper equipment plays a big role in edging. Crews need to be trained to only remove as much of the edge as necessary to achieve the desired result. This may be done through minimal trimming using a line trimmer, or even trimming with hand equipment. Our advice is the same as for a haircut: If you remove too much at one time the only remedy is to wait it out until more growth occurs. Soil contamination is another drawback of removing too much of an edge.

Weed invasion in the sand and surrounding slopes can be bothersome to golfers. Unless the weeds are pleasant in appearance, they can prove distracting to the aesthetic appeal of a bunker. When left unattended weeds can take over an area of a bunker. Besides edging, the proper use of herbicides is typically part of bunker care. Hand weeding is also an effective routine. A properly trained member of a crew will only need to devote a few hours per week to keep up with weeds in bunkers at most courses. Once the crew is on top of the problem, herbicide applications become much less frequent, as does the need to introduce edging. Weed control is a minimal expense with major aesthetic reward to be gained.

Irrigation around Bunkers

Irrigation is an integral part of bunker maintenance. Irrigation equipment installed around bunkers is there to maintain turfgrass on the slopes, the bumps, and the intricate fingers and knolls that are often a part of a bunker's design and shape. Irrigation plays a role in maintaining the growth of the turfgrass. The turfgrass plays a role in retaining the edge of a bunker. Without the grass and its root structure, the edges of a bunker are likely to crumble, either on their own or with the help of golfers climbing in and out on a daily basis.

Fig. 8-25 Remodeling needs to consider the layout of irrigation around hazards. The appropriate time to work out the aspects of irrigation is not after remodeling work is underway, or worse yet, finished.

In some climates, irrigation systems around bunkers are also used to wet the sand in order to provide a firmer surface. Whether or not this is intentional, any time irrigation water falls within a bunker, it will have this effect. Water in bunkers also wears out sand through the continual action of particles shifting as the water exerts pressure downward during drainage. And of course, drainage itself can pose a problem whenever water enters a bunker, no matter what its source. An irrigation consultant is the best defense against the unnecessary introduction of irrigation water into bunkers. Although it can never be completely prevented, through careful design, it is possible to attain the most efficient and practical system layout.

Mowing: *The Greenkeeper's Hazard*

Grass can be mowed to create a "hazard." Imagine the conditions possible when one sets the height of a mower lower or higher. An instant variation of play is afforded. Tightly mown lies can be created around greens and high roughs along fairways or even across them. Such "hazards" are not at all permanent, and they come to us at the pleasure of the greenkeeper. Even at a recently completed golf course, after the turf has grown in to satisfaction and the golf architect has painted out the lines for fairway mowing, the superintendent can sneak out within a few days and begin changing the course.

Fig. 8-26 The greenkeeper has great influence on the hazard aspect of grass heights and condition. In this example, tall grasses and wildflowers are left to grow high while the fairway, rough, and chipping areas are defined from tee to green. Coldwater Golf Club, Arizona, Forrest Richardson, golf course architect. (Photograph by Mike Houska, DogLeg Studios)

To quote Tom Doak, "In golf architecture, tightly mowed grass is the nearest thing we have to a land mine. The average golfer sees acres of manicured grass and is encouraged to swing without fear. But the clever architect can utilize short grass in several ways to increase the difficulty of the course, and it will have the greatest effect on better players who recognize and fear the problems it will present."

The practice of mowing different areas of a course to different heights is debated frequently. On one hand we have those who feel that the entire course should be of just two heights; they say that fairways should go forever, that there should be no roughs. The only contrast should be provided by the greens themselves. Others feel that the definition of fairways, the creation of separate cuts of rough and perhaps even other heights around greens and hazards, is preferred. There is no right or wrong. The beauty of mowing heights is that they are easily changed. If we do not like the way it looks or plays, we can correct it on the spot with just a few simple instructions.

Another surface that is drastically affected by mowing heights is the putting surface. Upon our greens we can have Augusta and Oakmont speeds like the Indy 500, or we can slow them down. For even faster greens, we can roll the surfaces with rollers. When we

Bunkers, Pits & Other Hazards

Fig. 8-27 This bunker has no less than four grass textures surrounding it: fairway, rough, deeper rough (on slopes), and tall fescues. Texture assists in bringing the hazard to the attention of the golfer.

Fig. 8-28 This fairway bunker is flanked by taller grass that will catch a slow rolling shot. However, the tightly mowed surrounds of the greenside bunkers funnel shots toward the bunkers. Bethpage Black Golf Course, New York. (Photo by Larry Lambrecht, Courtesy of Rees Jones, Inc.)

combine fairway heights, chipping areas, and slopes leading from greens, we are able to create terrific options and setups at our approaches. Whether you are for it or against it, mowing-height variation makes golf interesting. Our playing fields can be varied even more from one course to another. Not only does the golfer have the personality of the golf architect to contend with, but also the greenkeeper. And this greenkeeper is the same evil chap responsible for the daily location of the cup at the green.

Near bunkers, the effect of mowing heights can increase the reach of a bunker severalfold. A bunker of just 10 feet across can become a gaping chasm of nearly 100 feet if the surrounding area is mowed tightly and the terrain slopes down and toward the bunker in places.

While varied mowing heights can make a fairway defined and provide different textures, it can also create a superhighway. The yellow-brick-road approach can be limiting, to say the least. On the fairway, there is a great loss when we so narrowly constrict the player to only be "here." This is especially true when we have interesting terrain—contours—to play with. How wonderful it is to stand upon a tee and look out at the fairway, thinking of it almost as the surface of a very large green. In lieu of a putter, we hold a big club, and the thoughts are not just how far and how straight, but also which way the ball will break! Hitting the running shot that curves and banks in the fairway has been a dying art as golf courses have become less firm. Artificial irrigation has homogenized our turf into a single surface with like qualities no matter the season, the region, or the individual fairway. Perhaps it looks greener and more consistent, but does it make better golf?

The debate over "firm and fast" vs. "soft and green" will go on for a long time. A Boredom Links is not necessarily born when we water a golf course, trim it perfectly, and define the fairways. It is simply a different course from the alternatives. The greenkeeper plays a tremendous role in creating the "hazards" of a golf course. He or she is a golf course

CHAPTER 8 | RESTORATION & MAINTENANCE *of* HAZARDS

Fig. 8-29 Flat bottomed traps with steep side slopes offer a trade-off in terms of maintenance; the sand stays put, but the grass is more difficult to cut. Myopia Hunt Club, Massachusetts. (Courtesy Ran Morrissett)

architect in disguise—his or her role is that of an influential teacher. Where the golf architect has been the parent and brought the course to life, those who take care of the course and set it up every day expose the golfer to new and temporary "hazards" all the time.

Maintenance of Water Hazards

The most significant problem for maintaining water hazards is that it is largely impossible, without draining the water, to see what is going on within the hazard. "It's much like diagnosing a patient who is unconscious," says Phred Bartholomaei, a water feature designer and expert. "We look for signs and symptoms." The diagnostic signs of a pond or lake include odor, color, clarity, and the health of fish. "We also look at the algae color," notes Bartholomaei. "Green is a good indication of a healthy lake, whereas red algae—which is often brownish—means that there is not enough oxygen in the water."

An expert called to evaluate a water feature will also want a water test conducted. There may also be good cause to test soils below the water surface. Water quality is further assessed by temperature; higher water temperatures will increase the likelihood of problems associated with too little oxygenation. Circulation, movement, wave action, and depth of the water feature are extremely important factors.

The most common issues of water features—natural or artificial—include the following:

Nutrient Loading. A water feature that is too rich in nutrients can develop several problems. The two primary causes of nutrient loading are grass clippings and waterfowl droppings getting into the water. Methods for reducing clippings are fairly obvious: use catchers, reduce mowing along lakes, or create native zones that eliminate the need for mowing and help to catch clippings before they get into the water. Methods for reducing waterfowl are not as clear-cut. The best advice when waterfowl begin to muck up a lake or pond is to consult with a lakes expert. Regional resources, such as fish and game offices, can often offer suggestions based on specific species.

Cattails. Unwanted cattail plants growing in water features are often a problem, as they overtake the shoreline and can reduce visibility across the water. If a golf hole relies on visibility and cattails obstruct the shot, the problem must be rectified. The cattail (genus: *Typha*) rarely takes root in water deeper than 18 inches. When cattails are observed growing in deeper water, it is almost always the case that they have established themselves in shallower water and then sent runners down to the deeper depths. So you should keep shorelines deeper than 18 inches if you are not in the mood for cattails. Chemical treatments for cattail growth are available, but the drawback is that applications can also kill other aquatic plants, many of which compete for the cattail's habitat. Sometimes these other plants are desirable, even beyond their benefit in partially displacing the cattail. Burning cattails, a common solution, does a great job at getting rid of the stalk, but it leaves the plant below the water to begin growing all over again.

Fig. 8-30 Cattails have taken over this marsh. Believe it or not, there is a golf hole beyond this tee, but it is no longer visible due to the overgrown shoreline. Responsible aquatic management—even in protected wetlands—will yield better habitats for wildlife and certainly, better golf.

Leaks. Artificial ponds and lakes are known for leaking. Common methods of finding the leak include sending a scuba diver into the water to see if there has been penetration to a plastic liner. The diver can be assisted by fluorescent dyes that will gravitate toward the leak. By using high-intensity lights, it is possible to follow the currents of the dye. This doesn't always work. Draining a lake and relining it or adding a liner material is a more guaranteed method, but expensive. A soil sealing product, SS-14, can be added to soil-lined lakes. The SS-14 will seek areas where there are leaks and have the effect of expanding soils and making them more apt to seal.

Shoreline Deterioration. The shorelines of lakes, ponds, and streams can become compromised through erosion, continually moving water, drawdown (the lowering of a lake, such as when irrigation is being pumped out), wave action, and the ever-hungry, grass-eating carp. Golfers can also erode shorelines by hunting for golf balls and—yes, we've seen this—driving carts right along the edge of lakes. To combat shoreline erosion and deter further problems, it is common to line shorelines with rock gabions,[3] loose stone, erosion control matting, and concrete edges. Another problem of shorelines is tree root infestation. Tree roots can undermine the liners of

---

[3] A *gabion* is a wire mesh basket that is filled with stone and then stacked or placed in an interlocking fashion to stabilize a stream or watercourse, or to serve as a retaining wall. The benefit is that the gabion itself—the rectangular basket filled with rock—does not require any structural reinforcement other than its weight.

a water feature and cause leaks and breakage of decorative shorelines. The best way to combat this is to keep trees away from artificial water features.

Pollutants. Runoff across golf courses can contain pollutants, silts, and fertilizers. Since many golf courses serve as drainage basins for communities, this problem can only be dealt with by creating silt traps before lakes and ponds, and by creating native areas where grass and plants are able to provide filtration above water features. Blowing dust is another problem. Many golf courses are built in developing areas. New construction brings dust and loose soils. If these soils are not dammed and filtered, silts can enter lakes and ponds after rains. On golf courses in agricultural areas, fertilizers may be blown into lakes and water sources from fields and farm operations. Regardless of the source of pollutants, there is almost always a way to remove them or significantly reduce their occurrence.

Golf courses have made great progress in reducing their reliance on fertilization, herbicides, and pesticides. A large problem facing golf course maintenance now is from the aforementioned pollutants that emanate from off-site. Each of the solutions mentioned here should be considered if such problems occur. Filters installed on golf course drainage systems are becoming popular. The idea behind these filters is to trap pollutants before they enter water features, and in some cases to ensure the course is not discharging pollutants when water passes through the property on its way downstream.

There are numerous chemical additives and artificial fixes for lakes that are designed to rectify water-quality issues and improve the overall water quality. "Nature is always best," says Bartholomaei in reference to many of these products. "If algae is the problem, you are not addressing it by killing it, in fact you are adding to the biomass in the lake, which can cause even more problems later on." Bartholomaei prefers common-sense approaches whenever possible. But he is also practical. At Pebble Beach's famous 18th hole, for example, he was part of the design team that fortified the fairway with carefully engineered and textured artificial stone. "There was no other way in that case," he says. "Nature needed a hand, and we gave it to her."

Today, the philosophy with regard to water-feature maintenance and preservation is to work with simple methods and avoid overmaintenance.

Fig. 8-31 This created wetlands adjacent to a fairway is managed by the golf course for the betterment of the community. Not only does the wetlands provide open space that no one has to pay for, but it is an attraction for wildlife, too.

Water features now include created wetlands, recirculating ponds to keep water moving, and smaller bodies of water where evaporation is less of an issue. Water conservation in many areas has prompted a move away from decorative water. But even in the arid southwestern United States and portions of Mexico, large water features are often needed to both store water and handle large volumes of treated sewage (effluent).

Fig. 8-32 A narrow drainage ditch is staked as a hazard.

Maintenance of water features must also address such overlooked issues as adequate hazard demarcation, bridges, environmental compliance, thawing problems (thermacline[4]), and issues associated with trespassing. It may seem unnecessary to point out that water hazards cannot possibly be made safe against poor judgment by golfers or trespassers, but it is surprising how often we hear of just these types of instances. How is it that the golfer who slips while trying to hunt down a wayward shot on the edge of a water hazard sues the golf course "because there were no handrails" or "because it was slippery"? Of course it was slippery! It is wet and full of water. The next thing we know the golfer will sue because of poor club selection on the tee.

Tree Maintenance

Arbor care is very often overlooked in maintaining a golf course. Trees, after all, are natural objects. The attitude toward taking care of them is sometimes one of letting nature, therefore, take its course. But this is not always healthy for the tree or the golf course.

Trees can create wonderful strategy, but they can also choke out the turf, restrict the options in playing a hole, and become unwieldy if they are allowed to grow out of control. Individual specimens may become too large. Trees can also propagate and create a thick forest that blocks views and has the effect of corralling golf play along very defined alignments. It might also be pointed out that trees can become overgrown in groups when they are planted as small saplings and eventually grow to great sizes. Surprise! Your course is not the same anymore.

---

[4] Thermacline is a thin layer of water in a lake sandwiched between the upper layer of water (the epilimnion) and the lower, colder layer of water (hypolimnion.) During the summer months, surface water is heated by the sun, and the surface temperature can rise to 80 degrees or more. This floats over a layer of colder denser water called the hypolimnion. Between these two layers is a thin layer in which the water temperature drops fairly substantially. This will be the thermacline. During spring thaws, nutrients can suddenly come up to the surface as the water "turns over" when the layers exchange places. Fish kills and very unpleasant water quality results. A preventive measure is to keep water moving when this is about to occur.

Fig. 8-33 Restoration and maintenance should involve a certified arborist to assess the health of trees on a golf course. Far too often, funding limitations will cut out the tree expert on a project. This can lead to more being spent later in having to deal with disease, removal, and replacement of trees.

The essential advice in tree care is to consult with both a golf course architect and an arborist. If trees are considered an asset to your course, there is no reason why an investment should be withheld when it comes to their care and control. The advice we pass on about trees is quite simple and to the point:

We maintain golf courses for the game of golf to be played and not firstly as a home to trees. While trees can be great for golf, they can also take away from the experience when they are not managed. Manage your trees. Get a plan that considers not only their health, but what is best for the game as well.

Hazard Education

One of the biggest challenges connected with the maintenance of hazards is communicating the nature of hazards. The game of golf is appreciated for its unpredictability, and the term *rub of the green* means that occasionally bad lies and poor conditions are encountered on the golf course. These situations are avoidable for the most part. Courses spend thousands of dollars every year to achieve bunker predictability and consistency. Isn't the golfer better equipped to deal with inconsistencies? This challenge is what makes the game so very enjoyable and interesting.

Does this mean that we go back to the days of old where bunkers were sand pits created from sheep hiding from the elements? We don't believe so. But we do believe in finding a balance between the extremes. We would like to think that the priority in terms of maintenance and budgets should go mostly to greens, tees, and fairways. Hazards were not named so in golf because they were all the same and consistent. The word itself—*hazard*—comes from the French *hasard* which means, in essence, "chance."

We learn how golfers react to hazard maintenance and the idea of preservation through a variety of sources. Certainly the media—television—has affected our sense of hazards. Do you suppose that when TV commentators began uttering such lines as, "I'm sure he would rather be in the bunker, Peter—that grassy area beside the green is no place to be," we might have seen a new trend in hazard appreciation? How is it that our professional players have come to *want* to be in a hazard?

Fig. 8-34 Illustration by Charles Crombie as it appeared in the May 6, 1904, issue of Golf Illustrated.

Committees, member groups, and management hold the keys to understanding what is on the mind of the golfer. The golfer is a customer of sorts. While the golfer does not dictate the playing conditions, he or she has great influence. The ideas of playability, standards, and fairness must be communicated to these groups. So, too, must the architect's design intent for the course. How awful it is to see a great design become derailed by decisions made by committees—often without ever considering to ask the very creator of the design.

Fig. 8-35 Hazard education is essential if golfers are to appreciate what goes into a golf course. This event, "A Bunkered Weekend," brought golf enthusiasts and members to a full day of learning about bunkers. Participants try their hand at re-edging a bunker. (See Figs. 8-3 and 8-4.)

Is there too much opinion involved in setting up and maintaining our golf courses? Are hazards becoming maintained to a degree that is crossing a line? John Philip, head greenkeeper at Carnoustie, may have a good solution to the opinionated golfer. He recently placed a small suggestion box on the course and notified members that he would check it regularly. Oh yes, did we mention that the suggestion box rests on top of a metal pole? Or that the pole was installed in the middle of the water hazard at Carnoustie's famous Long Hole, the 6th?

CHAPTER 9

OPINIONS ABOUT HAZARDS

Bunkers, Pits & Other Hazards

It has been reasoned that the best time to ask a golfer's opinion about a hazard is right before a shot is contemplated. If you ask after the shot has been played, it could very well influence the answer.

In summing up our research, thoughts, and personal opinions about hazards, it only seems right that we also invite the opinions of others to grace these pages. We solicited the advice of golf architects, writers, and a few hybrids of the two.

As you read through the thoughts of our invited "panelists," you might do well to think of our little bunker—how each of these distinguished contributors might treat it differently. How would each mold the little bunker, position it, and shape it? Would it be alone, along the line of charm, or tucked tight against the green?

Most of the opinions here are from one-on-one interviews and surveys conducted just for this writing. Some of the opinions we gathered are short and sweet, while others are more detailed. All who answered our plea for their thoughts were passionate about hazards and their place in golf.

Fig. 9-1 "Golf In 2001" was the title of this cartoon that ran in Golf Illustrated over 100 years ago.

Mike DeVries

Mike believes hazards should offer a chance for some form of recovery, even if it is playing out sideways. His preference is for hazards that are in the line of play and offer options to make players think. He believes that rakes in bunkers should be optional, and that we have become way too fussy about keeping bunkers fair and in immaculate condition. To be blunt, he says, "It's a hazard. Deal with it."

The best bunkers are designed with a shovel, rake, and tamper in hand, according to DeVries. He thinks of bunkers in "three dimensions." His idea of the perfect bunker is one that heaves in and out, up and down, and ties in with the surrounding areas. According to DeVries, a simple, dished-out pit is usually a poor excuse for a bunker.

Mike's favorite hazards are the Scabs at Crystal Downs, hole No. 6; the Road Hole Bunker; and old stone walls. Mike believes contouring is the ultimate way to combat technology. By using the contour of the ground, it is possible to create hard and fast conditions. By taking the wind into account, one can make golf courses more interesting. And through the occasional blind shot, one can have a psychological impact on the golfer.

DeVries loves MacKenzie's work for its natural looking and psychologically effective hazards. He has also been influenced by Tillinghast (boldness and beauty), Thomas (great strategy), and Maxwell (deep and rugged).

Fig. 9-2 Kingsley Club. Mike DeVries, golf course architect. (© Mike DeVries)

As for modern designers, he agrees with many in saying Pete Dye has been a great influence and is always willing to take risks and try something different. "Pete is not afraid of severity," says DeVries.

Bill Coore

"The three most important things when it comes to a great golf course are the routing, the green complexes, and the hazards," says Coore. He maintains that hazards are the most important factor on a course, even more so than the greens. His belief is that no other element has as much visual impact on the golfer as the hazards of the golf course.

When Coore goes about laying out a golf course, he looks for the features on the ground that "look like golf," as he describes it. He searches for contours, exposed sandy areas (if they are so fortunate to be working on such a property), and so on. Once the concept of the course is established, hazards are used as strategic elements to create interesting and inspiring play and artistic stimulation. "Hazards influence how people feel about the golf course," he says.

Working with his shapers and design partner, Ben Crenshaw, Coore strives to make hazards look natural, as though the hand of man had never intervened. Coore has come to appreciate that hazards are the part of the golf course that gets remembered most. "They define the character of the holes."

"Making hazards look natural is easily stated, but it takes time," says Coore. If there is a "Coore secret" to bunkers, it involves this concept of time. His bunkers are usually roughed in, seeded around the edges, and then left alone for an extended period of time. Once they have grown in and aged, the team returns to work on them some more, finishing the edges and getting them ready for play.

Coore embraces three keys to good bunkers: (1) placement for strategic golf, (2) technically sound construction (such as drainage), and (3) aesthetic appeal. "It is the third element that is hardest to get right," he adds. "The greatest hazards are 'alive,' just sitting there saying, 'Here I am—I have always been here and you need to deal with me.'"

Fig. 9-3 Bandon Trails Golf Course at Bandon Dunes Resort, Oregon. Bill Coore, golf course architect.

According to Coore, there is nothing more thrilling than hitting your ball over or skirting along the side of an impressive or fearsome-looking hazard. On the issue of fairness, he is concerned that there is a tendency toward making hazards "fair," leading us toward standardization and eventually an erosion of the true spirit of golf. "Fairness leads to predictability, and that makes the game dull. One of the reasons you don't often see tournament courses with more natural-looking hazards is because of rulings—'Is the ball in the hazard or isn't it?' If they are clean around the edges, there is far less uncertainty. This is unfortunate because hazards are becoming sterile as a result."

Bill prefers sand to water hazards, as sand allows for a recovery shot and no lost ball. He prefers courses with lots of width. He likes to give golfers room to play and to create advantage through positioning. "I enjoy designing holes that don't tell you everything when you walk to the tee. The best courses withhold information that must be gained over time from playing the course."

The ultimate bunker might be one along the centerline of play, as long as there is room to negotiate it right and left, as well as short and long. "No element that creates interest can ever be considered unfair," notes Coore.

"There is nothing so set in stone in golf course architecture that you would never consider doing it," he says, referring to the shed on the Road Hole at St. Andrews and use of boundary holes, with out-of-bounds running right alongside the play.

"The best bunkers are often the ones that aren't maintained," says Coore. On many of his bunkers, he recommends as little mowing as possible, no use of mechanical bunker rakes, and edges left in a natural state. Among his favorite quotes is that of Claude Crockford, the famous former Superintendent at Royal Melbourne Golf Club, who once commented to Ben Crenshaw, "In the U.S. you try to grow grass, where we are trying to keep it from growing."

Coore will incorporate trees into the strategy of the golf holes, but generally he prefers to use them as landscape elements rather than as strategic design elements. "The problem with trees is that they are alive and people can influence their existence," he remarks. In clearing a wooded site, Coore strives for a feel of randomness and irregularity, a litmus test for creating an interesting design.

Coore has been inspired by MacKenzie, saying, "His hazards were not only strategic, but emotionally impacted the play of the game." When asked about the future of hazard design, Bill went back to his concern about the trend toward standardization. He is hopeful that the work of some architects such as Tom Doak at Pacific Dunes and the influence of more-natural courses such as Sand Hills will help move the game toward a more-natural style of design.

Mike Strantz

(Author's Note: We interviewed Mike Strantz for this book in early 2005. As it turned out, this interview about his design philosophy would be among his last. Strantz lost his battle with cancer in June of 2005, ending a career that was certain to produce many more innovative courses.)

"To me, the more you flirt with hazards—the closer you stay to hazards or successfully carry hazards—the shorter distance you should have to the hole with a better angle of approach. Let the person who has the ability execute a heroic carry. That is one of the most exciting things in golf," said Strantz. He believed in positioning exciting and daring hazards but also in having enough area to play so that those who choose can play around them.

Influences on Strantz's work included the bunkering at Pine Valley and Shinnecock; the Beardies at Royal County Down (specifically those at Nos. 2, 3, and 9); Rae's Creek at Augusta National; the ocean at Cypress Point; the bunker around the green at Pebble Beach's No. 7 (the way they looked back in the 1970s); the carry on the second shot at Pebble Beach's No. 8; the approach to the No. 14 green at National Golf Links; and the natural grasses combined into bunkering at Royal County Down and Royal Melbourne. Strantz reported, "I can honestly say that when designing a course there is never the occasion when at least one thought of a Pine Valley bunker will not pop into my head."

Strantz felt MacKenzie was probably the best at creating and using hazards, followed by Ross—especially his work at Pinehurst No. 2. About MacKenzie, Strantz said, "No one comes close to the way he shaped and moved a hole around hazards. The diagonal carries that must be negotiated in direct line of play to the hole are one of the things that make his courses so much fun and a challenge to play. Hazards are what is exciting to me about golf. They *are* the challenge."

Strantz looked to the dictionary to defend the use of what some might term an "unfair" hazard. "One of the definitions of 'unfair' is 'marked by injustice, partiality, or deception.' Mike felt that sounded like it could be part of the definition for the game of

Fig. 9-4
Tobacco Road Golf Club (see color insert). Mike Strantz, golf course architect.

golf. He believed that if you choose to play golf, you are, in his opinion, "knowingly subjecting yourself to the possibility of the above without singling out hazards."

Bob Cupp

Asked whether he maintains an overall guiding philosophy on hazards, Cupp says, "I subscribe to the theory that a good shot must be rewarded. But this is clouded in confusion because we often hear members, and many good players, suggest that a bunker should be placed on the edge of a fall-off or some other place where the player is not supposed to go. This is contrary to pure strategic design. A bunker, or any hazard, should be an invitation. The problem is that it is not a widely accepted precept. It leads certain players to believe, and some to say, that I design difficult courses. Well, I did not accept this idea academically. I learned it as a player, knowing that if I overcame a hazard to get a better angle to the green, or less distance, or even to secure a better stance, the idea occurred to me that the enjoyment of the game was greatly enhanced on a course that offered many of these situations. In fact, the idea has been with me my entire career."

Among Cupp's favorite quotes about hazards is that of James Balfour, a member at St. Andrews before Old Tom Morris did his part to change The Old Course. Balfour's seven words, "Hazards are the essence of the game," have stuck with Cupp throughout his work. "The only things I might add is that the stance is definitely a hazard, and hazards have degrees of difficulty. Like art, there is seldom anything that is solid black and white," says Cupp.

Cupp points out, "It costs the same to build a great bunker as it does a crappy bunker." He believes strongly that the strategic value of a bunker is not in its shape, but its location. While the height of the exit lip is a factor, nothing is so important as where a bunker gets placed in the context of a hole.

When asked what can be done on a limited amount of land to counteract the length that the best modern players hit the ball today, Cupp says, "As long as the hazards are meaningful, the amount of land is almost irrelevant."

Fig. 9-5 Newscastle Country Club, Washington (U.S.A). Bob Cupp, golf course architect.

Jim Engh

Engh describes his bunkering as "muscle" bunkering. It is typically big, bold, and intimidating. He strives to make the golfer take notice by building dramatic bunkers with aesthetic appeal. Engh's philosophy is to use bunkers sparingly, and to make each one very powerful—whether for aesthetic or strategic purposes.

His approach is to vary the lies within individual bunkers, creating some portions of bunkers to be very penal, with other parts less severe. "Sixty to seventy percent of the time the golfer will usually find their ball in a flat level lie and have a chance to recover," he says. "However, I believe in the theory that balls finding fairway bunkers should not necessarily be able to reach the green. When sheep dug themselves into hillsides to form the first natural bunkers they were not worried about getting to the green."

Engh integrates the slope of the bunker to make it part of the hazard. Among his design traits is a theme carried through the golf course, yet one that allows hazards to form distinctive holes. "The golfer should have to play the course a number of times in order to figure it out," he adds.

Engh is not a fan of blind hazards, although much of his inspiration for golf course design came from his trips to Ireland, where blind hazards are commonplace. MacKenzie was a major influence for him. Today, he loves the work of the late Mike Strantz and Pete Dye and enjoys taking walks around any new course to see the work of his contemporaries.

Jim accepts water hazards as a part of American golf but does not advocate a forced carry over water. He designs "bailout" areas and believes in the idea of a hazard being "hazardous," but at the same time he accepts the idea that it makes a difference who is playing the game.

The factors of wind and altitude need to be considered in the laying out of golf holes, according to Engh. He feels that these elements are hazards in their own right. In addition, he uses short grass as an effective "hazard" where conditions allow. "I hope that golf course design will continue in different directions and it will always evolve," he says. "Golf has evolved from one type of game into many different forms on a variety of different landscapes; I hope that trend continues."

Fig. 9-6 *18th hole at Fossil Trace, Jim Engh, golf course architect.*

Geoff Shackelford

If you ask Geoff Shackelford about hazards, the first thing he'll tell you is that, "Without hazards, golf would have become extinct long ago... No component of golf architecture is more important than the incorporation of hazards into the design."

Geoff likes to remind the golfer that hazards are supposed to be dangerous and unpredictable places to be. He also feels that the maintenance of hazards has gotten too precise and that uniformity has rendered many wonderfully placed hazards pointless. He considers it criminal that a bunker is often a better place to be than in the rough.

Fig. 9-7 *Rustic Canyon Golf Club (see color insert). Geoff Shackelford, design consultant.*

"Bunkers were placed on a golf course to wreak havoc; grass is planted as a playing surface. Yet on some courses, the grass provides the havoc and the bunkers provide the breathing room."

Shackelford feels it should require talent and not just luck to recover from most hazards. One of his favorite stories, and ours as well, is a situation that occurred at Augusta National's famous par-5 13th. For many years, the creek fronting the green was a combination of trickling water, pebbles, grass, and an occasional sand bar. This "irregularity" added to the temptations of a player who was not sure whether to risk going for the green in two shots. By offering danger and also the chance of recovery, the hazard in front of No. 13 created major headaches for the best players in the world. But then someone decided the hole would be better served if the creek were filled with several feet of water, thus eliminating the opportunity for those occasional recovery shots. This was supposed to make the short par-5 more difficult. But raising the water level actually made the hole simpler for the best players in the world. Now that the creek offered no chance of recovery, a good player who was 235 yards away with a hanging lie had virtually no temptation to go for the green. The decision was already made. Had the creek stayed unpredictable with an off-chance of recovery, the same player might well have attempted to reach the green in two. Fortunately, portions of that irregular element have been restored to this creek.

The concept of temptation is what Geoff feels is so important in the makeup of hazards. Tempting hazards seduce us into trying specific shots and prompt us to attempt something of which we may or may not be capable. This is the spirit and the essence of golf.

Tom Fazio

Tom Fazio was inspired by his uncle, George Fazio, and learned the business working with him on essentially all of his golf courses. Squires Golf Club is the first course they worked on together. At the publishing of this book, Tom entered his forty-second year in golf course design.

Fazio maintains that he does not have a philosophy when it comes to hazards, arguing there should be no rules in golf course design. He stresses variety and uniqueness.

"I like to build 'playable' courses. The game is hard enough without building extremely difficult and penal hazards such as those one might find on the classic courses in the British Isles." For Fazio, hazards where players might have to play backwards or sideways to extricate themselves, border on the unplayable.

Fig. 9-8 Ventana Canyon Golf Club, Mountain Course (see color insert). Tom Fazio, golf course architect.

Fazio describes his approach as site-specific and heavily influenced by the climate, the club, the owner, and ultimately the people who are going to play the course. These factors help dictate the type of golf course he designs, and consequently the difficulty of the hazards he employs. Fazio calls Victoria National one of the most difficult golf courses he has ever designed. "The site dictated part of this difficulty, as did the client and users of the layout. If it was to be a public golf course, I would have designed it very differently," he notes.

Fazio admits that modern golf architecture places an emphasis on fairness, although what is fair and unfair is very subjective. Fazio reasons that, "better players tend to play golf in the air, and the poorer players tend to play golf along the ground. As designers, we must be mindful of this." A Fazio design focuses on hazard placement, followed by aesthetic value. "There is a reason for each of our hazards," he notes. Fazio's hazards are located with a purpose in mind and where they will make the most sense, sometimes regardless of whether they will fit naturally into the landscape. At that same time, he suggests that the routing of a golf course is critical with regard to hazards. His philosophy is to do his best to fit holes and hazards into the natural terrain.

Fazio gives considerable weight to maintenance when it comes to hazards. "All hazards need to be maintained, and maintenance can be expensive. We must take this into account," he says.

Fazio varies bunker style from course to course. He says that he "enjoys the idea of using people who have never built a bunker before as this leads to new ideas and variety."

George Pepper

Pepper's favorite hazards include the Road Hole Bunker, Hell Bunker, Rae's Creek, the Church Pews, and the Devil's Asshole. Pepper is quick to credit Australia's Royal Melbourne with some of the best bunkering in the world.

Pepper believes in the concept of being able to see a reachable hazard from the tee. Are there unfair hazards? "Sure, a bunker with a tree in it would fit that definition," he says.

Pepper doesn't buy the notion that the hazards of classic courses are necessarily better than those on modern layouts. "Pacific Dunes has some of the greatest hazards in golf," he notes. At the same time, he agrees that modern courses generally place too much emphasis on clean and crisp hazards and practice excessive maintenance.

Pepper's list of unique hazards includes Hell's Half Acre at Pine Valley, bunkers within greens, the snake-line Barry Burn at Carnoustie's No. 17 and 18, the Church Pews at Oakmont, the quarries at Merion, the white sand beach at El Dorado in Mexico, and the Maiden Hole Bunker at Royal St. George's.

Pepper believes a hazard is not always a formal bunker or water. "There are plenty of conditions in golf which routinely cost between a half and a full stroke—the same as most hazards," he notes. As examples, he mentions the viciously contoured greens at Pinehurst No. 2, where the slope-away edges repel marginal approach shots, pine trees with limbs near the ground such as those at Winged Foot, and patches of ice plant, heather, and gorse.

Pepper relates the apocryphal tale of the American golfer dealing with one of the most intimidating opening hole hazards in golf: the Swilcan Burn at The Old Course. After topping his first four shots, the American finds his ball in the Swilcan Burn and turns to his caddie, saying "I'm so disgusted with my game, I could jump in there and drown myself." To which the caddie replies, "Aye, but you couldn't keep your head down long enough to do it."

Tom Doak

Doak begins his comments by saying, "There is way too much grooming of hazards in modern golf." Doak says he often asks himself "how much he can get away with" when it comes to making hazards more rugged. At Pacific Dunes, he explains, "The sand in the bunkers is different from bunker to bunker. Some are firm, some are soft." He reasons that he got away with this because of the sheer beauty of the site.

Fig. 9-9 Pacific Dunes Golf Course at Bandon Dunes Resort, Oregon. Tom Doak, golf course architect.

Doak says that he doesn't design hazards differently for public and private clubs, believing that it is bad policy to "dumb down" any golf course merely because the public golfer will play there. "Those golfers deserve a similar playing experience," he says.

In designing a fairway hazard, Doak wants the player to think twice about whether trying to reach the green from the hazard is a good bet. His philosophy is to set up the hazard and the hole where it may be possible, but with significant consequences if the recovery is not executed just so. The result may be a ball left in the bunker. He sometimes prefers hazards that aren't at all set up to allow for a full recovery shot.

"Water is the most overused hazard," he says. "I question sites where the only contour on the property was sadly turned into a pond or lake."

Doak argues, "Natural vegetation is the most underused hazard out there. Golfers are infatuated with having wall-to-wall manicuring." Doak doesn't believe in getting hung up on the "rules" defining hazards. "Some of the best hazards are, for example, short grass. If used properly, such condition can serve as a great hazard."

MacKenzie, according to Doak, was "the best of the classic architects at designing and building hazards." In general, Doak believes that hazards were better on older courses.

Maintenance practices have a significant effect on hazards, according to Doak. Whether positively or negatively, hazards change over time, and this is a part of golf that he accepts. "I often go back to see hazards, and they have changed dramatically from what they looked like when I visited just a few years before," he says.

Geoffrey Cornish

Cornish embraces the strategic approach to designing hazards, incorporating as many as 16 strategic or "bite-off" holes on an 18-hole course. Cornish does not like the idea of adding a penal hazard or condition to an otherwise strategic hole, "I do not like the double hazard," he says. An example in his view are some of the holes at Olympia Fields where a tree blocks a pending shot from a bunker. However, Cornish is quick to quote Harry Colt, who suggested there "is no such thing as a misplaced hazard."

Hell Bunker on the The Old Course's No. 14 is a favorite bunker. "It wasn't there originally, as it is only some 300 years old," he notes. "It has evolved over time and has played a major role in the golf course. Most golfers who play there frequently have failed to avoid it."

Cornish believes that there are plenty of hazards in golf that are not bunkers or water. He has always advocated the use of chipping areas and gives credit to Tillinghast for paying attention to the wind. "In my work, I have never hesitated to walk out into a field, even when there may have been an angry bull nearby, to check the direction of the wind," says Cornish.

Fig. 9-10 Waverly Oaks Golf Club, Massachusetts, a design by the firm of Cornish, Silva and Mungeam.

Ross, Tillinghast, and Willie Park were great at building and incorporating hazards into their golf courses, according to Cornish. "Ross talked about how the steepness of the face of a bunker can have a great impact on a golf shot, even more so than the depth," he notes. In modern times, Cornish points to the "Robert Trent Jones Era," from 1953 to 1990. According to Cornish, "This was followed by the 'Pete Dye Era' when many architects began copying what Pete had done."

Cornish believes that it is generally more exciting to see the hazard than to make it blind, but notes that "once you know where a hazard is, it really is no longer blind."

While water hazards have a finality about them, Cornish believes they can be made fair when designed properly. He has always liked using water in his designs.

Cornish, who worked with Stanley Thompson, noted that Thompson aimed for the spectacular in nearly all his bunkering. "Thompson felt that people should be impressed," says Cornish. He adds that the designers of the great links courses would likely laugh at the notion that the depth of bunkers should graduate depending on the shot. "Some of the deepest bunkers on links courses are fairway bunkers," he notes. "The lessons learned on the links courses are so important to golf course architecture. We must never forget them."

Cornish anticipates more random bunkering in the future of golf course design, but with ample attention paid to placement. He believes, "The new breed of architects will always come up with something new." One can easily tell that Cornish embraces innovation and clever thinking. "Allan Robertson introduced the concept of strategic architecture back in the 1840s when he began to widen the fairways at St. Andrews. This allowed golfers to play around hazards, instead of just over them," he reminds us.

Art Hills

Hills uses hazards in a variety of ways, but focuses on their strategic nature and not their penal implications. Typically, he will use just one or two fairway bunkers—not six or seven. Once in a while, he will introduce a penal bunker, placing it toward the middle of a fairway. He uses bunkers sparingly around greens, too. "A goal is to incorporate about 50 to 60 bunkers, maybe even less, on the whole golf course," he says.

A friend once told Hills, "Golf is like life. Sometimes you don't know when something will pop up at you that you will have to deal with." That idea has stuck with him in his design of golf courses and hazards. Hills likes using risk-reward hazards, angles, and "bite-off" holes that create an advantage if the hazard is challenged successfully. Hills admires Seth Raynor for designing bunkering with sharp angles to the player. He abhors the overused three-lobbed bunker. "They're trite," he says.

Fig. 9-11 Fiddler's Creek Golf Club, Florida (see color insert). Arthur Hills, golf course architect.

Hills likes width in his designs, feeling that it creates a better game. He believes it is more important than length for all but the best players in the world. "The best players are playing a different game than most golfers," he says. Hills likes holes where the golfer, particularly the average golfer, can stand up on the tee and rip a driver.

In terms of bunker style, Hills avoids flashed sand on faces, saying it causes maintenance challenges. "There is more of a permanency about flat-bottom bunkers with grass faces," he notes. His specifications often call for mist heads along bunker faces to help maintain the grass.

Hills favors the use of water hazards. "Augusta provides a great example," he says. "The 12th, 13th, and 15th are terrific holes defined by water. However, I really don't like fountains and waterfalls. They belong in shopping malls, not on golf courses."

"Golfers should have a feeling of accomplishment, so we work hard to design hazards for all levels of play, not just for the best players playing from the back tees," he says. Beyond the common hazards of sand and water, Hills uses low collection areas in his designs. And according to Hills, wind is one of the best hazards, especially for better players. "It gets them thinking and out of their routine. It forces creative shot making."

Hills is impressed with some new courses, such as Pacific Dunes and Sand Hills. "They used the land beautifully," he says. Among his favorite modern-age architects is Pete Dye, who Hills believes is great at creating and using hazards. He cites the TPC at Sawgrass as a prime example. "But overall I don't feel that golf architecture has improved over the years," he says.

A forced carry or cross-hazard can be unfair, according to Hills, as can bunkers that are repeatedly too deep or have severe overhangs. He doesn't care for beach bunkers or greens where a bunker is between the green edge and water. "The hazard should be either the bunker or the water," he maintains. Hills thinks hazards should be visible, but works to avoid making his courses too predictable hole after hole.

In the future, Hills expects to see more of what is being done on the top-ranked courses; more-natural features, less manicuring, and more-natural grasses on newer designs. "There is a tendency toward a more natural golf course," he says. Hills commented that if you built greens like those at Crystal Downs, "you would be sued." While he loves the greens there, he recognizes that most golfers today would not appreciate them.

Gil Hanse

Hanse's design styles and philosophies were heavily influenced by his time spent playing and studying the classic links courses in Great Britain. He was impressed with the way the land played a critical role in the routing and hazard formations of the golf courses there. He incorporates the same philosophy in his own designs, often allowing the land to determine where hazards will go and what type of hazards they will be.

CHAPTER 9 | OPINIONS ABOUT HAZARDS

When asked about some of his favorite hazards, Hanse mentions the Principal's Nose at St. Andrews for all its strategic implications; the Cardinal Bunker at Prestwick for how it impacts golf shots on multiple holes; and the bunker work at Pacific Dunes, especially on No. 13. "Sand Hills is one of the best bunkered courses in the world," he says. "The natural blowouts are unrivaled." Hanse has also been influenced by Macdonald's masterpiece, the National Golf Links, for its attention to the scale of the hazards and their strategic placement.

Hanse is a strong advocate of centerline hazards and always incorporates several into his designs. As with any design feature, however, he limits their use. Hanse believes that centerline bunkers should perhaps be the rule rather than the exception when it comes to fairway hazards. "It's a concept that American golfers may not be ready for, although I wouldn't mind testing the hypothesis," he adds. Hanse is a firm supporter of the older, classic approach to hazards. "Bunkers were natural hazards when they first appeared on golf courses, but most bunkers today are unnatural in location and appearance," he says. Hanse notes that the classic architects did all they could to try to make hazards look as natural as possible—as if they had always been there.

Fig. 9-12 French Creek Golf Club, Pennsylvania (see color insert). Gil Hanse, golf course architect.

Hanse feels that MacKenzie was best at designing and incorporating hazards into his golf courses. "He was a master of creating beautiful bunkers that were very strategic and natural in appearance," he says.

Short grass chipping areas are a quasi-hazard deployed by Hanse. As unofficial hazards they create shot options and variety and are pleasing to look at. Hanse feels that topography is a great way to create deception and obstructions that force precise shot making. For example, Hanse may have one side of a fairway offer a clear view of the green, while making the other side somewhat blind over a natural hill or landform.

As a rule, Hanse believes if a golfer finds one of his hazards, such as a fairway bunker, he should be able to advance the ball about half the distance he could have otherwise. He admits, however, that he doesn't always stick to that rule, but consciously thinks about the shot value of the hazard as he designs a hole.

Hanse will use water as a hazard when it occurs naturally on a site. He doesn't go out of his way to add ponds or streams. He is always amazed at the way golfers will accept water as a hazard even though a ball hit into it is lost for good, yet will complain about a deep bunker where a recovery shot is possible.

He doesn't mind incorporating a few blind hazards in his golf courses, reasoning that "they are only blind once." Hanse only uses hollows where they can drain naturally via the surface. He doesn't like catch basins or drains in the bottom of hollows where balls collect.

Hanse is always cognizant of the prevailing wind on his routings, especially on open sites where wind is more of a factor. He would love to see the word *fair* fall out of use in association with hazards.

Rees Jones

Rees considers the subject of hazards extremely complex and difficult to get one's arms around. He is not all that enamored with what he calls "the current trend of building scattered bunkers haphazardly placed around a golf course for no real rhyme or reason other than aesthetics." He also feels many of the rugged-looking bunkers that are being built today "will fall down over time" and calls them "the collapsing bunkers." He notes that golf architecture goes through trends, and this is another one, just as deep bunkers were once in vogue.

Fig. 9-13 No. 4 at The Bridge Golf Club, New York. The golfer can opt for a less penal approach, using the slope to feed the ball onto the green. Rees Jones, golf course architect. (Photo by Larry Lambrecht, Courtesy of Rees Jones, Inc.)

Says Jones, "The American version of golf, which is stroke play, vs. the British Isles version of the game, which is match play, dictates the way many hazards in this country are designed. In the U.S., golfers won't tolerate hitting their ball into a bunker and not having any kind of recovery shot. In the British Isles, the player simply picks up his ball out of the hazard and play continues on the next hole. Whether you like it or not, the original concept of hazards has evolved from what it once was."

Jones adds, "The 1950s ushered in an era of change in hazard maintenance. The use of gang mowers and the belief by many that the areas between bunkers and greens should be mowed with these large machines changed hazard design and their placement." Jones mentions "pockets" on older greens (from settling), saying "This kind of thing doesn't happen as often on modern greens."

On trees, Jones is opinionated. "The widespread removal of trees on golf courses is ridiculous," he says. "Many of these older courses were built on open farmland, and the architects always intended trees to be planted on them." Jones sees trees as legitimate hazards and one of the few ways to protect the difficulty of many designs. "Many water hazards came about because of the land that was given to architects to build their golf courses. They had no choice because of the low-lying nature of the properties but to build lakes and ponds."

Jones sees economics as a key driver of golf course design in the next ten years. He believes that high maintenance costs will impact what the architect can do in the design of hazards. As a result, hazards will need to be easier to maintain on many courses.

Graham Marsh

According to Marsh, one of the first things that comes to mind when he considers a new golf course is what kind of golfer will be playing the course, and equally important is the objective of the client. In most instances, this will determine what he does with the style and severity of the hazards. At Sutton Bay, Marsh explains, "The course was created to have a links character and a style similar to the older courses you would find in Scotland. That is what we tried to emulate." He designs his hazards differently depending on whether the golf course will be for the public, a high-end resort, or a private member

Fig. 9-14 Sutton Bay, South Dakota (see color insert). Graham Marsh, golf course architect.

club. He needs to know if the goal is to put 90,000 rounds per year through the course, or if it will be for championship play. "For public golf courses, the goal is often to get as many players around as possible. For a resort course, it might be to build a spectacular course or one that is very playable for beginners and intermediate players," he says.

"The depth and difficulty of bunkers, the size of the mounding, the number of blind shots, the use of forced carries is very much determined by the use of the golf course. If you start putting bunkers ten feet deep, the average golfer is going to die down there," he adds. One of Marsh's primary goals is to take a piece of land and design a golf course to satisfy the greatest number of golfers. "This is particularly difficult these days, because you are dealing with the wide variety of playing standards—from the professional to top amateurs to the beginners," he says. His hazard philosophy leans much more toward strategic design then penal design. He will limit forced carries and water, always being conscious of giving the average player a way out or a shorter carry. However, if asked to build a very tough golf course, he would probably employ more aspects of penal design.

There may be locations where Marsh is forced to use certain hazards because of the conditions at hand. "Sometimes it might be the only way to achieve a golf course on that particular piece of property," he says. "For example, if you only have 180 acres of land in Florida and you have to deal with wetlands, you may be left with hazards that you normally wouldn't elect to employ. In Australia, we often have to build courses in flood plains, and you need to create waterways to get fill to raise other areas of the course."

Marsh believes the larger the number of hazards on a golf course, particularly if they are in play, the slower the play will be. You also have to consider the maintenance of hazards. More hazards means higher maintenance costs, in his opinion.

Marsh utilizes grassy hollows, mounds, and other natural landforms that are found on the site as an alternative to sand bunkers. "These don't necessarily slow play down as much. Some of the best holes in the world don't have any bunkers at all."

Marsh says he is not averse to using hazards on the centerlines of holes but explains, "We allow various options of play over or around them, and different teeing locations."

MacKenzie inspired Marsh more than any other architect. "MacKenzie had a great visual style to his bunkering, and the playability of his courses, the size of his greens, and the strategic aspects were all terrific."

According to Marsh, "trees offer a wonderful asset on a golf course, and he will incorporate banks of trees into designs when he can." Many of his favorite courses, however, don't have any trees at all.

"One of your first responsibilities as a designer is to get the best out of a piece of property. The interesting thing about golf course design is that there are lots of designers out there doing all kinds of great, but different, work because we all see things a little differently. A golf course design is similar to asking ten different artists to sit down to paint the same landscape. You will get ten different pictures of that same landscape."

Pete Dye

When considering the use of bunkers, Dye lists three basic questions he needs to answer: "What purpose do I want the bunker to serve? What type of bunker is needed? What will be the best strategic position?"

"Strategic placement [of bunkers] subconsciously forces the golfer to head away from the bunkers, when the better route may be to hug them. . . . When you get those dudes thinking, they're in trouble," he says.

The philosophy of Pete Dye was certainly grounded, at least significantly, at Prestwick. This is where he first saw the use of railroad ties (sleepers). Dye was fascinated by their ability to add a striking and demanding dimension to the course, presenting the golfer with a highly visible obstacle as well as a means of controlling erosion. Dye eventually stopped using railroad ties and began using chicken wire hidden with vegetation to form his trademark steep banks along water hazards.

Among Dye's cherished golf experiences are the wide expanses at Turnberry; the pot bunkers at Prestwick; landscapes of multicolored heather; blind holes; narrow sloping fairways; and, at Prestwick, the menacing Pow Burn, a winding and weaving creek. At Carnoustie, Dye loves the uneven stances, undulating greens, and the center fairway bunker on the famed No. 6 hole.

Fig. 9-15 Prestwick Golf Club in Scotland inspired Dye in many ways. He has always been enamored with the movement of the land and its contours. (Courtesy of P. Burton)

Over the years, Dye has become a master of illusion. Greens where so much earth was removed in front that they appear elevated and wide fairways with angles of play to various golf pin locations are two such examples. Dye believes interesting approaches reward the ground game.

Dye claims to have always followed the words of MacKenzie in making "every one of his courses imitate the beauties of nature." But Dye's overall philosophy is to make sure a golf hole appears more difficult than it really is.

When deciding the purpose of a bunker, Dye takes into consideration the overall severity of the hole, whether water comes into play, the desired angle for the shot, and how best to challenge the aggressive player. Often, he will use a bunker to guide a golfer on the intended route to the green. Taking a cue from his tour of Scottish courses, rarely does he make use of opposing bunkers. Except on par-3s, Dye will rarely position bunkers directly in front of the green. He has built many lateral and rear bunkers to defend his holes from better golfers who hit their shots pin high or beyond.

He has used a wide variety of bunker types including shallow grassy-banked bunkers, waste bunkers,[1] steep-walled bunkers, and pot bunkers. Dye is thought of as a master of the psychological use of hazards to torment the golfer's mind. There may be no greater example than his famous island green at No. 17 of the TPC of Sawgrass. From the moment golfers step on the first tee—long before they face this delicate shot—they know they will have to contend with this hole. It's in their minds from the onset.

Mike Hurdzan

Hurdzan, like others, works at making golf holes "look hard and play easy" for average golfers, and "look hard and play hard" for the best players. "Golf is a game of visual messages and symbols. Hazards are symbols. So the 'how, where, and what kind of hazard' becomes the essence of the message. A hazard should not exclusively defend nor define, but rather communicate the challenge at hand," maintains Hurdzan.

Among Hurdzan's favorite hazards are holes where the ocean comes into play. He is fond of sod wall bunkers and feels that outcroppings of rock, boulders, and cliffs are great focal points as well as hazards. He is not an advocate of too many trees.

Hurdzan loves both past and present designs, saying, "MacKenzie gave lots of thought to angles of play and landing areas that were fair challenges for all skill levels. He thought about fairway slopes and how the ball moved on them. Other equally

---

[1] Dye explains that the term *waste bunker* was coined during the building of Harbour Town, when a sewer line break caused thousands of gallons of raw sewage to flood the unfinished 16th hole. "We saw the contractor was having a hell of a time, and so we told them they could let it run along the fairway," Dye explains. "We created some dams, and there the sewage sat for several days. In the end, we covered it up and compacted it into a flat bunker. Nothing would grow there, so I brought in a bunch of crushed seashells. We called it a 'waste bunker' for obvious reasons. And the name stuck."

Fig. 9-16 Devil's Paintbrush, Canada (see color insert). Mike Hurdzan and Dana Fry, golf course architects. (© 2001 Henebry Photography)

cerebral architects were Max Behr and Donald Ross. There always seemed to be a meaning to their madness." In modern times, Hurdzan believes Pete Dye is "the most creative guy alive. He has the courage to push the boundaries of design. The rest of us are followers."

As both golf architect and writer, Hurdzan has expressed his philosophy on hazards in practice and theory. "My favorite things are to use a wide variety of hazards in different ways, especially those which are naturally occurring," he says. "The only unfair hazard is a forced carry, a shot across a hazard with no bailout that is even too long for a golfer's best shot."

Are modern bunkers maintained so that they are too crisp and clean? "Yes," says Hurdzan. "And we spend too much time raking bunkers and building them to be nearly perfect."

Afterword

Many golf scholars have come to know Aleck Bauer's compilation of essays about golf hazards. Bauer's work was reprinted by Grant Books of England 80 years after his first edition hit bookstores in 1913. The reprinted edition was given a simple title: *Hazards*.

We bring this up for the purpose of stressing a point. Bauer's original edition was given a title much more meaningful than the short *Hazards*. Beautifully letterpressed on the front cover, on five separate lines of equally weighted and sized type, Bauer used these carefully crafted words for his original title:

It has been an honor to follow Bauer's work on hazards. Our hope is that each of us connected with golf architecture, course development, and the care and love of golf courses will continue to dig deeper into understanding how important hazards are to the heart and soul of the game.

—Forrest L. Richardson & Mark K. Fine

Glossary

Aa

aiming bunker Sand bunker placed to aid the golfer in aiming

aiming flag A flagstick and flag, usually of a different color than those used to mark hole locations on the course, set into the ground to denote a preferred landing or aiming alignment on a par-4 or par-5 hole prior to the green; aiming flags are typical on blind shots or fairways without reference points for aiming

aiming post A pole set within fairways as an aid in aiming

aerial golf General style of play on modern golf courses, especially American courses, where golfers tend to approach an intended target with a high lofted shot that lands and stops rolling abruptly; promoted by increased artificial irrigation of golf courses

aiming rock A painted stone or one of naturally contrasting color that is placed along a mound or ridge by a greenkeeper to indicate the preferred alignment for a shot that is blind or semi-blind, the locations of which may change daily depending on pin or tee position of a hole

aiming tree A tree left in place or planted with the primary purpose of aiding a golfer in aiming a shot or determining the line to a target

alpinization This concept emanates from a shift in thinking on how to place and create features when golf emigrated away from the linksland to the interior; the idea of creating large mounds and hollows was hit upon by J. H. Taylor with the help of Peter Lees in the Mid Surrey courses around 1911 (source: Tom Paul)

Alps Hole The par-4, 17th hole at Prestwick; also generally a hole mimicking the original Alps hole with an approach shot that must carry a very large mound that blocks the view to the green

alternate route Any pathway to a target if there are two or more fairly obvious choices

Amen Corner Portion of the routing of the back nine at Augusta National consisting of the second shot at the par-4 11th, the par-3 12th, and the tee shot at the par-5 13th; affectionately, any portion of a course with similar attributes to that of the real Amen Corner at Augusta

amoeba-shaped Shaped like a blob or with no organized shape at all

amphitheater Green set amongst mounds or hillsides so that the finished area mimics a genuine amphitheater

angle of approach Angle at which an approach shot is supposed to be played to the target for optimum scoring potential

angle of hole The angle of a dogleg hole; also the playing strategy of a hole in terms of its requirements, not related to its geometry

angle point A point on the design plans for a par-4 golf hole at which a shot played from the tee ideally ends and the second shot to the center of the green begins; or on a par-5 hole where the second shot ideally ends and the third shot begins; in the case of straight golf holes the lines connecting tees, greens, or other landing points do not always create an angle, yet the term is still used

angular Abrupt and contrasting due to noncurved surfaces, especially compared to the surrounds

anthill A uniform-shaped mound that resembles an anthill with a peaked top; often a pronounced bump in a green that creates impossible putts

approach The fairway and adjacent features immediately fronting a green that are within the path of a golf shot; the shot made by a golfer to a green from fairways, roughs, or hazards

approach side The side of a feature or hazard facing the golfer en route to a green or target

apron Grass that extends from the green outward toward the front, sides, or back, usually not cut as low as the green itself; aprons are generally not a consistent width and considerably wider in dimension than fringes or collars (see also: collar and fringe)

architectural feature A building, whether inhabited or abandoned, or any wall, dam, bridge, or other structure on a golf course that defines a hole or serves as an obstacle to play; common examples include stone cottages, old rock walls, bell towers, pump houses, castle ruins, and so on

arm A thinnish extension of a bunker, lake, or other feature that resembles an arm; an inlet of water that is typically long and relatively narrow, much more so than a bay

armpit Slang for a scraggly and usually deep bunker

arroyo Watercourse in an arid region; a gully or channel carved by water (Spanish; see also: barranca, wadi, and wash)

artificial feature A feature created by construction

artificial hazard Any hazard created by construction

artificial hole A golf hole not built into existing terrain and features, but created by significant earthmoving and artificial means

artificial ridge A pronounced ridge that extends across, or partially across, a green

artificial three-shot hole A par-5 hole that would ordinarily be reachable in two shots but because of an obstacle or obstacles forces a player to play to the side or lay up on one or more shots

artificial turf Carpet used in place of natural turfgrass

asymmetrical Without symmetry and therefore more natural-looking

atypical Not typical, and therefore more interesting than not

avenue Path to a target; slang for the linear heart of a fairway

Bb

ba Ball (Scottish)

backstop A mound, ridge, bunker, depression, slope, or other feature that helps stop a golf ball from rolling further; a typically ugly fence or net placed to help prevent errant balls from damaging life or property

backwater A small, generally shallow body of water attached to a main channel but with little or no current of its own

backwater pool A pool formed due to an obstruction in a stream or channel

bald mound A rounded mound with grass cut exceptionally tight to the ground

ball catcher A trap, grass depression, playable hazard, or mound that tends to stop balls and prevent errant or over-hit shots from continuing; a ball catcher is typically a savior to a golfer and results in a lie not as bad compared to the alternative had the ball continued beyond the feature that caught the ball

ball collector Any depression, including a sand bunker, that is intended and designed with inward slopes for the purpose of collecting balls hit to its general area; usually for the purpose of preventing balls from rolling further off line

ball magnet Any hazard or other area other than a tee or green that tends to attract shots hit by golfers

ball-to-target line The direct line from the position of a player's ball to the target

bank A slope of rather steep angle that divides an area, terminates to a lake or hazard, or forms the edge of a tee or green

bank shot A shot where a steep slope is used to manipulate the direction or speed of the ball

barber pole A bold striped pole set within fairways as an aid in aiming

barranca An otherwise dry channel, usually steep-walled, in which water flows during rainfall runoff; barrancas are usually covered in vegetation, which distinguishes them from washes (see also: arroyo, wadi, and wash)

baseball glove sand trap A sand trap that resembles a baseball glove; often used to describe bunkers by George C. Thomas, which were often characterized by gnarly "fingers" extending from the main body of the bunker

bay In reference to bunkers, an area that extends out from the main mass of a bunker and is defined by capes or areas of turf; an area of a surface, especially water, that extends outward from the main portion of the area to form a smaller area, mostly secluded

beach Slang for sand trap or bunker

beach bunker A large sand bunker with a relatively flat bottom and very slight edges surrounding; also, an improved sand hazard combined with the shoreline of a lake or pond (see: shoreline trap)

bear paw bunker A series of roundish bunkers that together form the appearance of a bear's paw; perhaps also a bunker created by the personal hand of Jack Nicklaus, although this usage is undocumented, thank goodness

beached whale A green that looks like it was shaped over the top of a beached whale

beeline The centerline of a golf hole or the direct line of sight between an area of a hole and the target, especially when such an imaginary line is unobstructed and free of obstacles; derogatory term for an unimaginative golf hole, usually straight and with little or no interest such that a golfer is only required to hit toward the target with lack of thought or challenge

beehive mounds From the geometric era of golf design in America, the very early 1900s; such mounds were abrupt at their bases, concentric, dome-shaped, and typically identical in addition to being spaced evenly over generally flat terrain; any mound shaped like a beehive

bell-shaped Shaped like a bell, being wider at the front and narrowing toward the back

bench terrace Flat area that interrupts a hillside

bend Refers to the angle created in a dogleg hole

berm A small rise in the terrain that is long and narrow; usually manmade but can be naturally occurring

bilevel A tee or green having two distinct levels

Biarritz Hole Name bestowed to an exceedingly penal and long par-3 hole, typically playing over a perilous hazard and seemingly impossible to reach from the tee; the name comes from a golf hole that course architect C. B. Macdonald saw at Biarritz, France, at the Biarritz la Phare Course built by Tom and Willie Dunn, Jr. (1888)

bite-off bunker Bunker so positioned as to beckon the player to "bite off" (carry) more of it in order to gain a better position or advantage on a particular shot

bite-off hole A hole, or portion of a hole, allowing a shot to be played that, by changing the angle of flight, will enable the golfer to reach the target or be closer for the next shot

blin Blind (Scottish)

blind A hidden area from which a golfer can see a target, but cannot generally be seen by others

blind approach Situation caused by a golfer hitting to an area outside of the planned landing area and therefore limiting visibility to the area of the green

blind green A green positioned such that it cannot be seen from areas that golfers are meant to be playing from to approach the green (note: although a particular green may not be visible from deep in the rough, for example, this does not mean it is a "blind green"; this is simply a "blind approach" caused by the golfer's mishap)

blind shot A condition where a golfer playing a shot from a tee or intended landing area cannot see the next intended landing area, be it a fairway landing area or the green itself

blow out A sand bunker set into a rise that has its sides and/or top flash extending, as if naturally, out into the surrounding terrain; usually a sand feature that is set into a natural dune land setting, in many cases a natural sand dune that has been somewhat formalized into a bunker

bomb crater Large circular bunker

boomerang green A green shaped in a wide arc like that of a boomerang, typically with the concave portion facing the line of play and the two "wings" on each side

boomerang hole A long dogleg hole that so severely plays around a feature or hazard that it appears to come back in the opposite direction

boondocks Rough country that is heavily brushed and usually inaccessible; any remote area of a course; derived from the Filipino word for mountain *(bundok)* introduced to America by returning servicemen from Asia following World War II

bottleneck Portion of a hole or fairway that narrows significantly; any elongated and narrow section of a golf course feature; also an area of a course at which play slows considerably due to course layout, difficulty of a hole, or other condition of the facility or course policies

boulder Any rock fragment larger than 60.4 cm (24 inches) in diameter

boundary hole Golf hole that borders a hard-edged property line, hazard, or other obstruction that significantly affects play strategy due to the peril on the opposite side of the boundary from the hole itself; a prime example is the Road Hole at The Old Course at St. Andrews, which closely borders and is interrupted by sheds and a hotel property separated by fencing and walls

bounds Short for "out-of-bounds"

bowl An area having a shape of a bowl; an area of a green where there is an undrained low point

Bradshaw's Bottle During the British Open in 1949, Harry Bradshaw, an Irish pro, pushed his drive and found it inside a broken bottle; the rules at the time did not permit relief, and he wasted a stroke to break the bottle and ultimately lost the tournament

bracketed bunkering Bunkering flanking both sides of a fairway or green, generally opposite to each side and somewhat congruent in terms of size and quantity of bunkers

brae A hill or hillside (Scottish)

break The direction that a ball will roll on a putting surface

breakneck green A green with slopes and breaks so confusing that a golfer might break his neck trying to read them

bridge Thin strip of turf between bunkers suitable for use in accessing the green or other area

broken ground Rough earth with rises and falls suitable for transformation to golf use, or for leaving as rough areas in between tees and fairways, alongside holes, and so on

broken nose Nose of a bunker that abruptly forms a steep slope

builder Construction entity of a golf facility

bulb A protrusion of a feature such as a sand trap or green

bulkhead A retaining wall along a waterfront; also used loosely to describe any artificial retaining wall or surface, such as that on a bunker face or steep embankment

bump A very small and usually gradual mound

bump and run Shot played into a slope or bank and then allowed to continue toward the target

bumps and hollows A scattering of small mounds and depressions

bunker Historically, a grassy mound or configuration of mounds located to influence and affect a golf shot regardless of whether it is faced with or contains sand; mostly in modern terminology, a depression filled with sand for the same purpose; a hazard when it contains sand unless otherwise noted by local rules; a protective embankment or dugout; a fortified chamber often lying mostly underground (see: sand trap and trap)

bunker complex A grouping of bunkers and mounds that, by nature of their proximity, work together to define an area of interest

bunker happy Characterized by too many bunkers

bunker island Any raised area within a bunker on which turf is grown; not technically a part of the hazard unless otherwise noted

bunker well The main body of a sand bunker, at which it is typically lowest in elevation

bunker-to-bunker Situation where bunkers are positioned such that a golfer may play from one to another and become frustrated doing so

bunkering The combination of bunkers at a green, hole, or course

buried elephant A large mound, usually in a green, that appears as though it was formed by covering a large animal carcass with earth; sometimes used sarcastically to describe a mound feature that is out of scale or not shaped well (see also: hogback)

Burn Hole No. 1 at The Old Course, St. Andrews, 376 yards, par-4; the Swilcan Burn loops across in front of the green

burn Scottish term for a creek or stream

burp An abrupt mound that seems to come up out of nowhere

butte An isolated hill or mountain with steep sides, smaller than a mesa or plateau

button hook A hole with a green set across a hazard or feature situated to the side of a fairway requiring play beyond the green and then back in a "looping" alignment if one is to avoid hitting over the hazard or feature; mostly used to describe a par-5 hole where the centerline of the third shot is nearly at a right angle to that of the second shot's centerline, taking its name from the looping shape of a button hook

Cc

cabbage Slang for very thick rough that entangles

cambuca A derivative of paganica, a twelfth-century game played with a wooden ball

canny Descriptive for a snugly situated green or tee; also a carefully situated feature

cant A slope in one general direction, such as seen in a "canting fairway," which slopes to one side or angle so as to influence balls hit to it in that direction; also, used to describe greens, but seldom tees (see also: double cant)

cape In reference to bunkers, extensions of turf that interrupt the main mass of a bunker and help to form bays (see: bay); the point or head of land projecting into a body of water; any rounded projection jutting out into an area of lower-lying terrain

cape hole Any hole longer than a par-3 designed on a "cape" of land mostly surrounded by peril (water, deep rough, etc.), with a tee shot that can be played further along the cape with more risk; the hole will typically end to a green set at the end of the cape above the hazard or rough

Cardinal Bunker The large fairway bunker on the 3rd hole at Prestwick

carpet-faced bunker A bunker with a steep face, sometimes vertical, that is stabilized and faced with layers of floor carpet that are capable of retaining the earth behind them

carry The distance that a golf ball travels in the air; often refers to the distance a golf ball must travel before landing to clear a hazard or feature

carry bunker A sand-filled bunker positioned such that the preferred line of play requires a direct hit over the bunker

carrying hazard Same as "carry bunker," but extended to any hazard positioned so that the preferred line of play requires a carry to clear its limits

Cartgate Hole In No. 15 at The Old Course, St. Andrews, 456 yards, par-4. So named because it is close to the cart track that crossed the fairway and led to the beach

Cartgate Hole Out No. 3 at St. Andrews, 397 yards, par-4. This hole shares its green with hole No. 3

catch A low spot or grass bunker designed to "catch" balls or drainage

catch bunker Bunker situated so as to "catch" a ball before it goes out of play, or otherwise into a worse position

catcher's mitt A roundish mound with a pronounced depression set into the face of one side slope; a bunker with the same general definition (see also: Thomas bunker)

catchment A low spot usually associated with drainage

cathedral effect Tall trees lining an area and creating the feeling of being within a cathedral

cauldron Exceptionally deep and treacherous hazard, usually a bunker

cavern A grass or sand bunker of exceptional depth and with steep side slopes; in geologic terms, a large underground opening in rock, usually formed by dissolved limestone

cementlike approach A hard or flat area fronting a green that allows balls to roll without impedance

centerline A line that connects the tee center point with angle points and green center points; used in planning a golf facility as the skeletal system of a golf hole; a centerline is a path assumed by the golf course architect to be one of the preferred alignments for play to properly negotiate a hole (see: course geometry)

centerline bunker A bunker placed along a common centerline of a golf hole

centerline hazard A hazard, usually a formal bunker, placed along the centerline of a hole

chainsaw shaping Shaping so naturally conducive to golf that it is said to require "only" a chainsaw with which to ready it for planting

chasm A deep bunker; a ravine or natural area that is deep and steep

Cheape's Bunker A formidable bunker on the No. 2 hole at The Old Course, it is named for Sir James Cheape who saved the course from the rabbit farmers in 1821 by buying the links. His descendant, another James, sold the links to the Royal & Ancient in 1892, which sold it to the town in 1893.

chicane An obstacle, usually in the form of sharp turns, built into a path or route to a target

chipping area Area designated for chipping practice, with or without a formal putting surface to accept shots

chipping swale A swale adjacent to a green that is mowed and slopes at a height conducive to chipping or putting onto the green

chocolate drop A mound with a pointed top resembling a drop of chocolate but much larger and not nearly as sweet; a typical American design trait as golf became popular during the very early 1900s, but eventually viewed as bad design by the celebrated architects of the golden age

chole A flemish game resembling golf and perhaps involved in golf's ancestry; two players bid on the number of strokes to reach a distant goal, such as a door or gate, by hitting a ball with a club; the lowest bidder gets three consecutive shots and then the opponent is allowed to strike the ball once to stymie the opponent or merely hit the ball backward; the goal is to reach the target with the amount of strokes bid

Church Pews A famous feature located between the third and fourth fairways at Oakmont Golf Club outside Pittsburg, Pennsylvania; a large, flat sand trap interrupted several times by low, narrow, grassy ridges placed perpendicular to the line of play, the appearance of which resembles church pews (see also: reverse church pews)

chute A rather narrow opening flanked by slopes or hillsides that creates a visual "tunnel" from the viewpoint of the golfer

cigar bunker A bunker shaped like a cigar, long and narrow, typically used during the geometric period of design influence in America

classic course A debatable definition, but generally a golf course built in the span from the 1900s through 1940s that exhibits golf course design traits common to courses of these early eras; such traits include natural use of landforms, simple earthmoving techniques, and bold hazards; "classic" in literal terms is typically the first rank or authority, constituting a standard or model; therefore, the term may be expanded to include a course of recent vintage that exhibits "classic" traits, although such a course is more appropriately called a "modern classic"

classic hole A famous golf hole that has been widely copied in design principal

cleavage A narrow opening between two mounds

climax The green of a hole; a point within a round or course where the most awaited and celebrated hole or holes are grouped

cloverleaf A bunker or green shape with three or four bulbs protruding from a central point

coffin bunker A long and slender bunker of straight proportions, usually about the size of a coffin and relatively deep-appearing

collar A relatively constant width of grass that surrounds a putting green but is not cut as low as the green itself (see also: apron and fringe)

collection area A grassy depression near a green where errant approach shots wind up

collection bunker A bunker situated to collect balls, usually stopping them from entering deeper trouble

compartment An area of a green defined by breaks, ridges, or the outer limits of the green, and which is distinguishable by the golfer from the balance of the green when playing a hole

containment Shaping that assists in keeping the ball in play through depressions, slopes, and mounds that are angled up and away from the golfer

contour An imaginary line that represents a series of points at the exact same elevation above a given reference point, such as the level of an ocean; contour lines are used to draw the vertical shape of the land in a two-dimensional representation; also used to describe the slopes and surfaces of a golf course, hole, fairway, or green

contour mowing Mowing that generally follows the contour of the fairways or roughs and works in and out around mounds and features as opposed to going up and over high points and slopes without regard for the natural flow of the course

convex slope Slope with increasing gradient as contours decrease in elevation

cookie-cutter greens Greens that are all similar on a course and usually uninteresting

cookie-cutter traps Sand bunkers that are relatively round and look so similar that they are said to have been "manufactured by the same mold"; also sand traps with a crisp edge as if cut with a giant cookie-cutter

cop bunker A sand bunker designed expressly to divert play around or over it away from a particular area; a cop bunker is usually penal in nature, placed so as to penalize even the poorest of shots

cop hazard Out-of-bounds stakes set along a hole to create a penalty, usually for the purpose of protecting another nearby hole or practice area, but sometimes out of pure spite

Corner of the Dyke Hole No. 16 at The Old Course, St. Andrews, 424 yards, par-4. A cluster of three bunkers makes up Principal's Nose on this hole, thought to be a reference to Mr. Haldine, principal of St. Mary's College in the early nineteenth century and endowed with a prominent, bulbous nose.

corrie Bowl-shaped hollow depressed into a hillside (Scottish)

corset A rigid and closely controlled restriction

craig A rugged rock or outcropping (Scottish, from the Gaelic word for "rock"); also spelled "crag"

crest The top of a mountain, hill mound, or bunker; an emblem adopted by a club or course to signify membership or origin

cross-hazard A sand bunker or other formal hazard that lies at a 90-degree angle to the line of play, usually requiring a shot to carry it; can also mean a pronounced feature or rough area having the same characteristics, but not necessarily a hazard per the Rules of Golf

cross-bunker A sand bunker that lies at a 90-degree angle to the line of play, usually requiring a shot to carry it

cross-over Point where the intended play of two holes intersects, common in early courses of the British Isles, now less common due to liability; also used informally for a place where parallel holes going in opposite directions meet a similar set of holes and play "crosses over" from one side to the other, in routing, a place where any series of holes "crosses over" another series between greens and tees

cupping area The available area for setting a cup on a putting surface; that area of a green on which it would be fair to set a cup, usually not the far edges of the green nor areas of severe slope where a ball could not be stopped

Dd

debris mound A landform created by piling debris (rock, layers of cut vegetation, etc.) and then covering the debris with compacted soil; can be an efficient way of ridding sites of unwanted materials without hauling to off-site locales

deception bunker A bunker so placed that it makes a target appear closer to a golfer than it actually is; usually an elevated bunker well short of a green that conceals the distance between the bunker and the green

deep ditch hazard An irrigation ditch or similar manufactured water course that is defined as a hazard

deep hollow A significant low area or nook created by and mostly surrounded by mounding

dell A secluded low-lying area or valley, usually having an intimate atmosphere

Dell Hole The par-3, 5th hole at Lahinch; also generally refers to a hole with a green almost completely surrounded by large mounds (like the aforementioned) with only a small portion visible from the tee

desert lateral rule Local rule common to Arizona and other desert regions where a player may choose to treat the native desert rough surrounding a target golf hole as a hazard and play from the last point the ball crossed the fairway, incurring a one-stroke penalty (coined by: Forrest Richardson, Phantom Horse Golf Club, 1985)

detour design One of the five basic strategies of golf design: holes and shot requirements may be predominantly open, heroic, penal, layup, or detour in nature; a detour design is one that gives the golfer obvious routing choices to reach the target that are defined pathways

developer Instigator of a golf project; one who "develops" golf courses

Devil's Asshole The menacing, small, deep bunker that fronts the par-3 10th green at Pine Valley

Devlin's Billabong The small pond water hazard located just in front of the 18th hole of the South course at Torrey Pines in La Jolla, California; the hazard, added in 1968, caused major grief to Bruce Devlin in the 1975 San Diego Open, where the pro attempted six strokes from the hazard and ultimately lost all chance of a win

diagonal bunker A bunker set diagonally to the line of play and usually within the line of play to the hole

diagonal hazard A hazard set diagonally to the line of play or approach

dimple A small indentation in a surface that adds character and is an intended feature

dip A depression in a green, but also in fairways; usually across the path of play rather than along it

dipsy-doodle Slang to denote a roll in the landscape, usually between two noticeably higher points; also used liberally to describe several bumps and hollows that would be too cumbersome to describe individually and with no valid purpose: "Bob, can you and your dozer give me another dipsy-doodle over here between the green and the tree line?"

do-or-die hazard A hazard from which recovery is impossible; a lake is typically a "do-or-die" hazard, as shots cannot be played from underwater

dog squeeze Particularly awful shaping work, as in "Listen, Bub, that mounding is dog squeeze, pure and simple."

dogleg A golf hole with an angled alignment; the term is believed to have first been used in a 1902 *Golf Illustrated* article in which a path was described as "rather like a dog's hind leg"

dog-paw bunker A bunker with multiple "bulbs" protruding off a larger area, resembling a dog's paw

double cant A cant that is sloped in more than one direction; a double-canted green is one that has two distinct slopes that are largely separate

double diagonal A two-shot or three-shot hole on which there is a diagonal hazard in the fairway and one again at the approach to the green (coined by Robert Hunter)

double dogleg A golf hole that has two doglegs in its centerline (see: zig-zag hole)

double fairway A hole with two pronounced fairways or paths that allows a golfer more than one option in playing

double green A green that serves as the target for two holes, each hole having its own flag

double jeopardy A situation caused when a hazard or feature penalizes a golfer and the escape route presents an equal or greater penalty, causing the golfer to potentially lose two shots (see: double hazard)

double penalty Literally two penalties incurred at one time or as a result of two infractions in succession; occasionally used interchangeably with "double hazard" or "double jeopardy"

driving hazard Any hazard placed so it will influence the tee shot on a par-4 or par-5 hole

drop area An area designated by local rules where a ball played into a hazard may be dropped under penalty; painted markings, stakes, or markers define drop areas

drum A narrow ridge or hill (Scottish)

dune A hill or ridge of sand that has been created and shaped by the wind; a duplication by construction of a natural dune

Dyke Hole No. 2 at The Old Course, St. Andrews, 413 yards, par-4. The "dyke" is the old wall that forms the boundary between the hotel and the 17th fairway

Ee

eccentric lie An unusual lie caused by interesting design or, perhaps, design that is too interesting

eddy A swale shaped against the natural flow of a fairway or green surface; a current of water or air that moves contrary to the direction of the main current, especially in a circular motion.

Eden Hole The par-3 11th on the Old Course at St. Andrews received its name from the River Eden that flows behind the green; any hole that plays to a slightly teardrop-shaped green with the "pointed" part facing the tee-box; in the strictest sense, such a hole will be guarded by a deep and high-faced sand bunker at the front of the green and positioned directly along the line of play to the heart of the green

elbow The bend of a dogleg hole

elbow hole A type of dogleg hole; a hole that bends at a defined point

elephant's nose A uniquely shaped mound, somewhat like a nose; often confused with "buried elephant"

elevated fairway A fairway elevated above a tee or green

elevated green A putting surface that is noticeably raised above its immediate surroundings

elevated tee A tee significantly elevated above the fairway or approach

elevation The measurement above sea level or some other constant point of a defined coordinate or series of coordinates; a contour line represents a constant elevation along a string of imaginary points on a landscape; also, a drawing showing what an object will look like from the side

Elysian Fields The portion of The Old Course at St. Andrews, Scotland, that defines playing options at the 14th, or "Long," hole; a relatively open area flanked by bunkers on all sides toward the line of play

environmentally sensitive area An area in which access is denied by a government or other appropriate agency from which relief with a penalty specified by the local rules must be taken by a golfer, as defined by the Rules of Golf

eroded bunker Whether planned or accidental, a bunker with edges that are random and appear to have been cut away by the forces of nature

excavation The cutting of earth, soil, or rock away from an existing or filled area

eyebrow The back lip of a bunker when arched and left to rough high grass that, when viewed from the front, resembles an eyebrow; any grading feature that resembles an eyebrow

eyewash Extra detailing or landscaping added to a golf hole or course that has no real value other than cursory aesthetics; typically a belittling term

Ff

F An abbreviation for "fairway" on early hole diagrams

face The upslope of the far side of a bunker when looking toward the target; the side of a slope or bank when facing the target

facelift Slang for remodeling work in which only the visible components of a hole or course will be reshaped or influenced

fair bunker As defined by Alister MacKenzie: "If a bunker is visible and there is an alternate route around it, then it is fair"; often used with reference to MacKenzie

fair hazard A hazard positioned and built such that it can be avoided

fairway An expanse of grass that serves as the connection between a tee and a green; the primary target for any shot that is not an approach shot to a green

fairway bunker A sand bunker that has a direct impact on the play of a golf shot other than an approach to the green

fairway flag A flagstick and flag placed within a fairway to aid in alignment, typical on holes where a blind shot may exist or confusion may arise as to the correct direction of play

fairway mounding Mounding located within a fairway; any mounding between the tee and the green that helps define the fairway

faithful restoration A rehabilitation or renovation of a feature or course that is intended to evoke the style and feel of the original course design, even though, from a technical point of view, the new result may be different from what was originally in place

fallaway green A green that is slanted so that the predominant slope is away from the approach to the hole

false front An approach to a green, or area prior to a green, that is improved to resemble a putting surface or guarded by bunkers or features to suggest that the green is closer to the golfer than it is

fan wall Timbers or railroad ties laid back against the face of a bunker or slope in a fanlike shape

fat part of the green The largest portion of a green where there are abundant cup positions; the area of the green where a safe shot is typically played to avoid surrounding hazards

faux restoration A restoration in which historic considerations are not observed; the effect is superficial and not faithful to the particular course or its history

feather To blend a mound or slope to a flatter area with no obvious point of transition

featherie An early golf ball with a core of compressed feathers inside a leather outer

feature Any hazard, mound, depression, natural condition, area, or portion of a golf hole or course that may be individually referenced; also a consistent design trend evident throughout a golf course; "Among the features of the course are its large, expansive greens."

featureless Course without features other than rudimentary tees, fairways, and greens

feel-good bunker A bunker so placed that it may be overcome, usually along the normal line of play, by most ordinary golfers with little or no difficulty

fell Mountain or hill (Scottish)

fill Material set over existing grades

finish grade The final grade of a golf course on which turf and hazard surfaces are established

floating Smoothing a surface for its final surface treatment, curing, or seeding

floating green A green held afloat on a body of water by means of a barge or other apparatus and capable of being relocated (architect Scott Miller is credited with developing this concept at Coeur d'Alene, Idaho, 1991)

fog Growth of long grass (Scottish slang)

folds Undulations, especially in the surface of a green

forced carry A condition that requires a golfer to execute a shot capable of clearing a hazard or feature with no alternative path to the target

forced dogleg A dogleg hole or portion of a hole that bends around an obstacle that cannot be hit over due to its size or height

fore bunker A bunker set to the front of others

formal hazard A sand, water, or other area demarked or otherwise subject to the Rules of Golf, or local rules, relating to play from hazards

formalizing Cleanly cropping and manicuring courses, especially around bunker edges and turf edges of fairways; formalizing is a modern golf course trend largely adopted in America in the 1960s as course conditioning became so popular

firth Large, but relatively narrow, inlet of the sea (Scottish)

finger A thin band of turf that extends into a bunker; any especially thin extension of a bunker, mound, or lake

framing Restricting the view of a golfer through plantings, clearing, and grading so as to border the "picture" seen from a tee or area; the practice is considered overrated by some golf course critics but it nonetheless remains a wholesome element of landscape architecture

freak green A green so severe in contour or shape that it may be unfair

freeway golf Golf holes with straight-edged fairways and parallel relationships that are highwaylike in appearance; such holes were typical of many post-WWII designs until strategic design became commonplace in golf architecture

fringe A ring of grass that surrounds a putting green but is not cut as low as the green itself; fringe may be the same width as a collar, but mowed at a different height, usually lower than the collar (see also: collar)

fronting A feature or area that is in front of another feature or area

funnel bunker A bunker that is graded such that balls are drawn to it as if "funneled"

furrow rake A specialized rake for raking sand traps, made famous through its use at the Oakmont Country Club, consisting of a two-by-four approximately two feet long with V-shaped notches cut into one side, later made from cut lengths of sickle-bar mower blades used on farm tractors; the furrow rake was also used at nearly all Pittsburgh-area courses prior to the 1960s

furrowed trap A sand trap, or sand-filled bunker, raked with furrows (see also: furrow rake)

Gg

gathering area An area on the approach side of the bunker that gathers rolling balls toward the hazard; the Road Hole Bunker at The Old Course has a gathering area that feeds balls into the steep-walled pit

gathering bunker A sand bunker set into the terrain with slopes that promote balls to roll into it, usually shaped with a wide opening faced toward the golfer

geometric design An early and novel approach to course construction in America where features were angular and evenly spaced; can now occur when computer-aided design is allowed to exclusively dictate form

geyser hazard A water hazard that cannot be seen except as a result of a fountain shooting water into the air

giggle bunker A bunker so situated that it is well out of play and makes one "giggle" at the thought of who placed it and why

Ginger Beer Hole No. 4 at the Old Course, St. Andrews, 464-yards, par-4, where Old Daw Anderson set up his refreshment stall in the 1850s, selling more potent brews than the name suggests

glen Valley with a stream or brook running through it, usually somewhat narrow and secluded (Scottish)

gnarly Having intensive bumps, roughness, and abruptness; particularly natural with no soft or finished qualities

goal posts A pair of features situated opposite one another through which a shot is played toward a target

golden age of golf course architecture Began with the opening of The National Golf Links in 1911 by C. B. Macdonald and lasted until the stock-market crash of 1929

golf course architect The individual responsible for the design of a golf course or facility, or for designs to remodel a golf course facility; a golf course architect should possess, according to the ASGCA, "a knowledge of the game, training, experience, vision and inherent ability, and be in all ways qualified to design and prepare specifications for a course of functional and aesthetic excellence"

golf course architecture The broad profession that encompasses golf course planning, design, specifications, and the supervision of construction of golf courses and golf facilities

golf course architorture Golf architecture carried to an extreme, usually an absurd one (coined by Ron Whitten)

golf course design The design of a golf course or facility

golf course designer Informal title given to a golf course architect; sometimes used to distinguish between a bona fide golf course architect and one who simply has had design input in a course

good-player bunker Bunker positioned to catch the good player, or make him think twice

gorse *Viex europaeus,* a native plant on the linksland of the British Isles (see: whins)

gotcha bunker Hidden bunker that "comes out of nowhere" (coined by Neal Meagher)

grade The finished or existing surface of an area; also the slope of an area

grading Relocating dirt from one place to another with mechanized or hand tools; the result of such activity

grass bunker A depressed area that is typically formed by one or more mounds; grass bunkers generally have low points

grass-faced bunker A bunker with a steep slope planted with grass (also called a grass-walled bunker)

grass mounds Mounds planted with grass; the term is usually reserved for instances where mounds are situated within nonturf areas, sand bunkers, or waste areas

grassy hazard An area that punishes a shot hit to it by way of its depth, the cut height of grass, or intricacies of slope; grassy hazards are generally surrounded by closer-cut grass and are isolated pockets or hillocks rather than formal hazards

grassy hillock A grass-covered mound, typical of links courses and linksland

grassy hollow A depressed or low point of a turfed surface, usually subtle and fitting harmoniously into surrounding slopes or mounds (see hollow)

green Smooth grassy area at the end of a fairway especially prepared for putting and positioning the hole; all ground of a hole that is specifically prepared for putting; also, an archaic term (through 1900) used to describe the entirety of the golf course, and source of such terms as greenkeeper, green fee, and so on; a green is also a grassy lawn next to a house or cottage (Scottish)

green complex The collective features and their interrelationship at the site of a green and the immediate surroundings

greenside bunker A sand bunker that has a direct strategic or penal impact on the play of a shot to a green

greenkeeper The individual charged with "keeping the green" by maintaining and caring for a golf course property

ground character The movement of the fairways on a hole or course that is apart from the features and greens, but integral to them by way of approaches and playing interest; also the natural movement of land before a golf course is built or shaped

ground contours The slopes of fairways that direct bounding balls; the use of ground contours was more common in early designs (pre-1950), before artificial irrigation began to soften fairways and limit the influence of slopes on shots to fairways

gully A watercourse created by running water, but normally dry; gullies are distinguished from rills by their depth

gully pot A catch basin (British)

gunch Tall, thick native rough on a golf course, from which a golfer normally has to accept an "unplayable lie"

Hh

H An abbreviation for "hazard" on early hole diagrams

ha ha A sunken fence or built land feature that typically retains earth on one side while being exposed on the other; such a feature is not visible from the upper side until one is close upon it, at which point the change in elevations becomes clear; also, a feature or hazard positioned such that it elicits surprise from the golfer upon discovery

haycock A mound resembling a somewhat rounded and conical pile of hay

haystack A mound that is pronounced and dome-shaped at the top, like a stack of hay

hazard An area of a golf course containing water, sand, or other terrain that is subject to the Rules of Golf pertaining to play from such areas; also used loosely to describe features that are in the path of a shot (i.e., trees, hillsides, etc.)

hazard marker Any device used for delineating a water hazard; the most common examples are posts made of wood or plastic and are driven into the ground directly or inserted into a sleeve; standard colors for hazard markers are yellow for regular water hazards and red for lateral water hazards

Heathery Hole Nos. 6 and 12 at The Old Course, St. Andrews. The Heathery "Going Out" is the 6th, a 412-yard par-4. The Heathery "Coming Home" is the 12th, a 314-yard par-4. Stroke Bunker on the 12th is so called because, once in it, you lose at least one stroke. The names of both holes are a reminder of the times when the landscape at St. Andrews was largely heather.

heathland An expansive area of interior land, usually wasteland that is relatively flat and poorly drained; likely from "heather," the Scottish plant that so defines such inland areas of "waste"

Hell Bunker The bunker on the par-5, 14th at The Old Course at St. Andrews, large and strategically placed approximately 100 yards short of the green

hemmed-in Tightly situated amongst bunkers, features, trees, and so on

heroic design One of the five basic strategies of golf design: a hole may be predominantly open, detour, penal, layup, or heroic in nature; a heroic hole provides the golfer an opportunity to attempt a high-risk shot in order to place the ball in a very desirable position; failure to successfully execute the heroic shot usually results in a highly penalized situation

herringbone A pattern of drainage ditches where there is a central ditch running in the direction of the flow and extension ditches running outward from either side of the central ditch; from above, a herringbone drainage pattern resembles the skeleton of a herring

hidden trap A sand bunker that cannot be seen from normal areas of play

hill In Britain, any pronounced rise in the landscape below 1,969 feet in height from its base, unless the rise is especially abrupt, in which case it may be termed a mountain even if just 984 feet in height (note: in the United States there is no official difference between a hill and a mountain); a pronounced rise created by earthmoving equipment, which, due to its mass, may not be sufficiently described by the term "mound"

hill hole An uphill hole

hillside The slope of a hill

hillock A small hill (Scottish in origin)

hinterland Land located away from coastal areas in the interior of a region

hinge point The angle point of a dogleg hole

hogback A mound that resembles the back of a hog in profile, usually smaller than a buried elephant

hogback ridge A ridge with a sharp summit and steep slopes of nearly equal inclination on both flanks, and resembling in outline the back of a hog

holding pond A small basin or pond designed to hold sediment-laden or contaminated water until it can be treated to meet water-quality standards or used in some other way

hole Short for "golf hole"; also, the specific and final target for the golfer; a 4 $1/2$-inch diameter by 4-inch-deep cylindrical space cut into the putting green of a hole

hole indicator A small flag, ball, or other attachment to a flagstick that may be slid up and down to visually represent the depth the pin is set from the front of a green; the higher the indicator is set on the flagstick, the further back the hole is positioned; indicators may also be in the form of signs or plaques configured at tees, with small pegs or markers showing where the pin has been set on a hole

Hole O'Cross In Hole No. 13 at The Old Course, St. Andrews, 430 yards, par-4. Likely the former site of a cross or a reference to the gulley that golfers had to cross to reach the green

Hole O'Cross Out Hole No. 5 at The Old Course, St. Andrews, 568 yards, par-5

hollow A depressed or low point of a surface; a small valley or basin, usually subtle and fitting harmoniously between surrounding slopes or mounds; hollows are not always fully depressed and may drain to other areas

hole strategy The end result when the art of devising plans for a golf hole have come together to create one or more approaches to playing a golf hole in the fewest strokes

horseshoe A bunker, mound, green, or other feature having the shape of a horseshoe; a U shape

hourglass shape The shape of a feature that has an extreme pinch in its middle

hump and bump A rise and fall occurring in combination; a series of such combinations

humpback A large bump or ridge; usually a raised area on the surface of a green creating interesting breaks

Ii

immovable obstruction Anything artificial that interferes with the line of play but is deemed immovable by the Rules of Golf or local rules (see also: movable obstruction and obstruction)

Jj

jail The position of a ball when advancement toward the target is nearly impossible

jeu de mail Archaic French game of Italian origin played within an enclosed court or roadway; thought to be partially responsible for the development of golf; combines elements from modern-day croquet, billiards, and golf

Kk

keeper of the green Alternative term for "greenkeeper" or "golf course superintendent"

kettle hole A golf hole largely depressed into the terrain due to a natural sink hole creating a round, deep, and bowl-shaped area like that of an old cast-iron kettle; any golf hole built through heroic earthmoving measures that resembles such a condition when finished

knob A small, isolated, and well-defined mound

knoll Small round hill

knowe A small rounded hill (Scottish)

knuckle Series of congruent mounds or bumps

kolf An archaic Dutch game with similarities to modern-day golf and played with a curved wooden club

Kruger Bunkers Famous bunkers at The Old Course, St. Andrews, built during the Boer War (1899–1902) when the British were fighting in the Transvaal, whose president was Paul Kruger

Ll

lake bunker A smallish pool, usually adjacent to a green; the term stems from sand bunkers that by some means filled with water or may have been intentionally filled with water to create a more penal hazard (see: water bunker)

lake hole Golf hole playing aside or over a lake

lakeside bunker Bunker located next to a lake

landform The form of a tract of land or region; also, used to refer to a smaller formation of land

landing area Typically, the area prior to the green of a golf hole, in which a golfer is expected to land a ball from the tee or fairway; also an imaginary circular area measuring approximately 200 feet in diameter that surrounds any point defined by the golf course architect at which properly executed shots will come to rest when a golfer plays a hole as intended based on its design; this definition includes the circular area surrounding fairway angle points and green center points

lateral water hazard A full or partial body of water or similar area parallel to a fairway that has been staked or defined as a lateral water hazard subject to the Rules of Golf; a lateral water hazard may be defined to include only a portion of a body of water, with the remainder being either a water hazard, through-the green, or out-of-bounds

layup area An area provided by the design of a golf hole, usually short of the eventual target or a hazard, crossing the line of a hole, that allows a golfer an alternative to a more aggressive line of play while perhaps sacrificing an opportunity for a lower score

layup design One of the five basic strategies of golf design; a hole may be predominantly open, heroic, penal, detour, or layup in nature; a layup design is one that demands that the golfer hit short of the intended target while enroute

layup hole A par-4 or par-5 hole on which it is expected that a predominance of golfers will hit an intentionally shorter shot from the tee than a full drive in order to stop short of an obstacle; a par-5 hole on which the second shot played is subject to the same expectation

light-bulb-shaped A green or other feature, shaped with a bulbous end tapering to a rounded point

line of charm An attractive and enticing line of play; a suggestion as to the alignment a golfer should play a golf hole that is implied by the design of the hole itself, especially as a result of the placement of hazards and features upon the hole; the line of play down a fairway that is most alluring to the golfer in that it yields the best position, although it may be subject to peril from a hazard or other feature; hazards contribute greatly to establishing an obvious line of charm by adding intrigue and a challenge to the alignment a golfer might decide to follow en route to the hole

line of flight The horizontal path a golf ball travels from impact by a club to its first contact with the ground

links A seaside golf course constructed on a natural sandy landscape that has been shaped by the wind and receding tides (a Scottish term from the Old English hlincas, or ridge meaning the undulating sandy ground near a shore); also used more generally as a synonym for a seaside golf course and sometimes for a golf course that is configured with nine holes extending outward and nine holes returning to the clubhouse, although there is no factual basis for such use; often incorrectly used to refer to any golf course

linksland Land near an open sea, or a bay that is connected directly to an open sea that possesses the characteristics of naturally rolling sand dunes or land features formed by the wind, the ocean and the receding tides

lip The vertical edge of a sand bunker; the visible band of soil beneath the turf surrounding the bunker to the point where the sand is placed; also, the upper edge of a hole cut into a green

long hole Any par-5 golf hole; also generically used to describe any hole of exceptional length regardless of its par

lone solider Any solitary mound, trap, hillock, or tree that serves to protect or guard an entrance to an area or target

Long Hole No. 14 at The Old Course, St. Andrews, 581 yards, par-5. It is the longest hole at The Old Course and has the largest bunker, Hell Bunker, positioned at about 100 yards from the pin. Others bunkers here are the Beardies, Kitchen, and Grave.

Mm

MacKenzie Bunker The fairway sand bunker on the 10th hole at Augusta National, which was a greenside bunker until the green was moved back considerably

MacKenzie green A putting surface with considerable contouring, but a natural appearance conforming to the adjacent terrain; not necessarily a green designed by Alister MacKenzie, but mimicking his style

MacKenzie school of design Conforming to the practice of Dr. Alister MacKenzie; strategic and playable designs with especially natural and irregular bunkers and sporting bold, contoured greens; examples include Cypress Point and Augusta National

man-made feature Any individual feature or collective features of a course or hole created through construction efforts

mental hazard A golfer's inner trouble dealing with a particular shot brought about through clever golf course architecture, which makes things appear much more difficult than they are

mine field Hole or fairway with an abundance of sand bunkers, especially one where such bunkers intrude into the fairway

minimalism A design and construction approach that involves the least disturbance, excavation, and improvements to a golf course or hole possible while still achieving aesthetic, playable, and interesting results (popularized by Ron Whitten)

mogul A small hill usually appearing in a cluster with others

molding Shaping by contouring

moon crater A depression with a faint ridge or lip surrounding

moonscape Broken and rough ground that looks like the surface of the moon; any area of exceptional roughness

moorland course A golf course built on land that is open and rolling, usually inland

mound A raised area of earth created by shaping; seldom used in reference to a natural rise in the ground, unless specified as "natural mound"

mounding Several mounds interrelated to one another visually or by proximity; the total of the mounds on a given course or area; the act of shaping mounds

movable obstruction Anything artificial that interferes with the line of play and is deemed movable by the Rules of Golf or local rules (see also: obstruction and immovable obstruction)

multiple fairway A hole with more than one fairway or ideal path that can be used to reach the green

Nn

native Having natural, indigenous qualities that are untouched or partially preserved

natural amphitheater A green set into an area that is naturally like an amphitheater

natural feature Any feature of a course or hole that is not manufactured

natural hazard A feature that existed on the site before the construction of the golf course and was incorporated into the design as a hazard; usually a body of water, topographical feature, or natural sandy area

natural hole A hole that fits so well into the natural landscape prior to construction that only minimal effort is required to ready it for play in terms of grading and shaping work

90-degree dogleg A par-4 or par-5 hole closely approaching a 90-degree bend at the first landing point, hopefully formed by a suitable hazard or obstacle and not other holes, houses, or private property

nose A feature extending into a bunker that is shaped like a human nose, being wider at the upper portion and tapering to its lower end; any mound that resembles a nose and extends into an area

notch An opening shaped into a fairway or between mounds that opens to a larger area; a naturally occurring opening in a valley

Oo

obstacle Any feature, tree, or condition in the way of a golfer's pursuit of a target or lower score

obstruction Anything artificial, including the artificial surfaces and sides of roads, paths, and manufactured ice, except: objects defining out-of-bounds, objects that are out-of-bounds and any construction declared to be an integral part of the course as specified by the Rules of Golf (see also: movable obstruction and immovable obstruction)

OB Abbreviation for "out-of-bounds"

open design One of the five basic strategies of golf design: a hole may be predominantly heroic, penal, layup, detour, or open in nature; an open design is not a preferred type, as it has no obvious obstruction en route to the target

optional carry A design where a carry over a hazard or feature is an alternative to a safer route, or to a carry over another area or feature, and produces a different result if successfully carried out by a player

optional hazard A hazard over or around which play must continue in order to avoid another hazard

orphan bunker An isolated bunker that is not integrated with other bunkers by way of mounding or features

outcropping A prominent protrusion of rock or natural terrain that juts up in the landscape

oxbow A looping bend in a river or stream that is geologically caused by water meandering on gradually sloping land; repetitive oxbows are called meanders and have opposite curves; anything in the shape of an oxbow

Pp

paganica Ancient Roman game similar to golf involving a leather ball stuffed with feathers and a bent stick; name means "the game of the countrymen"

pan bunker Small sand bunker that in plan view is the size and shape of a pot bunker but much less deep

pancake green Flat, boring green that is round

parkland course A course located on parkland or similar setting

peanut-shaped Having a shape resembling that of a peanut; rounded, elongated, and narrow or "pinched" in the middle

penal design One of the five basic strategies of golf design: a hole may be predominantly open, heroic, detour, layup or penal in nature; a penal design is focused on penalizing a golfer for a poor or mis-hit shot and can include either forced carries or fairways lined with hazards

peninsula green A green set on a raised area

personal bunker A deep pot bunker, large enough for only one golfer (see also: pot bunker)

pews Series of sand bunkers or traps set parallel to one another and generally linear in shape, as are church pews

pig-snout bunker A very, very small bunker or pair of shallow and round sand depressions that look like a pig's snout; such bunkers may only be 5 to 6 feet in diameter each

pimple Mostly used to describe an unsightly feature on a golf course, usually too small in relation to its location and out of place as a result

pine straw Bailed quantities of pine needles typically spread over areas in rough; sometimes used to control erosion and promote growth

pinnable area An area on a green where it is practical to set a hole

pit A deep bunker or grass depression with steep side slopes

plateau green A green set on a natural flat area or constructed to resemble such

playable hazard A hazard, such as a sand bunker or dry ravine, from which play is typically expected to occur in the course of completing play on a hole; an example of an unplayable hazard is a lake or deep gorge, from which a ball is presumed lost and not playable except under rare circumstances

popular bunker A bunker positioned or with characteristics such that it attracts shots into it

postage-stamp green An extremely small green, usually elevated and somewhat squared off on the sides; the par-3 8th hole at Royal Troon

pot bunker A small, round, especially deep sand bunker (see also: personal bunker)

pot green An old method of construction where a green was built in a depressed setting to aid in retention of water from surrounding areas

potato-chip green A putting green with contours that undulate similar to those of a potato chip

practice bunker A designated bunker created for the purpose of practicing, usually situated within a practice area, driving range area, or other practice venue

pregnant bunker A small bunker located above a larger bunker on a mound

preliminary grading Grading work performed in advance of feature shaping and finish shaping

principal hazards Hazards that are key to the playability or aesthetics

Principal's Nose The cluster of three small pot bunkers in the crook of the 16th fairway on The Old Course at St. Andrews

privacy mounds Mounds situated such that their primary purpose is to create a secluded area, such as to separate a tee or green from another area, activity, or use

prevailing wind The wind that predominates at a given locale

primary rough Grass cut to a consistent height that is immediately adjacent to the fairway, unless there is intermediate rough

protection bunker A sand bunker placed to assist in reducing shots being hit in its direction

protective hazard Any hazard positioned to keep balls away from its location

punch-bowl green A green that is located in a depressed area like a punch bowl; an archaic design used to help collect water onto the greens for better turf conditions

punch bunker A small deep bunker shaped as if a fist punched into a slope

Qq

quiddity The essential quality of a thing; in golf architecture, the essential function of a feature, such as strategy, aesthetics, or drainage

Rr

R An abbreviation for "rough" on early hole diagrams

radical bunker A sand bunker so large, expansive, and intrusive that it is radical compared to most others and will likely attract criticism

Rae's Creek The narrow creek at Augusta National Golf Club that runs behind the 11th green, in front of the 12th green, and along the left side of hole 13; its namesake is John Rae, who lived in a house on the Savannah River that he used to harbor residents who could not reach Fort Augusta safely during Indian attacks

railroad-tie embankment A wall or slope stabilized with railroad ties that creates a formal appearance along a bunker or other slope

ravine A narrow, steep-sided valley larger than a gully and smaller than a canyon; usually formed by flowing water

razorback clam bunker A shallow bunker resembling one-half of a razorback clam shell set into the ground, only, of course, much larger than the shell

rebunkering A remodeling that is restricted to changing bunkers on a hole or course

reshape To grade or shape to redo work already performed

re-veg The process of restoring vegetation to an area cleared or graded, usually with native species

redan green A green mimicking the Redan Green; a green with an angled hazard that limits the approach to a narrow line of play

Redan Hole The par-3 15th hole at North Berwick; also a hole mimicking the original Redan Hole, with the green slightly elevated and sitting at an angle to the line of flight, with a menacing hazard fronting the angled green; such a hole requires a golfer to carry the hazard to access a middle or back pin placement or play safe to the front of the green and accept a long and more difficult putt

remodel To change a feature, hole, or course, whether as a restoration, renovation, or a more complete alteration, such as a rerouting or significant rebuilding

renovation Change(s) made to a golf course or hole to improve conditions

restoration Careful rebuilding of a golf course, hole, or area to return it to its original form and character

reverse redan A Redan hole, or a hole with attributes of a Redan, that mirrors the original, on which shots played from the right toward the left will avoid the sand hazard to the front

revet To face a sand bunker with a revetment (see: revetment)

revetment An embankment, usually faced with stone or other material so as to hold back soil or sod; revetments are common on classic links courses where steep-faced bunkers are to be preserved

reverse church pews A series of relatively thin strips of sand traps set parallel to one another and perpendicular to the line of play; the term comes from the fact that such a feature (a series of sand traps set into the turf) is the reverse of the famous Church Pews at Oakmont Country Club in Pittsburgh, which is a series of grassy strips set into a large area of sand (see: Church Pews)

reverse tier An elevation change in a green creating two distinct levels, where the lower level is distal from the line of play into the green

riband bunker A bunker stretching entirely across the line of play (see also: cross bunker)

ridge A pronounced linear feature of generally consistent height that forms a division between two areas; on a putting surface, a linear alignment from which surface drainage will fall in opposite directions at any given point

ridge line A series of points of higher elevation that separate two adjacent lower areas or water sheds

ridgetop Top of a ridge of dunes or linear mounds

ringed Surrounded by bunkers or features

risk-reward A shot requirement, or series thereof, that involves initial risk on the part of the golfer in anticipation of a reward by virtue of the finishing position of the ball, shorter distance to be covered, or eventual reduction in further risk to be encountered; a heroic or strategic hole, which rewards the golfer with a better position or opportunity in exchange for a degree of risk (also known as risk and reward)

riverine Related to a river; being situated along the banks of a river

Road Bunker A deep, steep, sod-faced pot bunker at St. Andrews

Road Hole The par-4 17th hole on The Old Course at St. Andrews, with an extension of North Street located directly behind and bordering the back of the putting surface; the road leads directly into the center of the city of St. Andrews; played as a par-5 until the late 1960s; famous for its difficulty, and named after the roadway running behind the green, which has proved the downfall of many; perhaps its most memorable modern-day professional drama was in 1984, when it cost Tom Watson the Open

road An informal hazard unless otherwise marked

rough The taller grass that borders fairways and may include native areas that are unimproved; generally speaking, all parts of a golf course excluding greens, tees, fairways, hazards, and areas out-of-bounds

rough bunker A bunker languishing 10 to 20 yards outside the fairway line

running approach A shot played to a green that bounds along the ground prior to the green as opposed to being hit higher and landing upon the green's surface on the fly

rushes Any of various monocotyledonous, often tufted marsh plants with cylindrical and often hollow stems

Ss

sand A granular material composed predominantly of mineral sediments with diameters larger than 0.074 mm (0.0029 inch) and smaller than 2 mm (0.079 inch)

sandy waste area An informal sand area, not designated as a hazard

sand cliffs The portion of a sand bunker where sand is especially steep, such as under the lip of an elevated edge

sand-faced bunker A bunker with a steep face covered with sand (also known as "sand-walled bunker"); a natural-appearing bunker with sand continuing up the face and held in place with native grasses or natural conditions

sand green A putting surface constructed of compacted sand and no turf; the surface is often oiled to keep the sand in place; sand greens are constructed where no water is available or where no means exist to finance standard turfgrass greens

sand pit A "sand bunker," usually deep

sand trap A sand-filled depression strategically placed as a hazard and a deterrent to making an unimpeded recovery shot; term used regionally in place of bunker (see: bunker)

sandhill A hill all or partially covered with sand; a small dune stabilized partially with turf or tall grasses

saucer green A round, relatively small, usually uncontoured green

scab bunker A style of bunker that is carved into a mound or placed between two small mounds, with lips of varying heights and an appearance similar to that of natural sand dunes; particularly used to describe bunkers designed by Dr. Alister MacKenzie that had the appearance of scabs

seaside bunker A sand bunker formed by the wind and blowing sand, or one so built to resemble this appearance; not necessarily or typically bunker situated by the sea

seaside course A golf course located immediately adjacent to a sea or ocean; synonymous with "links" in modern times

semiblind A hole or shot requiring execution with only partial visibility to the target due to an obstacle or topographical condition

shaper An equipment operator who shapes features according to the plans created for a golf course or instructions given by the architect

shaping The process of moving or pushing dirt to create the shape of fairways, tees, greens, mounds, and hazards

sharp dogleg A dogleg hole with a second shot alignment at an angle to the tee shot in excess of 33 degrees

sheds Famous structures at the Road Hole at St. Andrews Old Course, that are hit over from the tee shot; the sheds were originally station sheds for the St. Andrews railway line; when they were torn down to build a hotel, an uproar ensued and replicas of the original sheds were rebuilt

shelf A tier or flat area that is situated within an incline and interrupts a slope

shelved An area that is graded to form a shelf in a fairway, green, or other area

sideburn An area of rough or longer grass extending from one area to another

signal bell A permanent bell mounted so that it may be used by players leaving a green or other area that is concealed from the golfers who follow, signaling that play is complete and it is now safe for the group following to play to the area

sinkhole A depression caused by the dissolving of underlying lime stone, salt, or gypsum or other unstable conditions

skillet bunker A sand bunker the size of a pot bunker but much less deep (coined by Cabel Robinson)

sleeper A hole that is astonishingly beautiful, interesting, or challenging within a layout; a course that gets little attention and is more deserving; timber, stone, or steel set into the ground to support railroad ties set to provide windbreak or hold back a slope (see: sleepered bunker)

sleepered bunker A bunker that has lumber or railroad ties holding back one or more banks

sleeping policeman British term for a speed bump, stemming from the passive method by which such bumps in roadways and parking lots control speed; in golf a long bump in a fairway or green

slight dogleg A dogleg hole with a bend that is hardly noticeable

slight hollow A grassy, subtle depression between mounds

snake pit A bunker, usually sand, that is so deep and defined that it is almost certain disaster for the golfer who hits into it

sod-faced bunker A bunker with a steep face, that is stabilized with layers of sod that are capable of retaining the earth behind it

spaded bunker A bunker with a clean edge, not uneven or natural

spine A pronounced ridge in a green, often feathering out to nothing

split fairway A fairway divided by one or more features or hazards along the linear direction of the play of the golf hole, creating alternatives for the golfer; one route usually offers a greater reward at a greater risk of penalty

split level Usually a fairway but sometimes a tee or green with distinct levels separated by an embankment in reference to greens and tees (see: bilevel and trilevel)

St. Andrew First disciple of Christ, believed to have been crucified by the Romans in Patras, Southern Greece; according to legend, St. Rule stole parts of St. Andrew's remains centuries later to take them to the "ends of the earth," as directed by divine influence; St. Rule's ship wrecked on the east coast of Scotland, the known "ends of the earth" at the time; namesake for the town of St. Andrews, Scotland

St. Andrews City on the east coast of Scotland; location of The Old Course at St. Andrews, regarded by many as the "home of golf"

stadium course A golf course design concept that facilitates tournament play, particularly the seating of spectators, giving the golf course a stadium feel

stair-stepped Having distinct levels with almost equal distance between each that give the appearance of steps to a green or other feature

step An area between levels of a green

stiff hazard A hazard that is especially difficult to avoid or recover from, and usually one that appears obvious and penal

stone wall Literally, a wall made from stone, usually stacked with no mortar or bonding

strait A small body of water, usually linear and narrow, that connects two larger bodies of water

strategic design A type of golf course design that is focused on providing alternate routes from which a golfer may choose to proceed based on risk versus the reward and allowing players with different skills to negotiate a hole commensurate with their particular skill levels; in actuality all golf architecture is strategic, even "open design" which is strategic by virtue of its assumed ease

Strath Bunker The bunker that guards the green at The Old Course at St. Andrews, the "High Hole Coming Home"; the name refers to the Strath brothers, especially Davie, a friend and golfing partner of Young Tom Morris.

Stroke Bunker A bunker at The Old Course on the Heathery Coming Home, the 12th hole, a 314-yard par-4; so called because once in it, you lose at least one stroke.

strip bunker A long and narrow sand bunker, usually aligned parallel to the line of play and bordering a fairway or green site

strip mine Slang for a long narrow bunker

subgrade The grade below the final finished grade

sunk green A green depressed into the surrounding landscape, if not entirely, at least visually from the tee locations

sunken Depressed into the surface with no obvious outfall

surrounds The entirety of the features and forms surrounding a green; also, the landscape and environs around a course property or any localized area

Sutherland Bunker The bunker at hole No. 15 at The Old Course, St. Andrews; the name refers to Mr. A. G. Sutherland, a keen golfer who in 1869 was so outraged when he discovered that the bunker had been filled in that he wrote to the R&A several times; two cousins went to the course one night and re-created the bunker, leaving a note with Sutherland's name on it

swale A visibly low area of linear proportions in which drainage may flow to an outfall or low point; the term is usually reserved for fairways and roughs

sward Grass-covered soil

swath A row of grass left after cutting; a long, broad strip or belt, such as a swath of grass between two bunkers

sweeping Characteristic of a mound, slope, green, or fairway in which there is a huge area of gradual grade that appears larger than it is

Tt

T An abbreviation for "trap" and occasionally "tree" on early hole diagrams

target An area at which the golfer is expected to aim, land, or end up; sometimes used interchangeably with pin or flag

target bunker A sand-filled bunker placed primarily for the purpose of directing a shot over or aside it to a preferred alignment

target moundings A group of mounds that suggests or implies the preferred line of play (either toward, aside, or over) or otherwise serves as a crutch in determining alignment of a shot to be played

terraced green A green with distinct levels or tiers

think-twice bunker A bunker positioned to cause doubt about a particular shot or route to a target

Thomas bunker A dramatic, jagged-edged, catcher's mitt sand bunker; this feature was a trademark of golf course architect George C. Thomas (1873–1932)

Thomas-Bell bunker A sand bunker with flashes of sand between jagged peninsulas of turf, or capes, named for the famous bunkers created jointly by golf architects George C. Thomas, Jr. and William P. "Billy" Bell

tight fairway A fairway that is especially narrow, because of encroaching hazards, features, trees, or rough

tile drainage Drainage by means of a series of tile lines laid at a specific depth and grade

tongue A narrow band of turf interrupting a bunker; on greens, an extension of green surface that spills out to a lower grade like a tongue hanging out of a mouth; any strip of turf or terrain that looks like a really big tongue

traditional design Golf course design that is stoic and resembles that of a classic course

transition area An area along a hole that serves to transition between the turf and native terrain; usually with a clean edge adjacent to the golf course and an undefined edge adjacent to the native surroundings; such areas have a twofold purpose as they help prevent both balls and irrigation from infiltrating the native area

transition bunker A formal bunker serving the same purpose as a transition area

trapping The combination of traps on a hole or course

tree island A raised area of land within a bunker or waste area on which a tree is growing

tree wall A mass planting of trees that is linear and wall-like

treed rough A deep rough area with trees and native terrain

triple fairway A hole with three pronounced fairways that allow a golfer several options in playing

triple green A putting surface that accommodates three different golf holes, each hole having its own flag

trough A noticeable linear depression that outfalls to a larger low area; often a fairway feature that feeds or collect balls and drainage; on greens, a subtly low area that is much longer than it is wide

tundra A rolling plain, devoid of trees, with subsoil that is frozen year-round

Uu

U-shaped Shaped to resemble the letterform U

undulation A wavelike motion to and fro in a fluid or elastic medium propagated continuously among its particles but with little or no permanent translation of the particles in the direction of the propagation

unplayable hazard A hazard such as a lake or deep gorge from which a ball is presumed lost and unplayable

Vv

v-ditch A drainage channel with a cross-sectional V shape

Valley of Sin The large, low area fronting the 18th green at The Old Course at St. Andrews; used reverently to indicate any similar design feature where the green extends well forward and to a low point from which balls must be putted or chipped a great distance and up a significant incline

volkswagen Slang for an abrupt mound in an isolated portion of a fairway that looks as if it has been created by covering a Volkswagen Beetle with dirt and sod

Ww

wall A face of a bunker; also, any of a variety of artificial walls, usually vertical, such as bulkheads, rock walls, concrete walls, railroad-tie walls, and so on

washout Erosion caused by a sudden gush of water, as from a downpour or flood; a channel created by such erosion

waste area Usually a flat-bottomed area with occasional vegetation or tall grasses, the surface of which is sand or smoothed soil, resembling a huge bunker, but not defined as a hazard

waste bunker Same as waste area, but defined as a hazard

water bars Berms or long swales strategically placed along slopes for runoff to other areas

water bunkers Historically sand bunkers that filled with ground water and were modified to become water hazards; prior to casual water rules, the term is likely to have referred to sand bunkers that filled with rainwater and were "in play" with no relief; today the term is sometimes used sarcastically to refer to very small lakes

water feature Any feature on a golf course, natural or man-made, that holds water, including creeks, streams, washes, lakes, ponds, and waterfalls; designed for golfing strategy, hazards, aesthetics, or auditory ambiance; often used to refer to a water fall or cascading stream

water hazard A full or partial body of water that usually crosses the path of a golf hole and has been staked or defined as a water hazard subject to the Rules of Golf; a water hazard may be defined to include only a portion of a body of water, with the remainder being either a lateral water hazard, through-the-green, or out-of-bounds

water hole A golf hole where water is designed to come into play; a small natural depression in which water collects, especially one used by animals for drinking

watery filth Standing water (from early St. Andrews Golfing Society Rules)

watery grave A water hazard in which

a ball has been hit and will not be found or played; any deep or especially menacing water hazard where the above may become a reality

waving mounds Mounds that are repetitive and appear to have been shaped by the wind

well trapped Having many or well placed bunkers; the term can be used to describe a hole, green, or fairway

wet meadow Grassland with waterlogged soil near the surface but without standing water for most of the year

wetland An area with hydrology, soils, or vegetation types that support habitat and oxygen exchange meeting a criteria established for determining such an area; the single feature that all wetlands have in common is a soil or substrate that is saturated with water during at least a part of the growing season; wetlands require that one or more of these attributes be met: (1) hydrology: at some point of time in the growing season, the substrate is periodically or permanently saturated with or covered by water; (2) hydrophytic vegetation: at least periodically, the land supports predominantly water-loving plants; (3) hydric soils: the area contains undrained, wet soil that is anaerobic, or lacks oxygen in the upper levels; other common names for wetlands are sloughs, ponds, swamps, bogs, and marshes

whins *Viex europaeus,* a plant native to linksland on the British Isles; another name for gorse

white stakes Out-of-bounds; derived from the customary use of white stakes to demark the limits of in-bounds ground

Yy

yawning bunker A bunker with a large surface area that can be seen, usually rising up at the back and appearing in the shape of an open mouth when yawning; a gaping bunker

Zz

zig-zag hole A hole with a double dogleg

Glossary contents from On Course — A Dictionary of Words & Terms Used by Golf Course Architects *(© 2002 Forrest Richardson)*

BIBLIOGRAPHY

Bahto, George. *The National School of Design.* Chelsea, Mich.: Sleeping Bear Press, 1997.

Balfour, James. *Reminiscences of Golf on St. Andrews Links.* Edinburgh: David Douglas, 1887.

Bamford, J. L. *Royal Portrush Golf Club, 1888–1988: A History.* Portrush, Northern Ireland: Royal Portrush Golf Club, 1988.

Barclay, James A. *The Toronto Terror: The Life and Works of Stanley Thompson, Golf Course Architect.* Chelsea, Mich.: Sleeping Bear Press, 2000.

Behrend, John, and Peter N. Lewis. *Challenges and Champions: The Royal & Ancient Golf Club.* St. Andrews, Fife, Scotland: Royal & Ancient Golf Club of St. Andrews, 1998.

Bauer, Aleck. *Hazards: Those Essential Elements in a Golf Course Without Which the Game Would Be Tame and Uninteresting.* Chicago: Tony Rubovitis, 1913, and Droitwich, Worcestershire, England: Grant Books, 1993.

Browning, Robert. *A History of Golf.* New York: E. P. Dutton, 1955.

Campbell, Malcom. *The Random House International Encyclopedia of Golf.* New York: Random House, 1991.

Chapman, Kenneth G. *The Rules of the Green: A History of the Rules of Golf.* Chicago: Triumph Books and the USGA, 1997.

Colt, H. S., and C. H. Alison. *Some Essays on Golf Course Architecture.* New York: Charles Scribner's Sons, 1920, and Droitwich, Worcestershire, England: Grant Books, 1993.

Cornish, Geoffrey S., and Ronald E. Whitten. *The Architects of Golf.* New York: HarperCollins, 1993.

———. *The Golf Course.* New York: Rutledge Press, 1981, 1982, 1984, 1987.

Cotton, Henry. *Henry Cotton's Guide to Golf in the British Isles.* Manchester, Greater Manchester, England: Cliveden Press, 1969.

Daley, Paul. *Golf Architecture: A Worldwide Perspective.* Vol. I. Louisiana: Pelican Publishing Company, 2002.

———. *Golf Architecture: A Worldwide Perspective.* Vol. II. Louisiana: Pelican Publishing Company, 2003.

Davis, Spencer H., Jr., Steven R. Langlois, and Louis M. Vasvary. *The Dictionary of Golf.* New York: Carlton Press, 1990.

Davis, William H. *Great Golf Courses of the World.* New York: Golf Digest, 1974.

de St. Jorre, John. *Legendary Golf Clubs of Scotland, England, Wales, and Ireland.* Wellington, Fla.: Edgeworth Editions, 1998.

Doak, Tom. *The Anatomy of a Golf Course.* New York: Lyons & Burford, 1992.

———. *The Confidential Guide to Golf Courses.* Chelsea, Mich.: Sleeping Bear Press, 1996.

Doak, Tom, Dr. James S. Scott, and Raymund M. Haddock. *The Life and Works of Dr. Alister MacKenzie.* Chelsea, Mich.: Sleeping Bear Press, 2001.

Dye, Pete, with Mark Shaw. *Bury Me in a Pot Bunker.* New York: Addison-Wesley, 1995.

Elliott, Mal. *Perry Maxwell's Prairie Dunes.* Chelsea, Mich.: Sleeping Bear Press, 2002.

Fazio, Tom, with Cal Brown. *Golf Course Designs.* New York: Harry N. Abrams, 2000.

Finegan, James W. *All Courses Great and Small: A Golfer's Pilgrimage to England and Wales.* New York: Simon & Schuster, 2003.

———. *A Pine Valley Golf Club, A Unique Haven of the Game.* Pine Valley, NJ: Pine Valley Golf Club, 2000.

Garrity, John. *America's Worst Golf Courses: A Collection of Courses Not Up to Par.* New York: Collier Books, 1994.

Glynn, Enda. *A Century of Golf at Lahinch, 1892–1992.* Galway, Ireland: Lahinch Golf Club, 1991.

Graves, Robert Muir, and Geoffrey S. Cornish. *Golf Course Design.* New York: John Wiley & Sons, 1998.

Gillum, John. *The Sacred Nine.* Suffolk, England: The Royal Worlington & Newmarket Golf Club, 1992.

Green, Robert, and Brian Morgan. *Classic Holes of Golf: A Grand Tour of the World's Most Challenging, Historic, and Beautiful Golf Holes.* New York: Prentice Hall, 1989.

Hawtree, Fred. *Aspects of Golf Course Architecture.* Droitwich, Worcestershire, England: Grant Books, 1998.

———. *Colt & Co. Golf Course Architects.* Woodstock, Oxford, England: Cambuc Archive, 1991.

Hobbs, Michael. *Golf in Art.* Edison, N.J.: Chartwell Books, 1996.

Hoffman, Davy. *America's Greatest Golf Courses.* New York: Gallery Books, 1987.

Hotelling, Neal. *Pebble Beach Golf Links.* Chelsea, MI: Sleeping Bear Press, 1999.

Hunter, Robert. *The Links.* New York: Charles Scribner's Sons, 1926, and Chelsea, Mich.: Sleeping Bear Press, 1999.

Hurdzan, Michael J. *Golf Course Architecture: Design, Construction, and Restoration.* Chelsea, Mich.: Sleeping Bear Press, 1996.

Jarrett, Tom. *St. Andrews Golf Links: The First 600 Years.* Edinburgh, Lothian, Scotland: Mainstream Publishing, 1995.

Joy, David. *St. Andrews and The Open Championship: The Official History.* Chelsea, Mich.: Sleeping Bear Press, 1999.

Jones, Robert Trent, Jr. *Golf by Design.* Boston: Little Brown, 1993.

———. *Golf's Magnificent Challenge.* New York: McGraw-Hill Publishing Company, 1988.

Jones, Robert Tyre. *Golf Is My Game.* Garden City, N.Y.: Doubleday, 1960.

Klein, Bradley S. *Rough Meditations.* Chelsea, Mich.: Sleeping Bear Press, 1997.

———. *Discovering Donald Ross, the Architect and His Courses.* Chelsea, Mich.: Sleeping Bear Press, 2001.

Klemme, Mike. *A View from the Rough.* Chelsea, Mich.: Sleeping Bear Press, 1995.

Kroeger, Robert. *The Golf Courses of Old Tom Morris.* Cincinnati, Ohio: Heritage Communications, 1995.

Labbance, Bob, and Gordan Wittaveen. *Keepers of the Green, a History of Golf Course Management.* Chelsea, Mich.: Ann Arbor Press; Golf Course Superintendents of America, 2001.

Lewis, Peter N., Elinor R. Clark, and Fiona C. Grieve. *A Round of History at the British Golf Museum.* St. Andrews, Fife, Scotland: Royal & Ancient Golf Club of St. Andrews, 1998.

Lewis, Peter, Fiona C. Grieve, and Keith Mackie. *Art and Architecture of the Royal and Ancient Golf Club.* St. Andrews, Fife, Scotland: Royal & Ancient Golf Club of St. Andrews, 1997.

Longstaff, J.R. *The First Hundred Years of Bishop Aukland Golf Club: 1894–1994.* Bishop Aukland, Durham, England: Bishop Aukland Golf Club, 1994.

Low, John L. *Concerning Golf.* London: Hodder and Stoughton, 1903, and Far Hills, NJ: USGA Rare Book Collection, 1987.

Lyle, Sandy, and Bob Ferrier. *The Championship Courses of Scotland.* Kingswood, Tadworth, Surrey: World's Work, 1982.

Macdonald, Charles Blair. *Scotland's Gift: Golf.* New York: Charles Scribner's Sons, 1928, and Stamford, Conn.: Classics of Golf, 1985.

MacKenzie, Alister. *Golf Architecture.* London: Simpkin, Marshall, Hamilton, Kent & Co., 1920; Stamford, Conn.: Classics of Golf, 1988; and Droitwich, Worcestershire, England: Grant Books, 1982.

———. *The Spirit of St. Andrews.* Chelsea, Mich.: Sleeping Bear Press, 1995.

Mackie, Keith. *Open Championship Golf Courses of Britain.* La: Pelican Publishing, 1997.

Muirhead, Desmond, and Guy L. Rando. *Golf Course Development and Real Estate.* Washington, D.C.: Urban Land Institute, 1994.

Muirhead, Desmond, and Tip Anderson. *St. Andrews: How to Play the Old Course.* Newport Beach, Calif.: Newport Press, 2000.

Mulvihill, David A., et al. *Golf Course Development in Residential Communities.* Washington, D.C.: Urban Land Institute, 2001.

Pace, Lee. *Pinehurst Stories: A Celebration of Great Golf and Good Times,* 2nd ed. Pinehurst, N.C.: Pinehurst, 1999.

Parascenzo, Marino. *Oakmont 100 Years.* Oakmont, Pa.: Fownes Foundation, 2003.

Park, Willie, Jr. *The Game of Golf.* London: Longmans Green and Co., 1896.

Peper, George, and the editors of *Golf Magazine*. *The 500 World's Greatest Golf Holes.* New York: Artisan, 2000.

Price, Charles. *The World of Golf: A Panorama of Six Centuries of the Game's History.* New York: Random House, 1962.

Price, Robert. *Scotland's Golf Courses.* Aberdeen, Scotland: Aberdeen University Press, 1989.

Redmond, John. *Great Golf Courses of Ireland.* Dublin, Ireland: Gil & Macmillan, 1992.

Richardson, Forrest L. *Routing the Golf Course: The Art and Science That Forms the Golf Journey.* New York: John Wiley & Sons, 2002.

Robertson, James K. *St. Andrews: Home of Golf.* St. Andrews, Fife, Scotland: J. & G. Innes, 1967.

Ross, Donald J. *Golf Has Never Failed Me: The Lost Commentaries of Legendary Golf Course Architect Donald J. Ross.* Chelsea, Mich.: Sleeping Bear Press, 1996.

Ryde, Peter, D. M. A. Steele, and H. W. Wind. *Encyclopedia of Golf.* New York: Viking Press, 1975.

Scott, Tom. *The Concise Dictionary of Golf.* New York: Mayflower Books, 1978.

Shackelford, Geoff. *Alister MacKenzie's Cypress Point Club.* Chelsea, Mich.: Sleeping Bear Press, 2000.

———. *The Captain: George C. Thomas and His Architecture.* Chelsea, Mich.: Sleeping Bear Press, 1997.

———. *The Golden Age of Golf Design.* Chelsea, Mich.: Sleeping Bear Press, 1999.

———. *Grounds for Golf.* New York, NY: St. Martin's Press, 2003.

———. *Masters of the Links: Essays on the Art of Golf and Course Design.* Chelsea, Mich.: Sleeping Bear Press, 1997.

Shackelford, Geoff and Michael G. Miller. *The Art of Golf Design.* Chelsea, Mich.: Sleeping Bear Press, 2001.

Shapiro, Mel, Warren Dohn, and Leonard Berger. *Golf: A Turn-of-the-Century Treasury.* Secaucus, N.J.: Castle, 1986.

Steel, Donald. *Classic Golf Links of England, Scotland, Wales, and Ireland.* Gretna, La: Pelican Publishing, 1993.

Steinbreder, John. *Golf Courses of the U.S. Open.* Texas: Taylor Publishing Company, 1996.

Stewart, John W. *William Clark Fownes, Jr. The Man, The Golfer, The Leader.* Fredericksburg: Sheridan Books, 2003.

Stobbs, John. *An ABC of Golf.* London: Stanley Paul, 1964.

Swift, Duncan. *The Golfer's Reference Dictionary Illustrated.* Dearborn, Mich.: Schaefer's Publishing, 1999.

Thomas, George C. *Golf Architecture in America.* Chelsea, Mich.: Sleeping Bear Press, 1997.

Tillinghast, A. W. *The Course Beautiful.* Warren, N.J.: Treewolf Productions, 1995.

———. *Reminiscences of the Links: A Treasury of Creative Essays and Vintage Photographs on Scottish and Early American Golf.* Warren, N.J.: Treewolf Productions, 1998.

———. *Gleanings from the Wayside.* Researched, compiled, designed, and edited by Richard C. Wolffe, Jr., Robert S. Trebus, and Stuart F. Wolffe. Warren, NJ: Treewolf Productions, 2001.

Travis, Walter J. *Practical Golf.* New York and London: Harper & Brothers, 1901.

Tulloch, W. W. *The Life of Old Tom Morris.* London: Werner, Laurie, 1908, and Far Hills, NJ: USGA Rare Book Collection, 1992.

Ward-Thomas, Pat, Herbert Warren Wind, Charles Price, and Peter Thomson. *The World Atlas of Golf: The Great Courses and How They Are Played.* New York: Random House, 1976.

Wethered, H. N., and T. Simpson. *The Architectural Side of Golf.* London: Longmans Green & Co., 1929; second edition, titled Design for Golf, London, 1952, and Grant Books, Droitwich, Worcestershire, England: 1995.

Wexler, Daniel. *The Missing Links: America's Greatest Lost Golf Courses and Holes.* Chelsea, Mich.: Sleeping Bear Press, 2000.

Resources

The following resources are listed for convenience to the reader.
Many of the organizations listed are referred to in this book.

American Society of Golf Course Architects (ASGCA)
125 North Executive Drive, Suite 106
Brookfield, Wisconsin 53005
(262) 786-5960
www.asgca.org
The premier organization of professional golf course architects in North America; profiles of golf course architects, a library of designs, current news, and so on

American Society of Irrigation Consultants (ASIC)
221 North LaSalle Street
Chicago, Illinois 60601
www.asic.org
An organization of professionals within the irrigation industry. Founded to keep those within the industry informed of irrigation design, installation, and product application issues.

British and International Golf Greenkeepers Association (BIGGA)
BIGGA House
Aldwark, Alne, York YO61 1UF
United Kingdom
44 1347 833800
www.bigga.co.uk
The professional association of greenkeepers in the United Kingdom.

Club Managers Association of America (CMAA)
1733 King Street
Alexandria, Virginia 22314
(703) 739-9500
www.cmaa.org
An association of over 5,000 members operating country, city, athletic, faculty, yacht, town, and military clubs.

European Golf Association (EGA)
Place de la Croix-Blanche 19
CH-1066 Epalinges
Switzerland
+41 21-784-35-32
www.ega-golf.ch
An organization whose membership is restricted to European national amateur golf associations or unions; observes the Rules of Golf and amateur status as directed by the Royal & Ancient.

European Institute of Golf Course Architects (EIGCA)
Merrist Wood House, Worplesdon
Guildford, Surrey GU3 3PE
United Kingdom
+44 1483 884036
www.eigca.org
The organization of professional golf course architects in Europe; members' profiles, news, education, and library.

First Tee
World Golf Village
425 South Legacy Trail
St. Augustine, Florida 32092
(904) 940-4300
www.thefirsttee.org
An organization committed to making the game of golf accessible and affordable to kids and minority youth.

Golf Club Atlas
www.GolfClubAtlas.com
A Web site to promote the frank commentary on the world's finest golf courses. Within this site, the subject of golf course architecture is discussed in several different sections, including course profiles, monthly interviews, and discussion groups.

Golf Course 1
www.golfcourse1.com
An affiliated Web site of the ASGCA; a resource for golf course developers and owners of new courses and remodeling projects.

Golf Course Builders Association of America (GCBAA)
727 O Street
Lincoln, Nebraska 68510
(402) 476-4444
www.gcbaa.org
A nonprofit trade organization of golf course builders and suppliers; includes member directory, certification information, application form, and news.

Golf Course Superintendents Association of America (GCSAA)
1421 Research Park Drive
Lawrence, Kansas 66049-3859
(785) 841-2240
www.gcsaa.org
The professional organization for golf course superintendents; career opportunities, learning center, resource center, news, and more.

Golf Course.com
www.golfcourse.com
An online magazine and database useful for finding golf course locations, prices, policies, public reviews, and so on.

Golf Digest
www.golfdigest.com
The official Web site of Golf Digest; includes course reviews, travel information, instructional tips, features from the magazine, and news (recommend www.golfdigest.com/courses).

Golf Illustrated
Curtis Circulation Company
730 River Road
New Milford, New Jersey 07646
(201) 634-7400
fax (201) 634-7499

Golf Online
www.golfonline.com
The official Web site of Golf Magazine; includes articles, travel information, instruction, and the golfcourse.com database.

Golf Range Association of America (GRAA)
www.golfrange.org
An organization dedicated to the advancement of the golf range and practice-facility industry; includes a national Top 100 list, Golf Range magazine, golf range directory, and membership information.

Golfing Scotland
Gateway East, Technology Park
Dundee DD2 12W
Scotland
+44 1382 429000
www.scottishgolf.com
A directory of courses and practice ranges, news, and webcam for Scottish courses.

Irrigation Association
6540 Arlington Boulevard
Falls Church, Virginia 22042-6638
www.irrigation.org
An association whose mission is to provide information about improving the products and practices used in the irrigation industry. Included are directories, conservation and water-management resources, a search engine, and education and job opportunities.

Japanese Society of Golf Course Architects
www.jsgca.com
An organization of leading golf course architects in Japan.

John Wiley & Sons, Inc.
111 River Street
Hoboken, New Jersey 07030
(201) 748-6000
www.wiley.com
Global publisher focusing on scientific, technical, and medical journals; textbooks; and professional and consumer books, as well as subscription services.

Ladies Professional Golf Association
100 International Golf Drive
Daytona Beach, Florida 32124-1092
(386) 274-6200
www.lpga.com
The organization of female professional golfers (includes club pros) in the United States; LPGA Tour news updates, information on touring and teaching pros, history, and pro shop.

Land Trust Alliance
1331 H Street NW, Suite 400
Washington, D.C. 20005-4734
(202) 638-4725
www.lta.org
The leading organization promoting and fostering the private land conservation movement by encouraging voluntary land conservation across the United States.

Michigan State University Turfgrass Information Center
www.lib.msu.edu/tgif
A database of over 76,000 publicly available turfgrass educational materials.

National Club Association (NCA)
www.natlclub.org
An association that provides legal advice and lobbyist services for private and recreational clubs.

National Golf Course Owners Association (NGCOA)
1470 Ben Sawyer Boulevard, Suite 18
Mt. Pleasant, South Carolina 29464
(843) 881-9956
An information source for member golf course owners, offering them data critical to their success in the golf industry; includes ADA and IRS information, upcoming association events, and Golf Business *magazine.*

National Golf Foundation (NGF)
1150 South US Highway One, Suite 401
Jupiter, Florida 33477
(561) 744-6006
www.ngf.org
The leading organization dedicated to researching the entirety of the golf industry; directory of member companies, infosearch, golf directory, course construction activity, and news.

Pace Manager Systems
4804 Elmdale Drive
Rolling Hills Estates, California 90274
(310) 791-7348
www.pacemanager.com
Pace Manager seeks to cure the problem of slow play on today's courses by finding its cause and proposing solutions.

PGA Tour
112 TPC Boulevard, Sawgrass
Ponte Vedra Beach, Florida 32082
www.pgatour.com
The organization of touring professionals (male, female, and senior) in the United States; tournament schedules, leaderboards, headlines, course travel information, and online store.

Professional Golfers Association of America (PGA)
100 Avenue of the Champions
Palm Beach Gardens, Florida 33410
www.pga.org
An organization of professional golfers (including club pros) within the United States; tournament headlines, schedules, and golf instruction.

Remodeling University
www.remodelinguniversity.org
An affiliated site of the ASGCA; the leading resource for golf course developers and owners on remodeling, renovation, and restoration projects.

**Royal & Ancient Golf Club
of St. Andrews (R&A)**
St. Andrews, Fife, KY16 9JD
Scotland
www.randa.org
The leading legislative body of golf in Europe, the site includes European tour news, information on St. Andrews, Rules of Golf, and frequently asked questions. Also included is information about the British Golf Museum.

Shivas Irons Society
P.O. Box 22239
Carmel, California 93922
www.shivas.org
A society dedicated to exploring the "beautiful and mysterious" side of golf, providing opportunities for personal and social transformation; based on Michael Murphy's novel Golf in the Kingdom.

Society of Australian Golf Course Architects (SAGCA)
www.sagca.org.au
The organization of professional golf course architects within Australia; members' profiles, golf and the environment, news journal, and contacts.

St. Andrews Links Trust
Pilmour House
St. Andrews, Fife, KY16 9SF
Scotland
+44 1334 466666
www.standrews.org/uk
The official Web site of the "home of golf." Information on all six St. Andrews golf courses, online booking, history, and store.

The American Golfer
Contact: I. Martin Davis
200 Railroad Avenue
Greenwich, Connecticut 06830
(203) 862-9720
e-mail: imd@aol.com

United States Golf Association (USGA)
P.O. Box 708
Far Hills, New Jersey 07931
(908) 234-2300
www.usga.org
The governing body for golf within the United States; information on USGA championship tournaments, Rules of Golf, handicapping, equipment, foundation for people with disabilities, news, and contacts.

USGA Green Solution
Contact: Kimberly Erusha or Jim Snow
(908) 234-2300
e-mail: kerusha@usga.org or jsnow@usga.org

USGA Rare Book Collection
Golf House
P.O. Box 3000
Far Hills, New Jersey 07931-3000
A library of rare golf books that are out of print and very hard to find. Great source for research work.

Urban Land Institute (ULI)
1025 Thomas Jefferson Street NW
Suite 500 West
Washington, D.C. 20007
(202) 624-7000
An organization dedicated to providing leadership and guidance with respect to responsible and environmentally enhancing land planning issues, techniques, and strategies.

World Golf Village
21 World Golf Place
St. Augustine, Florida 32092
www.wgv.com

Home of the World Golf Hall of Fame and Golf Museum
World Scientific Congress of Golf
www.golfscience.org
A collection of documented scientific research projects on golf by authors around the globe.

Index

Aberdeen Golf Club (Royal), 125
Addington Golf Club, 29
Ade, George, 101
Aeration, 201
Aerial Photography, 209, 212, 215
Aesthetics of hazards, 154, 157
Alison, Charles Hugh, xii, 99, 103, 116
Alpinization, 9–13
Alps Hole, 115, 120, 122, 143–144
Amick, Bill, 180
Annandale Golf Club, 100
Appleby, Stuart, 24
Architectural Side of Golf, 34, 125, 157
Arizona Biltmore Golf Club, 26, 156, 175, 212
Ashdown Forest Golf Club (Royal), 28
Augusta National Golf Club:
    Amen Corner, 47
    bunkers, 156
    green speeds, 229
    hole No. 12, 139
    influence on maintenance, 15
    Jones, Bobby, 112–113
    Jones, Robert Trent Sr., 208
    MacKenzie, Alister, 116, 200
    Rae's Creek, 19, 47–49, 175, 199–200, 208, 241, 244, 246
    water hazards, 250

Bahto, George, 122
Balfour, James, 242
Ballybunion Golf Club, 11, 23, 102, 125, 146
Baltusrol Golf Club, 44, 129
Bandon Dunes Golf Club, 195, 227, 240, 247
Bandon Trails Golf Course, 240
Banff Springs Golf Club, 128
Banks, Charles Henry, 99–100
Barry Burn, 175, 246
Bartholomaei, Phred, 56, 201, 202, 231, 233
Bauer, Alex, 224, 259
Beaman, Dean, 45–46
Beardies, 13, 175, 241
Behr, Max Howell, 100, 257
Bel Air Golf Club, 100, 195
Bell, William F., 101, 211
Bell, William Parc "Billy," 26, 87–88, 100–101, 126, 156, 175, 210, 212
Bellerive Country Club, 112
Bendelow, Thomas, 101–102
Bethpage Black Golf Course, 24, 129, 230
Biarritz Hole, 122, 165
Biarritz la Phare Course, 104
Black Rock Golf Club, 179
Boston Golf Club, 29, 153, 174
Boulders Golf Club, 172
Bradbury, Ray, 173
Braid, James, 75, 85, 94, 102
Brancaster (Royal West Norfolk Golf Club), 115
Bridge Hole, 50–51
Broken ground, 8, 14, 18, 24, 28–29, 37, 75, 78, 226
Brookline Country Club, 79
Brown, Lancelot, 21

Bruce's Billabong, 175
Bryan, Mike, 42
Bucknell Golf Club, 219
Buenaventura Golf Course, 172
Bulkheads, 23, 46, 201
Bulldozer(s), 178, 184, 186, 202
Bunker(s):
    cartoon, 170
    contamination, 221, 223, 225–226
    cross-bunkers, 104, 116, 125, 128, 130
    crusting, 198, 221
    definition of (USGA), 24
    drainage. *See* Drainage
    edges, 154, 186, 193–196, 227–228
    evolving from linksland, 8, 14
    fabric lining, 190–191
    fried-egg lie(s), 197
    irrigation around, 185, 202-204
    maintenance, 220–228
    naming, 175–176
    origin of word, 13, 183
    pace of play, 170
    placement, 153–155, 183
    probing, 212–213
    protocols for care, 220
    purpose, 38–40, 149–150
    raking, 222, 223, 224-227
    sand placement, 185
    sand specification, 196–198
    sand stabilization, 185, 191–192, 197
    shape, 154
    shaping, 181–185
    sod walls, 23, 187, 193
    specifications, 183
    walls, 192–193, 227
Burton, Patrick, 220

Calf Bunker, 93
Camouflage, 169
Campbell, Sir Guy, 7
Cape Bunker (Royal North Devon), 8
Cape Bunker (Westward Ho!), 120
Cape Hole (Mid Ocean Golf Club), 83–85
Cape hole(s), 165, 167
Cardinal Bunker, 73–75, 175, 251
Cardinal Hole, 75,
Cardinal's Nob, 74, 75
Carton House Golf Club, 30
Carnoustie Golf Club, 34, 36, 102, 120, 123, 236, 246, 255
Carry, 151–152, 159
Cascades Golf Club, 106
Chalmers, William, 6, 51
Chassard, John, 220
Cheape's Bunker, 175
Cherry Hills Country Club, 106, 217
Chicago Golf Club, 114
Chipping areas, vii, 124, 229, 230, 248, 251
Chocolate drops, 21, 79, 81, 82, 102
Church Pews, 13, 43, 57–59, 109, 175, 246
Clark, Robert, 53

Index

Clashing Rocks Hole, 22
Coffin Bunkers, 175
Coldwater Golf Club, 27, 194, 229
College Arms Golf Club, 21
Collier, James, 94
Colt, Harry Shapland, xii, 61, 63, 94, 98, 99, 102, 116, 248
Computer Aided Design (CAD), 172
Conditions of courses, 37, 155
Construction, 177–204
    bunkers, 181–191
    irrigation, 202–204
    lakes and ponds, 198–200
    preserving natural hazards, 180
    water hazards, 198–202
Contours, 29–31, 37
Coore, Bill, 35, 87, 152, 239, 240
Cop bunker(s), 11, 102, 109
Cornish, Geoffrey, 210, 248
Cornish, Silva and Mungeam, 248
Corsets Bunkers, 138
Cottage Bunker, 175
Crenshaw, Ben, 35, 88, 152, 239, 240
Crockford, Claude, 240
Crombie, Charles, 150, 236
Cross-bunkers. *See* Bunkers
Crossraguel Abbey, 74
Cruden Bay Golf Club, 3, 108
Crump, George Arthur, 11, 61, 63–65, 104, 132
Crystal Downs Country Club, 239, 250
Cupp, Bob, 22, 242, 243
Cypress Point Club:
    deception, 169
    design strategy, 40, 164
    hole No. 7, 111
    hole No. 16, 59–61, 139
    Hunter, Robert, 110–111
    MacKenzie, Alister, 112, 116
    ocean holes, 149, 241
    ranking for bunkering, 166

Daley, Paul, 11, 34, 35
Darwin, Bernard 10, 86, 96
Deacon Sime Bunker, 92
Deal Golf Club, 2
Deceiving Tactics, 38, 169
Dell Hole, 30, 32, 71–73, 120, 165, 168–169
Desert Mountain Golf Club, 182
Design of hazards:
    character, 174
    detour design, 39, 163
    methods, 171–174
Detour design, 160
Devil's Asshole, 13, 43, 61, 62, 63, 175, 246
Devil's Paintbrush Course, 257
DeVries, Mike, 238–239
Diagonal hazard, 78, 103, 124, 126, 129–130, 162, 241
Dickenson, Patric, 145
Ditch(es), 12, 22–23, 25, 27–28, 108, 110, 115, 128, 149, 202, 234
Doak, Tom, 145, 179, 195, 229, 241, 247
Dobrineiner, Peter, 145
Dogleg(s), 26–27, 54, 83, 117, 125, 156, 165, 166, 167, 229
Donaghadee Golf Club, 140
Dooks Golf Club, 22

Doonbeg Golf Club, 187, 192
Dornick Hills Golf Club, 118–119
Dornoch Golf Club (Royal), 10, 120, 123, 227
Dornoch, Scotland, 3, 123
Drainage:
    bunker(s), 185, 187–190, 223
    horizontal drain box, 190
Duel Hole, 218
Dunbar Golf Links, 35
Dunn, Tom, 104
Dunn, Willie Sr., 104, 122
DuPont Country Club, 110
Dye, Alice, 43–47
Dye, Pete, vii, 16, 24, 43–47, 193, 226, 239, 243, 248, 250, 255–257

Effluent, 199, 202, 234
Egan, Chandler, 54, 56, 69, 110
Eleanor's Teeth, 175
Emil "Dutch" Loeffler, 57, 109, 110, 219
Emmet, Devereux, 105, 110
End Hole, 53
Engh, Jim, 179, 243, 244
Everhard, H. S. U., 68

Fairness, 158–160, 236, 240, 246, 252
Faldo, Nick, 153
Farley, Floyd, 173
Fay, Michael, 124
Fazio, George, 34, 105, 106, 245
Fazio, Tom, 57, 106, 245
Fiddler's Creek Golf Club, 249
Fine, Mark, vii, 216–217
Firestone Country Club, 112
Fish kills, 234
Floral hazards, 151
Flynn, William, 106–108
    accuracy, carry, length, 151–152
    Cherry Hills Country Club, 217
    Lehigh Country Club, 107
    Merion Cricket Club, 131–132
    Pine Valley Golf Club, 65
    Toomey and Flynn, 110
    trees, 33–34
Forrest, Steve, 200
Forsgate Country Club, 99
Fossil Trace Golf Club, 244
Fourth Hole Bunker (Royal St. George's), 89–91
Fowler, William Herbert, 108, 125
Fownes, Henry C., 57, 82, 109
Fownes, William H., 57, 82, 109–110
Fox Chapel Golf Club, 193, 207
French Creek Golf Club, 251
Fried egg lie(s), 197
Frost, Robert, vi, 69
Fry, Dana, 257
Furrowed rake, 205, 226
Furrows, vii, 109–110, 226

Gabion(s), 232
Galen Hall Golf Club. *See* Wernesville Golf Club
Ganton Golf Club, 108
Geographic Information Systems (GIS), 172
Geometric design, 21–23, 102
Ginger Beer, 13
Glading, Reg, 91
Gleneagles Golf Club, 102

Global Positioning System (GPS), 180, 183, 220
Golden Age of Design, x, 20, 33, 110, 119
Golf Club Atlas, 150
Golf course architect:
    master plans, 215–218
    role, 214–215
    selecting, 213–214
Golf:
    development of, 4–6
    first mention of, 4
    format of play, 154
    rules: *See* Rules
    shot values, 160–161
Gordon, William F., 110
Gorse, 8, 10, 96, 103, 123, 135, 246
Grannie Clark's Wynd, 159
Grant's Bunker, 93
Grant, Douglas, 54, 56, 69, 180
Grasses:
    roughs, 37
    mowing, 229–231
Greens:
    hazards of, 31–32
    Riviera No. 6, 87–89
    speed, 170
Grubbing, 184
Gullane Golf Club, 149
Gumbleys Hole, 175

Hanse, Gil, 25, 153, 174, 250, 251
Harbour Town Golf Links, 256
Harper, R. J., 55
Harris, Sydney J., 206
Haultain, Arnold, 136, 148
Hawtree, Fred, 9
Hawtree, Martin, 94, 96
Hayling Golf Club, 12, 141
Headwaters Golf Club, 199
Heather, 30, 96, 103, 108, 139, 246, 255
Hell Bunker, 39, 40, 43, 66–69, 175, 246, 248
Hell's Half Acre, 13, 43, 63, 65, 129, 175, 246
Heroic design, 39, 112, 160–162
Het kolven, 4
Hideout Golf Club, 38, 165, 198
High Hole(s), 52, 198
Hills, Art, 249
Himalaya Bunker (Royal St. George's), 89–90
Himalayas, 85–86, 175
Hodge, Thomas, 53, 66
Hollins, Marion, 60
Home Hole, 53
Honorable Company of Edinburgh Golfers, 12, 157, 188
Hotchkiss Preparatory School Course, 99
Hoylake Golf Club, 25
Hunter, Robert, 110–112,
    Cypress Point Club, 59–61
    importance of hazards, 136, 153
    Pebble Beach Golf Links, 54, 56, 69
    standards for design, 155
    The Links, 8, 111–112, 153
Huntercombe Golf Club, 121
Hurdzan, Mike, 256–257
Hutchinson, Horace, 22, 66, 67, 77, 151, 158

Ice plant, 246
Integral obstructions, 32–33

Iron Bridge Golf Club, 200
Irrigation, 185, 202–204,
Island green, vii, 44, 45, 46, 176, 256

Jasper Park Golf Club, 128
Jetsons, The, 22
Jones, Rees, 24, 230, 252
Jones, Robert "Bobby" Tyre Jr., 14, 47, 112–113, 219
Jones, Robert Trent Jr., 85, 184–185
Jones, Robert Trent Sr., 45, 48, 85, 106, 112, 131, 184, 208, 248

Kaanapali Golf Course, 194
Kapalua Plantation Course, 142
Kasumigaseki Golf Club, 99
Kendal, John, 94
Khayyam, Omar, 178
Kidd, David McLay, 227
Kimball, Bruce, 176
King James II, 4
Kingsley Club, 239
Kitchen Bunker, 175
Kittansett Golf Club, 106
Knoll Country Club, 99
Kolf, 4

Lahinch Golf Club, 18, 23, 30, 32, 63, 71–73, 120, 168
Lakes:
    artificial, 198–200
    constructing, 200–202
    lining, 200–201
    slopes, 201
    volume, 201
    water quality, 201
Langford, William Boice, 113
Larrabee, Gary, 81
Las Palomas, The Links at, 27, 173
Lawsonia Golf Club, 113
Layup Design, 160, 163–164
Lee, Joe, 131
Leeds, Herbert, 79, 82, 196
Lees, Peter, 11
Lehigh Country Club, 106–107, 220
Leith Links, 6, 188
Lewin, Kurt, 218
Lewis, Peter, 53
LIDAR mapping, 220
Line of charm, 100, 152–154, 238
Linksland:
    alpinization, 9–11
    altered for golf, 9–11
    association with hazards, 8
    drainage, 187, 189
    formation of, 3, 7–8
    importance of, 6–9, 20
    origin of word, 6–7
    routing, 168
    sheep upon, 3
    trees, 33–34
    undulations of, 20, 30
Lippo Village, 22
Littlestone Golf Club, 115, 222
Long Hole, 66, 68, 236
Lord of Culzean, 74
Los Angeles Country Club, 126
Low, John, 114, 125, 159, 165

Index

Luck, 99
Lytham & St. Anne's (Royal), 108

Macdonald, Charles Blair, 114–116,
    Banks, Charles, influence on, 99–100
    Emmet, Devereux, work for, 105
    Golden Age, 20–22
    influences mentioned, 132, 251
    Mid Ocean Golf Club, 83–85
    Pine Valley Golf Club, influence on, 65
    raking sand bunkers, 224
    Raynor, Seth, work for, 122
MacKenzie, Dr. Alister, 116–118,
    Augusta National Golf Club, 112, 200, 208
    camouflage, 169
    Cypress Point Club, 59–61, 111, 164
    hazard importance along line of play, 155
    Hunter, Robert, work with, 110
    influences mentioned, 239, 241, 243,
        247, 251, 254, 256–257
    Maxwell, Perry, association with, 119
    Rae's Creek, 47–49
    ranked as most respected, 98
Maiden Bunker, 13, 115, 175, 246
Maintenance:
    bunker(s), 220–228
    change resulting from, 207
    education, 235–236
    mowing practices, 229–231
    preservation of hazards, 219–220
    trees, 234–235
    water hazards, 231–234
Mangrove Lake, 83–85
Marsh, Graham, 143, 194, 253
Martin, A., 49, 51
Match play, 15, 118, 154, 222, 252
Maxwell Rolls, 119
Maxwell, Perry, 20, 118–119, 146, 239
McCormick Ranch Golf Club, 45
McGovern, J. B., 110, 124
Mechanical raking, 175, 223, 225, 227
Medinah Golf Club, 102
Melbourne Golf Club (Royal), 43, 116, 240, 241, 246
Merion Cricket Club, 13, 43, 106, 107, 131, 132, 246
Mid Ocean Golf Club, 83, 84, 85
Mid-Surrey Golf Club (Royal), 9, 10, 11
Milwaukee Country Club, 102
Moorlands, 30
Morris, Old Tom, 3, 8, 36, 51, 53, 66, 71, 73, 97,
    102, 104, 119, 120, 123, 129, 158, 197, 198,
    216, 229, 242
Morrish, Jay, 172
Morse, Samuel, 180
Moselem Springs Golf Club, 34
Mucci, Pat, 150
Muirfield Golf Links, 45, 99, 102, 120, 125, 157, 158
Muirfield Village Golf Club, 43, 45
Muirhead, Desmond, 22, 45, 156
Myopia Hunt Club, 79–82, 196, 231
Mystery of Golf, 136, 148–49

Naming of hazards, 175–176
National Golf Links, 20, 115, 132, 241, 251
Natural features, 155, 180
NCR Country Club, 131
Neville, Jack, 54, 56, 69, 180
Newscastle Country Club, 243
Nicklaus, Jack, 45, 68, 71, 93, 162, 182

North Berwick Golf Club, 22, 23, 29, 31, 76
Northwood Golf Club, 142

Oak Hills Country Club, 123
Oakland Hills Golf Club, 123
Oakmont Country Club, 82, 211
    Church Pews, 43, 57–59, 246
    ditches, 23
    Fownes, W. C. and H. C., 109–110
    furrowed raking, 226
    green speeds, 229
    hazard maintenance, 219
Ocean Course at Kiawah Island Resort, 226
Old Course, The. *See* St. Andrews Links
Old Head Golf Links, 39
Old Man's Plateau, 175
Open design, 160, 164–165
Open, The, 5, 9, 19, 33, 61, 75, 90, 182
Orientation of holes, 166–167
Ouimet, Francis, 106
Out-of-Bounds, 35–36, 54, 92, 93, 170, 240

Pace of play, 169–170
Pacific Dunes Golf Course, 195, 241, 246–247, 250–251
Pacific Ocean, 54, 57, 59, 69, 154, 180
Palmetto Hall Plantation, 22
Par-6, 166
Park, Willie, 20, 110, 121, 158, 206, 248
Pasadena Golf Club, 100
Pasatiempo Golf Club, 117
Paton, Stuart, 114, 125
Patterson, Thomas, 54
Peachtree Golf Club, 112
Pebble Beach Golf Links, 180, 241
    bunker renovation, 208
    hole No. 8, 69–71, 139
    hole No. 18, 54–57, 154, 233
    Hunter, Robert, 110
Penal design, 160–162
Penetrometer, 197
Pepper, George, 246
Pern, Jeremy, 20, 140, 188
PGA, vii, 24, 45, 46, 105, 129, 130, 137
Phantom Horse Golf Club, 26, 33, 197
Philadelphia School of Design, 100
Philip, John, 236
Phoenician Golf Club, 176
Pilmoor Links, 49, 51. *See also* St. Andrews Links
Pinehurst No. 2, 123, 241, 246
Pine Valley Golf Club, 11, 96
    broken ground, 29
    Crump, George, 104
    Devil's Asshole, 43, 61–62
    Hell's Half Acre, 13, 43, 63–65, 129, 175, 246
    influences mentioned, 106, 111, 129, 132,
        241, 246
    ranking for bunkering, 166
Plainfield Golf Club, 123
Playfair, Sir Hugh Lyon, 53
Ponte Vedra Club, 46
Porthcawl Golf Club (Royal), 102, 125
Postage Stamp, 20
Pottawatomie Park Golf Course, 45
Pow Burn, 75, 175, 255
Prairie Dunes Country Club, 20, 119, 146
Presidio Golf Club, 108
Prestwick Golf Club, 22–23, 73, 75, 76, 78, 115, 120,
    143, 144, 251, 255

Principal's Nose, 13, 91, 92, 93
Psychological effects of hazards, 133–146
    attention, 143
    comfort zone of golfer, 137
    intimidation, 139
    perception of difficulty, 145–146
    resilience of golfer, 144–145
    stress, 138, 140–144
    swing, effect upon, 140–144
Purgatory Bunker, 175
Purves, Alexander Pattison, 89
Purvis, Laidlaw, 89, 222
Putter, Jurek Alexander, 51

Quaker Ridge Golf Club, 129

Rae's Creek, 19, 47–49, 175, 199–200, 208, 241, 246
Rae, John, 47
Railway lines, 32, 53, 54, 92
Raynor, Seth, 121–122
    Banks, Charles, association with, 99–100
    Cypress Point Club, 60
    Fox Chapel Golf Club, 193, 207
    influences mentioned, 249
    Yale Golf Club, 122
Redan, 23, 76, 77, 78, 79, 122, 165, 175
Reid, George, 3
Remodeling, 206–213,
    adding hazards, 218–219
    budgeting, 209, 217, 219–222, 235
    rebuilding, 208
    removing hazards, 218–219
    renovation, 208
    research for, 209–213
    restoration, 208–209
    shifting hazards, 218–219
Reservoir(s), 199
Restoration, 208–209
Retention capacity, 199
Richardson, Forrest, vii, 26–27, 33, 38, 112, 156, 165, 176, 194
Risk/reward, 103, 130, 165
Riviera Country Club, 87, 89, 100, 126, 154, 194
Road Bunker, 43, 49–54, 145, 192, 246
Road Hole, 35, 49, 51, 52, 53, 54, 145, 175, 192, 220, 239, 240, 246. *See also* St. Andrews Links (The Old Course)
Robertson, Allan, 9, 52, 119, 120, 123, 249
Robinson, Heath, 170
Robinson, Ted Sr., 199
Rock outcropping(s), 20, 155, 176
Rolland, Doug, 102
Ross, Donald, vii, 43, 82, 98, 123–125
    Gordon, William, work with, 110
    influenced mentioned, 241, 248, 257
    natural qualities, 180
    variety of hazards, 156
Roughs:
    cartoon, 158
    hazard, 37
    mowing, 229–231
    St. Andrews Links, 19
Routing of courses, 171
Routing the Golf Course, 28, 112
Royal & Ancient Golf Club, 6, 25, 51, 150. *See also* St. Andrews Links
Royal County Down Golf Club, 120, 174, 241
Royal North Devon Golf Club 8, 108

Royal Portrush Golf Club, 102, 120, 168
Royal St. George's Golf Club, 43, 85, 89, 90, 91, 138, 246
Rules:
    bunkers, 65, 182
    cartoons, 150, 236
    casual water in bunker, 188
    development of, 12, 25–26
    integral obstructions, 32–33
    out-of-bounds, 35–36
    USGA Rules, 24–25
Runcie, Sam Jr., 75
Rustic Canyon Golf Club, 244
Rye Golf Club, 102

Sadalla, Dr. Edward, 28, 133, 136, 151
Sahara Bunker, 13, 115, 143, 144, 175
Salem Country Club, 123
San Diego Country Club, 101
San Francisco Golf Club, 129, 218
Sand Hills Golf Club, 15, 19, 152, 166, 241, 250–251
Sand traps, 109, 189. *See also* Bunker(s)
Sand:
    stabilization in bunkers, 185, 191–192, 197
    type, 196–198
Sandwich. *See* Royal St. George's Golf Club
Saucon Valley Grace Course, 110
Sawgrass. *See* Tournament Player's Club at Sawgrass
Scabs, 175, 239
Scioto Country Club, 123
Scoonie Burn, 175
Scotch & Soda, 175, 176
Seminole, 123
Setup of Courses, 37–38, 154
Severity of hazards, 158
Shackelford, Geoff, 47, 87, 244
Shadow Creek Golf Club, 13
Shape of hazards, 157
Shawnee Country Club, 10, 129
Shinnecock Hills Golf Club, 80, 104, 106, 241
Shiskine Golf Club, 121
Simpson, Thomas, 3, 12, 34, 125–126, 157, 175
Size of hazards, 157
Sleeper(s), 23, 73, 75, 78, 91, 142, 193–194, 255
Snyder, Arthur Jack, 27, 38, 165, 194, 198
    bunker drainage, 188–189
    Oakmont Country Club, 58
Sod walls, 23, 187, 193
Somerset Hills Golf Club, 129
Southerland, John, 123
Spectacles Bunkers, 175
Spyglass Hill Golf Club, 112
Squires Golf Club, 245
St. Andrew's Golf Club (Yonkers, New York), 102
St. Andrews Links (The Old Course):
    A. Martin map, 51
    Beardies, 13, 175, 241
    Bridge Hole, 50–51
    Calf Bunker, 93
    cartoon, 170
    Chalmer map, 6, 51
    Cheape's Bunker, 175
    Coffin Bunkers, 175
    Cottage Bunker, 175
    Deacon Sime Bunker, 92
    Elysian Fields, 68
    End Hole, 53
    Grannie Clark's Wynd, 159

Index

St. Andrews Links (continued)
    Grant's Bunker, 93
    greens, 167
    Hell Bunker, 39, 40, 43, 66–69, 175, 246, 248
    High Hole(s), 52, 198
    Hodge map, 53
    Home Hole, 53
    influence on early golf, 5–9
    influences mentioned, 114, 116, 119–120, 123, 153, 159, 240, 242, 249, 251
    influences on design, 22, 34–36, 168
    Kitchen Bunker, 175
    Long Hole, 66, 68, 236
    maps, 51, 53
    Principal's Nose, 13, 91–93
    ranking for bunkering, 166
    Road Bunker, 43, 49–54, 145, 175, 192, 220, 239, 239, 246
    Road Hole, 23, 145, 175
    rough, 19
    sheds at Road Hole, 23, 145
    Spectacles Bunkers, 175
    Strath Bunker, 13, 76, 175
    Swilcan Burn, 7, 27, 50, 54, 175, 247
    Valley of Sin, 175
    Wig Bunker, 93
St. Enodoc Golf Club, 85–86, 90
St. George's Hill Golf Club, 94–96, 102
Stanford University Golf Course, 101
Stanwich Club, 110
Steel, Donald, 91
Stone Harbor Golf Club, 23
Stone Harbor Golf Club, 22
Stone walls, 23, 25, 32, 79, 120, 156, 201, 239
Stowe Country Club, 21
Strantz, Mike, 16, 202, 241–243
Strath Bunker, 13, 76, 175
Sunningdale Golf Club, 121, 125, 158
Sutton Bay, 143, 194, 253
Sutton, Martin, 98
Swilcan Burn, 7, 27, 50, 54, 175, 247
Swinley Forest Golf Club, 139
Swinstead, G. Hilliard, 5

Taft Bunker, 175, 196
Taft, William, 196
Talking Stick Golf Club, 35
Tarn's Coo, 93
Taylor, J. H., 9, 94
Tenby Golf Club, 179
That Damned Bunker, 94
The Bridge Golf Club, 252
The Old Course. *See* St. Andrews Links
Thomas, George C., 87, 100, 126, 157
Thompson, Stanley, 112, 128, 157, 249
Tillinghast, A. W., 10, 22, 34, 44, 64, 65, 98, 129, 130, 154, 166, 167, 239, 248
Tip O'Neil Bunker, 175
Tobacco Road Golf Club, 202, 242
Toll, A. H., 105
Toomey and Flynn, 110
Topographical mapping, 100, 102, 211
Topographical maps, 211–212
Tournament Player's Club at Sawgrass, vii, 43–47, 139, 250, 256
TPC at Sawgrass. *See* Tournament Player's Club at Sawgrass

Travis, Walter, 130–131, 158
Trees, 33–35,
    fairness, 159
    maintenance, 234–235
Troon Golf Club (Royal), 20
Truett, Philip, 224
Tulloch, W., 119
Turf dykes, 104, 120
Turnberry Golf Club, 255

U.S. Open, 13
USGA, 9, 24, 25, 45, 82, 166, 189

Valderrama Golf Club, 112
Valley of Sin, 175
van Schoel, Hensrick, 4
Vardon, Harry, 13, 75
Ventana Canyon Golf Club, 245
Victoria National Golf Club, 246
Visibility, 106, 144, 159, 168–169
von Hagge, Robert, 131

Walton Heath Golf Club, 108
Wannamoisett Golf Club, 123
Waste bunker(s), 202, 256
Water Hazards: 27–28
    aeration of, 201
    bulkheads, 23, 46, 201
    cattails, 232
    definition of, 26–27
    effluent, 199, 234
    fish kills, 234
    leaks, 232–233
    maintenance of, 231–234
    nutrient loading, 231–232
    pollutants, 233
    reservoir(s), 199
    retention capacity, 199
    shorelines, 232–233
    wetlands, 233
Watson, William "Willie," 23, 100
Waverly Oaks Golf Club, 248
Wee Burn, 175
Weed control, 221, 228
Weed, Bobby, 45
Wentworth West Golf Club, 102
Wernersville Golf Club, 166
West Norfolk Golf Club (Royal). *See* Brancaster
Weston Golf Club, 32
Westward Ho! Golf Club, 120
Wetlands, 233
White Faces of Merion, 13
Whitten, Ron, 210
Wig Bunker, 93
Wilson, Alan, 65
Wilson, Dick, 131
Wilson, Hugh, 44, 64–65, 106–107, 132
Wind, 36–37
Wind, Herbert Warren, 47
Winged Foot Golf Club, 129, 246
Woking Golf Club, 114, 125

Yale Golf Club, 122
Yates, Bill, 40, 169

Zareba Hollow, 74
Zimmer, John, 219